MW00771987

Essentials of Child and Adolescent Psychopathology

Essentials of Behavioral Science Series
Founding Editors, Alan S. Kaufman and Nadeen L. Kaufman

Essentials of Abnormal Psychology
by Andrew R. Getzfeld

Essentials of Child and Adolescent Psychopathology, Second Edition
by Linda Wilmshurst

Essentials of Psychological Testing, Second Edition
by Susana Urbina

Essentials of Statistics for the Social and Behavioral Sciences
by Barry H. Cohen and R. Brooke Lea

Essentials of Research Design and Methodology
by Geoffrey R. Marczyk, David DeMatteo, and David S. Festinger

Essentials

of Child and Adolescent Psychopathology

Second Edition

Linda Wilmshurst

WILEY

Cover image: Thinkstock
Cover design: Wiley

This book is printed on acid-free paper. ♾

Copyright © 2015 by John Wiley & Sons, Inc. All rights reserved.

Published by John Wiley & Sons, Inc., Hoboken, New Jersey.
Published simultaneously in Canada.

No part of this publication may be reproduced, stored in a retrieval system, or transmitted in any form or by any means, electronic, mechanical, photocopying, recording, scanning, or otherwise, except as permitted under Section 107 or 108 of the 1976 United States Copyright Act, without either the prior written permission of the Publisher, or authorization through payment of the appropriate per-copy fee to the Copyright Clearance Center, Inc., 222 Rosewood Drive, Danvers, MA 01923, (978) 750-8400, fax (978) 646-8600, or on the web at www.copyright.com. Requests to the Publisher for permission should be addressed to the Permissions Department, John Wiley & Sons, Inc., 111 River Street, Hoboken, NJ 07030, (201) 748-6011, fax (201) 748-6008.

Limit of Liability/Disclaimer of Warranty: While the publisher and author have used their best efforts in preparing this book, they make no representations or warranties with respect to the accuracy or completeness of the contents of this book and specifically disclaim any implied warranties of merchantability or fitness for a particular purpose. No warranty may be created or extended by sales representatives or written sales materials. The advice and strategies contained herein may not be suitable for your situation. You should consult with a professional where appropriate. Neither the publisher nor author shall be liable for any loss of profit or any other commercial damages, including but not limited to special, incidental, consequential, or other damages.

This publication is designed to provide accurate and authoritative information in regard to the subject matter covered. It is sold with the understanding that the publisher is not engaged in rendering professional services. If legal, accounting, medical, psychological or any other expert assistance is required, the services of a competent professional person should be sought.

Designations used by companies to distinguish their products are often claimed as trademarks. In all instances where John Wiley & Sons, Inc. is aware of a claim, the product names appear in initial capital or all capital letters. Readers, however, should contact the appropriate companies for more complete information regarding trademarks and registration.

For general information on our other products and services please contact our Customer Care Department within the United States at (800) 762-2974, outside the United States at (317) 572-3993 or fax (317) 572-4002.

Wiley publishes in a variety of print and electronic formats and by print-on-demand. Some material included with standard print versions of this book may not be included in e-books or in print-on-demand. If this book refers to media such as a CD or DVD that is not included in the version you purchased, you may download this material at http://booksupport.wiley.com. For more information about Wiley products, visit www.wiley.com.

Library of Congress Cataloging-in-Publication Data:

Wilmshurst, Linda, author.
[Essentials of child psychopathology]
Essentials of child and adolescent psychopathology / Linda Wilmshurst.—Second edition.
p. ; cm.—(Essentials of behavioral science series)
Preceded by Essentials of child psychopathology / Linda Wilmshurst. © 2005.
Includes bibliographical references and index.
ISBN 978-1-118-84019-1 (pbk. : alk. paper)
ISBN 978-1-118-84018-4 (Adobe PDF)
ISBN 978-1-118-84020-7 (ePub)
I. Title. II. Series: Essentials of behavioral science series.
[DNLM: 1. Adolescent. 2. Child. 3. Mental Disorders. 4. Adolescent Psychology—methods.
5. Child Psychology—methods. 6. Psychopathology—methods. WS 350]
RJ499
618.92′89—dc23

2014012663

Printed in Singapore

10 9 8 7 6 5 4 3 2 1

CONTENTS

SERIES PREFACE

In the *Essentials of Behavioral Science* series, our goal is to provide readers with books that will deliver key practical information in an efficient, accessible style. The series features books on a variety of topics, such as statistics, psychological testing, and research design and methodology, to name just a few. For the experienced professional, books in the series offer a concise yet thorough review of a specific area of expertise, including numerous tips for best practices. Students can turn to series books for a clear and concise overview of the important topics in which they must become proficient to practice skillfully, efficiently, and ethically in their chosen fields.

Wherever feasible, visual cues highlighting key points are utilized alongside systematic, step-by-step guidelines. Chapters are focused and succinct. Topics are organized for an easy understanding of the essential material related to a particular topic. Theory and research are continually woven into the fabric of each book, but always to enhance the practical application of the material, rather than to sidetrack or overwhelm readers. With this series, we aim to challenge and assist readers in the behavioral sciences to aspire to the highest level of competency by arming them with the tools they need for knowledgeable, informed practice.

Essentials of Child and Adolescent Psychopathology, Second Edition, provides an overview of child and adolescent disorders that begins with a look at the foundations of the discipline and the unique historical influences that played a role in the evolution of the field. This updated version of the book includes all of the changes in the criteria and conceptualization of disorders that can be found in the *Diagnostic and Statistical Manual of Mental Disorders*, Fifth Edition (*DSM-5*; American Psychiatric Association [APA], 2013). The book is divided into six parts. In Part I, readers are introduced to child and adolescent characteristics (e.g., family, school, economics, culture) that shape developmental pathways toward normal or deviant behaviors, and the role of theoretical perspectives in guiding our understanding of the underlying processes. Current trends and issues in the areas of professional ethics, research, assessment, diagnosis, and treatment are also addressed. Part II contains three chapters (intellectual and developmental disabilities, attention-deficit/hyperactivity disorder, specific learning disabilities) that focus on disorders representing a range of neurodevelopmental impairments and functioning from global (global developmental delay) to more specific deficits (executive functioning deficits).

The focus in Part III is on the internalizing disorders (anxiety and obsessive-compulsive and related disorders, disorders of mood and somatic symptom and related disorders), whereas Part IV discusses externalizing disorders, such as oppositional defiant disorder and disorders of conduct. Disorders that most likely have onset in later childhood or adolescence, such as eating disorders and substance-related disorders, are presented in Part VI. The final section, Part VII, contains two chapters devoted to special topics: trauma- and stress-related disorders and children of diverse cultures. Finally, the book provides three additional appendices that contain important information, regarding ethical codes of conduct, references for assessment instruments and resources, and the Individuals with Disabilities Education Improvement Act of 2004 (IDEA 04).

Alan S. Kaufman, PhD, and
Nadeen L. Kaufman, EdD,
Founding Editors
Yale Child Study Center,
Yale University School of Medicine

Part I

The Foundations

The following three chapters provide the basic foundations for understanding child and adolescent psychopathology. In the Introduction, readers will discover how child and adolescent psychopathology evolved as a unique discipline and the growing pains that were evident in achieving the early milestones, historically. Through the use of case examples, readers will gain an increased appreciation of important developmental considerations that are required in order to make clinical decisions regarding where a child's behavior is best represented on the normal versus abnormal continuum based on important information available from developmental expectations and theoretical perspectives.

The second chapter provides important information regarding ethical issues and challenges that practitioners face in their work with young children and adolescents, whether this takes place in a clinical or research setting. Issues of confidentiality can be daunting as practitioners attempt to determine who is the legal guardian for children under 18 years of age (or the age of majority in the state where the clinician is practicing), especially in cases where information regarding the custodial parent may not be readily accessible. The chapter ends with an important discussion about common risks and protective factors that can influence the trajectory of child development.

Finally, in the third chapter, readers are introduced to issues in diagnosis, assessment, and treatment as they relate to different systems of classification (empirical versus categorical), and how the recently revised *DSM-5* has attempted to address these issues. Different methods of clinical assessment will be discussed, as well as issues of obtaining parental consent and child assent for individual assessments.

One

INTRODUCTION TO CHILD AND ADOLESCENT PSYCHOPATHOLOGY

Development, Theories, and Influences

Recognition of clinical child psychology as a unique discipline has only emerged in the past 30 years, despite auspicious beginnings. The end of the 19th century ushered in an era of social reform that addressed the need to protect children's rights concerning health and education, to provide protection within the judicial system, and to free children from working within the adult workforce (Culbertson, 1991). In the wake of this movement, child labor laws and mandatory education became a reality. At the turn of the 20th century, Lightner Witmer established the first psychology clinic to treat children with learning disabilities, and by 1909 more than 450 cases had been seen at the clinic. However, Witmer fell out of favor with his colleagues, because of his refusal to adopt Terman's revision of the Stanford-Binet tests of intelligence and his reluctance to accept Freud's theories on behavior disorders.

William Healey, an English-born psychiatrist who shared America's enthusiasm for Freud's theories, opened the first child guidance clinic in Chicago in 1909. By 1933, 42 child guidance clinics were in operation at a wide variety of locations, including juvenile institutions, courts, hospitals, schools, and universities. As the popularity of the child guidance clinics grew, the emphasis shifted from delinquency to problems evident at home and at school, with a primary interest in parent–child difficulties.

The underlying philosophy of the time was that the source of children's problems could be found in parenting and the family (Horn, 1989, p. 27). In 1948, 54 child guidance clinics came together to form the American Association of Psychiatric Clinics for Children (AAPCC). According to Horn, this marked a shift from identification to training and treatment; a movement riddled with debate over standards, roles, and status among psychiatrists, psychologists, and social workers. For a summary of the timelines in historical perspective, refer to Rapid Reference 1.1.

Despite the popular rise of the child guidance clinics, the field of clinical child psychology encountered many roadblocks that delayed the establishment of child psychopathology as a unique discipline until only 30 years ago. One reason for the delay was the fact that theories of child development were firmly entrenched in the controversy over nature versus nurture.

Rapid Reference 1.1

Early Milestones in the History of Child Psychology

1892 American Psychological Association founded; G. Stanley Hall is first president.

1896 L. Witmer founds first psychology clinic, at the University of Pennsylvania, for children with learning disabilities and academic problems.

1897 Witmer's clinic offers four-week summer course in child psychology.

1905 Binet-Simon Intelligence Scale for measuring mental abilities in children published in France.

1907 Witmer establishes a residential school for retarded children and founds the first clinical journal, *The Psychological Clinic.*

1908 H. Goddard establishes first clinical internship program at Vineland Training School (New Jersey).

1909 Beers, supported by psychologist W. James and psychiatrist A. Meyer, founds the National Committee for Mental Hygiene, later renamed the National Association of Mental Health (NAMH).

1909 W. Healey establishes the first child guidance center, the Juvenile Psychopathic Institute (Chicago), to treat and prevent mental illness in juvenile offenders; later named the Institute for Juvenile Research.

1909 G. Stanley Hall invites Sigmund Freud to lecture on psychoanalysis at Clark University.

1910 Goddard translates the Binet-Simon Intelligence Test for use with "feebleminded children" at the Vineland School.

1911 A. Gesell appointed director of Yale's Psychoeducational Clinic; renamed Clinic of Child Development.

1912 J. B. Watson publishes *Psychology as a Behaviorist Views It.*

1916 Terman's Stanford-Binet Intelligence Test is published.

1917 APA section of clinical psychology is founded.

1920 Watson and Raynor demonstrate that fear can be conditioned in a child called Albert.

1922 NAMH funds eight pilot child guidance clinics established in various cities.
1926 Piaget publishes *The Language and Thought of the Child.*
1928 Anna Freud publishes *Introduction to the Technique of Child Analysis.*
1930 Kanner joins Johns Hopkins University and opens first pediatric psychiatric clinic, Harriet Lane Pediatric Clinic.
1932 M. Klein authors *The Psychoanalysis of Children.*
1935 Kanner publishes first textbook on child psychiatry.
1937 Adolescent psychiatric ward opens at Bellevue Hospital.
1944 Kanner describes autistic behaviors and attributes illness to "refrigerator mother."
1945 Studies by R. Spitz raise concerns about negative impact of institutional life on children.
1948 American Association of Psychiatric Clinics for Children (AAPCC) is formed as 54 child guidance clinics come together.
1950s Behavior therapy emerges as a treatment alternative for child and family problems.
1951 Bowlby publishes on attachment.
1952 American Psychiatric Association (APA) publishes the *Diagnostic and Statistical Manual of Mental Disorders (DSM).* The *DSM* contains two disorders of childhood: Adjustment Reaction and Childhood Schizophrenia.
1953 The American Academy of Child Psychiatry is established.
1968 *DSM-II* published and adds "hyperkinetic reaction of childhood."
1977 Thomas and Chess publish work on the nine categories of temperament.
1980 *DSM-III* is first version of *DSM* to make specific developmental recommendations regarding childhood disorders.
1984 Sroufe and Rutter introduce domain of child psychopathology as offshoot of developmental psychology; *Developmental Psychopathology Journal* is introduced.
1999 Clinical Child Psychology established as the 53rd division of American Psychological Association; renamed Society of Clinical Child and Adolescent Psychology (2001).

Note: See Nietzel, Bernstein, & Milich, 1994, and Slaff, 1989, for details.

Toward the end of the 19th century, there was a growing belief that mental illness had a biological basis, and Emil Kraepelin's (1856–1926) textbook published in 1883 argued that physical ailments could cause mental dysfunction. The disease model was a mixed blessing, with some practitioners intent on finding a cure, whereas others feared that diseases could be transmitted to others or passed on genetically to offspring. Fear and misunderstanding resulted in the placement of adults and children with mental retardation and mental illness in institutions for the next half-century.

CAUTION

The nature (heredity) and nurture (environment) debate has waged for centuries. John Locke, the 17th-century English philosopher, proposed that children came into the world as a blank slate (*tabula rasa*), and it was the parents' responsibility to fill the slate with the proper environmental controls and discipline. By contrast, the 18th-century French philosopher Jean-Jacques Rousseau envisioned the child as a flower that would grow and flourish, naturally, in a *laissez-faire* approach. Caring, nurturing, and opportunity were the parents' gifts to the growing child. Most psychologists today appreciate the interaction of both heredity and environment.

DON'T FORGET

Henry Goddard is credited with establishing one of the largest training schools for the mentally retarded. However, the belief system upon which the school was constructed did much to harm attitudes about the mentally retarded. Goddard's beliefs were summarized in his fictional book that chronicled two sets of offspring of Martin Kallikak: (1) descendants from his union with a barmaid, who were plagued by feeblemindedness, delinquency, and alcoholism, and (2) descendants of his union with a "nice girl," who all became respectable citizens.

Another roadblock to the establishment of clinical child psychology as a unique discipline was the shift in emphasis from treatment to identification. Psychologists became increasingly involved in intellectual assessments of children and adults for placement in education and the military. By 1918, psychologists had screened more than 2 million potential candidates for the army.

Abnormal behavior in children continued to be interpreted from the vantage point of adults, and thus childhood maladjustment was described in adult terms and treated with adult treatment methods (Peterson & Roberts, 1991). By the mid-1930s, child guidance clinics were firmly entrenched in linking child problems to adult problems. After years of viewing children's problems from the vantage point of adult psychopathology, the current trends are to refine our understanding of how many characteristic features of these child and adolescent disorders differ from adult disorders. Since the 1970s, several journals have emerged that are exclusively devoted to research about child and adolescent clinical concerns (e.g., *Journal of Clinical Child Psychology, Journal of Abnormal Child Psychology, Journal of the American Academy of Child and Adolescent Psychiatry, Journal of Child Psychology and Psychiatry and Allied Disciplines*).

In the mid-1980s, the field of clinical child psychology witnessed the evolution of yet another stage of development. At this time, the domain of developmental psychopathology (Sroufe & Rutter, 1984) emerged as an offshoot of developmental psychology, complete with its own journal, *Development and Psychopathology*. Within this framework, atypical behavior is conceptualized as deviating from the normal developmental pathway.

Organizational principles of developmental psychopathology define a system that considers human development as *holistic* (the interactive and dynamic concept of the total child) and *hierarchical* (movement toward increasing complexity; Cicchetti & Toth, 1998). Increased emphasis has been placed on determining processes that can inhibit (protective factors) or escalate (risks) the development of maladaptive behaviors.

DON'T FORGET

Conceptually, because normal and abnormal behaviors stem from the same developmental principles and are part of the same continuum, increased emphasis is placed on having knowledge of normal behavior (its stages and underlying processes) as a precursor to abnormal behaviors.

PRACTICAL APPLICATIONS: CASE STUDY ILLUSTRATIONS OF CHILD AND ADOLESCENT PSYCHOPATHOLOGY

The following cases will serve as an introduction to some of the practical issues faced by clinicians working with children and youth and provide a framework for better understanding the importance of considering developmental contexts and environmental influences in understanding child psychopathology.

The Cases of Jason, Winnie, and Brian

The psychologist is asked to observe three children in Mrs. Skill's fourth-grade classroom: Jason, Winnie, and Brian. All three children have been rated as demonstrating the following behaviors: has problems sustaining attention, loses things necessary for tasks, is easily distracted, is forgetful, is restless, doesn't seem to listen, is disorganized, doesn't complete assignments, and demonstrates poor follow-through. The psychologist's observations of the children verify information obtained from the teacher rating scales. A review of the children's cumulative folders reveals that all three children scored within the average range on the Otis-Lennon group intellectual screening test given during the previous third-grade school year.

Question: Is a diagnosis of attention-deficit/hyperactivity disorder (ADHD) an appropriate classification for Jason, Winnie, or Brian? Why?

According to the *Diagnostic and Statistical Manual of Mental Disorders*, fifth edition (*DSM-5*; APA, 2013), all three children demonstrate many symptoms associated with ADHD. The psychologist has verified the teacher's ratings of these behaviors through classroom observation, has reviewed the school records, and is fairly comfortable ruling out any contributing intellectual difficulties. Furthermore, these problems have been documented on an ongoing basis.

What's missing from this picture?

In order for the psychologist to diagnose whether the three children have ADHD—or rule out the possibility of ADHD in favor of a different diagnosis (a process called *differential diagnosis*)—information is required from several key sources, including the home and school environments. What is missing, therefore, is information from the child's home environment. The psychologist schedules interviews with all three parents to obtain additional information.

The Case of Brian

According to Brian's mother, Brian has "always been this way." His mother describes Brian as a "space cadet" who constantly misplaces things and often gets distracted when trying to do his homework. Brian eats standing up and is always on the go. His mother adds that Brian is just like his father, who is also restless, active, and distracted. Brian seems very capable (his mother and teacher both feel he is a bright boy), but he has problems completing assignments because of his distractibility. Everything seems to take his attention away from the task at hand.

After talking to the mother, the psychologist develops a *case formulation* (a hypothesis about why the problem behavior exists and how it is being maintained). The case formulation is based on information obtained from the family history, consistency in Brian's behaviors across situational contexts (home and school), and the longevity of the problem (he has always been that way). The psychologist is now more confident in suggesting that Brian does have ADHD, probably the Predominantly Inattentive Presentation, and discusses possible interventions with Brian's parents.

Based on all of the information, the psychologist makes a provisional diagnosis for Brian of ADHD, Predominantly Inattentive Presentation.

The Case of Winnie

Winnie's mother arrives at the interview out of breath and very anxious to hear about her daughter. Her mother describes Winnie as a "real worrier" and admits that she is that way herself. Winnie has always been very timid, and as an infant she was cautious, fearful, sensitive to noises and touch, and "slow to warm up to others." Socially, Winnie has a few close friends. Homework is a painful process, as perfectionistic tendencies get in the way of completing assignments, because Winnie keeps erasing her work. Because of the extent of her fears and anxieties, Winnie is often overwhelmed by tasks and appears inattentive, distracted, and forgetful.

Winnie's provisional diagnosis is general anxiety disorder (GAD), but the psychologist also needs to rule out possible obsessive-compulsive disorder (OCD).

The Case of Jason

Jason's foster mother arrives at the interview with her social worker. This is Jason's fourth foster placement in the past 2 years. Jason has been in his current foster placement for the past 6 months. According to the social worker, Jason was a witness to family violence from an early age. Jason's family was well known to Social Services, and Jason has been in care several times in the past for reported neglect and possible abuse. Shortly after Jason and his brother rejoined their parents 2 years ago, Jason's father shot his mother and then himself, while Jason and his younger brother slept in an adjoining bedroom. Jason has been receiving play therapy for the past 2 years. Jason continues to have trouble sleeping and is often agitated and restless. In relationships, his behavior vacillates between being overly inhibited (shy and withdrawn) or disinhibited (socially precocious). His ability to sustain his attention and concentration is impaired, and he is often forgetful and appears disorganized.

Jason's provisional diagnosis is chronic posttraumatic stress disorder (PTSD), but an attachment disorder (reactive attachment disorder [RAD] or disinhibited social engagement disorder [DSED]) and ADHD also need to be ruled out.

Summary of the Three Child Study Cases

Although the three children demonstrated similar symptoms in the classroom and in the home environment (pervasive across situations), only one of the three children was likely demonstrating ADHD.

Given high rates of *comorbidity* (disorders occurring together) in childhood disorders and the fact that many disorders present with similar symptom clusters, the need for developing a case formulation based on information from multiple sources cannot be overemphasized.

The Case of Matthew

The next day, the psychologist is asked to observe another child in the fourth grade: Matthew, an 11-year-old who is repeating the fourth grade. Matthew has a behavior problem, and his emotions often escalate out of control. This day is no exception. When the psychologist observes Matthew in the classroom, he demonstrates a full-blown temper tantrum, throwing himself on the floor, kicking, and crying.

The psychologist makes an appointment to meet with Matthew's father. She leaves the elementary school and stops on her way home to pick up her 3-year-old daughter, Rachel, at the daycare center. To the psychologist's dismay, Rachel is lying on the floor, kicking and screaming because another child took her favorite toy from her.

When the psychologist meets with Matthew's father, he states that Matthew's behavior problems have been ongoing from an early age. Matthew can be aggressive, moody, and irritable. Tantrums are frequent and often unpredictable. Matthew is oppositional and defiant at home and at school, and he often refuses to comply with even the smallest request. Often Matthew seems to deliberately annoy others.

Question: Are the temper tantrums produced by Matthew and Rachel indicative of a disruptive behavior disorder?

Disruptive behavior disorders, classified as conduct disorder (CD) and oppositional defiant disorder (ODD) by the *DSM-5* (APA, 2013), are highly prevalent in children and adolescents. Of these disorders, ODD is represented by a constellation of symptoms of aggression, anger, and disobedience. Children with ODD have recurrent displays of negative behaviors toward authority that are defiant, disobedient, and hostile (APA, 2013). Matthew's provisional diagnosis is ODD or depression.

The Case of Rachel

The psychologist's 3-year-old daughter throws tantrums at the daycare center when she is frustrated. These tantrums have been increasing in frequency for the past 6 months. Talking to the daycare staff, the psychologist finds out that one particular child, Arty, seems to trigger these tantrums in her daughter. Arty joined the daycare center about six months ago. Rachel does not throw tantrums at home and is a relatively easy-to-manage child. The psychologist is aware that, developmentally, tantrum behavior in toddlers normally peaks at around three years of age. The daycare center staff members are not concerned and see Rachel's behavior as reactive to increasing frustration. The provisional diagnosis is a developmentally appropriate response to frustration.

DON'T FORGET

Although Matthew and Rachel displayed the same behavioral response to frustration (temper tantrums), when viewed within a developmental context, tantrums are a normal expression of frustration at 3 years of age but more deviant behavior at 11 years of age.

DISTINGUISHING NORMAL FROM ABNORMAL BEHAVIOR

Although many of the professional skills and competencies required to distinguish normal from abnormal behavior are shared by clinicians who serve adult and child populations, several unique skills and competencies distinguish these two populations as separate clinical fields.

Determining whether a behavior pattern is normal or abnormal requires, at a minimum, a fundamental understanding of normal expectations and the range of behaviors that constitute the broad limits of the average or normal range. In order to determine whether a behavior falls outside of the normal range, clinical judgment is often based on a series of decision-making strategies. One way of measuring how the behavior compares to normal expectations is the use of "the four Ds" as a guideline to evaluating the behavior: *deviance, dysfunction, distress,* and *danger* (Comer, 2013).

Rachel, the psychologist's 3-year-old daughter, was previously observed throwing a temper tantrum at the daycare center. Consider the severity of Rachel's tantrum behavior in relation to the tantrum behavior of another 3-year-old child, Arty.

The psychologist observes Rachel throwing a temper tantrum because Arty has taken her favorite toy. Rachel is lying on the floor, crying and kicking her legs into the floor mat. This behavior occurs whenever Arty takes this toy away (about twice a week) and lasts until the teacher intervenes. Rachel's mother has not seen this behavior at home. Arty also causes a similar reaction from Sara, another child in the program. Arty is constantly fighting with other children. Arty takes what he wants, when he wants it. If stopped, Arty throws temper tantrums that escalate in proportion and can last up to half an hour. On two occasions, Arty has injured a teacher by throwing an object wildly into the air. When frustrated, Arty will strike out, and he has bitten others to get his way. Arty's mother has asked for help with managing Arty's behavior. She is afraid Arty will injure his new baby brother.

DON'T FORGET

Clinical decisions are often based on measures of the *intensity, duration*, and *frequency* of a behavior relative to the norm. In addition, evaluating whether a behavior is pervasive across situations can also provide information regarding the nature and severity of the behavior in terms of eliciting *mild, moderate*, or *severe* levels of concern.

In evaluating Rachel's and Arty's behaviors, we know that tantrum behavior peaks at 3 years of age and that biting is not uncommon among preschoolers. However, although Rachel's tantrum behavior would likely be considered to fall within the range of normal expectations, Arty's behaviors are more concerning, because the behaviors demonstrate deviance from the norm on all measures: intensity (he has injured others), frequency (he has done so repeatedly), and duration (his tantrums last at least half an hour). In contrast, Rachel's behaviors are isolated to the school situation and to Arty's advances in particular. Rachel's tantrums would likely elicit a mild level of concern and possibly result in the development of a behavioral intervention plan to assist Rachel in coping with Arty's advances.

However, in addition to all the aforementioned concerns, Arty's behaviors would also be considered more severe because of the pervasive nature of the behavior, which is evident at home as well as at school. Furthermore, the behaviors pose a danger to those around him (he has injured a teacher), and Arty has not developed appropriate skills in areas of self-control or social relationships (dysfunction). Arty's ease of frustration, low frustration tolerance, and habitual tantrum behavior all signal high levels of distress. In addition, Arty's behaviors are disturbing and distressing to others. Based on the nature of Arty's problem behaviors, a more intensive treatment program would be required to modify his behavior.

CAUTION

There has been an increasing awareness of the need to integrate cultural variations into our understanding of deviant behaviors and psychopathology (Fabrega, 1990; Rogler, 1999). The *DSM-5* (APA, 2013) includes sections acknowledging cultural factors and cultural reference groups in describing disorders.

DON'T FORGET

Symptoms of inattentiveness, lack of concentration, restlessness, fidgeting, forgetfulness, and disorganization may signal a case of ADHD. However, differential diagnosis may be required to rule out anxiety, depression, post-traumatic stress disorder, child abuse, learning problems, and a host of other potential problems that share similar features.

The use of the four Ds can provide helpful guidelines in determining normal from abnormal behavior in the following ways:

- *Deviance.* Determining the degree that behaviors are deviant from the norm can be assisted through the use of informal assessment (interviews, observations, symptom rating scales) or more formal psychometric test batteries (personality assessment). Classification systems can also provide clinicians with guidelines for evaluating the degree of deviance. Clinicians working with children and adults must also be aware that several disorders can share common features, and often additional data gathering is required to rule out or confirm the existence of a specific disorder (*differential diagnosis*). In addition to disorders sharing similar features, some disorders also occur together more frequently, a condition known as *comorbidity.*
- *Dysfunction.* Once a disorder is identified, the relative impact of the disorder on the individual's functioning must be determined. Child clinicians may be interested in the degree of dysfunction in such areas as school performance (academic functioning) or social skills.
- *Distress.* An area closely related to dysfunction is the degree of distress the disorder causes. Children often have difficulty articulating feelings and may provide little information to assist the clinician in determining distress. Interviews with parents and teachers can provide additional sources of information. Some disorders may present little distress for the individual concerned but prove very distressing to others.
- *Danger.* In order to determine whether a given behavior places an individual at risk, two broad areas are evaluated: risk for self-harm and risk of harm to others. Historically, the focus has been on victimization and maltreatment of children (abuse or neglect) or the assessment of risk for self-harm (suicide intent). However, more recent events, such as the 1999 Columbine shootings and increased awareness of bullying, have raised concerns regarding children as perpetrators of harm. Accordingly, emphasis has been placed

on methods of identifying potentially dangerous children and conducting effective threat assessments.

Normal and Abnormal Behaviors: Developmental Considerations

Evaluation of psychopathology from a developmental perspective requires the integration of information about child characteristics (biological and genetic) and environmental characteristics (family, peers, school, neighborhood). Therefore, understanding child psychopathology from a developmental perspective requires an understanding of the nature of cognitive, social, emotional, and physical competencies, limitations, and task expectations for each stage of development. This understanding is crucial to an awareness of how developmental issues impact psychopathology and treatment. Examples of developmental tasks, competencies, and limitations are presented in Rapid Reference 1.2.

The Impact of Theoretical Perspectives

The ability to distinguish normal from abnormal behavior and to select developmentally appropriate child interventions can be guided by information obtained from various theoretical frameworks. Different theoretical perspectives can provide the clinician with guidelines concerning expectations for social, emotional, cognitive, physical, and behavioral outcomes. In addition, a therapist's theoretical assumptions will also influence how the disorder is conceptualized and guide the course of the treatment focus.

Rapid Reference 1.2

Examples of Developmental Tasks, Competencies, and Limitations

Age or Stage of Development	Task or Limitations
Birth to 1 year	Trust vs. mistrust (Erikson) Secure vs. insecure attachment (Bowlby) Differentiation between self and others Reciprocal socialization Development of object permanence (Piaget: objects exist when out of sight) First steps; first word

Age or Stage of Development	Task or Limitations
Toddler: 1–2.5	Autonomy vs. shame and doubt (Erikson) Increased independence, self-assertion, and pride Beginnings of self-awareness Social imitation and beginnings of empathy Beginnings of self-control Delayed imitation and symbolic thought Language increases to 100 words Increase in motor skills and exploration
Preschool: 2.5–6	Initiative vs. guilt (Erikson) Inability to decenter (Piaget: logic bound to perception; problems with appearance/reality) Egocentric (emotional and physical perspective; one emotion at a time) Increased emotion regulation (under-regulation vs. over-regulation) Increased need for rules and structure Can identify feelings: Guilt and conscience are evident Emergent anxieties, phobias, fears
School age: 6–11	Industry vs. inferiority (Erikson) Sense of competence, mastery, and efficacy Concrete operations (Piaget: no longer limited by appearance, but limited by inability to think in the abstract) Can experience blends of emotions (love-hate) Self-concept and moral conscience Realistic fears (injury, failure) and irrational fears (mice, nightmares)
Teen years	Identity vs. role confusion (Erikson) Abstract reasoning (Piaget) Emotional blends in self and others (ambiguity) Return of egocentricity (Piaget/Elkind: imaginary audience and personal fable) Self-concept relative to peer acceptance and competence

Neurobiological Theories

Neurobiological and physiological theories are concerned with the impact of biological and genetic factors on individual differences. There has been increasing recognition of the interactive contribution of environmental (health, nutrition, stress) and genetic influences. Emphasis has been placed on several factors in this area, including temperament, genetic transmission, and brain structure and function.

In defining abnormal behavior, a neurobiological model would seek to determine which parts of the body or brain were malfunctioning, whether genetics, brain chemistry, or brain anatomy. Twin studies have been instrumental in providing information concerning the role of genetics, while refined neurological approaches, such as magnetic resonance imaging (MRI), have also contributed to our knowledge of underlying brain-based differences in some disorders.

Psychodynamic Theories and Theories of Attachment

Freud initially envisioned abnormal behavior resulting from fixations or regressions based on earlier unresolved stages of conflict. His psychosexual stages provide potential insight into unconscious drives and conflicts that may influence the underlying dynamics of certain pathologies. These unconscious defense mechanisms serve to protect the vulnerable ego and stem from battles between the id (more primitive pleasure principle) and the superego (moral conscience). These defense mechanisms add depth to our understanding of more primitive child defenses, such as denial, or more socially constructive defenses, such as humor.

DON'T FORGET

Historically, psychoanalytic applications have been very difficult to support empirically. Influenced by Bowlby's theories of self-development and attachment, recent research by Fonagy and Target (1996) has provided empirical support for psychodynamic developmental therapy for children (PDTC). Working through the medium of play, therapists assist children to develop skills in the self-regulation of impulses and enhanced awareness of others.

Erik Erikson (1902–1994) also supported the notion of stages; however, his psychosocial stages outline socioemotional tasks that must be mastered to allow for positive growth across the lifespan. As can be seen in Rapid Reference 1.2, theorists have adapted the concept of developmental tasks and stages of development to explain and predict a wide variety of behaviors based on competencies and limitations (social, emotional, cognitive, and physical) evident at each of the stages.

According to Erikson, in the first year of life, the major task is to develop a sense of basic trust versus mistrust. From the foundation of a secure attachment, the preschooler is free to explore the environment. Either a growing sense of autonomy develops or the insecure child may shrink from these experiences, producing feelings of shame and self-doubt. The school-age child masters school-related subjects and peer socialization, which increase a sense of industry versus inferiority. In adolescence, the task becomes one of identity versus role confusion.

John Bowlby's (1908–1990) *adaptation theory* was influenced by Darwin's theory of evolution and Freud's emphasis on internal working models. Bowlby believed that early attachment relationships carry a profound influence throughout the lifespan. Later, Mary Ainsworth explored attachment issues using the Strange Situation experiments and revealed that securely attached infants were more independent and better problem solvers than were insecurely attached infants. Infants who demonstrated avoidant attachment rarely showed distress when separated from caregivers, whereas infants who demonstrated resistant attachment often demonstrated clingy behaviors and greater upset at separations from caregivers who responded with unpredictable behavioral extremes (love and anger). In the late 1970s, working with a population of maltreated infants, Main and Weston (1981) ultimately added a fourth category of disorganized behavior to describe distressful and frightened responses to caregivers.

CAUTION

Although attachment theory was developed to explain how children develop an organized schema of relationships (internal working models), Main and Hesse (1990) reasoned that disorganized responses were the result of an inability to construct a schema, because attachment in these maltreated infants activated two competing and irreconcilable response systems: attachment (approach) and fear (avoidance).

Behavioral Theories

Behavioral theory is based on the fundamental credo that behavior is shaped by associations (contingencies) resulting from positive (reinforcement) and negative (punishment) consequences. Consequences are *positive* if they achieve one of the following goals:

- They add a benefit (positive reinforcement; e.g., finish your work in class and you will be given 10 minutes of free activity time).
- They remove or avoid (escape) a negative consequence (negative reinforcement; e.g., if you finish your work in class, you will not have to stay after school).

DON'T FORGET

The concept of negative reinforcement is more difficult to understand than positive reinforcement because negative reinforcement is often confused with punishment. Remember that punishments deliver negative consequences and reduce rather than increase behaviors.

Consequences are *negative* if they achieve one of the following goals:

- They add an adverse or negative consequence (punishment).
- They remove or avoid a positive consequence (penalty).

DON'T FORGET

Behaviors can also be categorized as a *behavioral excess* (externalizing, acting-out behaviors) or a *behavioral deficit* (internalizing, withdrawn behaviors).

CAUTION

Parents or teachers can be very frustrated when a child continues to engage in repeated negative behaviors despite warnings, punishments, and various other acts of negative consequences. However, what they fail to understand is that all the nagging and cajoling serves as a positive reinforcement to the child, because the outcome is increased adult attention. Therefore, the more nagging continues, the more the behavior is reinforced and will be sustained.

Some punishments can be so severe that behavior is eliminated altogether, a condition known as *extinction*. If behavior is no longer reinforced and continually punished, then extinction is often the result. Determining whether the behavior is an excess or deficit also requires knowledge of what to expect based on developmental level. Optimally, a behavioral plan will target increasing a deficit behavior rather than reducing an excessive behavior. For example, it is preferable and often more successful to attempt to increase on-task behavior than to attempt to reduce off-task behavior, because increasing the positive behavior will ultimately reduce negative consequences.

Although the majority of learned behavior occurs through operant conditioning or observational learning, behaviorists use the paradigm of classical conditioning to explain the development of irrational fears or phobias. For example, a child may develop a fear of sleeping alone if he or she is awakened by a very loud thunderstorm. Furthermore, the fear might generalize to fear of the dark, fear of loud noises, or fear of his or her own bed or bedroom. Pairing the loud noise with sleeping alone can result in the child's developing a conditioned response of fear of his or her own bed.

Cognitive Theories

Cognitive theorists are primarily interested in the relationship between thoughts and behaviors and how faulty assumptions can impact on social relationships, as well as influence self-attributions in a negative way. Jean Piaget's stages of cognitive development are outlined in Rapid Reference 1.2. Piaget was highly influential in his attempts to chart the course of cognitive development. According to Piaget, children in the preoperational stage (ages 2 to 7) can be easily misled by dominant visual features because of their inability to consider two aspects simultaneously, what Piaget calls an inability to decenter. A very young child will say that there is more liquid in a tall, thin glass than a short, fat one, even though the child witnessed the same amount of liquid being poured into the two glasses. Visual dominance also contributes to difficulties separating appearance and reality (a dog wearing a cat mask is now a cat). Taking another's perspective or point of view is also very limited because of the child's egocentrism or self-focus. The school-aged child (the concrete operations stage) is capable of reasoning beyond that of the preschool child; however, this stage is limited by concrete observations. According to Piaget, abstract thinking is not achieved until adolescence, when hypothetical and deductive reasoning emerges. Although Piaget believed that all children progress through a series of fixed stages, recent research has recognized that children of differing abilities may progress at different rates and that Piaget's stage theories may not be universal.

Social cognitive theories. Albert Bandura's (1977, 1986) contributions to the field of social cognition stem from his early work on social learning processes, observational learning, and aggression. Bandura's (1977) understanding of the social aspects of learning has been instrumental in increasing our awareness of observational learning. Children's observation and subsequent modeling of adult behavior can have positive (nurturing and empathic caring behaviors) or negative consequences (aggressive responses; e.g., witness to domestic violence).

DON'T FORGET

The concept of *triadic reciprocity* was developed by Bandura to explain the complex nature of people, behaviors, and the environment. According to Bandura, behavior not only is the outcome of the person in a given environment or situation, but it also influences the person and the environment.

Person ⇄ Environment

⇅

Behavior

Research concerning children's understanding of social relationships has also been applied to the development of social skills and problem solving in social situations. Studies in this area have revealed that children who are rejected by their peers are often aggressive, argumentative, and retaliatory toward others (Dodge, Bates, & Pettit, 1990). Furthermore, negative behaviors often resulted from tendencies to misinterpret ambivalent social situations as hostile, or what has come to be known as the ***hostile attribution bias***.

DON'T FORGET

Aggression from the social cognitive perspective might be explained by observational learning (the child is potentially a witness to violence at home; Bandura) or as resulting from an interpretation of a situation based on faulty attributions, *hostile attribution bias* (Dodge et al., 1990).

Cognitive-behavioral theories. The cognitive-behavioral approach seeks to understand associations between thoughts and behaviors. Therefore, emphasis is placed on understanding how the child's faulty belief system contributes to maladaptive behaviors, such as aggression, depression, and anxiety. Cognitive theorists, such as Aaron Beck (1976), posit that depression develops and is sustained by self-attributions arising from a *cognitive triad* producing thoughts of helplessness, hopelessness, and worthlessness. Seligman and Peterson (1986) suggest that learned helplessness can develop from repeated negative self-attributions, which produce feelings of powerlessness and lack of control that ultimately become a self-fulfilling prophecy.

Theories of Parenting and Family Systems Theory

Baumrind (1991) also investigated *parenting styles* and found three approaches to parenting that impacted on child behaviors for better or worse. Children raised by authoritarian parents (high on structure, low on warmth) tend to react with behaviors that are aggressive and uncooperative, tend to be fearful of punishment, and are generally weak on initiative, self-esteem, and peer competence. Children who are raised in permissive households (high on warmth, low on structure) often fail to develop a sense of responsibility and self-control. Authoritative parents (high on warmth and high on structure) provide the optimum conditions for growth, and as a result children often demonstrate high degrees of self-reliance, self-esteem, and self-controlled behaviors.

Family systems theory is represented by a variety of approaches that emphasize the family unit as the focus of assessment and intervention. This theoretical framework acknowledges the family system itself, as a unit made up o systems: parent and child, marriage partners, siblings, extended fami on. Within families, behaviors are often directed toward maintaining or ing boundaries, alignment, and power. Boundaries are the imaginary lines define the various subsystems. A family's degree of dysfunction can often be dete mined by boundaries that are poorly or inconsistently defined or those that are too extreme (too loose or too rigid). Salvador Minuchin (1985), a proponent of structural family therapy, has suggested that enmeshed families (lacking in boundaries) may interpret a child's need to individuate as a threat to the family unit.

DON'T FORGET

A theorist from a family systems perspective might view the aggressive behaviors of a child in the context of behaviors motivated to undermine the importance of the primary marital relationship. Triangular relationships that shift the balance of power include the parent–child coalition (parent and child versus parent), triangulation (child caught between two parents), and detouring (maintaining the child as focus of the problem to avoid acknowledging marital problems).

DON'T FORGET

An understanding of developmental pathways includes an awareness that several possible pathways may produce the same outcome, an occurrence known as *equifinality* (e.g., many factors may cause a single outcome, such as childhood depression), and that similar risks may produce different outcomes, which is known as *multifinality* (e.g., childhood neglect may result in aggressive behavior in one child and withdrawal in another; Cicchetti & Rogosch, 1996).

Influences and Developmental Change

Most clinicians today recognize that in addition to understanding child characteristics (temperament, developmental stage), it is equally important to consider environmental influences (family, peers, school, community, economics, and culture) when evaluating child and adolescent disorders. Ultimately, the importance of including the developmental context in understanding child and adolescent disorders is crucial to comprehending not only the child's present level of distress or dysfunction but also how the difficulties came to be (developmental pathway).

The child clinician must also consider the impact of environmental influences as predisposing, precipitating, and maintaining (reinforcing) factors regarding the ough theoretical assumptions can guide our under- of developmental change, our knowledge of individual development, personality or temperament) can refine our child's unique nature. Ultimately, our awareness and under- these forces are embedded in the child's environmental context key to fully comprehending child psychopathology.

ing to Bronfenbrenner (1979, 1989), developmental contexts consist series of concentric circles emanating from the child, who occupies the innermost circle. At the core are the child's individual characteristics (biological context, such as genetic makeup, temperament, intelligence). Moving outward, the child's immediate environment (*microsystem*: family, school, peers, community, neighborhood), the surrounding social and economic context (*exosystem*: poverty, divorce, family stress), and the cultural context, beliefs, and laws (*macrosystem*), provide additional ripples and sources of influence. Within this framework, understanding a child's mental disorder requires an appreciation of the influences of all contextual variables. More recently, Bronfenbrenner and Morris (1998) have referred to the model as a *bioecological model* in order to emphasize the importance of biological factors. In addition, Bronfenbrenner ultimately included a fifth level (*chronosystem*) to refer to the impact of one's cumulative experiences over the course of a lifetime.

Understanding multiple levels of influence also requires emphasizing the dual nature of influence, because child and parent mutually influence each other. Therefore, the bidirectional nature of these influences, or *reciprocal determinism* (Bandura, 1985), becomes a crucial aspect of interpreting how interactive effects of these influences may be instrumental in constructing different developmental pathways.

> **CAUTION**
>
> One major influence that has often been overlooked is the compatibility between the environmental systems. According to Bronfenbrenner, the *mesosystem*, which represents the interaction between two microsystems (e.g., home and school environment), predicts the degree to which a system remains healthy, functional, and in balance.

Sameroff's *transactional model* (Sameroff & Chandler, 1975) captures the ongoing and interactive nature of developmental change between the child and the environment. A transactional model is also crucial to understanding the dynamics of various disorders in order to trace the developmental pathway and construct meaningful case formulations and relevant treatment alternatives. For example, in their discussion of depressive disorders in children and adolescents, Cicchetti and Toth (1998) stress the need to use an ecological transactional model in order to comprehend the complex nature of depressive disorders in children and youth and t the diverse and multiple influences that contribute to the emerge disorder.

DON'T FORGET

Several theories have been developed to assist our understanding of the complex dynamics that exist between individual and environmental influences. Bandura developed the concepts of *triadic reciprocity* (1977) and *reciprocal determinism* (1985) to emphasize the bidirectional nature of the influence. Bronfenbrenner (1979, 1989) envisioned ecological influences from the inner child to the outer world (family, community, culture). Sameroff's transactional model (Sameroff & Chandler, 1975) focuses on how interactive forces can shape the course of developmental change, while Cicchetti and Toth (1998) have applied the model to explain potential pathways for the development of depressive disorders in children and adolescence.

Theories in Context

Viewing the child within the contexts of developmental influences provides an enhanced level of insight into the underlying dynamics of potentially disordered behaviors and can guide and improve our ability to make case formulations that have ecological validity.

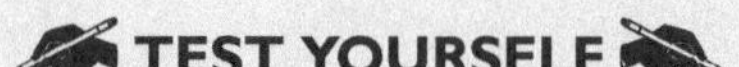

TEST YOURSELF

1. **The establishment of child psychology as a unique discipline**
   (a) occurred early in the 1900s.
   (b) was ushered in by the reform movement.
   (c) met with many road blocks.
   (d) was assisted by the intelligence testing movement.
2. **Which of the following is not considered one of the four Ds of clinical decision making?**
   (a) Dysfunction
   (b) Distress
   (c) Danger
   (d) Denial
3. **According to Erikson, the first psychosocial task sets the stage for development of**
   (a) autonomy versus shame.
   (b) trust versus mistrust.

ority.

le confusion.

several possible pathways that may produce the same g., many factors may be responsible for depression) is an f

ltifinality.

equifinality.

(c) triadic finality.

(d) triadic reciprocity.

5. According to Bronfenbrenner, the sphere of influence most concerned with culture and laws, is the

(a) macrosystem.

(b) exosystem.

(c) mesosystem.

(d) chronosystem.

6. Negative reinforcement is the same as

(a) punishment.

(b) a negative consequence.

(c) a penalty.

(d) escape.

7. According to Piaget, preschool children's reasoning is faulty because

(a) they have limited memories.

(b) they can only consider one visual feature at a time.

(c) vision acuity is not clearly established.

(d) they have limited attention spans.

Answers: 1. c; 2. d; 3. b; 4. b; 5. a; 6. d; 7. b

Two

ISSUES IN CHILD AND ADOLESCENT PSYCHOPATHOLOGY

Ethical Issues in Research and Practice

Mental health professionals working with children and families are guided by ethical principles and professional standards developed and monitored by their professional organizations. Psychologists' scientific, educational, and professional activities are guided by an ethics code (Ethical Principles of Psychologists and Code of Conduct) developed by the American Psychological Association. The most recent amended revision of the ethics code (American Psychological Association, 2010) includes a set of general guiding principles, as well as specific standards to be enforced across a wide variety of psychological roles (clinical, counseling, school psychology) and applied practices (research, education, test construction and design, or administrative or supervising capacities).

Other professional bodies, such as the American Counseling Association (ACA, 2005), the American School Counselors Association (ASCA, 2010), and the National Association of School Psychologists (NASP, 2010), have also developed ethical guidelines and principles for professional practice in schools and mental health settings. The aforementioned ethical codes are all available in their entirety on the Internet and can be accessed using the contact

> **DON'T FORGET**
>
> The five general principles are considered to be aspirational goals. Although these general principles are not considered to be enforceable rules, they provide the foundation from which psychologists can seek direction in making ethically based decisions. The five general principles are as follows:
>
> - Beneficence and nonmaleficence
> - Fidelity and responsibility
> - Integrity
> - Justice
> - Respect for rights and dignity of others

information provided in Appendix A. Common general principles among these different practicing bodies include principles of beneficence and nonmaleficence, fidelity, justice, and autonomy.

The American Psychological Association's ethical standards cover issues in 12 areas of practice, including resolving ethical issues, competence, human relations, privacy and confidentiality, advertising and public statements, record keeping and fees, education and training, research and publications, assessment, and therapy.

DON'T FORGET

Common principles across ethical codes of the American Psychological Association, ACA, and NASP, include the following:

- Beneficence and nonmaleficence (do not harm)
- Fidelity (maintain relationships of trust and ethical compliance)
- Justice or competence (fairness, equality, minimization of bias, and recognition of boundaries of professional competence)
- Autonomy (self-direction) and respect for the rights of others

RELATIONSHIP BETWEEN ETHICAL GUIDELINES AND LAWS

The majority of mental health laws and statues that apply to mental health practitioners fall within the realm of civil rather than criminal law. Ethical guidelines are not laws and, as such, are not legally binding. However, the professional bodies do monitor and sanction violations of their members. Although a professional body such as the American Psychological Association may sanction its members for violation of the ethics code, it can also inform other professional groups or state and federal associations of nonmembers who violate the ethics code.

Ethical Dilemmas

Ethical principles become very important when practitioners are faced with ethical challenges, such as ethical dilemmas. Practitioners face ethical dilemmas when two or more ethical principles are in conflict with one another. These principles can result in challenging decision-making choices that can become even more complex when one of the clients is a child.

PUTTING IT INTO PRACTICE

Balancing a client's right to fidelity (maintaining relationships of trust) with the principle of beneficence (benefit) and nonmaleficence (doing no harm) might occur if a therapist is faced with the following dilemma. A teenager (15 years of age) is receiving counseling at a private clinic, and her parents are paying for the sessions. The girl has disclosed to the counselor that she is having unprotected sex with a 17-year-old male. The teen has asked that the counselor not tell her parents. The parents suspect that their daughter might be sexually active, but they have no proof. They demand that the counselor provide the information to confirm their suspicions. In this case, the therapist must face several ethically challenging questions, including "Who is the client?"

ETHICAL ISSUES IN ASSESSING, TREATING, AND CONDUCTING RESEARCH WITH CHILDREN

One of the key clinical considerations in obtaining children's consent for involvement in assessment, treatment, or research is determining their level of competence in understanding the nuances and nature of what they are agreeing to. However, although the concepts of competency and informed consent overlap to a degree, one argument could be that competency is actually a necessary precursor to obtaining informed consent (Koocher & Keith-Spiegel, 1990). From this perspective, informed consent requires that the child demonstrate sufficient comprehension of the decision, which includes weighing potential outcomes and anticipating possible future consequences. Therefore, understanding how cognitive limitations might compromise decision making developmentally is a necessary precursor to obtaining informed consent.

Ethical Considerations in Research

- Research programs involving children as subjects must adhere to standards set by professional organizations such as the American Psychological Association (2010), NASP (2010), and the Society for Research in Child Development (2007).
- Another safeguard is a requirement that the research program be subject to an ethical review board to ensure compliance with the American Psychological Association's guidelines for research with human subjects and to evaluate the benefits and any potential risks. If there is no ethical review committee, NASP (2010) suggests the use of peer review ("preferably a school psychologist") of the research proposal and methodology.

- Children with physical vulnerabilities due to their diminutive size and cognitive limitations may also have a limited ability to comprehend significant issues such as the full nature of their participation or inherent appearance/reality distinctions.
- Due to cognitive limitations, informed consent for participation is obtained from the parents of children who are minors. However, even under these circumstances, the child's assent, or consent and willingness to participate, should be obtained by providing explanations of the process to the child in language suited to the child's developmental level.

DON'T FORGET

Although the age of majority is typically 18 (34 states), it can range up to 21 (Mississippi, D.C., New York) in the United States and between 18 (50% or six provinces) and 19 in Canada. The Canadian Code of Ethics for Psychologists recommends that children 12 years of age or older be involved in providing informed consent for their participation in research or assessment.

Ethical Considerations in Practice

Since children rarely self-refer, therapists are most often asked to see a child at the request of an adult (parent, teacher, guardian). Although parents or guardians are assumed to be acting in the best interests of the child, many situations can place professionals in a position of a conflict of interest. The Putting It Into Practice case study illustrates how a parent's wishes may not be in the best interest of the child and may actually infringe on the psychologist's ethical standards to do no harm and to demonstrate fidelity and integrity.

Issues of Confidentiality

In the vast majority of cases, parents or legal guardians of children under 18 years of age (or the given age of majority in the practicing state or province) are responsible for signing releases of information and/or obtaining or releasing reports pertaining to a child's medical or educational records. However, ethical issues can often result, especially when working with parents and adolescents regarding the limits of confidentiality. Clinicians working with adolescents or older children should always define the limits of confidentiality at the onset of the therapeutic relationship. Limits of confidentiality include ethical duties to report any indications of harm to self or others or reports of abuse. However, the limits of confidentiality with respect to parent access to other information discussed during therapy sessions may be far more difficult to address.

PUTTING IT INTO PRACTICE

Nancy and George have recently separated. Nancy is afraid that her son Joel is not responding well to the separation, and furthermore she does not approve of his visiting his father on the weekends. Nancy feels that Joel is more upset when he comes back on Sunday evenings and complains that it takes him all week to get over the visit, and then it is time to leave again.

Nancy is hoping that the psychologist can interview Joel to determine that the visits with his father are not in Joel's best interests. Nancy also does not want the psychologist to give any feedback to Joel's father about the assessment, because she intends to use this information in court to stop the visitation.

In this case, the therapist is faced with a case of parent interests that are not necessarily in line with the best interests of the child. Furthermore, the parent is also asking the psychologist to compromise ethical standards.

CAUTION

When working with adolescents and older children, a therapeutic rule of thumb is to discuss and negotiate rules of confidentiality and issues of privacy (between parent and child) prior to beginning therapeutic sessions.

Parents who seek therapeutic resources for older children and adolescents can often be persuaded that the clinician's ability to establish a trusting relationship with the child may initially require the therapist not to disclose information to the parents. By building a sense of rapport and trust, the psychologist will likely be able to develop the child's gradual understanding that sharing these private thoughts and feelings with parents will ultimately improve the parent–child relationship.

Confidentiality does not outweigh the therapist's mandated duty to report. The majority of mental health practitioners are legislated by state law

CAUTION

In obtaining parental consent for children whose parents are divorced or in custody litigation, the therapist must exercise special care in determining who is the custodial parent.

CAUTION

Be aware of state laws for reporting abuse. For example, failure to report abuse in the state of Florida is a misdemeanor of the first degree, subject to one year's imprisonment or a $1,000 fine.

to report issues of child abuse, neglect, or abandonment. Lack of reporting a suspected case of abuse can often result in legal ramifications.

RESEARCH METHODS IN CHILD PSYCHOPATHOLOGY

Clinical child researchers seek scientific truths guided by the four objectives of the scientific method: description, prediction, control (prevention), and understanding. Hypothesis testing can take two broad forms:

1. An investigation of the relationship among a set of variables (e.g., age, gender, aggression, leisure habits), known as *correlational research*
2. Attempts to demonstrate a cause-and-effect relationship between two or more variables (e.g., how leisure activities might influence aggressive tendencies)

DON'T FORGET

Researchers are primarily concerned with seeking answers to *nomothetic* truths, regarding the causes, nature, course, and treatment of childhood disorders.

CAUTION

Correlation does not imply causation. Although correlational research need only establish a relationship (either positive or negative) between the variables, experimental research has the more daunting task of delineating a cause-and-effect relationship.

DON'T FORGET

In an experiment, the researcher manipulates a variable and observes the effect of that variable on another variable. In the following experiment, the *independent variable* (violent versus nonviolent TV program) is manipulated by the experimenter, while the *dependent variable* (level of aggression) is the variable (behavior) that is monitored for expected change resulting from manipulation of the independent variable.

The Experimental Method

In conducting a true experiment, the researcher puts his or her hypothesis (hunch) about a behavior to the test. The researcher manipulates the experimental situation by randomly assigning subjects to one of two grouping conditions: a control group (which is not exposed to the variable in question) and an experimental group (which is exposed to the variable).

In the example provided in the Putting It Into Practice box, a researcher wants to examine the relationship between TV viewing and aggressive behavior. The research hypothesis is that watching TV violence increases aggressive behavior. In order to test this hypothesis, the researcher would set out to disprove (or reject) the null hypothesis. The null hypothesis would reflect a condition of no difference in level of aggressive behavior in children who watch violent versus nonviolent TV programs. One possible way to examine this research question would be to randomly assign subjects to the two conditions presented in the Putting It Into Practice box.

Several research questions can be generated about the study:

1. Does the study have *internal validity*? How well has the researcher linked increased aggression to the TV program that children watched (cause-and-effect relationship)?
2. Does the study have *external validity*? To what extent can the results of this study be generalized beyond the clinical laboratory?

PUTTING IT INTO PRACTICE

One hundred 4-year-old low socioeconomic status (SES) boys are randomly assigned to one of two groups: violent cartoon group (VCG) and nonviolent cartoon group (NCG). Each group is observed in the playroom (25 children at a time) while raters obtain a 15-minute baseline record for aggressive versus nonaggressive play for each child. Children are then exposed to a 15-minute cartoon: In the VCG group, the cartoon's main character is involved in several fight scenes involving swords, guns, and body contact, whereas the NCG group watches a Winnie the Pooh cartoon. Observations of play behaviors after cartoon watching are recorded for aggressive versus nonaggressive play. Results reveal that aggressive acts increased significantly for children who were in the VCG during the second play period and continued to be evident when the children returned for a third observation period 2 weeks later.

Internal Validity

The researcher has made a good attempt to match his samples for age, SES, and gender, as well as limiting the extraneous confounds. Objective measures were taken of play behaviors before and after TV viewing. The researcher has also included a repeat observation 2 weeks later to evaluate longer-term effects. In evaluating internal validity, it would be informative to know how observations were conducted to rule out any potential observer/experimenter bias effects (e.g., were observers aware of the group affiliation, or was the rater unaware of group affiliation? How was interrater reliability established?).

External Validity

Can findings be generalized to different populations? Although this experimental design produces high internal validity (experimental control), the artificial or contrived nature of the experimental situation may detract from ecological validity (validity of context). Generalizability of results would improve as the study was replicated, if findings were similar for males at different age levels, females at any age, and populations other than low-SES populations.

CAUTION

It could be strongly argued that the hypothetical study violates the ethical principle of beneficence and nonmaleficence, or the clinician's duty to do no harm. Ethically, the researcher's exposure of children in the experimental group to the violent cartoon condition resulted in increased and prolonged negative behaviors (aggression), which might produce long-term maladaptive consequences.

Quasi-Experimental Design

In clinical studies, randomized placement is often difficult to achieve, and in some cases may not be advised. One way to circumvent this problem is the use of a matched control group.

PUTTING IT INTO PRACTICE

A researcher wants to investigate the role of maternal depression on child abuse. Children who have been abused are matched to a group of children with the same demographics and characteristics (e.g., age, gender, SES, birth order) who have not been abused. Comparing prevalence rates of maternal depression for the two groups would provide an index of whether mothers of abused children were more depressed.

Empirically Based Treatments

There has been growing emphasis on empirically based treatments, specifically what works best for children who present with specific problems. In 1995, the

American Psychological Association's Task Force on Promotion and Dissemination of Psychological Procedures produced a report on empirically validated psychological treatments. *Well-established treatments* documented treatment effectiveness in comparison to another form of treatment, or placebo, in at least two between-group experimental studies. Further criteria included the need for inclusion of a treatment manual and clear delineation of subject characteristics. *Probably efficacious treatments* were those that demonstrated that the treatment was superior to a wait-list control group.

DON'T FORGET

The report of the American Psychological Association Task Force (1995) suggested classification of treatment efficacy based on several research criteria. Treatments were identified as *well-established treatments, probably efficacious treatments*, and *experimental treatments.*

DON'T FORGET

An *experimental treatment* is an empirically supported treatment approach that has been validated by comparisons of a treatment group with a no-treatment or alternative treatment control group.

DON'T FORGET

The wait-list control group is used in quasi-experimental studies where treatment facilities keep a wait list for services. Treatment effects for children benefiting from treatment (experimental group) are compared to a no-treatment condition (wait-list control group). Ethically, this approach is satisfactory because children in need of service are not deprived of treatment, since wait-list children will benefit from treatment once their wait-list status is removed.

Single-Subject Experiment

Clinical studies that focus on intervention may also use the subject as their own control, in what is called a *single-subject design.* In this case, the variable to be manipulated (independent variable) would be a clinical intervention, and the subject would be observed prior to intervention (for baseline data) and again after the intervention was introduced. A comparison of behavior before and after intervention would provide an index of the degree to which the intervention was responsible for the behavior change.

CAUTION

Many researchers strengthen the single-subject design by including a second set of measurements to rule out the possibility that behavioral change may be attributed to some other factor. In this case, a *reversal design* or *ABAB design* is used. Behavior is measured prior to intervention (condition A) and immediately following intervention (condition B). Intervention is removed for a specified time period, and behavior is again measured at the end of this no-intervention time (condition A). Intervention is then reintroduced, and the behavior is measured once again (condition B). The ABAB design provides a fail-safe approach to linking behavioral changes to intervention versus no-intervention periods.

Correlational Research

Researchers who are interested in how characteristics co-vary set out to compare how characteristics of one sample (participants) relate to characteristics in the same sample or another comparison sample. Correlations vary from −1 to +1, with +1 indicating a perfect positive correlation and −1 indicating a perfect negative correlation. Characteristics at zero are unrelated. In the hypothetical research study in the Putting It Into Practice box, the researcher investigates the relationship between studying and grades.

External and internal validity. Correlational studies have high external validity, meaning that a wide variety of variables can be generalized across large samples of subjects and replicated to include greater sample variance. However, due to the descriptive nature of the correlational research and the inability to draw inferences of causation between variables, internal validity is low.

PUTTING IT INTO PRACTICE

A researcher wants to study the relationship between time spent studying and grades on a multiple-choice psychology exam. Students are randomly assigned to one of three groups: group 1 (60 minutes), group 2 (90 minutes), and group 3 (120 minutes). Groups are given an introductory psychology chapter to study, and after the allotted study times they are given a multiple-choice test. The researcher plots the results to find an upward-sloping line: As study time increases, test scores increase. Results of study 1 confirm a strong positive correlation (.80) between study time and test scores. In study 2, students' study times are reduced by 30 minutes across the board. Results reveal a modest negative correlation (−.40) between decreased study time and test scores, producing a downward-sloping line.

Based on the researcher's study, can the researcher say that studying causes better grades? The answer is no.

Epidemiological studies represent one form of correlational research that is important to clinical studies. These studies inform clinicians of the incidence and prevalence of disorders in the population.

Naturalistic observation. When a laboratory study is neither possible nor desired, the researcher may choose to observe children in their natural environment, such as in their homes or on the playground, in order to document naturally occurring behaviors. This method can be used in research or clinical practice. As a research design, emphasis is not on controlling the environment but rather on systematically controlling how behaviors are defined (operationalized) and the methods used to record the observations.

CAUTION

It is important to remember that *correlation is not causation*, because two characteristics might be caused by a third factor. In the research program about studying and grades, other factors, such as anxiety, might impact on the outcome as well. Students with less study time might have had greater test anxiety, which contributed to lower scores.

DON'T FORGET

- *Incidence rate* refers to the number of new cases of a disorder within a given time period (e.g., the number of new cases in a year).
- *Prevalence rate* refers to the total number of cases of a disorder in the population within a given time frame.
- *Lifetime prevalence rate* refers to the number of cases of a disorder that might be expected to occur in one's lifespan.

Prevalence rates may differ significantly depending on the populations described (clinical versus nonclinical), how the disorder is classified (categorical versus dimensional), and how the disorder is measured.

DON'T FORGET

Some problems that may interfere with reliability of observed data include observer bias, observer drift, poor categories for coding, and central tendency (tendency to pick the middle category more frequently when rating behaviors).

DEVELOPMENTAL CONSIDERATIONS IN CLINICAL CHILD RESEARCH

The Study of Behavior Over Time

Research studies in the area of child psychopathology are often concerned with the study of how maladaptive behavior unfolds over the course of time, or the developmental pathways that serve as detours to normal development. These studies often seek to chart the course of maladaptive behavior by attempting to uncover factors that may protect (buffer) the individual from harm or that place the child at greater risk of harm. Other studies may concentrate on the various forms (symptoms and behaviors) that maladaptive behavior may take at various ages as they are evident in the behavioral transformations that might be demonstrated at various stages of development (Sroufe, 2007). For example, depression may be expressed as acting-out behaviors at 2 years of age and as social withdrawal at 11 years. The study of developmental pathways has also emphasized the need to consider the role of *equifinality* (the possibility that different pathways can lead to the same outcome) and *multifinality* (the possibility that similar paths can produce different outcomes) in determining outcomes.

DON'T FORGET

Equifinality is the possibility that many pathways can lead to the same disorder. For example, pathways to depression can be very different: loss of a loved one, academic failure, peer rejection, and so on. *Multifinality* is often best understood in the context of risk and protective factors. Although two children may experience peer rejection, one child may be more vulnerable to depression because of other risk factors (low self-esteem, poor family support), whereas another child who also faces peer rejection may be more resilient due to protective factors that act to buffer the negative experience, such as academic success, intelligence, and positive home supports.

Longitudinal, Cross-Sectional, and Accelerated Longitudinal Designs

A clinical researcher is interested in studying the impact of insecure attachment across the lifespan. In particular, he is interested in how insecure attachment might impact academic achievement and social popularity with peers in preschool, in elementary school, and at the completion of the first year of high school. One method available to study long-term development is the *longitudinal study*. In this particular case, the researcher would be committed to a research program that would require approximately 15 years of data input. Using this method, the researcher would probably select two groups of infants (infants who were securely attached and infants who were insecurely attached) that were matched for demographic characteristics (SES, family constellation, etc.) and follow the children over the next 20 years of development, collecting data at specified periods. Although the value of this approach is self-evident, there are also significant drawbacks to the longitudinal approach, namely in the potential for subject shrinkage over the longevity of the research (subject attrition) and the cost of the research program.

DON'T FORGET

The cross-sectional approach allows researchers to study different groups of children (matched for similar demographics) simultaneously at different developmental times. In the study described, the researcher could follow two groups of children at the end of each of the following age levels: 5, 8, 11, and 14 years. Disadvantages of this approach are loss of information regarding developmental pathways and the potential for cohort effects (generational effects).

A combination of the longitudinal and cross-sectional approaches, the *accelerated longitudinal design* reduces the time involved while protecting against potential cohort effects. Using this approach, the researcher would study several age groups of children at the same time and then follow these groups for the next several years. In our hypothetical example, the researcher might select groups at three time periods (5, 8, and 11 years) and follow these groups at 3-year intervals. In this manner, depending on the researcher's intent, the study could be completed within 3 to 6 years instead of 15 years.

Prevention: Risk Factors and Protective Factors

Improved research methodology and advances in technology (such as brain imaging and molecular biology) have all increased our understanding of the role of multiple influences (behavioral, psychological, and biological factors) in the etiology and course of child psychopathology. In addition, increased recognition that multiple influences can affect the trajectory of development for better or for worse has led to a greater emphasis on understanding how certain risk factors can contribute to vulnerability while other protective factors can buffer a child from harm.

DON'T FORGET

Bronfenbrenner's (1979, 1989) emphasis on the contextual nature of development has expanded our awareness of the role of external forces in shaping developmental pathways. This knowledge has led to a greater understanding that the child's individual (biological) characteristics are continually influenced by the child's immediate environment (family, school, peers, community, neighborhood), social and economic environment, and cultural environment, in a reciprocal and mutual way.

In his review of more than 1,200 prevention outcome studies, Durlak (1998) identified several common risk and protective factors that were shared across six areas of concern: social or behavior problems, academic problems, child maltreatment, physical injuries, drug use, and physical health problems (sexuality, teen pregnancy, etc.). One major contribution of Durlak's review is the presentation of findings sorted by level of influence: individual, family, peer, school, community, and other. This analysis is particularly well suited to the models of environmental influence discussed in Chapter 1. Durlak's meta-analysis reveals 10 common risk factors and eight shared protective factors that influence behavior problems and school failure. A very brief summary of these findings is presented in Rapid Reference 2.1.

Rapid Reference 2.1

Common Risk and Protective Factors for Behavior Problems and School Failure

Environmental Context	Risk Factors	Protective Factors
Community	Poverty-stricken neighborhood Ineffective school policies	Adequate social norms Effective school policies
School	Poor-quality schools	Quality schools
Peers	Negative peer influence or role models	Positive peer influence or role models
Family	Low SES History of parent psychopathology Marital conflict Harsh or punitive rearing	Positive parent–child relationship

Environmental Context	Risk Factors	Protective Factors
Individual	Early onset of problem Additional problems	Good social skills Self-efficacy
Other	Direct or indirect stressful conditions (any or all levels)	Direct or indirect social support (any or all levels)

Note: Data are from Durlak's (1998) meta-analysis of 1,200 prevention outcome studies.

The following discussion provides a description of how risk and protective factors can impact on the trajectory of development at different levels of influence.

Inner Circle

The inner circle represents the child's individual makeup and includes the biological beginnings, including the DNA code that makes the individual unique. Newborns present with varying levels of activity and wariness, and some researchers believe that these traits are genetically determined and enduring. Newborns also present with varying levels of curiosity and attentiveness, which have also been attributed to varying degrees of later intellectual development. Other risk factors at this level can include male gender, difficult temperament, low birth weight and/or birth trauma, intellectual level, and genetic links to psychopathology. Protective influences have been associated with normal ability and good health.

Immediate Environment (Microsystem)

The family system becomes the child's world and can either buffer the child from harm or be unable to provide the protection and support the child needs. Violence in the home or inconsistent parenting can lead to poorly developed mechanisms of self-control, impulsive responding, and tendencies to act aggressively, which will also impact on social contacts. Children who are aggressive are often rejected by peers. As the child develops, the influences of the school (teachers and peers) and community (extracurricular contacts) begin to assert greater influence on development. Research has demonstrated that peer relationship problems are predictive of long-term outcomes of maladjustment in areas of school dropout, criminal behaviors, and delinquency (Blum et al., 2000; Parker & Asher, 1987).

Risk factors at this level might include maternal depression, insecure attachment, poor parenting style, domestic violence, poor peer relations, and academic lags. Protective factors might include successful peer relations, involvement in extracurricular activities, and having a supportive parent.

Social and Financial Context (Exosystem)

Families feeling the strain of financial or emotional hardship, or teenage mothers faced with their own personal distress, may be unable to provide solace or comfort to a distressed and challenging child. Living in poverty or unsafe neighborhoods can add to an already stressful environment. In addition, disadvantaged children often lack opportunities or experience barriers to participation in organized recreation (Jones & Offord, 1989) and may experience limited access to nutrition and health care (H. R. Rogers, 1986). Low parent education can also be associated with greater risk for reduced academic expectations in children (Stevenson, Chen, & Uttal, 1990).

Cultural Context (Macrosystem)

Since low income is often associated with single-parent families and ethnic minorities, many studies have confounded the influence of these factors. However, when children are both impoverished and members of an ethnic minority, the long-term implications of living in poverty increase dramatically (Wilson & Aponte, 1985). Culturally, there may be a need to integrate potentially conflicting belief systems involving family, school, and peer norms or expectations. Children may be stressed by environmental pressures and forced to develop conflicting sets of behaviors in an attempt to accommodate diverse systems, behaving in different ways with family members, teachers, and peers.

> **CAUTION**
>
> Ethnicity can influence a number mental health issues for children and adolescents: parental beliefs about what constitutes mental illness, how symptoms are likely to be expressed or repressed (internalizing, somatization, externalizing), and whether seeking assistance for mental health issues outside of the family is an acceptable alternative (Gibbs & Huang, 2001).

Some risk factors related to cultural context include high risk for suicide in native populations and dropout rates for ethnic minorities.

A review of research concerning risk factors across the areas of influence reveals that additional risks can have a multiplier effect, such as the combined effect of poor school performance and social maladjustment on later maladjustment (Sameroff, 1993). Knowledge of potential protective factors can also guide our observation and understanding to assist in enhancing positive mental health and in the design of preventative interventions.

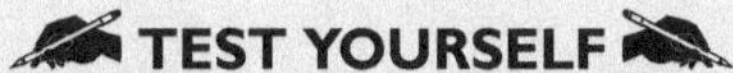

TEST YOURSELF

1. **Which of the following is *not* one of the five general principles of the American Psychological Association Code of Ethics?**
   (a) Beneficence and maleficence
   (b) Fidelity and responsibility
   (c) Justice
   (d) Integrity
2. **Which of the following is *not* true regarding informed consent in working with minors?**
   (a) Due to cognitive limitations, informed consent is required from parents of children who are minors.
   (b) A child's assent or willingness to participate should also be obtained.
   (c) In situations of divorce with two custodial parents, obtaining permission from one parent is adequate.
   (d) The clinician should encourage parents of adolescents in a therapeutic relationship to waive their access to privacy information in the initial stages of rapport building.
3. **In a correlational study of eating habits and obesity, a researcher concludes that eating bananas causes obesity in males. This statement is faulty because**
   (a) bananas are a low-calorie food.
   (b) the researcher did not include information about the age of the subjects.
   (c) the researcher's finding are limited only to males.
   (d) correlation does not imply causation.
4. **Which of the following is true regarding experimental studies?**
   (a) Studies have good ecological validity.
   (b) Studies have strong internal validity.
   (c) Studies have strong external validity.
   (d) All of the above
5. **The term *incident rates* refers to**
   (a) the number of new cases in a lifetime.
   (b) the number of existing cases in a decade.
   (c) the most recent number of cases cited.
   (d) the number of new cases within a given time period.
6. **Which of the following family characteristics was *not* considered a risk factor for behavior problems in Durlak's (1998) meta-analysis?**
   (a) Low SES
   (b) History of parent psychopathology
   (c) Number of siblings
   (d) Harsh parenting practices

Answers: 1. a; 2. c; 3. d; 4. b; 5. d; 6. c

Three

ISSUES IN CLINICAL DECISION MAKING: DIAGNOSIS, ASSESSMENT, AND TREATMENT OF CHILDHOOD AND ADOLESCENT DISORDERS

The assessment process involves several key steps, including determining individual differences and diagnosing signs and symptom presentations that are suggestive of specific mental disorders (U.S. Department of Health and Human Services [USDHHS], 1999). The purpose of diagnosis is to classify the problem within the context of other known behavioral clusters or disorders for the purposes of being able to draw on clinical knowledge regarding potential etiology, course, and treatment alternatives. The primary purpose of an assessment is to diagnose the nature of the problem in order that the most appropriate treatment can be selected.

> **DON'T FORGET**
>
> Assessment, diagnosis, and treatment are the fundamental steps in treatment planning. Monitoring and evaluation are often keys to how successful a treatment will be.

GOALS OF ASSESSMENT AND DIAGNOSIS

Assessment is a process. The initial stages of the process focus on clinical decision making regarding differential diagnosis (determine the specific nature of the disorder while ruling out the possibility that symptoms are not better explained by another disorder). The following sections summarize current issues and trends in areas of assessment (what should be assessed and how assessment should be conducted), diagnosis (how to categorize or classify childhood disorders), and treatment (clinical interventions).

Kronenberger and Meyer (2001) present a framework for diagnosis, assessment, and treatment that revolves around three pivotal questions that must be answered by the child clinician, regardless of the presenting problem:

1. What are the characteristics of the child's problem?
2. How should the clinician conduct an in-depth evaluation of the problem?
3. What are the appropriate intervention strategies?

DON'T FORGET

Three Questions That Guide Assessment:

1. What is the nature of the child's problem?
2. How should I evaluate the problem?
3. How should I intervene to correct the problem?

CAUTION

Contrary to our concept of the clinician as expert, research has demonstrated that clinicians' judgments can actually reflect underlying personal biases toward such areas as gender, SES, race, and age (Rosenthal & Berven, 1999).

THE NATURE OF THE CHILD'S PROBLEM: ISSUES IN DIAGNOSIS

Kronenberger and Meyer (2001) suggest that each of the questions addresses a specific issue or aspect of child psychopathology. Clinicians respond to the first question when they choose to characterize a child's problem through the use of a diagnostic category or provide a provisional diagnosis or case formulation based on presenting information of symptoms and features. As will become increasingly apparent, the diagnostic method used can predict what types of measures might be selected.

Furthermore, clinicians can and do disagree regarding a patient's diagnosis. Because psychology is not an exact science and is subject to personal opinion and interpretation, there have been concerns about the negative impact that certain labels might have. In addition, fears that labels can become a self-fulfilling prophecy have been supported by research. The classic study by Rosenthal and Jacobson (1968) is a case in point (see Putting It Into Practice).

Diagnosis as Classification: The Nature of Defining Outcomes

Although most clinicians would agree that a major goal of child assessment is to determine where the child's presenting behavior fits within the realm of adaptive or maladaptive behaviors, how the behavior is classified may vary depending on the classification system used.

Two main systems are currently used for classifying child and adolescent disorders or problem behaviors: the categorical classification system and the empirical or dimensional classification system. The main comparative features of each of these classification systems are presented in Rapid Reference 3.1.

PUTTING IT INTO PRACTICE

In order to demonstrate the impact of teacher expectations on student achievement, Rosenthal and Jacobson (1968) administered IQ tests to students at the beginning and end of the school year. The researchers then labeled 20% of the students as having exceptional potential for intellectual growth in the upcoming school year. In fact, selection of these students was random and was not related to IQ scores. However, at the end of the school year, students identified as intelligent actually demonstrated significantly greater gains in IQ on retest than the students who were not so identified. The researchers reasoned that inflated teacher expectations had become responsible for this Pygmalion effect in the classroom, so-called after the teacher in George Bernard Shaw's play *Pygmalion*.

The *Diagnostic and Statistical Manual of Mental Disorders*

Historical Background and Theoretical Orientation

Although the most widely used classification system in the United States is the American Psychiatric Association's *Diagnostic and Statistical Manual of Mental Disorders* (*DSM*), in Europe the *International Classification of Diseases* (*ICD*), published by the World Health Organization, is the most commonly used system. Both systems rely on a categorical approach to defining disorders based on a medical model that views disorders as present or absent (discrete categories with mutually exclusive boundaries). The *DSM* was originally published in 1952. The *DSM-5* (APA, 2013) provides the most current conceptualizations of mental disorders

DON'T FORGET

The approach to classification adopted by the *DSM* is a clinical or categorical approach that determines whether an individual meets the criteria for a specific disorder. The disorder is present or absent based on whether a specified number of symptoms match the defining criteria.

based on empirical investigations and clinical consensus. Clinicians use the *DSM* to evaluate whether symptoms meet established criteria in order to warrant a specific diagnosis.

The original version of the *DSM* (*DSM-I*) contained only two childhood disorders: Adjustment Reaction and Childhood Schizophrenia (APA, 1952). The *DSM-IV-TR* (APA, 2000) contained more than 20 disorders that may *first* appear in childhood (Disorders Usually First Diagnosed in Infancy, Childhood, or Adolescence).

Rapid Reference 3.1

Systems of Classification

System	Bases of Classification	Conceptualization of Disorders	Strengths and Weaknesses
Categorical Classification (*DSM*)	• Observation • Matching symptom criteria • Medical model: diagnostic categories • Structured and semistructured interviews (NIMH DISC-IV, K-SADS, CSI-4)	• Present or absent (all or nothing) • Qualitative and distinct entities of homogeneous features • Mutually exclusive: distinct boundaries	**Strengths** • Widespread usage among professionals in clinical practice (often an insurance requirement) and clinical trials (research) • Comprehensive documentation of disorder features **Weaknesses** • Subjectivity • Dichotomous (yes/no) • Mutually exclusive and comorbid disorders • Reliability and validity issues

(Continued)

System	Bases of Classification	Conceptualization of Disorders	Strengths and Weaknesses
Dimensional Classification (ASEBA, BASC, Conners)	• Multirater scales • Research-based statistical model (factor analysis) • Dimensions: levels or degree • Multirater rating scales (e.g., ASEBA, CRS, BASC)	• Continuum or degree of disorder • Adaptive to maladaptive range • Uses empirically based normative benchmarks (age, gender) • Multirater format • Focus on syndromes of co-occurring problems • Quantitative and continuous • Two broad-band behavioral dimensions • Externalizing and internalizing	**Strengths** • Can compare present status to normative peers (whether deviation is clinically significant) • Can compare degree of change pre- and posttreatment (whether change is statistically significant) • Use of multiple raters • Quantitative rating system **Weaknesses** • Not as well accepted by some clinical entities (e.g., insurance companies) • Problems integrating reports from multiple raters • Reliability and validity issues

DON'T FORGET

Many other disorders throughout the *DSM* can also have early onset (e.g., depression, anxiety, stress disorders, eating and sleeping disorders). In these cases, when applicable, the manual outlines symptom presentations that may vary due to age or gender effects in sections devoted to specific culture, age, and gender features.

Application of the DSM *Categorical Classification System for Child and Adolescent Disorders*

Structured and semistructured interviews have been developed to assist child clinicians in identifying *DSM* criteria in children and adolescents. Some of the instruments that have been developed to assist with *DSM* classification are outlined in Rapid Reference 3.2 and include the following:

- Anxiety Disorders Interview Schedule for *DSM-IV*: Child and Parent Versions (ADIS for *DSM-IV*; Silverman & Albano, 1996). Semistructured interview: 7–17
- Schedule for Affective Disorders and Schizophrenia for School Age Children (K-SADS; Ambrosini, 2000). Semistructured interview: 6–18
- National Institute of Mental Health (NIMH) Diagnostic Interview Schedule for Children (DISC), Version IV (NIMH DISC-IV; Shaffer et al., 2000). Structured interview: 6–17

Rapid Reference 3.2

Common Structured and Semistructured Interviews

Interview	Ages	Child Version	Adult Version
Anxiety Disorders Interview Schedule for *DSM-IV* (ADIS for *DSM-IV*: C/P; Silverman & Albano, 1996; Silverman et al., 2001)	7–16 years	Yes	Yes
NIMH Diagnostic Interview Schedule for Children Version IV (NIMH DISC-IV; Shaffer et al., 2000)	9–17 years	Yes	Yes
Schedule for Affective Disorders and Schizophrenia for School-Age Children (K-SADS; Ambrosini, 2000)	6–18 years	Yes	Yes

Note: References for all instruments can be found in Appendix B.

Strengths of the Categorical System for Child Populations

Benefits of using the *DSM* system include widespread usage and comprehensive documentation of the disorder, including diagnostic features; specific culture, age, and gender features; prevalence; course; familial patterns; and aids to differential diagnosis. Increased emphasis on empirically based treatments has increased the need for a common classification system across studies (Holmbeck, Greenley, & Franks, 2004; Ollendick & King, 2004). Furthermore, identification of *DSM* diagnostic categories are most often mandated by third-party payers in clinical practice.

CAUTION

More recent revisions of the *DSM* have recognized the need to incorporate *heterogeneity*, or individual differences in symptom presentation, by including several symptoms for each disorder, from which only a subset of items is required for the diagnosis.

PUTTING IT INTO PRACTICE

Are Parents or Youth More Reliable Informants in Predicting *DSM* Disorders?

Bird, Gould, and Staghezza (1992) compared parent and child responses to the DISC and found that, although parents are better predictors than youth of externalizing behaviors (attention deficit disorder, oppositional disorder), parents and youth were equally effective informants of internalizing disorders (separation anxiety, overanxious disorder, dysthymia).

Limitations of the Categorical System for Child Populations

As was previously discussed, the categorical approach has several self-limiting features. Although the categorical system works well for medical diagnosis (discrete and mutually exclusive), this is rarely the case with mental disorders. Conceptually, the system is especially problematic when considering high levels of comorbidity of disorders in child and adolescent populations. Limitations in applying the categorical system to child and adolescent disorders were summarized in Rapid Reference 3.1.

Developmentally, the *DSM* approach has several shortcomings, including the fact that defining features do not take into account symptom presentations that change with age (Wenar & Kerig, 2000). This issue is discussed at greater length later in the chapter.

Dimensional (Empirical) Classification

Historical Background and Theoretical Orientation

An alternative method of classification and diagnosis, the dimensional or empirical approach, looks at behavior in terms of a continuum rather than in discrete all-or-nothing categories. Proponents of the dimensional approach conceptualize maladaptive behaviors as symptom clusters, patterns, or syndromes. Statistically, when two populations are compared (normative and referred children), behaviors that go together and are pronounced in the referred population become identified as clinical patterns or clusters of symptoms. Whereas the *DSM* categorical system relies on structured and semistructured interview schedules to obtain information regarding potential diagnoses, the dimensional system assesses behaviors through the use of behavior rating scales or problem checklists. Three widely used behavioral ratings scales that use the dimensional approach are the *Achenbach System of Empirically Based Assessment* (ASEBA; Achenbach & Rescorla, 2001), the *Behavior Assessment System for Children* (BASC-2; Reynolds & Kamphaus, 2004), and the Conners Rating Scales (Conners, 2008). These multi-informant rating scales produce several sets of subscales, which were derived through empirical methods (factor analysis).

DON'T FORGET

Two broadband dimensions of behavior that have been revealed from factor and cluster analysis are the dimensions of internalizing behaviors and externalizing behaviors. Internalizing behaviors, which have also been referred to as *overcontrolled behaviors*, include such behaviors as anxiety, depression, social withdrawal, somatization, and shyness. Externalizing behaviors, also referred to as *undercontrolled behaviors*, include acting-out behaviors, such as aggression, rule breaking, and delinquency.

The Achenbach System of Empirically Based Assessment (ASEBA)

The ASEBA is one of the most popular rating scales used clinically and in research to identify problem behaviors in children and youth. The system includes a series of parallel rating scales for parents (Child Behavior Checklist [CBCL/6–18]), teachers (Teacher Rating Form [TRF]), and youth between 11 and 18 years of age (Youth Self Report [YSR]). The CBCL 2001 is a revision of an earlier version (Achenbach, 1991). The behavioral categories, clinical cutoff scores, and T-scores were derived from two samples of children: normative children (children across 40 U.S. states, the District of Columbia, one Australian state, and England who participated in the 1999 national survey and who had not been referred for behavioral or emotional help in the past 12 months) and children receiving mental health services from 20 outpatient and inpatient facilities. Almost 5,000 children contributed to the norms for this scale. The syndrome scales, as well as the Internalizing, Externalizing, Total Problem, and *DSM*-oriented scales, were obtained from normative (nonreferred) data available from the national survey sample. Children whose T-scores are within a range of 40 to 60 are considered to score within normal limits.

In addition to the narrow band scales or syndromes, the ASEBA also includes three broadband scales, and composite scores can be obtained for Internalizing Problems, Externalizing Problems, and Total Problems. Two additional scales, Adaptive Functioning and Social Competence, can provide information concerning a child's overall success academically and in the social arena.

DON'T FORGET

T-scores have a mean of 50 and a standard deviation of 10. Children who score above a T-score of 70 on the ASEBA syndrome scales are said to be within the *clinical range* (2 standard deviations above the mean and at the 98th percentile) relative to peers of similar ages and gender. A score between 65 and 69 (1.5 standard deviations beyond the mean, or the 93rd to 97th percentiles) is considered to be in the borderline clinical range.

Empirical Support for the Dimensional Classification System

Multivariate studies of child and adolescent behavioral and emotional problems provide support for the identification of two broad groupings of problems: externalizing behaviors (disruptive behaviors such as aggression, delinquent or rule-breaking behaviors, and hyperactivity) and internalizing behaviors (anxiety, depression, somatic complaints, and withdrawal).

Children with externalizing problems are referred more often than children with internalizing problems. They have been found to score significantly lower than internalizers on measures of intelligence, academics, and social acceptance.

Although the behaviors listed can be grouped into two different types of problems, recent research has also noted that children can and do demonstrate co-occurring externalizing and internalizing behaviors (Angold, Costello, & Erkanli, 1999; McConaughy & Skiba, 1993; Wilmshurst, 2002).

PUTTING IT INTO PRACTICE

In her evaluation of 86 Canadian youth with severe emotional disabilities (SED) referred for treatment at a mental health facility in Ontario, Wilmshurst (2002) found that 90% of the population showed clinical elevations for externalizing disorders (T-score 70+), with 74% having co-occurring internalizing disorders. Almost half the population (47%) had a cluster of four co-occurring disorders, with the most commonly occurring cluster involving oppositional defiant disorder (ODD), ADHD, conduct disorder (CD), and, not surprisingly, depression. In this study, those children with elevated levels for the anxiety disorders actually got worse when assigned to the residential rather than the home-based treatment alternative.

Application of the CBCL Dimensional/Empirical Classification System for Child and Adolescent Disorders: A Cautionary Note on the Use of Rating Scales

Several concerns arise regarding the use of rating scales in general. The first concern is that the reliability of the behavioral observation depends on the rater's perception, which in turn can be influenced by numerous extraneous variables (e.g., mood, recent history, stress). In their review of more than 119 studies using the CBCL, Achenbach, McConaughy, and Howell (1987) found that agreement among informants from similar settings (interparent agreement) were much higher (.66) than correlations of observations (.28) collected from informants in different settings (parent and teacher). These results suggest the importance of collecting information across contexts in order to enhance our understanding of how environmental contexts might influence the behavior in various settings (Frick & Kamphaus, 2001).

CAUTION

Gender Effects and Rating Scales

Parents and teachers tend to report more problem behaviors in males compared to females at all age levels, although adolescent girls tend to self-report more problems than adolescent males (Stanger & Lewis, 1993). Within deviant populations, research has consistently shown that emotionally disturbed adolescents (typically male) tend to rate themselves as socially adequate (Matson & Ollendick, 1988; Versi, 1995).

In addition, ratings have also been noted to vary across age levels, gender, and type of problem rated. Research has also noted that parents are more likely to identify more troublesome or external behaviors than less observable internalizing disorders, and that parent and child agreements are better for observable behaviors and for older (rather than younger) children (Offord, Boyle, & Racine, 1989).

Recent Trends in Combining Information From Categorical and Dimensional Systems

While proponents of the dimensional system have gained increased appreciation of this system's usefulness in classifying childhood disorders, increased pressure has been placed on the rigorous use of *DSM* categories to establish empirically based treatments (Ollendick & King, 2004). Within the wake of these movements, the debate regarding which system best serves the needs of children and adolescents has given way to more recent concerns regarding how to combine the merits of both systems. Rubio-Stipec, Walker, Murphy, and Fitzmaurice (2002) investigated the probability of being classified with a psychiatric disorder (dichotomous classification) using empirically derived (dimensional) symptom scales. The authors ultimately suggest that a full description of a child's mental health status should contain not only the dichotomous measure of whether a child meets the diagnostic criteria (nosology) but also valuable information regarding dimensional status, such as the probability of meeting the diagnostic criteria.

The current revision of the ASEBA, like the Conners Scales (2008), include information concerning both syndrome scales as well as *DSM* categories. As is discussed shortly, the *DSM-5* has responded to these concerns with greater emphasis on the combined use of categorical and dimensional aspects of classification.

THE *DSM-5*: ISSUES AND TRENDS

As was apparent in the historical review, the increasing awareness of the presence of mental disorders in children and youth witnessed has increased diagnostic consideration in the *DSM,* evident in the number of disorders cited, as well as increased descriptions of how symptom presentations for some disorders (e.g., anxiety, depression) may appear in children and youth. However, controversy remains regarding the degree to which the *DSM* diagnostic criteria apply to disorders in children and adolescents. A central issue has been the use of the categorical approach for problems conceptualized within a developmental framework, which is better suited to a perspective that endorses a continuum of severity approach (dimensional classification), which is more amenable to viewing symptoms of disorders along a developmental trajectory. Additionally, some clinicians are of the opinion that previous versions of the *DSM* did not include references to family and environmental factors that placed children at increased risk for psychopathology, such as insecure attachment, family dysfunction, or social skills deficits. However, it is important to note that the newly revised *DSM-5* (APA, 2013) addresses some of these issues (pp. 10–17) and does represent significant improvement in its attempts to conceptualize childhood disorders and apply symptom criteria within a developmental perspective in several important ways, with increased recognition and emphasis on the following:

- *Developmental and lifespan considerations.* The *DSM-5* has attempted to present disorders using a lifespan orientation, progressing from disorders that have early onset (neurodevelopmental disorders), to those most common in adolescence and young adulthood (bipolar, depressive, and anxiety disorders), and ultimately focusing on disorders most often associated with adulthood and later life (neurocognitive disorders). However, some would argue that the placement of schizophrenia spectrum and other psychotic disorders appearing as the second entry of disorders is not in keeping with the low incidence of these disorders in childhood. The separation of bipolar and related disorders from depressive disorders and placing the bipolar disorders before depressive disorders in the *DSM-5* has also been received with mixed reviews.
- *Comorbidity and clustering of disorders along internalizing and externalizing dimensions.* Unlike its predecessors, the *DSM-5* provides an increased emphasis on dimensional aspects of diagnosis relative to more traditional emphasis on categorical classification. Within this context, the *DSM-5* recognizes the influence of "neural substrates, family traits, genetic risk factors, specific environmental risk factors, biomarkers, temperamental antecedents, abnormalities of emotional or cognitive processing, symptom similarity, course of illness, high comorbidity and shared treatment response" (*DSM-5*, APA, 2013, p. 12). This shift in emphasis, clustering disorders along dimensions of internalizing (a response deficit, such as anxiety, depressive, and somatic symptoms) and externalizing factors (a response excess, such as impulsive, disruptive, and substance use symptoms), is consistent with research that supports similarities in environmental and genetic risk factors based on these two dimensions.
- *Supporting diagnosis using dimensional cross-cutting symptoms measures.* Moving away from the multiaxial approach of previous versions of the *DSM*, the revised edition suggests the use of a questionnaire targeting more

general symptoms common to several psychological disorders and difficulties (13 domains for adults, 12 domains for children and adolescents). The adult form consists of 23 questions in a self-report measure, indicating the extent to which problems are evident for the 13 domains, ranging from not at all (0) to severe (4). The Parent/Guardian symptom measure is used for children aged 6 through 17 years. The addition of this questionnaire supports an enhanced approach to collecting important information that goes beyond matching symptom presentation to a specific set of diagnostic criteria.

- *Reconceptualization of childhood disorders and unique diagnostic criteria for some disorders with onset in early childhood.* In the previous version, the *DSM-IV-TR* (APA, 2000) contained a separate category for childhood disorders, Disorders Usually First Diagnosed in Infancy, Childhood or Adolescence, which included disorders of intellectual disability (mental retardation), learning disorders, motor skills disorder, communication disorders, pervasive developmental disorders, attention-deficit and disruptive behavior disorders, feeding and eating disorders of infancy or early childhood, tic disorders, elimination disorders, and other disorders of infancy childhood or adolescence (separation anxiety disorder, selective mutism, reactive attachment disorder, stereotypic movement disorder). The *DSM-5* has replaced this category with the category of Neurodevelopmental Disorders, which includes intellectual disabilities, communication disorders, autism spectrum disorder, attention-deficit/hyperactivity disorder, specific learning disorder, motor disorders, and other neurodevelopmental disorders.

  The category of Anxiety Disorders has seen a number of changes. Childhood disorders of separation anxiety and selective mutism previously included in the section on disorders of childhood or adolescence have been relocated within the general category of Anxiety Disorders, while other disorders previously housed in this section have been relocated elsewhere. Obsessive-compulsive disorders have been removed from the category of Anxiety Disorders and exist in a new chapter created specifically for Obsessive-Compulsive and Related Disorders (body dysmorphic disorder, hoarding disorder, trichotillomania, and excoriation disorder). Additionally, the newly created chapter on Trauma- and Stressor-Related Disorders contains disorders of stress, including posttraumatic and acute stress disorders (previously listed as anxiety disorders), as well as the adjustment disorders. In addition to reorganizing the placement of disorders, the

DSM-5 now includes unique diagnostic criteria for posttraumatic stress disorder (PTSD) for children 6 years of age and younger.

Other new diagnostic categories include "disruptive mood dysregulation disorder," an early-onset depressive disorder marked by severe recurrent (three or more times, weekly) temper outbursts (verbally or behaviorally), which may serve as an alternative diagnosis for children previously thought to exhibit pediatric bipolar disorder. A new diagnostic category of "avoidant/restrictive food intake disorder," with onset most likely in early childhood, joins the chapter on Feeding and Eating Disorders, replacing the previous diagnosis of feeding disorder of infancy or early childhood.

Finally, conduct disorder and oppositional defiant disorder, which were previously classified as Disruptive Behavior Disorders found in the section on Disorders First Diagnosed in Childhood and Adolescence, can now be found in the category of Disruptive, Impulse-Control, and Conduct Disorders, which also includes intermittent explosive disorder.

- *Risk and prognostic factors.* The *DSM-5* has added a section on Risk and Prognostic Factors, which can be found after sections on associated features, prevalence, development, and course. The section provides unique diagnostic considerations resulting from influences of temperament, environment, and genetic physiological factors.
- *Clinical case formulation.* In keeping with the emphasis away from simply matching symptom presentations to diagnostic criteria, the *DSM-5* emphasizes that "it is not sufficient to simply check off the symptoms in the diagnostic criteria" but that emphasis must be placed on the development of a clinical case formulation. Developing a case formulation requires the ability to recognize the constellation of "predisposing, precipitating, perpetuating and protective factors' that have contributed to the development of psychopathology and utilizing this information for effective treatment planning" (p. 19).

Is One System Superior to the Other in the Diagnosis of Children and Adolescent Psychopathology?

Coghill and Sonuga-Barke (2012) explore the question of "whether child and adolescent mental disorders are best classified using a dimensional or categorical approach" (p. 469). In their paper, the authors discuss the relative merit of using a categorical versus dimensional approach to classification, relative to the types of disorders discussed. They state that, based on their review of taxometric studies, "taken together, they demonstrate that within the field of developmental psychopathology, there are likely to be situations where a categorical solution is appropriate and others where a dimensional approach is both more correct and more useful" (p. 482). Coghill and Sonuga-Barke (2012) conclude that both classification systems have value depending on the specific disorder that is discussed.

ISSUES IN ASSESSMENT: HOW THE CLINICIAN SHOULD EVALUATE THE PROBLEM

Assessment is the process of conducting an in-depth evaluation to determine the nature of the child's problem. Assessment requires knowledge of appropriate interview and observational techniques, as well as general assessment instruments (e.g., measures of cognitive, behavioral, and emotional functioning) and specific assessment inventories (e.g., measures of anxiety, depression, etc.). Information obtained using these assessment techniques will assist the clinician in confirming certain hypotheses while providing sufficient evidence to rule out other potential diagnoses (differential diagnosis).

Individual Clinical Assessment

While the underlying theoretical assumptions discussed in Chapter 2 provide a framework for understanding child psychopathology at a general or nomothetic level, clinicians must apply this understanding in their assessment of the unique aspects of psychopathology evident in the individual child (the ideographic level). For the child clinician, this investigation requires not only assessing the individual child but also obtaining information regarding important environmental influences, such as the child's family, peers, and school community. In addition, the clinician must also weigh the role of developmental considerations, such as the impact of the child's age level and gender, in evaluating the relative normalcy of the child's behaviors, thoughts, and feelings.

DON'T FORGET

A primary goal of the assessment process in child psychopathology is to develop a *case formulation*, or hypothesis, concerning the underlying influences that cause and maintain the maladaptive behavior, including the impact of environmental influences such as family, school, and community.

DON'T FORGET

Assessment is a multimodal or multimethod process of obtaining information from a variety of informants (e.g., parents or caregivers, teachers, child, peers) using a multitude of procedures (e.g., interviews, questionnaires, rating scales, standardized tests, self-report inventories) across a variety of settings (e.g., home and school).

Methods of Clinical Assessment

The process of clinical assessment can be conducted in several ways, and various clinicians will favor different approaches and instruments based on the nature of the problem and their own theoretical bias and training.

Why Use a Multimodal Assessment Model?

There are several reasons for using a multimethod assessment model, especially in the assessment of child and adolescent problems, including the nature of the problem (observable versus more covert), developmental limitations (parent report versus child self-report), and the need to verify the impact of situational influence. The multimodal assessment model provides a checks-and-balances approach to determining the nature of the problem. Multiple informants provide different perspectives on how the problem may appear or not appear in different settings. Ultimately, the clinician faces the ultimate challenge of defining the nature of the problem by integrating information from a variety of sources, settings, and instruments.

The Clinical Interview

The clinical interview is a goal-directed interaction between the clinician and the client (or the client's parent or teacher) and provides the opportunity of obtaining information that will assist in the clinical decision-making process. Interviews can vary considerably regarding the degree of structure: They can be unstructured, semistructured, or structured (Edelbrock & Costello, 1988). Clinical interviews can be very helpful in obtaining background information and in providing contextual information to assist in evaluating the severity (duration and intensity) and pervasiveness (existence across situations) of the child's problems.

DON'T FORGET

The *mental status evaluation* uses a series of questions as probes to determine a child's general orientation (name, place, date, and time), long- and short-term memory (general information and personal history), insight (abstract reasoning), and concentration or attention. This type of interview is often used to determine the potential of brain injury or thought disorders.

Advantages and Disadvantages

While the interview can be a rich source of information, there are several concerns regarding the reliability and validity of this technique, especially in the unstructured format. The interviewer's theoretical background may bias the direction of the questions or interpretation of the responses. Informants may also misinterpret questions or provide faulty information based on poor recall.

DON'T FORGET

The structured interview attempts to increase reliability and validity through the use of formatted questions, however most of the structured interviews (such as the DICA-IV) are modeled on the categorical classification system (*DSM*). Since this system considers disorders as discrete units that are either present or absent, information concerning the degree of symptom presentation along an adaptive-to-maladaptive continuum may be lost.

Behavioral Observation

Once the goals of the assessment are established, the clinician may have several potential hypotheses to consider regarding the nature and severity of the child's problem. One method of obtaining an overall impression of the child's behavioral responses is to conduct a behavioral observation. Although the first step in observation might be to perform a general observation of overall behavior (e.g., classroom behaviors), inevitably systematic observation will require selecting specific behaviors (target behaviors) for later in-depth observation and specifying the type of observational technique used (e.g., time sampling, event recording). For example, Sattler (2002) presents several coding systems that have been developed for observing children's behavior ranging from a two-category system (e.g., on-task versus off-task behavior) to a comprehensive 10-category list of inappropriate classroom behaviors (see Sattler for a complete review).

The Use of Clinical Tests: A Retrospective View

The tendency to equate assessment with testing produced a ripple effect—an equally strong tendency to equate testing with aptitude or achievement testing. Beginning with Goddard's translation of the Binet-Simon Intelligence Test in 1910 for use with "feebleminded children" and culminating in the famous *Larry P. v. Riles* case, issues in child assessment have resulted in strong opposition toward psychometric tests at many levels.

DON'T FORGET

The *Larry P. v. Riles* case (1972) in California found the use of standardized IQ tests on Black children unconstitutional for the purposes of placement in programs for the educable mentally retarded (EMR), unless the court provided approval prior to testing.

Professionally, dissatisfaction with testing was based on the disproportionate amount of time school psychologists were spending in conducting aptitude or achievement tests or in conducting *administrative assessments* (assessments designed to determine eligibility, placement, and diagnosis) instead of *functional assessments* (assessments designed to develop and evaluate interventions; Batsche & Knoff, 1995).

DON'T FORGET

Other issues contributing to the negativism surrounding psychometric assessment concerned potential stigmatization of labeling, categorizing, and placing of children in diagnostic categories.

Issues Regarding What Should Be Assessed and How Assessments Should Be Conducted

The questions of what should be assessed and how the assessments should be conducted are inextricably tied together. Similar to the way research questions often determine the research design, different procedures are required to obtain different types of information. Similarly, the way in which we conduct assessments is instrumental in determining the types of information we obtain.

CAUTION

It is important to note that the goals in conducting a functional assessment are different from those of a norm-based assessment. A clinician conducting norm-based assessments will be concerned with the degree to which a behavior is deviant relative to the norm (nomothetic formulation), while the clinician who conducts a functional assessment will be more concerned with the reason the specific behavior is occurring and the situational determinants of the behavior (ideographic or case formulation).

DON'T FORGET

Contemporary efforts toward the most recent (2004) reauthorization of the IDEA have continued to lobby for increased reliance on applied behavioral analysis and the replacement of standardized assessments with curriculum-based measures (CBM). This trend continues earlier efforts to shift the emphasis from assessment (testing) to consultation (problem solving) and from standardized tests to the use of data from CBM to measure intervention efforts and treatment effects (Rechsley, 2003).

Functional Versus Norm-Based Assessment

With the 1999 reauthorization of the Individuals with Disabilities Education Act (IDEA) Amendments of 1997, functional behavioral assessments (FBAs) and behavioral intervention plans (BIPs) became mandatory for students with emotional difficulties. Although aptitude or achievement tests are still required to determine eligibility for special education services, the inclusion of a functional analysis of a child's problems within the context in which they were occurring was seen as a major victory for many child advocates.

Proponents of functional assessments stress the need to develop intervention plans that have ecological validity relative to what is causing and sustaining the problem behavior. The referral question, they say, should firmly address why behaviors were occurring. Within this paradigm, the need for normative testing or linking behaviors to systems of classification or diagnostic categories has little merit or value.

Question of How Much or Degree

Norm-referenced assessment measures (psychometric tests) intend to answer questions relative to how much or the degree to which a given behavior deviates from the norm. The focus is on determining the severity of the problem. Psychometric instruments are available to evaluate a given child's functioning, relative to peers of similar age, in several areas: intellectual functioning, neurological functioning, behavior, emotional status (anxiety, depression, etc.), personality, and social functioning. Psychometric tests may be administered in the form of rating scales or paper-and-pencil tests, and they may be administered to a group or as an individual test battery.

Proponents of psychometric assessment value the availability of measures that can provide a reliable and valid index of the severity of the child's problem relative to similar-aged peers. The wide range of available instruments enhances a multimodal approach. In addition, parallel forms of rating scales exist for many instruments that allow for a comparison of evaluations across a number of different informants (parents, teachers, child self-report).

Critics of psychometric assessment have been most vocal regarding the overemphasis on aptitude or achievement testing in the schools. Many criticisms are also levied at inherent weaknesses in psychometric measures, such as cultural bias and the role of environmental stimulation on performance outcomes. Concerns might address the snapshot quality of a test result that portrays merely a point in time or, at best, a point within a definable range, rather than a dynamic ongoing process. At a conceptual level, critics may suggest that knowledge of the severity of a problem does not address issues concerning why a problem is occurring or how to intervene.

Why Assess Intelligence?

Historically, intelligence scales have been used as well-standardized, valid, and reliable predictors of academic achievement. The two most popular intelligence scales, the Wechsler Scales and the Stanford-Binet, have both seen recent major revisions. The Wechsler Intelligence Scale for Children—Fourth Edition (WISC-IV) provides a measure of overall intellectual functioning, based on scores obtained for four general indices: Verbal Comprehension, Perceptual Reasoning, Processing Speed, and Working Memory. The Stanford-Binet, now in its fifth revision, provides an index of overall intellectual functioning, as well as separate indices of functioning in the visual and verbal areas. Results of an intellectual assessment can also provide information regarding strengths and weaknesses in information processing as well as providing information concerning brain dysfunction or thought disorders.

A Question of Why

Functional behavioral assessments (FBAs) purport to answer questions relative to why a given behavior exists. Proponents of FBAs emphasize the ecological validity of an assessment approach that is linked to the situational determinants of behavior. Framed within a problem-solving approach, several steps might be involved in conducting FBAs, including gathering information from multiple sources regarding problem behaviors, determining probable functions, formulating hypotheses regarding causes, and ultimately generating and monitoring interventions. An example of an FBA is presented in Rapid Reference 3.3.

> **DON'T FORGET**
>
> An FBA can be defined as the identification of important, controllable, causal functional relationships applicable to a specific set of target behaviors or an individual client (Haynes & O'Brien, 1990, p. 654).

Once the FBA information is completed, the BIP is developed, which outlines specific goals and proposed interventions and designates the persons responsible for implementing the plan. An example of a BIP is also available in Rapid Reference 3.3.

Rapid Reference 3.3

Functional Behavioral Assessment (FBA) and Behavior Intervention Plan (BIP)

Josh is referred to the psychologist because he is aggressive toward his peers. After observing Josh and interviewing the teachers, the psychologist assists in the completion of the FBA worksheet, adding the following information:

Specific problem behaviors	• Verbal aggression: name calling • Physical aggression: pushing, shoving
Precipitation conditions	• Teacher is working with another student (independent work time) • Teacher is correcting homework (student has not done homework)
Consequences	• Teacher sends Josh to the office (removal from class)
Function of the behavior	• Removal from class (escape/avoidance) • Office is at hub of activity (attention)

Once the FBA is completed, then a BIP can be developed for Josh.	
Specific goals	1. Josh will increase positive comments. 2. Josh will complete daily homework assignments with 80% accuracy. 3. Josh will complete independent seatwork with 80% accuracy.
Interventions	1. Contract for positive comments + 1 bonus star. 2. Parent will sign completed homework assignments. 3. 15 minutes of independent work completed (80% accuracy) earns 3 minutes of free computer time at the end of the day.
Person responsible for monitoring	Intervention #1: teacher Intervention #2: parent Intervention #3: teacher

Critics of the FBA approach emphasize the lack of norm-referenced information and subjectivity involved in this assessment procedure. Although behavior is assessed from multiple vantage points, linking behaviors to situational determinants may result in incorrect assumptions. For example, a child may be frustrated at home and act out in school or vice versa. A high level of expertise is needed to assimilate and integrate assessment information from multidisciplinary sources and to select intervention strategies that are developmentally appropriate.

It is important to note, however, that despite current emphasis on behavioral assessment in the schools, behavioral analysis is a multisituational analysis requiring the gathering of information concerning the child's behavior, cognitions, and affects as they present across various situations and as seen by various informants. Despite the undisputed importance of attention to situational variables in conducting behavioral assessments, giving situational factors their due importance has often been neglected in child assessment (Mash & Terdel, 1997).

CHILD TREATMENT INTERVENTIONS

Issues in Treatment: Intervention and Prevention

Many adult therapies are also available for children. The most common therapeutic techniques used for children are psychodynamic (play therapy), ego-supportive, behavioral and cognitive-behavioral, interpersonal (social skills), and family systems. More than 400 different forms of psychosocial therapies currently exist (Comer, 2013). Given the complexities inherent in child treatment issues, it is not surprising to find that current trends have revealed an increased emphasis on the use of combined and multimodal treatment methods (Kazdin, 1996). The issue of treatment effectiveness can be addressed by posing questions at three levels:

1. Is therapy generally effective?
2. Are particular therapies generally effective?
3. Are particular therapies effective for particular problems? (Comer, 2013, pp. 107–109)

Treatment Effectiveness

Are Particular Therapies Generally Effective?

Meta-analyses of treatment effectiveness have produced the following summation: Therapy effects are strongest for outcome measures that target specific problems; effects for behavioral interventions are stronger than nonbehavioral approaches; and effects are strongest for adolescent girls (Weisz, Weiss, Han, Granger, & Morton, 1995). However, since the majority of studies analyzed were laboratory-based (analogue) interventions, the authors caution that results might not reflect child and adolescent practice as it existed in clinical settings.

DON'T FORGET

Treatment Effectiveness and the Dodo Verdict

In *Alice's Adventures in Wonderland,* Lewis Carroll's Dodo bird announces that "everyone has won, and all must have prizes" (Carroll, 1865/1988). This phrase has become a popular summation in psychological writings, called the *Dodo verdict.* In essence, the quotation has often been used as an analogy to demonstrate the lack of research support for specificity of treatment effects. Child and adolescent outcomes studies (Weisz et al., 1995) have demonstrated that treatment is more effective than no treatment or placebos.

Are Particular Therapies Effective for Particular Problems?

Family preservation using multisystemic therapy (MST) has been demonstrated to be an effective treatment approach for substance-abusing adolescents (Henggeler, Melton, & Smith, 1992) and as an alternative to hospitalization for seriously emotionally disturbed youth (Schoenwald, Ward, Henggeler, & Rowland, 2000). Multimodal programs that combine parent education, psychosocial treatment (behavior and contingency management), and pharmacology have proven effective for children with ADHD (Barkley, 1997). Promising approaches to anxiety reduction have been demonstrated by the use of cognitive-behavioral training techniques (Kendall et al., 1992), while parent training in behavioral methods has been determined as the most effective treatment method for dealing with disruptive disorders (Spaccarelli, Cotler, & Penman, 1992).

The American Psychological Association Task Force and Evidence-Based Treatments

In order to address the need for greater accountability regarding evidence-based treatment, the American Psychological Association convened two special task forces. After conducting an extensive research review, the Task Force on Psychological Intervention Guidelines (1995) developed two sets of criteria to assist in the classification of treatment programs. The first set of criteria, which is the most rigorous, classifies treatment programs that are deemed *well-established psychosocial interventions*. The second set of less-demanding criteria defines programs that are *probably efficacious psychosocial interventions* (Lonigan, Shannon, Saylor, Finch, & Sallee, 1994). Within these guidelines, emphasis has been placed on evaluating treatments with respect to treatment efficacy (internal validity) and treatment effectiveness or clinical utility (external validity).

DON'T FORGET

The goal of the American Psychological Association Task Force was to focus on identifying psychosocial interventions for high-frequency problems encountered in children's mental health, such as depression, anxiety, ODD, CD, ADHD, and autism.

Addressing issues of internal validity, the Task Force recommended the use of clinical trials or randomization, comparisons of alternative treatment approaches, and replication by different research teams. Clinical utility issues addressed questions about a program's feasibility, generalizability, and cost-benefit analysis. Results of the Task Force review can be found in a special issue on empirically supported psychosocial interventions for children appearing in the June 1998 *Journal of Clinical Child Psychology*.

Overall, the Task Force found more research initiatives directed toward the treatment of externalizing disorders (conduct problems, ADHD) than internalizing disorders (anxiety, depression) and significantly more studies that matched the probably efficacious treatment category than the category for well-established psychosocial treatments.

Does Specific Therapy Work for Specific Groups of Children?

According to Ollendick and King (2004), significant progress in recent years has effectively abolished the Dodo verdict and moved toward investigating "efficacy of specific treatments for children who present with specific behavioral, emotional and social problems" (p. 4). The authors go on to emphasize the need to incorporate more rigorous scientific methods, such as randomized clinical trials (RTC), in research programs designed to verify empirically supported treatments. In their review of well-established and probably efficacious psychosocial treatments for children and adolescents, Ollendick and King (2004) point out several continuing areas of concern. The authors suggest that there is a lack of identified empirical support of treatments for some of the most common disorders, such as anxiety and depression. In addition, verification of efficacious treatments has largely relied on cognitive-behavioral or behavioral treatments, whereas other theoretically based treatments, such as psychodynamic or family systems, have had less opportunity for scrutiny. Ultimately, the authors summarize three areas of controversy between clinicians and researchers that have been problematic and have presented obstacles in the past:

- Some treatments are more effective than others.
- There is a need for treatment manuals to ensure treatment fidelity.
- The portability of laboratory findings to real-life clinical settings is important.

Recently, there has been more focus on *translational* research, or research that can be used to inform public policy for children and adolescent concerns or to inform treatment alternatives for children and adolescent problems (Guerra, Graham, & Tolan, 2011).

Developmental Issues in Treatment

Although significant emphasis has recently been placed on the need to develop a wider body of research concerning empirically based treatments for child and adolescent concerns, Holmbeck et al. (2004) suggest that it is equally important that treatment alternatives also consider methods that are sensitive to developmental issues. The authors point out several developmental trends that can influence and direct the course of therapeutic involvement.

CAUTION

Holmbeck et al. (2004) raise several red flags concerning the portability of treatment plans across developmental levels, especially cognitive-behavioral programs, which emphasize higher-level thinking (such as self-reflective thinking, recursive thought and metacognition, or thinking about thinking).

In addition to level of cognitive appraisal, the authors also stress the need to consider the impact of the disorder in three other developmental areas:

- The role of the disorder in inhibiting normal development in other areas
- The use of a developmental perspective to prioritize targets for intervention
- Predicting the potential for children and adolescents to revisit earlier problems from a new cognitive vantage point

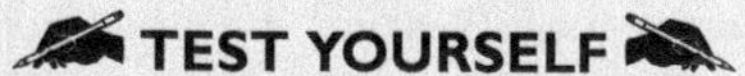

1. In Europe, the most common system used for diagnosis is

(a) the *Diagnostic and Statistical Manual of Mental Disorders.*
(b) the *Abridged Mental Health Index.*
(c) the *International Classification of Diseases.*
(d) the *Mental Health Primer for International Codes.*

2. One of the major criticisms regarding the use of the *DSM* for childhood disorders is that, historically,

(a) the *DSM* considered mental disorders as present or absent.
(b) the *DSM* did not take different developmental presentations of disorders into consideration.
(c) the *DSM* was primarily designed to diagnose adult disorders.
(d) all of the above

3. The Achenbach System of Empirically Based Assessment (ASEBA) provides behavioral ratings according to the

(a) dimensional system.
(b) categorical system.
(c) medical model.
(d) dimensional and categorical systems.

4. When a child is brought in for emergency treatment, the psychiatrist asks a series of questions as probes to determine the child's general orientation, long- and short-term memory, insight, and concentration or attention. The psychiatrist is conducting a

(a) projective evaluation.
(b) mental status evaluation.
(c) functional assessment.
(d) behavioral plan.

5. The outcome of the *Larry P. versus Riles* case was that

(a) projective assessments were banned in California.
(b) clinical child interviews were deemed unconstitutional.
(c) special education programs were closed to minorities.
(d) the use of IQ tests on Black children for educational placement was deemed unconstitutional.

6. In their study of the Pygmalion effect in the classroom, Rosenthal and Jacobson (1968) found that at the end of the school year random students identified as intelligent

(a) were given preferential treatment by teachers, resulting in increased IQ scores.
(b) were ignored by teachers, who then concentrated on less advantaged students.
(c) actually lowered their IQ scores due to lack of teacher input during the year.
(d) were less popular with peers than students not so identified.

7. Which of the following is a criticism of the Functional Behavior Assessment (FBA) approach?

(a) Lack of norm-referenced information
(b) Lack of multiple vantage points
(c) Linking behaviors to situational determinants
(d) Lack of research support

8. The Dodo verdict refers to

(a) inadequate research to support treatment effects.
(b) lack of specificity of treatment effects.
(c) improper use of multimethod effects.
(d) inadequate assessment techniques.

Answers: 1. c; 2. d; 3. d; 4. b; 5. d; 6. a; 7. a; 8. b

Part II

Neurodevelopmental Disorders

The fifth edition of the *Diagnostic and Statistical Manual of Mental Disorders* (*DSM-5*; American Psychiatric Association [APA], 2013) encompasses many changes from the previous edition (*DSM-IV-TR*; APA, 2000). One of the most significant changes to the *DSM-5* that impacts how disorders are conceptualized for child and adolescent psychopathology is the removal of the category Disorders Usually First Diagnosed in Infancy, Childhood or Adolescence. In the previous edition, this category contained 10 subcategories of disorders, including mental retardation, learning disorders, motor skills disorder, communication disorders, pervasive developmental disorders, attention-deficit and disruptive behavior disorders, feeding and eating disorders of infancy or early childhood, tic disorders, elimination disorders, and other disorders of infancy childhood or adolescence (e.g., separation anxiety disorder, selective mutism, reactive attachment disorder of infancy or early childhood, stereotypic movement disorder, and disorder of infancy, childhood, or adolescence not otherwise specified [NOS]). In its place, the *DSM-5* has relocated separation anxiety disorder and selective mutism within the chapter on Anxiety Disorders and moved the disruptive behavior disorders to the chapter on Disruptive, Impulse-Control, and Conduct Disorders. Feeding and eating disorders of infancy or early childhood can now be found in the chapter on Feeding and Eating Disorders.

Although inclusion of a chapter on Neurodevelopmental Disorders had been widely supported, perhaps the biggest challenge facing those involved in the revision process was what to include or exclude from this category. Andrews, Pine, Hobbs, Anderson, and Sunderland (2009) conducted a meta-analysis regarding several potential candidates, including conduct disorder (CD), separation anxiety disorder (SAD), attention-deficit/hyperactivity disorder (ADHD), intellectual disability (previously mental retardation), pervasive developmental disorders (autism spectrum disorder), motor disorders, communication disorders, and learning disorders. Their analysis revealed that some disorders were outliers with respect to the fit (CD and the impulsive hyperactive component of ADHD), while other disorders shared common features due to etiology, symptom similarity, age of onset, and course persistence. Based on their results, Andrews et al. (2009) suggested five potential disorders for inclusion in the neurodevelopmental category: intellectual disability, autism spectrum disorders, motor disorders, communication disorders, and learning disorders. Ultimately, six disorders were included in the neurodevelopmental category, as ADHD was added to the mix. According to the *DSM-5*, the six disorders were included in this category, since they met the following conditions:

1. They often share comorbidity (intellectual disability and ASD; ADHD and specific learning disorders).
2. The disorders represent a range of neurodevelopmental impairments and functioning from global (global developmental delay) to more specific deficits (executive functioning deficits).

The following three chapters discuss some of the most prevalent neurodevelopmental disorders, evident in childhood and adolescence, including intellectual and developmental disabilities (autism spectrum disorder), ADHD, and specific learning disabilities or disorders.

Some changes to look for in the presentations of these disorders, new to the *DSM-5*, are briefly discussed as follows. Clinical criteria and any alterations to diagnostic considerations will be discussed at greater length in the chapters to follow.

- *Intellectual disability or intellectual developmental disorder and developmental disorders (autism spectrum disorder).* Intellectual disability (previously mental retardation) has deviated significantly from previous discussions of ranges of intellectual functioning (mild, moderate, severe, and profound). Currently, the specifiers (mild, moderate, severe, and profound) are used to refer to levels of supports required for adaptive functioning across three domains: conceptual (academics, problem solving), social (social judgment, communication and relationships), and practical (life skills) domains.

Global developmental delay has been added as a category for children under 5 years of age who may demonstrate delays in the acquisition of developmental milestones and is considered to be a temporary category, pending further assessment.

- *Other developmental disorders: autism spectrum disorder (ASD)*. The category of pervasive developmental disorders (PDD) has been replaced by ASD, which now includes all disorders previously included under PDD, including autism, Asperger's disorder, and PDD-NOS. The *DSM-5* has reduced the previous three symptom categories to two broad categories, combining the two categories of impairments in social interaction and social communication into one category. Disorders within this category share features of two broad symptom categories, describing qualitative impairments or deficits in the following areas: (1) social communication and social interaction and (2) restricted, repetitive patterns of behaviors or interests. The *DSM-5* states that a diagnosis of ASD should replace any previous diagnoses of autistic disorder, Asperger's disorder, or PDD-NOS.
- *ADHD*. Although the *DSM-5* has not changed the diagnostic symptoms required for ADHD, it has changed the onset criteria (now evident prior to 12, instead of 7 years of age) and has reduced the number of symptoms required for individuals 17 years of age or older (five instead of six symptoms).
- *Specific learning disabilities or disorders (SLD)*. With respect to specific learning disorders, although the *DSM-5* no longer requires a significant discrepancy between intellectual functioning and achievement (previously a discrepancy of two standard deviations was required), it introduces the concept of academic skill levels being "significantly below age expectations" as determined by a standardized assessment (APA, 2013, p. 67).

Four

INTELLECTUAL AND DEVELOPMENTAL DISABILITIES

This chapter begins with a discussion of intellectual disabilities (ID) and finishes with a discussion of the developmental disability of autism spectrum disorder (ASD).

INTELLECTUAL DISABILITIES

Clinical Description and Associated Features

Background Information

It is important to note that intellectual disabilities (ID) or intellectual developmental disabilities (IDD), previously known as *mental retardation*, are not actually considered a medical condition or psychiatric diagnosis. Advocacy groups do not consider the condition to be a psychiatric disorder, although it is listed in psychiatric diagnostic manuals (Gillberg & Soderstrom, 2003). In reality, ID is most often used as an administrative label to designate individuals who have subnormal intellectual functioning (usually an IQ below 70) with associated deficits in other areas of adaptive functioning.

The use of intelligence tests to identify children with below-normal intelligence was introduced at the turn of the 20th century, when Alfred Binet was commissioned by the French government to develop an instrument (the Binet Scale) to assist in identifying children with inferior mental ability for purposes of special school placement. Although Binet cautioned against the use of a single score to describe intelligence (Gould, 1981), when the instrument was translated into English by Goddard and subsequently revised by Terman (Stanford-Binet), both authors promoted the strong belief that the IQ score was a valid measure of intelligence and, furthermore, that intelligence was itself fixed and genetically determined.

By the middle of the 20th century, use of the IQ measure as the sole determinant of ID met with increasing disfavor on several fronts. The American Association on Mental Retardation (AAMR) lobbied hard for inclusion of multiple criteria in the determination of mental retardation. However, intelligence testing continued to be the major defining criteria for some years to come. Rampant use of IQ testing to qualify students for special education placement throughout the 1960s and 1970s met with increasing controversy, culminating in the classic case in California of *Larry P. v. Riles*. As a result, severe restrictions were placed on the use of intelligence tests to place African American children in special education programs in California.

Ultimately, lobbying for the rights of all children to have a free and appropriate education, including children with disabilities, resulted in the passing of Bill PL 94-142. Finally, in 1992, the criteria were narrowed to include an IQ level that was two standard deviations below the mean (IQ 70), to be accompanied by deficits in adaptive functioning and with onset prior to 18 years of age (AAMR, 1992).

The AAMR changed its name to the American Association on Intellectual and Developmental Disabilities (AAIDD) in January 2007 to reflect contemporary changes in how the the disability is conceptualized and to reinforce the new terminology that was being used on a worldwide basis. In keeping with this movement, the *DSM-5* has also replaced MR with intellectual disability or intellectual developmental disability.

Current Classification of ID

There are currently three primary systems for classification of ID in North America: the *DSM-5* (APA, 2013), the AAIDD (2009a), and the educational system (IDEA, 2004; see Federal Register, 2006). The following sections provide a very brief description of the similarities and differences among these three systems. All three systems agree that three important factors need to be considered in the identification of ID, including IQ cutoff scores, deficits in adaptive functioning, and age of onset (prior to 18 years of age). However, there are also subtle differences among these three systems.

American Association on Intellectual and Developmental Disabilities (AAIDD)

The most recent classification of the AAIDD (2009a) emphasizes the degree and nature of support services required as the defining feature of ID based on whether an individual requires services that are intermittent, limited, extensive, or pervasive. The AAIDD system is based on the belief that proper supports will effectively enhance the functioning and quality of life for individuals with ID:

> While intellectual functioning, adaptive behavior, and age of onset remain the criteria for evaluating intellectual disability, supports remain the cornerstone of the AAIDD Definition System. AAIDD believes that once a diagnosis of intellectual disability is made, planning and providing supports is the key to reduce the mismatch between a person's capabilities and the skills, and what is required to successfully participate in all aspects of daily life. (AAIDD, 2009b)

It is important to note that AAIDD has been lobbying to raise the IQ cutoff score from 70 to 75.

DSM-5 *(APA, 2013)*

According to the *DSM-5*, three criteria are necessary for a diagnosis of an intellectual disability, including (1) significantly subaverage intellectual functioning (below an IQ of approximately 70, approximately two standard deviations below the mean, including a margin of +/− 5 points for measurement error, e.g., 65–75); (2) concurrent deficits or limitations in adaptive functioning (conceptual, social, practical domains), limiting functioning in one or more life activities (e.g., communication, independent living); and (3) onset before the age of 18 years. The reason that the score is suggested as "approximately 70" is to allow for the standard error of measurement. Intelligence test scores can predict within a 95% accuracy rate. In the case of an IQ score of 70, that would translate to an IQ range of 65 to 75.

The current criteria differ in many ways from how ID was previously conceptualized. In the *DSM-IV-TR* (APA, 2000), the range of intellectual functioning defined that nature and extent of the disability, placing it within mild, moderate, severe, or profound ranges, which were predictive of the expectations and necessary interventions.

In keeping with AIDD's emphasis on defining ID by the extent and nature of supports required, the *DSM-5* has removed any reference to levels of functioning related to ranges of IQ and replaced this with specifiers for mild, moderate, severe, and profound that are based on adaptive functioning levels, which are used to inform clinicians of the level of supports required to enhance functioning to the best ability possible. See Rapid Reference 4.1 for some examples. The current diagnostic criteria are more in line with the criteria supported by AAIDD noted previously.

Also new to the *DSM-5* is the category of *global developmental delay*, a diagnosis that is only given to children under the age of 5 years and is used to indicate that a child is not meeting developmental expectations in some areas of intellectual development. This category is subject to change when a valid and reliable reassessment of functioning can be conducted. This addition conforms more closely to the concept of "developmental lags" incorporated into definitions found in IDEA (2004).

Educational System (IDEA, 2004)

The Individuals with Disabilities Education Improvement Act (IDEA; *Federal Register*, 2004) is the latest revision of IDEA, an education act that provides federal funding for children who are deemed eligible for special education and related services. Intellectual disability is one of 13 possible categories of eligibility for disability services. Although the educational system also recognizes the need to include social and adaptive features of ID, most state education codes allocate funds for special education to children with disabilities, such as ID, based on IQ score cutoffs to determine eligibility for services. Currently, the actual IQ used to determine eligibility varies across states, but most states accept an IQ cutoff between 70 and 75 to designate ID.

DON'T FORGET

Bill PL 94-142 (Education for All Handicapped Children, 1975) emphasized the need to protect the rights of the handicapped and supported the AAMR's focus on including adaptive as well as intellectual measures in determining MR in children.

Under Part C of IDEA 2004 (Sec. 631), financial assistance is provided to the state for infants and toddlers with disabilities (birth to 2 years). Within this section is the provision to meet the needs of infants and toddlers with developmental delays or at risk for developmental delays. Within this context, *developmental delay* is considered to be a delay of 35% or more in one of five developmental areas (cognitive, motor, speech and language, social/emotional, or adaptive functioning) or 25% or more in two or more of the developmental areas. Part B of IDEA 2004 discusses services for students aged 3 to 21 years of age. Within this context, IDEA states that children 3 to 9 years of age *may* receive special education and related services if services are needed because of the developmental delays in one of the five areas noted previously. However, it is important

DON'T FORGET

Various skills can be considered as part of adaptive functioning. According to the *DSM-5*, adaptive skills in one or more areas that can limit functioning of those with ID include communication, social participation, and independent living, which can influence the quality of daily living experiences at home, school, work, and in the community.

to note that services are not mandated, are at the discretion of the state, and represent a "temporary" category, pending identification of one of the 13 disabilities required for eligibility for services. The section on developmental delay is similar to that noted in the *DSM-5* as *global developmental delay*, which is also a temporary category.

CAUTION

Children who lack stimulation or have been deprived of adequate opportunity to develop their cognitive skills may also score very low on IQ tests. It is therefore essential to determine whether deficits are the result of true limitations in capacity or lack of opportunity.

CAUTION

Adaptive functioning may also be influenced by many factors other than intellectual ability, including motivation, comorbid conditions, deprivation, opportunities to access supportive services, and family support.

Rapid Reference 4.1

Severity Levels for Intellectual Disability Across Domains

Degree of Severity	Conceptual	Social	Practical
Mild	Support needed academically	Immaturity; lack of social cues	Supports needed in daily living (e.g., shopping, money management)
Moderate	Increased supports; academic deficits	Immature social judgment, communication	Independent employment with mentoring
Severe	Limited achievement & understanding	Minimal language, gestures	Support required in all daily living; self-injurious behavior
Profound	Motor & sensory impairments	Limited communication	Dependent on others

DON'T FORGET

The AAIDD emphasizes that ID is not a mental disorder or a medical disorder but a state of functioning beginning in childhood that is characterized by limitations in intellectual and adaptive skills. The most recent definition emphasizes the need to consider multidimensional and ecological influences in developing interventions. Therefore, the AAIDD is strongly supportive of interventions aimed at individualized supports to enhance productivity.

Prevalence and Course

The overall prevalence of ID is approximately 1% to 3%. Males are probably more highly represented in this population. Eighty-five percent of the ID population have a mild degree of disability, requiring mild level of supports. By definition, onset is before 18 years of age, and earlier identification is associated with more severe forms of ID. Mild delays may not be detected until formal schooling begins. Rates for those with more severe ID are approximately 6 per 1,000 (APA, 2013).

There are wide variations in the presenting features of ID depending on the severity and associated personality and behavioral characteristics. Developmental delays vary widely with the nature of the disability. For some individuals, incapacity is limited to impaired academic performance (once called *6-hour retardates*), while adaptive skills are adequate in all other areas. Other individuals have concomitant aggressive features and behavior problems that exacerbate their limitations and reduce their ability to adjust and adapt successfully. Some of the negative features that can predict more serious problems include self-injurious behavior, aggression, stereotypical movements, communication problems, and overactivity (Aman, Hammer, & Rohahn, 1993).

CAUTION

Although the majority of states accept the ID cutoff at an IQ between 70 and 75, some states, like Iowa, have retained higher cutoff levels, for example, IQ of 85 (MacMillan & Forness, 1998).

Cognitively, depending on the level of severity, some individuals with mild ID (such as those with upper-level Down syndrome) can be quite capable of adequate functioning at a slower pace with modified goals. Typically, cognitive limitations are less noticeable in predictable and structured environments and most noticeable in novel situations or when abrupt changes disrupt predicted routines.

According to the *DSM* (APA, 2013), individuals with ID are at risk for comorbid disorders at a rate three to four times higher than the general population.

In addition, diagnosis may be more complex, as the common disorder features may be modified by the presence of ID. Some of the most common comorbid disorders include ADHD, depression, bipolar disorder, anxiety disorders, autism spectrum disorder, and disorders of impulse control.

CAUTION

In consideration of comorbid ADHD features, it is important to remember that many children with ID are often inattentive and active. An important distinction regarding ID populations is that a diagnosis of ADHD is only made if these symptoms are excessive for the child's *mental age, not chronological age.*

Etiology

Biological and Genetic Factors

ID can be the result of *genetic defects.* One of the most well-known types of ID, Down syndrome, results from a chromosomal abnormality involving chromosome 21 (incorrect number of chromosomes or damaged chromosomes). Children with Down syndrome usually have classic features, including short stature, round face, almond-shaped eyes, flat facial features, and low muscle tone. They can be socially engaging and affectionate, but they can also be stubborn. Speech problems are common, and health problems (especially heart) are also common. Children with Down syndrome can vary widely in their IQ potential, with some children scoring into the upper limits of the low average range (upper-level Down syndrome). The risk for Down syndrome increases with the maternal and paternal age. The risk for women over 45 years of age is 1 in 25 births.

DON'T FORGET

Risk factors for ID may also be related to having another medical condition at birth, such as cerebral palsy or a seizure disorder, such as epilepsy.

Prader-Willi syndrome is often recognized at birth because of low muscle tone and low reflex responses. A disorder of chromosome 15, Prader-Willi syndrome is recognizable in school-aged children, not only in physical features (short stature, small hands and feet), but by the accompanying problems of impulsivity, temper tantrums, compulsive eating, and some degree of ID (IQ scores generally in the 60 to 80 range).

Williams syndrome (WS), also known as Williams-Beuren syndrome (Morris, 2006a) in Europe, is a genetic neurodevelopmental disorder that occurs in approximately 1 in 7,500 births. The disorder is the result of a random genetic mutation in which part of chromosome 7 is deleted. However, individuals with WS have a 50% chance of passing on the gene to their children (Bellugi et al., 2007). The vast majority of individuals with WS have developmental delay (95%), although there are wide ranges in IQ scores from mild delays to severe ID. The vast majority (80%) will experience cardiovascular problems (Morris, 2006b). Strengths include verbal short-term memory, remarkable musical talent, and hypersociability, which might also be a weakness if people with WS are too socially disinhibited (Wang, 2006). Weaknesses are evident in poor visual-spatial abilities and visual motor integration.

Environmental Factors

During prenatal development, environmental factors can cause birth defects. Environmental toxins, called *teratogens*, can cause considerable harm to the fetus. Approximately 33% of all babies born to mothers who are heavy consumers of alcohol will be born with fetal alcohol syndrome (FAS). Clinical features of FAS include slow growth, central nervous system dysfunction (ID, hyperactivity, irritability), and unusual facial features (underdeveloped upper lip, flattened nose, widely spaced eyes). Although facial features become less pronounced with age, cognitive deficits remain.

Other causes of ID that may occur postdelivery include premature birth, lack of oxygen at birth (anoxia) resulting from a difficult delivery (cord wrapped around neck), head injuries, encephalitis, or meningitis. Children can also acquire diminished brain capacity from pollutants in the environment, such as developing lead toxicity as a result of consuming lead-based paint.

Assessment and Interventions

Assessment of ID requires a full developmental and medical history in order to determine the potential etiology, onset (prior to 18), and to rule out other competing diagnostic possibilities. Obtaining information regarding when the child achieved developmental milestones is an important part of the interview process for the identification of ID, since many of these children will demonstrate developmental delays in the acquisition of milestones. Individual assessment of intellectual functioning and adaptive functioning are also a necessary part of the identification and diagnostic process.

Intellectual assessment should be conducted using the age- and culture-appropriate instrument. Common intellectual instruments used to assess intelligence in English-speaking children are summarized in Rapid Reference 4.2.

There are several scales that can be used to measure adaptive functioning. These instruments provide information concerning how the individual's level of adaptive functioning compares to developmental expectations. Although information is obtained through structured interview format, results provide standard scores that can be used to directly compare adaptive levels with intellectual expectations. The instruments also provide age-equivalent scores to assist in determining developmental expectations. A list of common adaptive measures is available in Rapid Reference 4.2.

Interventions for children and adolescents with ID focus primarily on either behavioral/emotional issues or educational issues.

Behavioral Interventions

Behavioral programs have been very successful in targeting and altering problematic social, emotional, and behavioral concerns. The reason for the success of the behavioral programs can be linked to the program focus on breaking down problem behaviors into component parts (simplicity) and to systematically shaping behaviors into more socially adaptive skills through contingency management.

Empirical support for the use of behavioral methods with ID populations is well documented (Handen, 1998). Several techniques are available to create programs across the developmental spectrum to suit a variety of problem behaviors (behavior chaining, secondary rewards, token economies). Contingency programs can be developed to reduce excess behaviors (aggression, noncompliance) and increase deficit behaviors (compliance, social skills) at school and in the home (Wielkiewicz, 1995).

Approximately 7% of children and youth with ID will also exhibit challenging behaviors (Kiernan & Qureshi, 1993), although the rate increases significantly (as many as 22%) for those who are enrolled in special education programs (Kiernan & Kiernan, 1994).

Programs that have been most successful are those that use functional analysis based on applied behavioral analysis (ABA). These programs are successful because they can provide simplistic solutions to aggravating and disruptive problems, such as using praise to increase or ignoring to decrease negative behaviors. They can also be made more complex by chaining behaviors and increasing the number of contingency-based components.

DON'T FORGET

Adaptive functioning can differ based on environmental demands; therefore, it is advised that adaptive information be collected from different (home and school) sources.

Although behavioral treatment programs can be developed to either increase a deficit behavior or decrease an excessive behavior, it is always preferable to increase a deficit behavior, because this relies on positive reinforcement. The use of token economies (students can earn tokens or coupons for good behavior) and other contingency programs have met with success, especially in populations of younger children or children with ID.

Parent Training Programs

Research has demonstrated that including a parent component in the behavioral program can enhance success by increased consistency and transfer of effects between home and school or treatment facility (Handen, 1998). Parent training programs have been proven successful regardless of whether they are administered in a group or individual context (Clark & Baker, 1983).

Rapid Reference 4.2

Common Intellectual Assessment Instruments

Instrument/Age Level	Assessment	Measures
The Wechsler Preschool and Primary Intelligence Test (WPPSI-III): ages 2:6 to 7:3 (Wechsler, 2002)	Individual	Full Scale IQ, Verbal IQ, Performance IQ
The Wechsler Intelligence Scale for Children (WISC-IV): ages 6 to 16:11 (Wechsler, 2003)	Individual	Full Scale IQ: Verbal Comprehension, Perceptual Reasoning, Processing Speed and Working Memory Indexes
The Stanford-Binet, 5th Edition: ages 2 years to 85 (Roid, 2003)	Individual	Full Scale IQ, Verbal IQ, Performance IQ
The Differential Ability Scales Test (DAS:2; Elliott, 2007) Preschool level: ages 2:6 to 5:11 School age level: ages 6 to 17:11	Individual	Verbal Ability, Nonverbal Ability, Spatial Ability, and General Conceptual Ability

Common Adaptive Behavior Instruments

Instrument/Age level	Assessment	Measures
Vineland Adaptive Behavior Scales: ages birth to 18:11 (Sparrow, Balla, & Cichetti, 1984)	Interview Survey Interview Expanded Classroom Edition	Adaptive behavior in four domains: Communication, Daily Living Skills; Socialization, and Motor Skills
AAMR Adaptive Behavior Scales—School, 2nd Edition (ABS-S:2): ages 3 to 18:11 (Lambert, Nihira, & Leland, 1993)	Behavior Rating Scale	Five factor scales: personal self-sufficiency, community self-sufficiency, personal-social responsibility, social adjustment, and personal adjustment
Adaptive Behavior Assessment System (ABAS II): ages birth to 21 (Harrison & Oakland, 2003)	Parent and Teacher Rating Scales	Assesses 10 specific adaptive skills (*DSM-IV-TR*), plus three general areas (AAMR)

Note: References for all instruments can be found in Appendix B.

Educational Programs

The debate regarding whether children with ID are better served within separate special education programs or regular classes (a practice referred to as *mainstreaming* or *inclusion*) has waged over the past 20 years or more. Although some studies show minimal effects of special education programming (Hocutt, 1996), other studies suggest that mainstreaming does not sufficiently address academic concerns (Taylor, 1986). IDEA (2004) emphasizes the need to provide educational services for children with disabilities in the least restrictive environment, ensuring that children are integrated into the regular classs program for as much of the school day as possible. More recently, advocates have pushed for *full inclusion*, citing results from a meta-analysis conducted by Carlberg and Kavale (1980), which demonstrated that children with mild intellectual disabilities had better outcomes when they remained in the regular classroom, and that placement in special education (pull-out) programs resulted in feelings of isolation and lacked the inclusion of normative role models (Ysseldyke, Thurlow, Christenson, & Muyskens, 1991).

The debate continues, because researchers such as Hocutt (1996) have discredited earlier research based on methodological flaws and emphasized that the program itself (intensive, individualized instruction) rather than the placement is the key to successful intervention. However, whether this is best applied within a setting that has a lower student:teacher ratio remains to be seen.

Prevention Programs

Prevention programs have been instituted at all levels of intervention, from prenatal awareness campaigns (effects of drug abuse and alcohol, genetic counseling) to early intervention programs targeting parenting skills and early stimulation programs, such as Head Start programs. The impact of early intervention programs within the first five years of life has been clearly documented in the prevention of increasing cognitive declines (Guralnick, 1998).

DEVELOPMENTAL DISABILITIES: AUTISM SPECTRUM DISORDERS (ASD)

Clinical Description and Associated Features

The *DSM-5* made significant changes to the way it conceptualizes and defines autism spectrum disorders (ASD). Previously, the category of pervasive developmental disorders (PDD) was used to describe four disorders that shared features of *restrictive range of activities* (i.e., stereotypical behaviors, restricted interests), *lack of reciprocal interaction*, and *limitations in communication skills*. The four disorders that were included under the PDD umbrella were autistic disorder, Rett's disorder, childhood disintegrative disorder, and Asperger's disorder. Individuals who met some but not all of the criteria or who had atypical features were labeled as PDD, Not Otherwise Specified (NOS).

Currently, the *DSM-5* (APA, 2013) used the term *autism spectrum disorder* to refer to disorders that meet criteria evident in two broad symptom categories:

- Deficits in social communication and social interaction
- Restricted repetitive patterns of behavior

Using the previous classification system (*DSM-IV-TR*; APA, 2000), the majority of individuals diagnosed with autism (75%) also met criteria for intellectual disability. However, given current criteria, it is not known if this will continue to be the case, since individuals previously diagnosed with Asperger's disorder (a less severe form of autism) will now be reclassified as part of the autism spectrum. However, the *DSM-5* has included specifiers to designate whether the disorder is accompanied with or without intellectual impairment or with or without language impairment.

Onset is during the early developmental period, around 2 years of age, however, symptoms may not manifest until later in some individuals with more mild variations, or may manifest earlier in those with more severe variants of the disorder.

DON'T FORGET

What were previously conceptualized as two separate categories, communication and social interaction, have now been consolidated into one category. Within this category, deficits are required in three areas: social-emotional reciprocity, nonverbal communication, and the development and maintenance of relationships. For the second symptom category (restricted and repetitive behavior patterns), two out of a possible four symptoms must be present (motor movements, rituals, fixated interests, hyper/hypo response to sensory information).

DON'T FORGET

Autism, and the variations thereof, have been conceptualized in different ways by different researchers. Although Asperger's disorder was less well known than autism, Hans Asperger actually published his account of atypical children with similar features in a paper the year following Kanner's publication. However, it was not until Wing (1981) published a paper comparing Kanner's syndrome with Asperger's syndrome that Asperger's disorder gained recognition in its own right. According to Rutter (1978), during the next 30 years, several different diagnostic labels were suggested to account for these atypical features (infantile autism, childhood psychosis, childhood schizophrenia) and were applied to children who had all, some, or a few of the features described by Kanner.

DON'T FORGET

Controversy surrounding the autism/Asperger's debate has been ongoing. Some theorists have suggested that Asperger's disorder represents a less-severe type of autism (Schopler, 1985), while others (Howlin, 1987; Wing, 1981) have recommended retention of the separate categories, specifically due to the language-based differences noted in the previous criteria.

Prevalence and Course

The prevalence rates for ASD have increased dramatically in recent years. Although the *DSM-IV-TR* (APA, 2000) suggested a medium prevalence rate of 5 cases per 10,000, with rates ranging from "2 to 20 cases per 10,000" (p. 73), with four times more males than females being diagnosed with the disorder, the Center for Disease Control (CDC, 2009) reported a prevalence rate of 1%, or one child in 110, in the United States having the disorder. The current *DSM-5* also quotes the 1% estimate but states that "it remains unclear whether higher rates reflect an expansion of the diagnostic criteria of the *DSM-IV* to include subthreshold cases, or increased awareness, differences in study methodology," which have led to these increases (APA, 2013, p. 55).

CAUTION

Several studies did not support the previous *DSM-IV-TR* (APA, 2000) diagnostic criteria. Some researchers found children who met the criteria for Asperger's who had language problems (Eisenmajer et al., 1996; Prior et al., 1998), while others found autistic children who did not demonstrate significant language delay (Eisenmajer et al., 1996; Miller & Ozonoff, 2000).

DON'T FORGET

In their review, Macintosh and Dissanayake (2004) noted that although different language patterns were evident, the group with high-functioning autism (HFA) demonstrated more atypical speech patterns [*echolalia, noun reversals, atypical gestures*], while the Asperger's group tended to have more verbal rituals and asked odd questions. The review of studies demonstrated little basis for differentiation solely on the basis of diagnosis.

PUTTING IT INTO PRACTICE

Nancy loves chocolate milk. Nancy always brings her chocolate milk to school in a blue container. Today Nancy leaves her container of milk on the desk and leaves the room. Millie loves chocolate milk too, but she only has white milk in her container. While Nancy is out of the room, Millie drinks Nancy's chocolate milk and replaces it with white milk. The container is dark blue, so Nancy cannot see the color of the milk. When Nancy comes back into the room, will she think the milk in the blue container is chocolate or white?

This is an example of a Theory of Mind Problem. Children with more severe forms of autism cannot solve this problem, while those with milder forms are able to understand that Nancy would think that the container still had chocolate milk in it, since she was not present when the change was made.

DON'T FORGET

Ultimately, Macintosh and Dissanayake (2004) suggested that best clinical practice might be to consider both disorders as part of the *autism spectrum disorders* and then to specify the subtype of the disorder as either autistic disorder or Asperger's disorder, which is very close to what the *DSM-5* has done with including specifiers for intellectual and language functioning.

Rapid Reference 4.3

DSM-5 Criteria for Autism Spectrum Disorder (ASD)

A total of five symptoms are required from the following list:

Symptom Category	Examples
Qualitative and persistant impairment in social interaction and communication, across three broad areas (3 symptoms)	Deficits in social reciprocity: sharing, social referencing, initiating, maintaining interaction Deficits in nonverbal communication: lack of eye contact, gestures, facial expression Deficits in maintaining and developing social interactions: adapting behavior to context; imaginary play; engaging with peers

(*Continued*)

(Continued)

Symptom Category	Examples
Restricted, repetitive patterns of behavior, activities (2 symptoms)	*Repetitive, speech, nonfunctional activities (lining up), echolalia* *Need for sameness; rituals* *Preoccupation and fixedness on topics or parts of objects or themes* *Hyper- or hypo-responsiveness to sensory stimuli*

DON'T FORGET

Developmentally, *referential looking* (shifting gaze between caregiver and object of interest) occurs around 6 to 9 months and is followed by the active use of gestures to engage adults in reciprocal interaction.

DON'T FORGET

When their senses are overwhelmed, these children may find solace in hyper-focusing on a repetitive nonfunctional task (spinning wheels on a truck, lining up toys) or in the rigid adherence to the familiar.

ETIOLOGY

As early as the late 1960s, autism was thought to be caused by mothers who shaped their child's future by their cold and non-nurturing ways. The term *refrigerator mother* was used to describe the mothers of autistic children.

Biological, Neurological, and Neurotransmitter *Factors*

Studies have demonstrated that if one monozygotic twin has autism, then the chances of the second twin also having autism are at least one in three. Furthermore, in families where the second twin does not have autism, the nonautistic twin has autistic features but to a lesser extent (Bailey, Phillips, & Rutter, 1996).

As of yet, no specific genes have been isolated. The neurotransmitter serotonin has been implicated. However, unlike other disorders that were linked to a low level of serotonin (depression, obsessive compulsive disorder), studies have demonstrated elevated levels of serotonin in approximately 25% of those with autistic disorder (Klinger & Dawson, 1996).

CAUTION

In view of the escalating rates of autism, there has been significant controversy and debate regarding whether autism can be caused by a childhood vaccine (particularly the measles-mumps-rubella vaccine [MMR]) or a mercury-containing preservative (thimerosal) used in some childhood vaccines since 1930. Evidence, however, does not support the connection of thimerosal causing autism. Jick and Kaye (2003) suggest that increases are likely the result of improved practices for diagnosing the disorder and increased awareness of the disorder. It is also important to note that, coincidentally, the MMR vaccine is typically administered around the time that symptoms of ASD become more noticeable (12–15 months and 3–5 years).

Assessment and Treatment/Intervention

The assessment of ASD can be aided by the use of a number of behavioral rating scales that have been designed specifically to evaluate the likelihood that symptoms represent ASD. Of course, a medical and family history are essential to chart the course of the disorder as well as obtaining information to evaluate potential comorbid disorders. A summary of some of the most commonly used rating scales can be found in Rapid Reference 4.4.

Rapid Reference 4.4

Common Assessment Measures for Pervasive Developmental Disorders

Instrument/Age level	Assessment	Measures
Gilliam Autism Rating Scale (GARS): 3 years through 22	Behavior Rating Scale	Autism quotient, four scales: stereotyped behaviors, social interaction, communication, and developmental disturbance
Childhood Autism Rating Scale (CARS): 2 years+	Behavior Rating Scale	Classifies autistic symptoms into mild-moderate-severe range
Asperger Syndrome Diagnostic Scale (ASDS): 5 through 18 years	Behavior Rating Scale	Asperger quotient, five scales: cognitive, maladaptive, language, social, and sensorimotor
Gilliam Asperger's Disorder Scale (GADS): 3 through 22 years	Behavior Rating Scale	Four scales

Individuals with ASD represent a wide range of functioning. Although most children will demonstrate difficulties that conform to the key symptom clusters, how the disorder is manifested and the degree of severity will vary markedly. Therefore, it is very difficult to suggest any one program for all children with ASD. The importance of conducting an assessment that targets the areas of need is a crucial precursor to developing an appropriate treatment plan.

Autism was one of the disorders of childhood that was reviewed as part of the APA Task Force on evidence-based treatments. In her extensive review of programs for children with autism, Rogers (1998) did not find a specific program that matched the more stringent criteria, although the investigation did reveal eight comprehensive programs that obtained positive outcomes. The programs were intensive (involving anywhere from 15 to 40 hours per week), focused on early intervention (5 years or younger), and used behavioral methods. Significant gains were noted in decreased symptoms of autism, enhanced language skills, achievement of developmental goals, and social relations.

Dawson and Osterling (1996) conducted a similar meta-analysis and found that approximately half of the children who participated in the programs were able to bypass special education and enroll in the regular elementary school classroom. The authors suggest several characteristics common to successful programs, including targeting specific deficits (attention, compliance, appropriate play), use of a highly structured and predictable program with low teacher:student ratio, integration of programs across situations (clinic, home, school), engagement of parents as cotherapists, and careful monitoring of transitions between programs.

Although there is some controversy regarding which program is the best for autistic children, there is agreement that beyond early intervention, at a minimum, educational programs should provide opportunities for intense engagement in the process of learning, individualized and systematic instruction, and parental involvement (Hurth, Shaw, Izeman, Whaley, & Rogers, 1999).

Lovaas and the UCLA Applied Behavioral Analysis Program

One pioneering program in the area of intervention programs for autistic children was the program developed by Ivar Lovaas (1987) at UCLA. Modeled on principles of applied behavioral analysis (ABA), the program was intensive (three-year duration, 40 hours per week), pervasive (home and clinic), and relied heavily on behavioral methods of operant conditioning, imitation, and reinforcement. Initially, the focus was on appropriate behavior (reducing disruptive behavior and increasing compliance and imitation). In the second year, language training (increased use of appropriate expressive language) and social play were emphasized. The third year provided opportunities for fine-tuning skills for integration into the school system (emotional expression, preacademic skills, etc.). Average age on entrance to the program was approximately 2.5 years.

When the children were approximately 7 years of age, outcomes were compared for children enrolled in the most intensive group with those who received less intensive programming. Almost half (47%) of the children in the intensive group increased their IQ scores an average of 37 points (placing them in the average range) and were promoted to the regular second grade. Unfortunately, children who received less intensive services, or only special education, demonstrated minimal gains overall. Gains were maintained at follow-up six years later.

TEACCH Program

Another program that has gained increasing popularity is the Treatment and Education for Autistic and Related Communication Handicapped Children program (TEACCH; Schopler, 1994). The program focuses on close collaboration between parents and professionals and is based on the underlying belief that children are motivated to learn language as intentional communication, in a means-end association. For example, a child learns to say the word *eat* or *cookie* to obtain a favorite treat. The pragmatic approach of this program is evident as language becomes contextualized and integrated into ongoing daily activities rather than being taught as a discrete skill. The TEACCH program also translates abstract concepts (e.g., time, space) into visually meaningful alternatives (visual schedules and charts) that provide children with a visible way to track and predict the order of events, thereby alleviating anxiety generated by preoccupations with the need for sameness and rigidity of routines.

The TEACCH program is a functional approach (Schopler, 1994) that has been used internationally to assist in the integration of children with autism into regular classroom activities. Empirically, the TEACCH program has been identified as a successful treatment for reducing self-injurious behaviors (Norgate, 1998), for enhancing skills in individuals with high-functioning autism and Asperger's disorder (Kunce & Mesibov, 1998), and more effective than a nonspecific educational alternative (Panerai, Ferrante, & Zingale, 2002).

TEST YOURSELF

1. **The AAIDD considers an intellectual disability (ID) a medical condition and a psychiatric disorder.**

   True or False?

2. **Currently, the intellectual threshold for ID is considered to be**

   (a) 65 to 70.
   (b) 75 to 80.

(c) 65 to 75.
(d) 70 to 85.

3. According to the *DSM-5* the severity of ID is identified

(a) by degree of intellectual deficits.
(b) as intermittent, limited, extensive, or pervasive.
(c) as mild, moderate, severe, or profound supports.
(d) by both a and c.

4. The term Global Developmental Delay

(a) Is used to refer to a temporary condition until a complete intellectual assessment can be conducted
(b) Refers to specific delays in motor milestones
(c) Is reserved for ID where mild levels of support are required
(d) Refers to the fact that intellectual delays are recognized on a world-wide basis

5. Which of the following is FALSE regarding Williams syndrome

(a) 80% will have cardiovascular problems
(b) they are hypersocial
(c) they are talented musically
(d) none are false; all the above are true

6. According to IDEA (2004),

(a) Intellectual disability is not recognized as one of the 13 categories of disability
(b) Intellectual disability is the same as developmental delay
(c) States are mandated to provide special education services for children with delays until they are 9 years of age
(d) Children with ID who meet eligibility requirements for special education and related services, can receive these services until they are 21 years of age

7. Current estimates suggest which of the following prevalence rates for autism spectrum disorder?

(a) 25 cases per 10,000
(b) 7 cases per 10,000
(c) 1 case per 110
(d) 1 case per 1,000

8. Lovaas Program for ASD, developed at UCLA, relies on methods of

(a) cognitive behavioral therapy
(b) intentional communication
(c) theory of mind
(d) applied behavioral analysis

Answers: 1. False; 2. c; 3. c; 4. a; 5. d; 6. d; 7. c; 8. d

Five

ATTENTION-DEFICIT/HYPERACTIVITY DISORDER (ADHD)

Historically, in the 1930s and 1940s, "restless and inattentive" behaviors currently associated with ADHD were attributed to minimal brain dysfunction (MBD) resulting from brain trauma to the frontal lobe. However, the MBD theory lost momentum when research evidence failed to support the claims. Several years later, the *DSM-II* (APA, 1968) categorized the symptoms of "overactivity, restlessness and inattention" as the hyperkinetic reaction of childhood. Controversy and debate continued about the heterogeneity of seemingly incompatible symptoms of this disorder, which affected some children with passive inattentive symptoms while unleashing hyperactive and impulsive behaviors in others.

In the third revision of the *DSM*, the *DSM-III* (APA, 1980), an attempt was made to address both versions of the disorder by replacing the unified hyperkinetic reaction of childhood with a new category, called attention-deficit disorder (ADD). The disorder of ADD would recognize two distinct subtypes: ADD with hyperactivity and ADD without hyperactivity. However, by the time the *DSM* was revised (*DSM-IIIR*; APA, 1987), the disorder was once again the topic of significant debate. Lack of research support for subtyping from *DSM* field trials reversed thinking, and once again a single categorical domain prevailed: attention-deficit/hyperactivity disorder (ADHD).

CLINICAL DESCRIPTION AND ASSOCIATED FEATURES

The *DSM-5* (APA, 2013) maintains the conceptualization of the disorder from the previous version (*DSM-IV-TR*; APA, 2000) and continues to subtype the disorder into symptom presentations based on two predominant symptom categories: inattentive symptoms and impulsive-hyperactive symptoms. Currently classified as attention-deficit/hyperactivity disorder, based on the number and constellation of symptoms, individuals with the disorder may be classified as meeting criteria for one of three presentations, based on the degree to which the child demonstrates three core features of the disorder: inattention, hyperactivity, and impulsivity. The three presentations include:

1. Primarily Inattentive Presentation
2. Primarily Hyperactive-Impulsive Presentation
3. Combined Presentation

The diagnostic criteria have changed minimally from the *DSM-IV-TR* (APA, 2000), in the following ways: (a) Symptoms must now be evident prior to 12 years of age (rather than 7 years as noted previously); and (b) only five symptoms are required for individuals 17 years of age and over, instead of the six symptoms required for children and youth younger than 17 years of age.

What has mainly changed about the disorder is where it is located within the *DSM*. Previously housed in the chapter on Disorders First Diagnosed in Infancy, Childhood, and Adolescence, the disorder's placement was controversial, because it was positioned in the subsection on Attention-Deficit and the Disruptive Behavior Disorders. Some practitioners were opposed to this placement, because it could be misconstrued that those with ADHD were among the disruptive behavior disorders. However, with the addition of the chapter on Neurodevelopmental Disorders in the *DSM-5*, ADHD has been more appropriately relocated to this chapter.

DON'T FORGET

Although adding the category of Neurodevelopmental Disorders was readily agreed upon by those involved in the revision of the *DSM*, it was not self-evident which disorders should be housed in this category. Based on their meta-analysis of shared features, onset, and etiology, Andrews and colleagues (2009) found that some disorders were an easy fit based on validating criteria, while others were more controversial. Currently, the *DSM-5* includes six disorders under the category of Neurodevelopmental Disorders: intellectual disability, communication disorders, autism spectrum disorders (ASD), attention-deficit/hyperactivity disorder (ADHD), specific learning disorder, and motor disorders.

PUTTING IT INTO PRACTICE

For the third time in the past 5 minutes, Jeremy's fourth-grade teacher has had to tell him to sit in his seat and keep his hands to himself. It is as if Jeremy's feet are attached to springs. He doesn't walk; he bounces. He doesn't sit; he squirms. It's not just the motor activity that sets him apart from the rest of the class: Jeremy also has a motor mouth. He talks incessantly. He can't resist sharing his ideas with the class, whether they are welcomed or not. As soon as he thinks about them, regardless of whether the time is right, Jeremy blurts out answers, disrupts the classroom, and adds considerable stress to his teacher's already stressful job.

Jeremy is almost the polar opposite of his classmate Leonard. For Leonard, Jeremy's antics just fade into the background of other classroom stuff. Unlike Jeremy, Leonard is very quiet and rarely participates in classroom discussions, unless the discussions are about something that really interests him. Leonard spends most of his time staring out the window or off into space. The word *daydreamer* seems to fit Leonard perfectly.

Leonard always seems to be at least one step behind everyone else. Leonard is rarely on task; he drifts off in the middle of assignments; often he has to be reminded to return to earth. Leonard is doing poorly academically. He just doesn't seem to tune into whatever channel the rest of the class is on. Initially, the teacher thought that Leonard was a slow learner, until the class began to discuss different computer programs. The teacher was shocked at Leonard's sophisticated knowledge base and expertise in the area. That was when his teacher began to think that there was something else getting in the way of Leonard's academic success.

In this case study, Jeremy and Leonard share more than the same classroom and same teacher. As incredible as it might seem, they both probably share variations of the same disorder: attention-deficit/hyperactivity disorder (ADHD). How can two children who seem so different fall into the same diagnostic category? This is a question that has plagued theorists for the past 100 years. Although ADHD is among one of the most prevalent disorders in childhood, it continues to challenge professionals. It has been a topic for considerable discussion and controversy, especially regarding the overprescription of stimulant medications (Diller, 1996).

Predominantly Inattentive Presentation

The *DSM-5* lists nine possible symptoms for the inattentive presentation:

1. Careless attention to details
2. Problems sustaining attention over time
3. Does not appear to listen

4. Poor follow-through (schoolwork, homework, chores)
5. Poorly organized
6. Poor ability to sustain mental attention (e.g., homework, independent seatwork at school)
7. Loses necessary materials (e.g., pencils, notebooks, assignment sheets, homework)
8. Easily distracted
9. Forgetful

In addition to children and youth having six of the nine symptoms listed here, the *DSM* also stipulates that a diagnosis requires that (a) the symptoms are pervasive across situations (two or more settings); (b) they interfere with performance (academic social, work-related); and (c) they have been evident prior to 12 years of age.

DON'T FORGET

The *DSM* requires only six of nine possible symptoms in order to allow for some latitude in symptom presentation. Practitioners can indicate whether symptoms represent a mild, moderate, or severe manifestation of the disorder, based on the number of symptoms present and the resulting impairment.

DON'T FORGET

There are several reasons why the *DSM* would include additional qualifiers concerning onset and the pervasive nature of symptoms. As was discussed in Chapter 1, several disorders share the same features as ADHD. These additional criteria assist in making differential diagnoses. Symptoms occurring later in childhood (after age 12) may indicate an emotional response to maltreatment, an anxiety disorder, or recent changes in the family constellation. Symptoms that are evident only at school may signal a more specific learning disability.

CAUTION

Undiagnosed, the inattentive presentation is to education what high cholesterol is to those with heart problems: It can be a silently destructive force.

Unlike their highly active and highly visible counterpart, children with the inattentive presentation of ADHD are often misunderstood and undiagnosed; they often suffer painful consequences of internalizing disorders and have academic problems (Weiss, Worling, & Wasdell, 2003).

Reviewing the symptoms associated with the inattentive variant of ADHD, it is not difficult to understand why these children would encounter academic problems. One of the major developmental tasks of the school-aged child is to develop a sense of competence, mastery, and efficacy. However, children with ADHD face significant challenges in meeting increased academic and social demands.

According to Barkley (1998), children with predominantly inattentive symptoms may be characterized by a "sluggish" information-processing style (slow to process information) and problems with focused or selective attention. Therefore, against the backdrop of "academic noise," these children are unable to filter essential from nonessential details. Lack of attention to details often results from information overload and an inability to selectively limit the focus of attention. This processing deficit also reduces grade scores resulting from careless errors. Other academic concerns are evident in difficulties completing homework assignments (sustaining attention for boring tasks) and apparent lack of motivation. If homework assignments are completed, often under intense parent scrutiny, the disorganized student may forget to bring them to school or lose them somewhere in the mess of papers at the bottom of his or her backpack. Academic endeavors are a frustration for these children, their parents, and their teachers.

DON'T FORGET

The symptoms of ADHD must cause significant impairment, must be in excess of developmental expectations, and must occur in more than one setting (e.g., home and school). Symptoms must be evident prior to 12 years of age.

Predominantly Hyperactive-Impulsive Presentation

The *DSM* requires six of a possible nine symptoms for a diagnosis of ADHD Hyperactive-Impulsive Presentation, in children and adolescents (under 17 years of age). The nine symptoms include six hyperactive and three impulsive symptoms. The following are the symptoms of hyperactivity:

- Fidgety or squirmy behavior
- Problems remaining seated
- Excessive motion
- Problems engaging in quiet play

- Constantly being on the go
- Incessant talking

The following are the symptoms of impulsivity:

- Blurts out answers, comments
- Is impatient, has problems with turn taking
- Is intrusive to others

In the Putting It Into Practice case study, Jeremy demonstrates many of the symptoms of ADHD hyperactive-impulsive presentation: problems remaining seated, squirminess, always being in motion, incessant talking, blurting out answers, and problems with turn taking. If during the parent interview the clinician determines that Jeremy has always been that way, that Jeremy is the same way at home and at school, and that this behavior is causing problems across situations (home, school, church), then it becomes increasingly likely that Jeremy has the hyperactive-impulsive presentation of ADHD. In addition to their social problems, children with the hyperactive-impulsive type of ADHD also experience academic problems because of their impulsive nature. These children tend to rush through their assignments and often emphasize speed over accuracy. They often approach tasks incorrectly because they do not wait until all the directions are provided.

DON'T FORGET

Children with the hyperactive-impulsive variant of ADHD are at risk socially. Their inability to wait their turn does not make them very popular with their peers. Socially, children with ADHD often present with poor social skills and experience difficulty making and maintaining friendships. These children often gravitate toward other troubled children, and they may engage in various forms of rule breaking and other behavioral problems.

DON'T FORGET

According to the *DSM-5* diagnostic criteria, youth and adults over 17 years of age require only five symptoms from the impulsivity-hyperactivity presentation, although they still must satisfy conditions of significant impairment (social, academic, work-related), evidence of symptoms across more than one situation, and onset prior to 12 years of age.

Practitioners can indicate mild, moderate, and severe levels of the disorder, based on the number and severity of symptoms and degree of impairment.

Combined Presentation

Individuals who meet criteria for the combined presentation must meet criteria for both the predominantly inattentive presentation and the predominantly hyperactive-impulsive presentation, which means that children and youth prior to age 17 would require at least 12 symptoms (six from each presentation), and those older than 17 would require a total of 10 symptoms (five from each presentation).

ADHD From a Developmental Perspective

For children with ADHD, the core features of overactivity, impulsivity, and inattention will impact on learning and relationships based on the nature of developmental tasks emphasized at each stage of development.

DON'T FORGET

Developmentally different symptoms appear at different stages. Although it may be possible to detect symptoms of hyperactivity-impulsivity by 3 years of age, problems with inattention are not likely to surface until school age.

Early Precursors to ADHD Hyperactive-Impulsive Presentation

Although ADHD is very difficult to diagnose prior to 3 years of age, retrospective parent interviews have identified a number of early precursors to the hyperactive-impulsive variant of ADHD. As infants, children with difficult temperaments tend to be at greater risk for developing ADHD later. Other early risk factors include excessive activity, poor sleep patterns, and irritability. Parents also report that these infants are more difficult to soothe when upset than their non-ADHD peers (Barkley, 1998). During the toddler period (1–2.5 years), children with ADHD demonstrate higher levels of underregulated behaviors (lack of self-control), and in the transition to preschool (3 to 6 years), lack of self-control persisted, at a time when non-ADHD peers were demonstrating increased maturity and greater self-control. During the preschool period, children with ADHD are described by parents and teachers as being more demanding, stressful, and problematic than their non-ADHD peers, especially in "free play" or unsupervised activities (Campbell, March, Pierce, Ewing, & Szumowski, 1991).

ADHD and the School-Aged Child (6 to 11 Years)

In the Putting It Into Practice scenario, Leonard and Jeremy demonstrate many of the characteristic difficulties that children with ADHD exhibit during the school-age period. School-aged children are faced with the developmental task of increasing their sense of competence and mastery. However, children with ADHD face significant challenges in meeting increased academic and social demands. Although all children with ADHD are academically vulnerable, the nature of academic problems varies depending on how the symptoms of ADHD manifest.

School-aged children with the hyperactive-impulsive presentation of ADHD also experience academic difficulties, but the nature of their academic problems relates more to these children's impulsivity and their inability to inhibit responses that may compete with effective learning. Learning problems are evident in their tendencies to jump into tasks prior to listening to all the directions and to rush through assignments, sacrificing accuracy for speed. These children often demonstrate low frustration tolerance and tend to abandon tasks that do not have an immediate solution. Their impulsive behaviors also place this group of children at greater risk for accidental injury (Barkley, 1998).

CAUTION

Children with the inattentive presentation of ADHD are often misunderstood. Frequently, inattention is misinterpreted as lack of motivation. Problems sustaining their attention, poor organizational skills, and ease of distractibility contribute to poor educational outcomes. These children often seem to be one step behind and regularly drift off into daydreaming when the task is monotonous or boring. Homework and seatwork assignments are often poorly attempted and incomplete. These children often do poorly on tests, not only because of their tendency to miss important details but also because they have a very poor concept of time and time management. Many children with ADHD do not complete tests in the allotted time, and their lack of organizational skills also contributes to academic difficulty.

ADHD and the Adolescent (12–19)

At least half of the children diagnosed with ADHD will continue to meet the criteria for the disorder throughout adolescence. Adolescents with ADHD are poorly equipped to meet the challenges of managing the curriculum in middle school and high school, with its emphasis on increased workload and independent study skills. These students find that their poor work habits, lack of organizational skills, and poor follow-through often result in significant academic difficulties during this period.

DON'T FORGET

Children with the hyperactive-impulsive presentation are also socially at risk. These children often experience social problems because of their intrusive behaviors and tendencies to let their behavior escalate out of control.

CAUTION

A major developmental task in adolescence is the formation of a sense of personal identity, which includes the consolidation of a self-concept built on a foundation of peer acceptance and competence. Teens who have a history of poor academic outcomes and concomitant social problems are at increased risk for development of comorbid internalizing problems, such as anxiety and depression (Biederman, Faraone, & Lapey, 1992), and externalizing problems, such as aggression, defiance, and forms of delinquent behavior (Barkley, Fischer, Edelbrock, & Smallish, 1990).

Other social and emotional concerns prevalent at this developmental stage include increased risk for reckless driving accidents and participation in other high-risk behaviors, such as substance use, that are reported to be higher in ADHD populations (Barkley, 1998).

Prevalence and Course

According to the *DSM-5* (APA, 2013), estimates of ADHD in school-aged children range from 3% to 7% of the total population. Ninety percent of children identified with ADHD will be diagnosed with the hyperactive-impulsive symptom presentation. However, this figure may be somewhat misleading in terms of actual prevalence statistics, since many more children with inattentive symptoms can go undiagnosed because of the subtle nature of this variant of the disorder.

ADHD and Gender

Ratios of male-to-female frequency have been reported from 2:1 to 9:1. Currently, the question of whether there are gender differences in the prevalence

> **DON'T FORGET**
>
> Prevalence rates may vary widely among different reports. The variation in rates can result from several factors, including whether the samples refer to a clinical or general population, the methods used to classify the disorder, and the assessment instruments used. Unless otherwise stated, all prevalence data reported in this text refer to data noted in the *DSM* (APA, 2013).

rates for particular subtypes of ADHD symptoms continues to be an area of debate. Research suggests that females with ADHD may be more impaired than males in areas of psychosocial functioning, evident in higher rates of depression, anxiety, self-esteem, and levels of stress (Rucklidge & Tannock, 2001). It may be possible that since 90% of those diagnosed with ADHD demonstrate impulsive-hyperactive or combined symptoms, female rates of identification may reflect the presentation of different types of symptoms for ADHD. A recent review of clinical data for 143 inattentive and 133 combined presentation with ADHD revealed that children who had the inattentive presentation were more likely to be female (Weiss et al., 2003), whereas another study demonstrated that females are twice as likely to have the inattentive type (Biederman, Mick, & Farone, 2002).

According to Barkley (1998), the earliest age at which a diagnosis of ADHD might be possible is approximately 3 years, although symptoms of inattention are not likely to be noticed until much later. Approximately two-thirds of elementary school-aged children who are diagnosed with ADHD have an additional diagnosable disorder (Cantwell, 1994). High rates of comorbidity with both internalizing and externalizing disorders make the course of this disorder particularly prone to poor outcomes. Given the comorbid nature of the disorder, the course of ADHD is best understood within the context of the different developmental pathways that might result based on the comorbid features.

ADHD and Comorbidity

Academic and Learning Problems

Academic problems are common in children with ADHD, due to difficulties in impulsivity, poor attention to detail, problems with concentration, and the executive functions, which are discussed later in this chapter.

ADHD and Specific Learning Disorders Prevalence rates for comorbid ADHD and specific learning disabilities (SLDs) are difficult to predict accurately, due to wide variations among published studies regarding how SLDs are defined and measured. Controversies surrounding the definitions and measurement of SLDs will be addressed at length in Chapter 6. Comorbid rates have been estimated to be between 16% and 21% for these two disorders (Frick et al., 1991).

ADHD and Internalizing Problems

As is discussed at greater length in Chapter 8, symptoms of depressive disorder and bipolar disorder present differently in children and adults. In children, symptoms of depression and bipolar disorder often overlap with symptoms of ADHD, making differential diagnosis difficult. One of the major symptoms of depression in children is irritability. Irritable behaviors often manifest in restlessness, agitation, short attention span, problems concentrating, and impulsive responses, which resemble symptoms of ADHD. Unlike the lengthy highs and lows of adult bipolar disorder, children with bipolar disorder often experience rapid cycles of shifting moods (elation to irritability), with brief and multiple mood swings. Bipolar symptoms of pressured speech (incessant talking), distractibility, and overactivity can be easily mistaken for symptoms of ADHD. Symptoms of anxiety (e.g., distractibility, nervous agitation, restlessness, poor concentration) are also similar to symptoms of ADHD.

DON'T FORGET

As many as 30% of children with ADHD will repeat a grade; as many as 40% will be placed in special education programs; and as many as 30% may never finish high school (Barkley, 1998).

DON'T FORGET

Internalizing problems represent the continuum of overcontrolled responses indicating "problems within the self, such as anxiety, depression, somatic complaints without known medical basis, and social withdrawal from contacts" (Achenbach & Rescorla, 2001, p. 93).

In one study, Biederman and colleagues (1995) found that up to 70% of depressed children also had comorbid ADHD. In another study, approximately 90% of the younger (prepubertal) children and 30% of the adolescent population referred for bipolar disorder had comorbid ADHD (Geller & Luby, 1997). Other studies have found higher rates of comorbidity for overanxious disorder and somatic complaints (e.g., headaches, stomachaches) than in children without ADHD. In addition, many children who have ADHD also suffer from problems falling asleep and staying asleep.

CAUTION

Differential diagnosis between ADHD and the internalizing disorders can be a complex process, since the three core features of ADHD (i.e., inattention, overactivity, and impulsivity) share many of the same characteristics as symptoms of depression, bipolar disorder, and anxiety. In addition, high rates of comorbidity exist among these disorders.

CAUTION

One concern regarding the treatment of children with ADHD through the use of stimulant medication has been the underlying fear that this will lead to an increased rate of substance use later on. However, research does not support this concern. In fact, successful treatment of ADHD actually serves as a protective factor for later substance abuse, since adults who were not treated for ADHD are associated with much higher rates of substance abuse (Biederman, Wilens, Mick, Spencer, & Faraone, 1999).

ADHD and Externalizing Disorders

Children and adolescents with comorbid ADHD and disruptive behavior disorders (ODD and CD) are more seriously maladjusted (Moffit, 1990) and have significantly worse outcomes compared to children with ADHD alone (Barkley et al., 1990). Studies show that as many as 35% to 60% of children with ADHD will also have ODD, while as many as 50% of children with ADHD will go on to develop CD (Szatmari, Boyle, & Offord, 1989).

It has been suggested that a diagnosis of ADHD in childhood can be as strong a predictor for substance use as having a family history of substance abuse. Barkley and colleagues (1990) found that hyperactive teens with ADHD were significantly more likely to use cigarettes and alcohol than were their nonhyperactive peers. A longitudinal study tracking children with ADHD into adolescence found higher levels of substance use (across all substances) than in their non-ADHD peers (Brooke & Pelham, 2003).

ADHD and Social Relationship Problems

At least half of children with ADHD will also have problems in their relationships with peers. There can be a significant discrepancy between social skills and cognitive ability. Using this discrepancy criterion, Greene, Biederman, Faraone, Sienna, and Garcia-Jetton (1997) labeled this subtype "socially disabled" (ADHD+SD).

Compared to children who have ADHD alone, Green and colleagues found that children with ADHD+SD demonstrate higher levels of substance abuse, family problems, anxiety, mood problems, and conduct problems.

ETIOLOGY (CAUSES)

Although ADHD is one of the most prevalent childhood disorders, significant controversy remains regarding the exact cause of ADHD. It is most likely that the etiology involves a complex interaction between biological and environmental factors (Wolraich, 2000).

Biological and Neurological Features

Increased research into the potential neurobiological basis for ADHD has focused on four potential sources of information: structural regions of the brain, genetic transmission, neurotransmitter functions, and neurocognitive processing.

Brain Structures

With the advent of functional magnetic resonance imaging (fMRI) and single-photon emission computed tomography (SPECT), brain scans have revealed less activity in the frontal brain regions and more activity in the cingulate gyrus in children with ADHD compared to children without ADHD.

While the frontal system is responsible for executive functioning, the cingulate gyrus is involved in focusing of attention and in directing response selection. Three areas of executive functioning that can be particularly problematic for individuals with ADHD are working memory, sense of time, and sustained effort. Altered perception of time, associated with reductions of dopamine in the basal ganglia, may be accountable for poor time management in individuals with ADHD; however, this area is still in need of exploratory research. In addition to the basal ganglia, the parietal lobe has also been associated with governing sense of time, and there is some support that defective

> **DON'T FORGET**
>
> There is growing recognition that ADHD involves a deficit in executive functions, the higher-order cognitive functions that process information without conscious awareness (Brown, 2005). The executive functions are self-directed actions used to modify behavior and are responsible for initiating and maintaining problem-solving behaviors that manage, direct, and control the course of brain activity.

perception of time might be related to dysfunction in these areas (Rao, Mayer, & Harrington, 2001). Problems with prospective memory (remembering to remember) can result in poor follow-through and incomplete tasks (Barkley & Gordon, 2002).

Genetic Transmission

Approximately 50% of children with ADHD have a parent who also has the disorder (Biederman et al., 1995), and studies suggest that as much as 75% of etiology might be attributed to genetic factors (Sherman, Iacono, & McGue, 1997).

Neurotransmitters

Research has identified low levels of catecholamines (dopamine, norepinephrine, epinephrine) in children with ADHD. The catecholamines are associated with attention and motor activity. Medications prescribed for ADHD, such as Dexedrine (dextramphetamine), Ritalin (methylphenidate), and Cylert (pemoline), increase the number of catecholamines in the brain (Barkley, 1998).

Neurocognitive Processing

There has been increasing interest in examining how executive functioning and arousal levels in children with ADHD contribute to cognitive, emotional, and behavioral processing deficits. Inherent in executive functioning processes is the need to be flexible and readily shift focus between tasks when required and to adapt strategies as needed. Another important factor in problem-solving success is the ability to monitor, evaluate, and revise strategies. Ultimately, the task of being able to hold information in memory while performing these problem-solving tasks involves the use of *working memory*.

Developmentally, increased self-regulatory functions are evident as toddlers transition to the preschool stage. Increased self-control results from the child's ability to internalize good role models provided by parents and the increased utilization of inner language, which guides and directs appropriate behavior and inhibits inappropriate responses.

DON'T FORGET

Executive functioning tasks include initiation or inhibition, flexibility in shifting focus, and monitoring, evaluating, and adapting strategies as needed. In addition to organizing and managing cognitive functions, executive functions are also involved in the management and control of other regulatory functions, including behavioral and emotional control, and self-regulation of motivation or persistence of effort (Barkley, 2006b).

DON'T FORGET

The central feature of this model is the concept of *behavioral inhibition*. Barkley conceptualizes behavioral inhibition as the ability to inhibit a response (i.e., to refrain from responding or institute a delay) or stop an active response, and to maintain the delay over time. The delay (or termination) of the response is necessary as a manner of interference control, in order that goal-directed behavior can be initiated and maintained (Barkley, 1997).

Barkley's Model of ADHD

Barkley's (1997) model of ADHD focuses on understanding ADHD through the executive functions. The model is built around the concept of *behavioral inhibition*, a central feature of the disorder, and the ways deficits in behavioral inhibition relate to other executive functioning deficits and problems with sustained attention. Barkley is clear in delineating that this model was developed specifically to address deficits in processing that apply to the hyperactive-impulsive presentation of ADHD. Barkley emphasized that this model does not attempt to explain the inattentive variant of ADHD.

In Barkley's model, the child's degree of success in behavioral inhibition is central to determining the nature of outcomes of four central executive functioning tasks: (1) working memory (permits tasks of sequential ordering and planning), (2) self-regulation (modulates activity states to initiate goal-directed behavior and sustain effort), (3) internalization of speech (slows down reactivity and promotes inner reflection), and (4) reconstitution (analyzes and synthesizes information). Deficits in behavioral inhibition result in poor problem-solving strategies based on an inability to integrate and coordinate information generated by the four central processes. Deficits in these areas can result in negative outcomes for academic performance. In one longitudinal study, one-third of students with the hyperactive-impulsive presentation failed to graduate from high school, while only 21% enrolled in college, compared with more than 80% of their nondiagnosed peers (Barkley, 2006c).

DON'T FORGET

Barkley considers behavioral inhibition as the necessary first step in problem solving. Developmentally, behavioral inhibition is a precursor to the development of the other higher-order functions. The behavioral delay allows sufficient time to develop skills in the four major areas, which are in turn focal points for the development and refining of other essential skills.

CAUTION

Barkley has emphasized that the behavioral inhibition model was developed to explain the hyperactive-impulsive symptoms of ADHD, not the inattentive symptoms.

PUTTING IT INTO PRACTICE

Josh cannot concentrate on his homework and has to be continually monitored in order to stay seated, stop fidgeting, and get to work (sustained attention for effortful task). When he is playing videogames, Josh is riveted to the screen and can play for an hour at a time (sustained attention for self-rewarding task).

Barkley addresses the role of inattention in his model by distinguishing between two forms of inattention that are qualitatively distinct: sustained attention and selective attention. While Barkley attributes deficits in selective attention (i.e., inability to filter essential from nonessential details) to the inattentive version of ADHD, he contends that children who have the hyperactive-impulsive variant have problems with sustaining their attention over time. Barkley further distinguishes between sustained attention for essentially effortful tasks and what he calls "contingency based attention" or self-rewarding attention. For these reasons, ADHD may be less noticeable in unfamiliar settings or when tasks are particularly novel, which may lead to the misattribution that these children can be focused when they want to (Barkley, 2006a).

Assessment and Treatment/Intervention

Although an exhaustive review of assessment instruments is beyond the intention of this book, it is essential that clinicians obtain an accurate clinical picture of ADHD in order to rule out competing hypotheses. As has been discussed, ADHD shares many characteristic features with other disorders (depression, bipolar disorder, anxiety, posttraumatic stress disorder) and other problems of childhood and adolescence (abuse, maltreatment).

Detailed Clinical and Developmental History

A semistructured interview, such as the ones discussed in Chapter 3, should be conducted with the parent(s) or caregiver(s) to obtain information about the child's developmental history, including birth history, developmental milestones, medical history, educational history, social and emotional history, and family dynamics (including family stressors, clinical features, sibling relationships, and extended family). Obtaining parental expectations and impressions about the child's presenting problem is also important.

CAUTION

When conducting an assessment of suspected ADHD, clinicians must ask several key questions, including whether symptoms can be better accounted for by another disorder and whether comorbid disorders are also present.

DON'T FORGET

Assessment involves using multiple methods to obtain information from multiple sources and across multiple situations.

Parent, Teacher, and Youth Rating Scales

An important criterion of ADHD (APA, 2013) is that the disorder manifests across situations (home, school, etc.). Therefore, it is very important to obtain input from home and school to determine how symptoms present across different situations. In addition, given the high rates of comorbidity with other disorders, it is also essential to obtain information concerning other areas of potential diagnostic concern. Thus, an important part of the assessment process involves taking a comprehensive look at other major dimensions of child and adolescent psychopathology.

There are a number of behavioral rating scales that provide measures of ADHD characteristics in addition to other diagnostic categories. The rating scales have parallel forms that can be completed by parents, teachers, and older children, allowing for a comparison across informants. Three of the more popular behavioral rating scales are the ASEBA (Achenbach & Rescorla, 2001), the Conners Rating Scales (CRS-3; Conners, 2008), and the Behavior Assessment System for Children (BASC-2; Reynolds & Kamphaus, 2004). The scales included in each of these rating scales are summarized in Rapid Reference 5.1.

The ASEBA and CRS-3 scales provide information from both a dimensional and categorical approach to the classification of ADHD, as well as evaluating several other major problem areas. The BASC-2 scales provide an index of functioning based on a dimensional classification system.

In addition to the behavioral rating systems, other scales are designed to evaluate executive functioning. The Brown Attention-Deficit Disorder Scales (Brown, 2001) are available as parent and teacher questionnaires (3–12 years) and a self-report form (8 years to adult). The scales measure executive functioning in six areas: organization, attention, sustained effort, modulating emotions, working memory, and monitoring or evaluation. A comprehensive diagnostic form is also available to assist clinicians in integrating information from the clinical history and to provide guidance in screening for comorbid disorders.

The Behavior Rating Inventory of Executive Function (BRIEF; Gioia, Isquith, Guy, & Kenworthy, 2000) is also available in parent and teacher rating forms. This measure provides a rating of executive functions in two broad areas: behavioral regulation (inhibit, shift, emotional control) and meta-cognition (initiate, working memory, plan/organize, organize materials, monitor). The instrument is available in school-age (5–18) and preschool versions (2–5:11).

CAUTION

The individual assessment session can mask symptoms of ADHD because of the inherent "contingent attention" involved in the novelty of the testing process (Barkley, 1998).

Other Areas of Assessment

Academic difficulties are often part of the profile of children with ADHD. Therefore, individual intellectual and academic assessments may also be an important part of the assessment process in order to rule out other potential diagnostic categories (e.g., intellectual disability) or to assist in identifying comorbid features (e.g., learning disability). Cognitive assessment may also be helpful in evaluating processing deficits in areas of cognitive efficiency, processing speed, or working memory.

Rapid Reference 5.1

Behaviors and Disorders Evaluated by the ASEBA, CRS-3, and BASC-2 Scales

ASEBA	CRS-3	BASC-2
DSM-Oriented Scales	**DSM Diagnostic Categories**	**Dimensional Scales**
Affective Problems Anxiety Problems Somatic Problems	ADHD Inattentive Type ADHD Hyperactive-Impulsive Type	Externalizing Problems: aggression, hyperactivity, and conduct problems

ASEBA	CRS-3	BASC-2
DSM-Oriented Scales	**DSM Diagnostic Categories**	**Dimensional Scales**
Attention-Deficit/ Hyperactivity Problems Oppositional Defiant Problems Conduct Problems	ADHD Total (Combined Type)	Internalizing Problems: depression, anxiety, somatization School Problems: attention, learning Adaptive Behaviors: social skills, leadership, study skills Other Behaviors: withdrawal, atypicality
Other Problems That May Be Evaluated (Syndrome Scales)	**Other Problems That May Be Evaluated**	
Anxious/depressed Withdrawn/depressed Somatic Complaints Social Problems Thought Problems Attention Problems Rule-Breaking Behavior Aggressive Behavior Total Internalizing Total Externalizing Total Problems	Anxiety or Shyness Perfectionism Social Problems Psychosomatic Complaints Family Problems Emotional Problems Conduct Problems Cognitive Problems Anger Control Problems Hyperactivity Adhd Index	

Note: References for all instruments can be found in Appendix B.

Treatment Alternatives

Treatment alternatives for ADHD will vary depending on associated targets (comorbid features), symptoms, and the nature and extent of functional impairment. Interventions can be applied at home (parent training and family interventions), at school (behavior management and increasing on-task behaviors), and in interactions with peers (social skills training). Evidence-based research has for the most part focused on the effects of stimulant medications.

Stimulant Medications

A large-scale investigation of stimulant medications versus behavior therapy initially revealed that, for children with ADHD, stimulant medication was more effective in alleviating the core symptoms of the disorder (MTA Cooperative Group, 1999). However, follow-up of long-term effects, 6 and 8 years after enrollment in the 14-month program, revealed that enrollment in the program did not predict level of functioning on follow-up. Instead, symptom trajectory was the best predictor, with children showing the best behavioral and sociodemographic profiles demonstrating the best responses to any treatment. Although outcomes for those with the combined type of ADHD were initially promising, this group had the worst outcomes in adolescence, regardless of treatment program (Molina et al., 2009).

DON'T FORGET

The catecholamines (dopamine, norepinephrine, epinephrine) are the three neurotransmitters that have been associated with attention and motor activity. There are three main classes of stimulants currently in use for ADHD: amphetamines (Dexedrine, Adderall, Dextrostat), methylphenidates (Ritalin, Focalin, Concerta, Metadate, Methylin), and pemoline (Cylert). Recently, the U.S. Food and Drug Administration (FDA) has approved the first nonstimulant medication for ADHD: Strattera, a selective norepinephrine reuptake inhibitor.

CAUTION

Although there has been considerable research support for medical intervention in the treatment of ADHD, there is some indication that this form of treatment may not be equally effective for all types of comorbid associations. In one large-scale study, anxious youth with ADHD receiving behavior therapy responded as well as anxious youth who received medications alone (MTA Cooperative Group, 1999).

Stimulant medications can be found in various forms, including short-acting (Dexedrine and Ritalin) and slow-release forms (Ritalin-SR), and longer-acting forms (Ritalin-LA). Numerous studies have demonstrated positive effects of stimulant medication in controlling the core symptoms of ADHD in areas of impulsivity-hyperactivity (increased sustained attention, reduced restlessness) and inattention (increased attention, decreased off-task behavior, increased academic output; Elia & Rapoport, 1991; Pelham & Milich, 1991). In addition, behavioral benefits of stimulant medication have been demonstrated in reduced aggressive behaviors (Hinshaw, Heller, & McHale, 1992) and improved parent–child interactions (Barkley & Cunningham, 1978).

However, stimulant medication is not without its negative outcomes, such as the lack of height gain in some individuals. In the MTA study, long-term follow-up revealed that the group who took medication the longest demonstrated a 20% reduction in stimulant-related height gain (approximately 2 cm), compared to their peers who did not take medication, which has prompted researchers to continue to monitor height- and weight-related issues over 10- to 12-year periods (Swanson et al., 2008).

Behavior Management Programs and Functional Behavioral Assessments

Given that medical treatment or medical treatment alone may not be adequate or sufficient, researchers continue to look for behavioral programs that can work as an adjunct to medical treatment or in cases where medication is not accepted or advised. Results from the long-term follow-up of children enrolled in the MTA study (Molina et al., 2009), especially children with the combined type of ADHD, prompted researchers to investigate innovative methods in the treatment of this hard-to-serve population.

Interventions in the Home and School Environments

Empirically, studies have demonstrated that parent training (PT) programs can be an effective method of improving parenting skills while reducing parent stress, core symptoms of ADHD, and noncompliance (Sonuga-Barke, Daley, Thompson, Laver-Bredbury, & Weeks, 2001). Successful interventions in the home and school environments often involve the use of contingency management programs based on information provided from a functional behavioral assessment. Treatment manuals are available to assist clinicians in developing programs for parents of children with oppositional behaviors, social problems, and parent–child conflict (Barkley, 1997; Bloomquist, 1996).

DON'T FORGET

Contingency management programs are developed to address specific systems of positive and negative consequences to ensure behavioral change. Children with ADHD respond best to programs that have immediate reinforcers for good behavior and that have clearly defined goals and specific target behaviors.

Although PT programs have demonstrated improved functioning at home, including teacher consultation in the PT program can also be helpful. Combining

PT programs with teacher consultation allows for generalization of behaviors from the home to school environment. One of the more positive outcomes of parent and teacher collaboration is the enhanced communication between home and school that is monitored through the use of daily communication (often a student agenda can serve as the daily report for notes between parent and teacher). Studies have revealed that this combined approach can result in significant improvement in home and school behaviors (Pelham, Wheeler, & Chronis, 1998).

The concept of "coaching" as a therapeutic alternative was introduced by psychiatrist Ned Hallowell (1995) to assist adults with the disorder, although there has not been much empirical investigation of the treatment effectiveness of this procedure until recently (Goldstein, 2005). In 2009, the Edge Foundation (https://edgefoundation.org/) funded a two-year national study of the effectiveness of coaching for more than 250 randomly selected college students with ADHD. Initial results of these investigations (Parker, Hoffman, Sawilowsky, & Rowlands, 2011) look promising.

TEST YOURSELF

1. Historically, it was thought that ADHD symptoms were associated with

(a) poor parenting practices.
(b) trauma to the frontal lobe.
(c) problems with visual motor integration.
(d) poor teaching.

2. Which of the following is TRUE about ADHD?

(a) More males than females are identified.
(b) Ninety percent of children with ADHD will be diagnosed with the hyperactive-impulsive type.
(c) ADHD can be identified as early as 3 years of age.
(d) All of the above.

3. Which of the following disorders is least likely to be associated with ADHD?

(a) Bipolar disorder
(b) Oppositional defiant disorder
(c) anxiety disorder
(d) eating disorder

4. According to Barkley, the difference between those with predominantly inattentive symptoms and those with predominantly impulsive-hyperactive symptoms is that

(a) those with Inattentive Type have deficits in sustained attention.
(b) those with Impulsive-Hyperactive Type have problems with sustained attention for self-rewarding tasks.

(c) those with Inattentive Type have deficits in selective attention.
(d) both a and c are correct.

5. **Which of the following is NOT one of Barkley's four executive functioning components?**
   (a) Reconstitution
   (b) Externalization of speech
   (c) Self-regulation
   (d) Working memory
6. **Results of the MTA Cooperative Group Study (1999) revealed that**
   (a) PT groups were as effective as medication in reducing ADHD symptoms.
   (b) anxious youth with ADHD receiving behavior therapy responded as well as anxious youth taking medications alone.
   (c) medications were least effective for children with impulsivity.
   (d) behavior therapy did not assist with other symptoms such as poor social skills.
7. **Which of the following is NOT an executive function?**
   (a) Ability to shift between tasks
   (b) Ability to monitor and revise strategies
   (c) Rigidity
   (d) Working memory
8. **Contemporary theories of ADHD believe that ADHD is most likely caused by**
   (a) heredity.
   (b) environment.
   (c) a complex interaction between biological and environmental factors.
   (d) frontal lobe trauma.

Answers: 1. b; 2. d; 3. d; 4. c; 5. b; 6. b; 7. c; 8. c

Six

SPECIFIC LEARNING DISABILITIES

Throughout this text, there has been some discussion of the wide variations in definitions for childhood disorders depending on the nature of the defining source and/or geographic region. Definitions for specific learning disabilities are perhaps the most discrepant in this regard. Since our understanding of prevalence rates and the nature of research outcomes is contingent upon how the disorder is defined, a significant portion of this chapter is devoted to presenting an overview of the current controversies and trends in defining specific learning disabilities.

CLINICAL DESCRIPTION AND ASSOCIATED FEATURES

Issues in the Definition, Identification, and Classification of Specific Learning Disabilities (SLD)

There is considerable controversy regarding how to best define specific learning disabilities and the implications of terms of usage in different parts of the world. The differences in definitions can be found based on the nature of the defining source (e.g., the *DSM*, U.S. Federal Educational Register, National Joint Committee for Learning Disabilities) and on the country of origin. In many countries of the world, the term *learning disability* continues to be equated with intellectual disability. Furthermore, *specific learning disability* or *specific learning disorder* has also become equated with *developmental dyslexia* (Demonet, Taylor, & Chaix, 2004), which is primarily used to describe a reading disability.

The Changing Definitions of SLD

Traditionally, specific learning disabilities were identified and defined using a discrepancy criteria; namely, a student was considered to have a learning disability if there was a significant discrepancy between intellectual functioning (on an IQ test) and academic performance (in areas of reading, writing, or mathematics, as measured by a standardized academic test). Discontent with that method and introduction of an alternative method of identification (Response to Intervention, or RTI) has resulted in significant controversy regarding the conceptualization and identification of specific learning disabilities.

The Discrepancy Criterion

Formerly called academic skills disorders, criteria for SLD were clustered in the *DSM-IV-TR* (APA, 2000) under Learning Disorders in the chapter entitled Disorders Usually First Diagnosed in Infancy, Childhood, or Adolescence. At that time, the *DSM* used the discrepancy criteria to determine the existence of a learning disorder, based on the discrepancy between an individual's intellectual functioning and his or her academic functioning based on the use of standard scores. An individual was considered to have a learning disorder if the discrepancy between intellect and academic functioning was in excess of between 1 and 2 standard deviations (a standard deviation is equivalent to 15 points on the standard scale). At the time, this definition was consistent with the definition used by the *Federal Register* for learning disabilities, according to the 1999 reauthorization of the Individuals with Disabilities Education Act (IDEA), which was published in the *Federal Register*, on March 12, 1999.

Response to Intervention

However, there was growing discontent with the exclusive use of the discrepancy criterion for the identification of students with SLD because of (a) problems in the definition and application of the discrepancy criterion (lack of a universal rule as to how much of a discrepancy was required), (b) criticisms of the system favoring older children and those with higher IQs, and (c) concerns with the model being failure based. As a result, the latest reauthorization of IDEA (IDEA, 2004) added an alternative method of identification for students with SLD called Response to Intervention (RTI). The RTI approach allows a tiered system of empirically supported interventions to be applied, and failure to respond would be a criteria for identification of SLD for students who would require more specific and more intense interventions (*Federal Register*, 2006, 300.307(a), p. 46789).

Current Status

There continues to be a high level of controversy regarding the issues of definition and identification of children with SLD, with some experts, such as Kavale (2005), arguing that "changes to the operational definition, without changes to the formal definition are indefensible," resulting in a "disconnect between the formal definition and the operational definition" (p. 553). Furthermore, it has been noted that the RTI approach lacks information about IQ, which compromises the development of appropriate interventions (Semrud-Clikeman, 2005). In 2010, the Learning Disabilities Association of America (LDA) prepared a White Paper based on the expertise of 56 professionals in the field and recommended that the identification procedures for SLD be strengthened to include cognitive and neuropsychological assessments necessary to identify strengths and weaknesses for the purposes of developing appropriate interventions (LDA, 2010).

DON'T FORGET

A learning disorder is evident if achievement in one of the key academic areas (reading, mathematics, writing) is substantially below what would be expected based on age, however, *substantially below* is no longer specifically defined as a discrepancy between achievement and intelligence.

Despite this movement, the *DSM-5* (APA, 2013) has altered its criteria by removing reference to the discrepancy criteria and replacing it with reference to academic skills that are "substantially and quantifiably below those expected for the individual's chronological age . . . as confirmed by individually administered standardized achievement measures and clinical assessment" (p. 67). Many consider this definition to be more in line with IDEA (2004), but others consider the description to be more vague and less powerful than how it was previously stated.

DON'T FORGET

The *DSM* acknowledges SLD in several areas, with impairment in reading (accuracy, fluency, comprehension), written expression (spelling, grammar and punctuation, organization), and mathematics (number sense, facts, calculation, or math reasoning). Although the *DSM* acknowledges that associated processing deficits in areas of visual perception, linguistic processes, attention, and memory may accompany a learning disorder, if a sensory deficit is evident, then the learning disorder must be in excess of what would be expected, given that deficit.

DON'T FORGET

The discrepancy criterion provided a key defining feature in making a differential diagnosis of intellectual disability and SLD. For those with an intellectual disability, although academic achievement is low, it is considered to be commensurate with level of intellectual functioning, while in the learning-disabled population, SLD exists because there is a significant discrepancy between IQ and achievement.

DON'T FORGET

Kavale, Forness, and MacMillan (1998) suggest that theorists have lost sight of the biophysiological nature of the disorder and that, without reference to the nature of the central nervous system impairment, the disorder has been reduced to an empty concept used to refer to academic failure.

GENERAL PREVALENCE RATES AND COURSE

It is very difficult to determine prevalence rates for SLD because published studies vary widely regarding how SLD is defined and measured. For example, in studies that have used a *discrepancy criterion* (standard score differences between achievement scores and IQ scores), prevalence figures for comorbid ADHD + SLD have ranged from 16% to 21% (Frick et al., 1991)—in a study where a 20-point discrepancy between intelligence (IQ) and achievement was used—to a prevalence of 38% to 45%—in a study where a 10-point discrepancy was used between the standard reading scores and the IQ (Dykman & Ackerman, 1992; Semrud-Clikeman et al., 1992). Overall, prevalence rates for SLD are considered to be between 2% and 10% of the population (APA, 2000).

LEARNING DISABILITIES AND SOCIAL SKILLS DEFICITS

For the past 30 years, research has documented that children with learning disabilities encounter more social difficulties than their non-learning-disabled peers. The association between learning disabilities and social difficulties is so prevalent that Rourke (1989) suggested inclusion of the fact that these children have "significant difficulties in mastering social and other adaptive skills" (p. 215) as part of the definition. The Interagency Committee on Learning Disabilities (ICLD) conducted a massive evaluation of available research concerning learning disabilities and social skills and concluded that social skills deficits can represent an SLD (ICLD, 1987). As a result, the ICLD suggested that the National Joint Committee on Learning Disabilities (NJCLD) definition be altered to include social skills among the other areas of skill acquisition deficits (e.g., listening, speaking, reading, writing, reasoning, mathematical abilities, or social skills). However, opposition to potentially defining SLD as a social deficit was voiced about concerns that an individual could have a social SLD and not have an academic deficit (Forness & Kavale, 1991).

In their study of learning-disabled children, Stone and La Greca (1990) found that children with SLD not only had significantly lower sociometric scores compared to nondisabled peers, but they also were overly represented in the rejected and neglected sociometric groupings. The authors also found that social skills deficits impacted not only on social competence but also on academic achievement.

DON'T FORGET

Studies of children's social status groups have determined five distinct social classification groups: popular, rejected, neglected, average, and controversial (Coie, Dodge, & Coppotelli, 1982). Children who are neglected are considered to have low social impact scores (low social visibility), while those who are rejected score high on social impact but low on social preference (likability).

Furthermore, social skills deficits may emerge in kindergarten, prior to diagnosis of SLD (Vaughn, Hogan, Kouzekanam, & Shapiro, 1990), and persist into adulthood (Gerber & Reiff, 1994). Gresham and Elliott (1990) outline three ways in which social competence can be undermined: (1) *skill deficit* (individual has not learned required skill), (2) *performance deficit* (individual has the skill but does not apply it), and (3) *self-control deficit* (individual demonstrates aversive behaviors that compete or interfere with the acquisition and performance of appropriate social skills).

CAUTION

The difference between social skills and social competence has been distinguished based on the following accepted criteria. *Social competence* is a trait that determines the probability of completing a social task in an acceptable way; *social skills* are the requisite behaviors that are exhibited in social situations that produce socially acceptable outcomes (McFall, 1982).

Kavale and Forness (1996) conducted a meta-analysis of 152 studies concerning social skill deficits in children with SLD. Of the 6,353 students involved in the meta-analysis, 72% were male, and the average IQ was 95. Results revealed that almost .75 of the students (74%) received negative assessments of their social skills that would clearly discriminate them from their peers without SLD. The authors found that *teachers* perceived the students with SLD to be less academically competent and as having less social interaction than their peers without SLD. Teachers also rated 70% of the population with SLD as demonstrating anxiety. *Peer assessments* (peers without SLD) revealed that 8 of 10 students with SLD were rejected by their peers, with 7 of 10 not considered as friends by peers. Other findings were that peers without SLD rated the children with SLD as less popular, competent, communicative, and cooperative than their peers without the disorder. *Self-assessment* results indicated that 70% of students with SLD identified social skills deficits, while 80% identified lack of academic competence as their biggest concern. Eighty percent noted social competence deficits in areas of understanding social situations and generating appropriate solutions to social problems. As might be anticipated, 70% admitted to poor self-concept and lack of self-esteem. Measures of external-internal locus of control and attributions revealed that the majority of students with SLD were externally driven (attribute outcomes to outside influences rather than their own effort) and attribute their success to luck rather than effort. Failure was attributed to lack of ability rather than effort.

As a result of their meta-analysis, Kavale and Forness (1996) concluded that although the majority of students with SLD exhibit social skills deficits, resulting from a wide variety in deficits, they could not determine why the deficits occur. The authors call for further research to investigate the relationship between social and academic deficits, as well as the potential contribution of underlying mechanisms (language, memory, perception, cognition) to the development of social dysfunction. Given the results of their meta-analysis, the authors suggest that although social deficits are evident in the majority of children with SLD—and as such constitute an associated feature of many SLD profiles—inclusion of social deficit as a criterion for SLD is not recommended at this time.

LEARNING DISABILITIES AND SUBTYPES

There are several different types of learning disabilities. This discussion focuses on five specific types that have been studied, including disabilities in reading, writing, and mathematics, and less well-known disabilities involving nonverbal learning and motor skills deficits (related to coordination and handwriting). The five types of specific learning disabilities are presented in Rapid Reference 6.1.

Rapid Reference 6.1

Specific Learning Disabilities

Disability	Nature of Deficit	Associated Features and Difficulties
Dyslexia	Reading	Decoding, comprehension, fluency; left-hemisphere dysfunction
Dysgraphia	Written expression	Organization, spelling, grammatical structure, punctuation
Dyscalculia	Mathematics	Number sense, estimation, problem solving
Nonverbal learning disability	Visuospatial areas	Right-hemisphere dysfunction: weak math skills, propriception (body sense), balance, social pragmatics
Dyspraxia	Developmental coordination disorder (DCD)	Balance, fine and gross motor tasks, manual dexterity

SPECIFIC READING DISABILITY: DYSLEXIA

Clinical Description and Associated Features

Although learning disabilities are recognized as a heterogeneous group of disorders (NJCLD, 1987), specific reading disability is the most prevalent (80% of learning disabilities) and well-researched SLD to date. Children who have dyslexia encounter difficulties reading, which may be evident in problems *decoding* (problems associating the sound to the symbol) or *comprehending* what they have read. Because reading is often labored, their *fluency* is significantly compromised and results in increased difficulties with consolidating information they have read. Reading problems are not caused by general cognitive limitations or other environmental factors, such as inappropriate instruction, socioeconomic disadvantage, or sensory deficits. The disability impacts on the acquisition of basic reading skills from simple phonological processing (sound–symbol association) to word identification and passage comprehension.

CAUTION

Individuals with dyslexia are compromised in several ways, since reading often provides the foundation for learning about our world. As a result, a fluid reader can obtain more information about many topics than an individual who struggles with the written word. Stanovich (1986) labeled this process the "Matthew effect" to refer to the increasing gap in knowledge that can exist between good and poor readers. According to Ferrer et al. (2010), this gap can influence the development of IQ over time, because measurement of IQ often includes an assessment of our acquisition of vocabulary and general knowledge.

Definition of Dyslexia

In a recent paper produced by the International Dyslexia Association, Lyon and Shaywitz (2003) present a definition of *developmental dyslexia* that expands on the original working definition developed in 1994. The current definition differs from that derived in 1994 by specifying the disability as neurobiological in origin and conceptualizing the reading disability as a specific type of disability rather than one of several general disabilities. The definition characterizes the disability manifested in difficulties with accurate and/or fluent word recognition and by poor spelling and decoding abilities as a result of deficits in phonological awareness. The disability is not predicted by either cognitive abilities or instructional methods. Associated features may also include problems in reading comprehension and poor vocabulary development resulting from lack of reading. The current definition is clear in its recognition of fluency as a major and long-term outcome of dyslexia. Although many readers with dyslexia increase their reading accuracy as a result of intervention, lack of fluency produces long-term problems resulting in effortful, slow, and laborious reading (Shaywitz, 2003). Shaywitz and Shaywitz (2008) emphasize the need to recognize the impact of dyslexia on students taking high-stakes tests such as the GRE and GMAT, and they argue for the need to provide extra time for these students with dyslexia to perform to their potential.

Prevalence and Course

Dyslexia is the most common form of SLD. It is estimated that between 5% and 17% of the population meet criteria for the disorder (Ferrer et al., 2010). Developmentally, signs of dyslexia may be subtle until the child enrolls in school, however early problems with learning the alphabet, recognizing letters and numbers, rhyming activities, following instructions or directions, or difficulty writing his or her own name may be early signals of dyslexia. Some children may escape detection if they use strong memory skills and "appear" to be reading. Others may develop behavior problems to escape the inevitable task of having to read in front of a class. Children with dyslexia often also exhibit many of the executive functioning problems noted in children with ADHD, and it is not surprising that the comorbidity between these two disorders has been estimated to be as high as 38% to 45% in some studies (Dykman & Ackerman, 1991).

Etiology

Biological, Neurological, and Genetic Transmission

Twin studies have found that dyslexia was evident in 68% of monozygotic twins (DeFries & Alarcon, 1996), and genetic effects seem most pronounced in children with high IQs compared to those with low IQs (Knopik, 2001). Researchers have suggested that between 23% and 65% of children with dyslexia have a parent with the disorder, while the rate of co-occurrence among siblings is estimated to be 40% (Pennington & Gilger, 1996).

Several neurological systems have been associated with dyslexia, including systems responsible for processing expressive and receptive language (Pennington, 2009), verbal working memory (Swanson, 2009), and executive functions and processing speed (Johnson, Humphrey, Mellard, Woods, & Swanson (2010). Through the use of functional magnetic resonance imaging (fMRI) techniques, Shaywitz and Shaywitz (2008) have mapped the developmental path of good versus poor readers. In the normally developing brain, the path for increased reading fluency is from the posterior regions (visual perception, letter/word naming) to the frontal regions (responsible for comprehension), and from the right (spatial) hemisphere to the left (verbal). Results have demonstrated that the left-hemisphere posterior brain system in dyslexics does not respond appropriately when reading (Frith & Frith, 1999). Studies have determined that two different systems operate to develop reading ability: an initial more laborious system of phonetic awareness (parietotemporal region) and a more rapid decoding system used by more-skilled readers (e.g., sight vocabulary, from the occipitotemporal region). Apparently, dyslexic readers demonstrate underactivation of both of these areas, with an increased activation of the frontal gyrus (letter-to-sound decoding), which carries the entire decoding load for the dyslexic population (Shaywitz, 2003).

> **DON'T FORGET**
>
> Reading involves *visual recognition* of an array of letters as meaningful, recalling (*memory*) the meaning of the word, and integrating that word within a greater context (*comprehension*).

In those with dyslexia, the left posterior systems show low activation levels, resulting in the use of both posterior regions (left and right), instead of progressing to the frontal regions.

The revised definition of dyslexia proposed by Lyon and Shaywitz (2003) recognizes the neurological basis of the disorder that relates processing deficits to actual locations in the brain. Cognitively, the linguistic and visual coding processes should work together to provide links between the written and spoken word. From a cognitive perspective, both permanent memory and working memory are involved in learning to read.

Increased research effort and technological advances have also confirmed that deficits in the phonological components of language are at the basis of dyslexia. Lyon and Shaywitz (2003) suggest that phonemic awareness is at the basis of understanding how to break the reading code. This deficit in phonology is the most specific factor in predicting dyslexia to date (Morris et al., 1998).

Assessment and Treatment/Interventions

Historically, assessment of SLD has involved the process of exclusion; for example, assessment is driven by differential diagnosis to rule out competing hypotheses to explain why the child has an SLD, ruling out other possible explanations for an SLD, and often entails assessment of intellectual, sensory (hearing, vision, language), familial, developmental, emotional, and school history (e.g., absenteeism, number of schools attended, interventions attempted, etc.). Although the importance of conducting an initial intellectual or cognitive assessment has been a point of controversy, especially for proponents of RTI, those who favor early inclusion of cognitive measures in the assessment of SLD emphasize the importance of identifying the underlying cognitive skills (profile of strengths and weaknesses) to assist in developing an appropriate intervention. To this end, Johnson et al. (2010) suggest that cognitive assessments are vital to the identification and intervention process for individuals with dyslexia in order to address the following:

- The range of intellectual functioning
- Any deficits in reading achievement and the specific nature of the deficits
- Strengths and weaknesses in cognitive processing
- Processing deficits not caused by environmental conditions

Intervention

Experts in the field of SLD emphasize that it is important to dispel the myth that "reading problems are outgrown or somehow represent a developmental lag" (Shaywitz, Morris, & Shaywitz, 2008, p. 470), and that those with dyslexia will not improve over time, unless specific and intense interventions are applied. In their work with second- and third-grade children with dyslexia, Shaywitz and Shaywitz (2008) found that 50 minutes of daily tutoring specifically for sound–symbol associations (phonemic instruction) not only enhanced reading ability but also improved neural connections by increasing brain activation patterns in these children that mimic patterns of normal readers.

Early Intervention

Programs that target phonemic awareness and context in the early years (kindergarten, first grade) have been instrumental in reducing the risk of reading difficulties to less than 5% (Shaywitz et al., 2008), regardless of whether programs were embedded in the classroom, offered in a resource room, or a combination of both (Fuchs & Fuchs, 2005; Vaughn, Linar-Thompson, & Hickman, 2003; Vellutino, Scanlon, Small, & Fanuele, 2006).

Later Interventions

Unfortunately, interventions applied later are not as successful. Although direct instruction and practice in phonological processing can improve accuracy of decoding (Lovett, Barron, & Benson, 2003), the majority of those with dyslexia continue to be plagued by fluency issues and problems with labored reading, which impedes progress and hinders comprehension. Programs that target reading for comprehension and repeated reading approaches (student reads the same passage multiple times, trying to beat his or her earlier time) have been successful in enhancing reading fluency and critical thinking in some students (Kuhn & Stahl, 2003).

Kim, Vaugh, Wanzek, and Wei (2004) reviewed 21 group studies regarding the effectiveness of using graphic organizers to improve comprehension in students with SLD. In their review, the authors acknowledge that studies have demonstrated that graphic organizers are most effective when they are created by the students, positioned after the text, and used for a longer period of time (Dunston, 1992). It has been suggested that the use of graphic organizers might be particularly helpful for SLD students, because of their documented problems organizing and recalling verbal information (Wong, 1978) and their noted strengths in spatial or visual reasoning (Witelson, 1977).

Results of the meta-analysis by Kim et al. (2004) suggest that, despite methodological difficulties (lack of standardized reading measures and variety of methods used), the use of graphic organizers seemed to have a beneficial effect for students with dyslexia in enhancing reading comprehension through the use of semantic organizers. The authors conclude that visual displays of information, such as graphic organizers, may assist readers with SLD to organize information, aiding in comprehension and subsequent recall. However, the authors also stress the need for more in-depth and comparative research in this fruitful area, which has only produced three studies in the past 10 years.

SPECIFIC LEARNING DISABILITY OF WRITTEN EXPRESSION: DYSGRAPHIA

Clinical Description and Associated Features

While much is known about dyslexia, far less information is available about dysgraphia or disorders of written expression. Part of the problem is that while methods used to detect deficits in reading and mathematics are readily available, written expression is an area that is not as well defined, since the process is more difficult to quantify. As a result, the underlying neurocognitive processes are less well known and understood (Hooper, Swartz, Wakely, de Kruif, & Montgomery (2002).

Definition of Dysgraphia

Children with SLD in the area of written expression may manifest a variety of symptoms and profiles, since the writing process involves a number of different skills, including planning, organizing, revising, transcribing, and translating ideas into written content (Reid & Ortiz-Lienemann, 2006). As a result, some may struggle with handwriting (not caused by motor coordination problems) but exhibit problems attempting to copy notes from the board or another source. Others may experience problems with spelling due to an inability to correctly recall letter sequences and produce errors due to letter reversals (b/d), letter transpositions (*frist gril*, instead of *first girl*), or letter inversions (u/n). Others may suffer from more global deficits and experience problems with organization of their ideas and then transcribing these into written form. Still others may encounter problems with grammatical structure and punctuation. In all cases, written expression would be substantially below the level anticipated given their grade level and level of intellectual functioning, and similar to all other specific learning disabilities in that the deficit is not the result of environmental conditions (e.g., lack of teaching/schooling).

Prevalence and Course

Most children evidence some initial difficulties with letter and number reversals, however, in children with SLD in written expression, these difficulties will persist beyond an age when they should self-correct (approximately 8 years of age). It is very difficult to diagnose dysgraphia at an early age, since expectations for written expression are minimal in the early school grades. However, warning signs may be evident even in younger children if they have problems completing work on time, despite the effort, or have difficulty copying words and cutting and coloring within the lines.

Children who experience disabilities in written expression encounter increasing difficulties as they enter the higher grades, since more is expected in the area of written expression. Prevalence rates for dysgraphia in the early (primary) grades have been estimated to be between 1.3% to 2.7%, however, these rates climb to as high as 6% to 22% by middle school (Berninger & Hart, 1992; Hooper et al., 2002). It is not uncommon for children to experience both dyslexia and dysgraphia, since both involve similar neurocognitive processes (Mayes & Calhoun, 2007).

Etiology

Less is known about the cause of disorders of written expression, however, increased investigations have found several neurological factors involved in the process, including executive functions, such as memory, attention, graphomotor output, sequential processing, and higher-order verbal and visuospatial functions (Hooper et al., 2002). The role of the prefrontal cortex has come under increased investigation, since many children with ADHD also demonstrate significant problems in transcribing (handwriting, note taking) and spelling relative to peers who do not have ADHD (Imhof, 2004).

Assessment and Treatment/Intervention

As was previously mentioned, assessment of written expression is far more difficult than assessment of reading or mathematical ability, which are far more amenable to a quantitative assessment. Within the area of written expression, assessing a composition for clarity, ideation, and expression is also far more difficult to quantify than evaluating spelling or grammar errors. In one study, Mayes, Calhoun, and Lane found that using one assessment instrument identified 35% of children as having a written expression disability, while use of a different instrument identified 78% as suffering from dysgraphia.

DON'T FORGET

Dysgraphia involves three different aspects of the writing process: (1) the actual transcription process (copying from one source to another; putting ideas on paper); (2) the mechanical or technical aspects of the process (grammar, punctuation, spelling accuracy); and (3) the organization of information to be transcribed (clarity of presentation, sequencing of ideas, flow). Individuals with a specific disability in the area of written expression can experience problems in any or all of these areas.

Several different types of interventions can be used based on the nature of the SLD. Some students may benefit from direct instruction on how to plan the writing process, and several programs are available that use different mnemonics and embed different components into the process (guided feedback, self-regulatory procedures). For example, Reid and Ortiz-Lienemann (2006) used a Self-Regulated Strategy Development (SRSD) program to enhance the quantity and quality of written output in children with ADHD. Other modifications can be put in place to assist children with more severe output problems, such as the use of a scribe for note taking, allowing children to dictate their assignments, reduced output for written tests (filling in the blanks instead of an essay exam), and the use of speech recognition software (Graham, Harris, & Larsen, 2001; MacArthur, 2000).

SPECIFIC MATHEMATICS DISABILITY: DYSCALCULIA

Clinical Description and Associated Features

Children who experience problems with dyscalculia have deficits in their ability to process information related to numbers and mathematical procedures.

Definition of Dyscalculia

A mathematics learning disability (MLD) refers to limitations in mathematical understanding that can best be described as a deficit in understanding number sense, which impedes an ability to perform activities that involve problem solving or retrieving mathematical information (number facts). The disability has not been researched to the extent that dyslexia has, but investigators are beginning to probe neurocognitive factors and executive functions involved in the process (Geary, 2004; Swanson & Jerman, 2006).

Prevalence and Course

Prevalence rates are difficult to establish, because while some children have problems with specific math concepts (e.g., division, geometry) in some parts of the curriculum, they do not have problems with other math concepts. As a result, depending on the specific assessment instrument used, prevalence rates vary, since some instruments are more general and others focus on more specific mathematical problems. It is estimated that 5% to 10% of children enrolled in school would meet criteria for MLD (Barbaresi, Katusic, Collagin, Weaver, & Jacobson, 2005).

Individuals with MLD demonstrate persistent difficulties in the acquisition of the majority of math concepts due to deficits in neurocognitive processing in areas of number sense (estimating quantity, sequencing) and calculation frequency (Gersten, Jordan, & Flojo, 2005). At a young age, children demonstrate problems with counting, one-to-one correspondence, learning basic number facts, and understanding quantitative concepts such as more or less. As children get older, their problems are compounded by greater emphasis on problem solving using word problems and being presented with more complex mathematical procedures.

Etiology

Consistent with the majority of those with SLD, individuals with MLD often inherit the disorder (Kovas et al., (2007), with rates as high as 43%, suggesting high rates of genetic influence comparable with those for dyslexia (47%). Researchers have been divided on their investigations of causes of MLD, with some focusing on general neurocognitive processes, such as executive functioning deficits, while others have focused on specific deficits such as those inherent in the Approximate Number System (ANS).

Executive Functioning and Neurocognitive Processing Deficits

In his investigations of MLD, Geary (2000, 2003) suggests that deficits in executive functions, such as attention and short-term memory, and weaknesses in visuospatial functioning are at the core of MLD. Children who are weak in these areas have difficulties with alignment, place value, and orienting to information in charts and maps. He cites examples of children who use their fingers to count as an example of poor working memory.

Research on Number Sense

At a more specific level, researchers such as Mazzocco, Feigenson, and Halberda (2011) have investigated the ANS and its role in the acquisition of number sense.

According to the researchers, the ANS is a system that we access on an implicit and regular basis when we make quick decisions, such as picking the quickest and shortest checkout line in the grocery store. In their research, they found that children with MLD have a poorly established ANS relative to their non-disabled peers.

DON'T FORGET

Geary (2003) suggests that faulty visuospatial processing may be at the core of MLD, influencing such tasks as alignment of numbers or contributing to faulty place values.

Assessment and Treatment/Interventions

Children who have deficits in executive functioning (attention and short-term memory), neurocognitive processing (visuospatial analysis), and have poor number sense experience escalating problems with the math curriculum, because math is a cumulative body of knowledge.

Early screening is important; one such measure that has met with success is the Number Knowledge Test (Okamoto & Case, 1996), which taps such key areas as basic concepts, number sense, and counting. Bryant et al. (2008) found that in order for prevention and intervention programs to be successful, sessions need to be frequent and intense to provide optimum benefit (20-minute sessions, four days per week over 23 weeks). The incorporation of practical exercises to enhance facility with numbers, such as the use of number lines, practice in exchanging and counting money, and using measurements (recipes) to learn fractions, have all been beneficial classroom strategies.

NONVERBAL LEARNING DISABILITIES (NLD)

Clinical Description and Associated Features

Although many individuals are familiar with dyslexia and, to a lesser extent, specific disabilities of written expression and math, far fewer have heard of nonverbal learning disabilities (NLD). Individuals with this specific form of disability have a unique profile of strengths and weaknesses that may confuse the clinician who has never encountered this SLD. Whereas individuals with dyslexia often have intellectual profiles that show strengths in the performance areas (visual analytical skills) and weaknesses in the verbal portion (vocabulary and comprehension), those who have NLD show the opposite profile: significant strengths in the verbal areas and significant weaknesses in the performance (visuospatial) areas.

Definition of NLD

NLD is attributed to right-hemisphere dysfunction (Mattson, Sheer, & Fletcher, 1992) with associative problems in visuospatial processing. According to Rourke, a primary researcher and expert in the field, the syndrome is characterized by "significant primary deficits in some dimensions of tactile perception, visual persception, complex psychomotor skills and in dealing with novel circumstances" (Rourke et al., 2002, p. 311). In the literature, the disability has also been referred to as *developmental right-hemisphere syndrome* (Gross-Tsur, Shalev, Manor, & Amir, 1995), and visuospatial learning disability (Cornoldi, Venneri, Marconato, Molin, & Montinari, 2003).

Prevalence and Course

NLD is a low-incidence disorder, with a prevalence rate of approximately .1%; however, since many people are unfamiliar with this form of disability and because there is symptom overlap with Asperger's disorder, the prevalence rate may be underestimated. Although the male-to-female ratio for dyslexia is approximately 8:1, the likelihood of being diagnosed with NLD is equal for females and males.

Children with NLD often may appear clumsy and have poor coordination because of a poor sense of proprioception (sense of a body's position in space) and evidence slow speed of processing information, both cognitively and motorically. They excel at reading but are poor at math (dyscalculia), and they have a weakness for facial recognition and other visuospatial tasks. In the social arena, they share many similarities to individuals with Asperger's disorder (poor sense of social cues, pragmatic speech). As youth, they may feel isolated because of their weak social skills and may be prone to depression (Rourke, 1995).

Etiology

Although the majority of those with SLD have a high genetic component, for individuals with NLD, the disorder seems to be more related to brain dysfunction. According to Rourke (1995), the degree of deficit of the disorder is related to the amount of damage to the right cerebral hemisphere and white matter contained in this area (long myelinated fibers). Through the use of collaborative medical histories, Rourke suggests that the damage was likely caused by some form of acquired insult to the brain, or congenitally.

DON'T FORGET

Rourke and colleagues (2002) proposed the *white matter model* as an explanation for NLD. This model suggests that, as a result of insult to the right hemisphere of the brain (acquired or congenitally), the amount of white matter (myelinated fibers) is reduced, resulting in a disconnect between the left and right hemispheres of the brain, which do not communicate with each other.

Assessment and Treatment/ Intervention

Since NLD, by definition, is a neurological disorder related to brain dysfunction, the importance of a neurological assessment cannot be overemphasized. Such an assessment would include such measures as family history, medical history, assessments of intelligence and neuropsychological functioning, including such tests as measures of set shifting (category test), finger tapping, and trail making, as well as academic and behavioral assessments.

Given the long-range problems associated with NLD, it is also recommended that children diagnosed with NLD be evaluated for social skills and related abilities to assist with enhancing skills and preventing later tendencies toward increased isolation and potential for depression.

DEVELOPMENTAL COORDINATION DISORDER (DCD): DYSPRAXIA

Clinical Description and Associated Features

Whereas children with dysgraphia have difficulty transcribing information from one medium to another (ideas to written word; copying information from one source to another), those with dyspraxia or developmental coordination disorder (DCD) demonstrate immaturities in fine and gross motor skills, which may influence writing but also influence other activities that involve smooth muscle movements.

Definition of DCD

Children who are diagnosed with dyspraxia or developmental coordination disorder (DCD) experience problems in areas of posture, movement, and coordination. Globally, *dyspraxia* is the term most commonly used in Europe and the United Kingdom, whereas DCD is most commonly used in North America. The *DSM-5* considers DCD as a neurodevelopmental disorder, more specifically, a motor disorder characterized by poorly coordinated motor skills (clumsy, dropping or bumping into things, slow or inaccurate attempts to catch, cut, or copy). The disorder interferes with daily living and compromises success academically and socially.

Prevalence and Course

The prevalence of DCD is estimated to be between 5% to 6% of children ages 5 to 11, with the disorder occurring more frequently in males than females (2:1 vs. 7:1) (APA, 2013). The rates of comorbidity for CDC, dyslexia, and ADHD are high (Sugden, Kirby, & Dunford, 2008), with comorbidity for ADHD and DCD estimated to be as high as 50% by some researchers (Kadesjo & Gillberg, 1998).

Because children with DCD exhibit difficulties in the planning and executing of motor movements, early warning signs include difficulty with buttoning clothes or tying shoes, limited athletic ability (catching or throwing a ball), and difficulty completing tasks requiring precision, such as cutting or coloring. Motor milestones are often delayed (e.g., late crawling, walking).

Etiology

Although the exact cause for DCD has not been clearly identified, several potential sources of central nervous system dysfunction have been suggested, including premature birth or other birth complications, such as a lack of oxygen at birth (anoxia), and sensory integration issues (Vaive-Douret et al., 2011). More than half of college students with motor issues also report significant problems with handwriting and executive functioning problems in areas of time management, organization, and decision making (Kirby, Sugden, Beveridge, & Edwards, 2008).

Assessment and Treatment/Interventions

Since DCD falls primarily within the area of expertise for occupational therapists, which is beyond the scope of this text, interested readers are encouraged to seek out Barnett's (2008) excellent review of instruments available for the assessment and screening of DCD. These screening and assessment devices have been developed to evaluate the extent and nature of impairment related to DCD and to provide a profile for the development of intervention strategies. As for early intervention and target goals for children with DCD, Sugden and colleagues (2008) highlight the need to stress participation and engagement of children with DCD in activities that focus on school tasks, peer and recreational activities, and self-care.

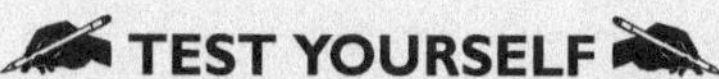

TEST YOURSELF

1. **The most common form of specific learning disability is**
   (a) mathematics disability (MLD).
   (b) nonverbal learning disability.
   (c) reading disability, dyslexia.
   (d) developmental coordination disorder (DCD).
2. **According to Kavale, Forness, and McMillan, current definitions of specific learning disabilities fail to acknowledge the role of central nervous system impairment.**
   True or False?
3. **The discrepancy model has come under current criticism because this model**
   (a) does not work well with the middle range IQ scores.
   (b) is biased in favor of children with higher IQs.
   (c) is compromised by underlying processing problems.
   (d) has the characteristics of both (b) and (c).
4. **A deficit in social competence is currently considered as one of the SLDs disabilities by the NJCLD.**
   True or False?
5. **Which of the following is TRUE?**
   (a) Children with SLDs usually do not have problems with peer relationships.
   (b) Children with SLDs are perceived as being too sociable by their teachers.
   (c) Children with SLDs are rated as less socially capable than non-SLD peers.
   (d) Children with SLDs are very capable of understanding social situations.
6. **Children with nonverbal learning disabilities (NLDs)**
   (a) are readily recognized as a specific learning disability by the educational system.
   (b) are more socially adept than traditional types of SLD peers.
   (c) excel at math.
   (d) are at risk for depression and suicide if intervention is not sought.
7. **Studies of children with dyslexia have found that**
   (a) fluency is a major and long-term outcome of dyslexia.
   (b) dyslexic readers exhibit underactivation of the areas of the brain associated with phonetic and visual awareness.

(c) reading failure can be reduced by intensive and effective early intervention.
(d) all of the above are true.

8. Stanovich (1986) coined the phrase *Matthew effects* to refer to

(a) the cumulative effect of poor reading skills.
(b) poor readers tend to compensate by being better listeners.
(c) the majority of children with dyslexia are male.
(d) the majority of children with dyslexia come from poverty.

Answers: 1. c; 2. true; 3. d; 4. false; 5. c; 6. d; 7. d; 8. a

Part III

Internalizing Disorders

Internalizing problems result from behaviors that are *overcontrolled*, compared to externalizing or *undercontrolled* behaviors (Achenbach, 1966; Cicchetti & Toth, 1991). Internalizing behaviors are "problems within the self, such as anxiety, depression, somatic complaints, without known medical cause, and withdrawal from social contact" (Achenbach & Rescorla, 2001, p. 93). By definition, internalizing problems are more covert in their nature and, therefore, they are often more difficult to detect and assess.

INTERNALIZING DISORDERS

There are several practical reasons for discussing anxiety, depression, and somatic problems from an internalizing perspective, including high rates of comorbidity, shared features of negative affectivity, shared assessment difficulties, and common problem areas associated with these disorders, such as social withdrawal, peer neglect, poor self-efficacy, and low self-esteem.

DON'T FORGET

Anxiety disorders, depression, and bipolar disorder, as well as somatoform disorders, share internally oriented symptoms: depressed mood states, anxious and inhibited responses, and tendencies to express emotional distress as physical discomfort. Factor analysis of syndrome scales of the ASEBA (Achenbach & Rescorla, 2001) yielded an internalizing dimension comprising three syndrome scales: Anxious/Depressed, Withdrawn/Depressed, and Somatic Complaints.

Prevalence Rates for Internalizing Disorders

Although younger boys and girls have similar prevalence rates for internalizing disorders (7% to 9%), in adolescent populations (12 to 16 years), females are approximately four times more likely (15.7%) than males (3.9%) to have internalizing disorders (Offord, Boyle, & Szatmari, 1989). The following patterns have also emerged:

- As many as 10% to 15% of children and youth experience symptoms of depression (Smucker, Craighead, Craighead, & Green, 1986).
- In any one year, 13% of children are diagnosed as having an anxiety disorder (Costello et al., 1996).
- Approximately 25% of children attending clinics for headaches or low energy have a somatoform disorder (Garber, Walker, & Seman, 1991).

PUTTING IT INTO PRACTICE

Kerry is a very quiet little girl and a C student. Kerry's thoughts often drift away from the task at hand, and her teacher feels that Kerry is probably a slower learner who is readily overwhelmed by task demands. On occasion, Kerry complains of stomachaches and headaches, and she misses about four days of school per month because she is not feeling well.

Robby is in Kerry's class, but unlike Kerry, Robby is a disruptive force in the class. Robby is also a C student, but his teacher feels that he would get better grades if he would just focus on his work. Robby can be bossy and often interrupts class lessons and routines. When the teacher is asked to bring children's names for discussion to the next team meeting, she immediately thinks of Robby and two other boys who are disruptive and disturbing. Kerry's name does not come to mind.

Two years later, Kerry is referred to the school psychologist because she is in danger of failing the fifth grade. An assessment at that time reveals that Kerry is actually a bright girl who is overwhelmed by worries, fears, and her own feelings of inadequacy. Furthermore, Kerry has developed several avoidance behaviors to deal with her growing anxiety and depression, resulting in increased fears, somatic complaints, and frequent absenteeism.

Given the high rates of comorbidity between anxiety and depression, there has been significant debate over the past two decades concerning whether anxiety and depression represent distinct diagnostic categories or whether symptoms might be better explained by a broadband notion of negative affectivity. In 1991, Clark and Watson proposed the tripartite model of anxiety and depression, in which *negative affectivity* (emotional distress) is conceptualized as a common underlying symptom shared by both anxiety and depression, while low positive affectivity is considered to be unique to depression, and physiological arousal is considered to be unique to anxiety.

DON'T FORGET

Comorbidity rates as high as 60%–70% have been reported between anxiety and depression. Developmentally, onset of anxiety is a precursor to depression (Kovacs & Devlin, 1998).

Subsequent research has supported only the first two hypotheses, since physiological arousal was not evident in all forms of anxiety. Research has demonstrated that low positive affectivity (anhedonia) can discriminate between children with depressive disorders and anxiety disorders (Lonigan, Carey, & Finch, 1994), while negative affectivity is a feature shared by both anxiety and depression (Chorpita, 2002; Chorpita, Plummer, & Moffit, 2000). Anxiety and depression often occur together in young children, with *negative affectivity* considered to be "a broad temperamental factor of emotional distress that is related to mood states such as sadness, fear, guilt and anger," relative to *positive affectivity*, which is a term used to refer to a mood state of elation or enthusiasm (Ebesutani, Smith, Bernstein, & Chorpita, 2011).

DON'T FORGET

The tripartite model suggests a three-part solution to the depression and anxiety debate: a feature common to both anxiety and depression (negative affectivity), a feature unique to depression (low positive affectivity), and a feature unique to anxiety (physiological arousal).

Emotion Regulation, Behavior Inhibition (BI), and Internalizing Disorders

In their discussion of the development of depression in children and adolescence, Cicchetti and Toth (1998) proposed a complex model based on attachment theory, framed within Bronfenbrenner's (1979) ecological transactional model. Cicchetti and Toth described how self-regulation in infancy and childhood develops across biological, socioemotional, and cognitive systems in response to sensitive parenting within a secure attachment relationship, where a child learns how to self-soothe, reducing the tension in the system, and maintain equilibrium, based on the mother's successful ability to respond to the child when in a stressful situation. "As the infant's brain develops, the infant becomes increasingly self-sufficient in modulating arousal generated by physiological tension" (Cicchetti & Toth, 1998, p. 228). If the parent is not sensitive and responsive to the child and the child forms an insecure attachment to the parent, then the child's systems of emotion regulation do not develop properly, resulting in increased activation of the right brain, resulting in negative affect expression, and rather than increasing dominance of the left brain in normal development, which "may strengthen inhibitory effects on negative arousal." Emotion regulation has been recognized as an important set of skills necessary for successful adaptation, especially within the realm of social interactions (Macklem, 2008) and the development of positive representational models of the self, whereas emotion dysregulation has been associated with the development of internalizing problems, such as the increased risk for depression (Ciccheti & Toth, 1998).

Researchers investigating anxiety sensitivity, or the tendency to anxiety bias, have explored the cognitive (biased or negative thought processes) and biological (neurodevelopmental and hormonal determinants, as in the fight-or-flight response (Barlow, 2002) factors in their influence on anxiety responses. Individuals who experience high anxiety sensitivity perceive anxiety-provoking situations or events as having the potential for severe and negative consequences and are at increased risk for the development of anxiety disorders (Reiss, 1991). From a cognitive perspective, adults and adolescents can use two important cognitive strategies when faced with a potential stressor, including *cognitive reappraisal* (occurring early in the process, in the form of potentially downplaying a threat evaluation) and *suppression* (regulation of the emotional impact by inhibiting physiological or behavioral responsiveness [Gross, 2002]). This ability to suppress or inhibit a response can be helpful when situations call for a more calm and socially appropriate response, however, when used to the extreme it can result in less adaptive responses and less successful adjustment (Bonanno, Papa, Lalande, Westphal, & Coifman, 2004).

For example, child temperament factors such as behavioral inhibition (BI) have been linked to increased risk for anxiety disorders (Perez-Edgar & Fox, 2005). Infants with BI have been found to demonstrate increased activation of the right hemisphere (associated with processing novel responses), while toddlers with BI have been found to withdraw from exposure to novel or unfamiliar social situations, which can ultimately lead to increased avoidance behaviors, resulting in peer rejection (Fox & Pine, 2012), and set the stage for social anxiety in early adolescence (Fox, Henderson, Marshall, Nichols, & Ghera, 2005). From a perspective of cognitive neuroscience, increased vigilance, or attention bias to threat, can result in overactivation of the amygdala and increased focus on the threat registered in the ventrolateral prefrontal cortex (Pine, Helfinstein, Bar-Haim, Nelson, & Fox, 2009). Research has demonstrated that children who have dysregulated emotions are at increased risk for internalizing problems, exhibit difficulties expressing their emotions appropriately, especially the negative emotions, such as anger or sadness (Zeman, Cassano, Perry-Parrish, & Stegall, 2006), and are more likely to develop depression than their peers without emotion regulation issues (Hsieh & Stright, 2012).

Somatic complaints are frequently reported complaints of physical distress by children and adolescents evident in 4% (boys) to 11% (girls) of youth 12 to 16 years of age (Offord et al., 1987). The most common symptoms include headaches (25%), low energy (23%), and stomach pains (15%; Eminson, Benjamin, Shortall, Woods, & Faragher, 1996). Approximately one-third to one-half of all children diagnosed with somatization disorder (discussed at length in Chapter 9) also meet criteria for other internalizing disorders, such as anxiety or depression (Garralda, 1999). Zolog et al. (2011) found significant positive associations between somatization and symptoms of anxiety and depression in their community sample of more than 1,500 children 10 to 12 years of age.

Studies of child psychopathology have supported the use of the two broad higher-order categories of internalizing and externalizing problems for child and adolescent populations (Cosgrove et al., 2011). Disorders most often included in studies of internalizing problems include those that encompass characteristics of "anxiety, fear, and misery" associated with "major depressive disorder (MDD), generalized anxiety disorder (GAD), separation anxiety disorder (SAD), panic disorder (PD), and phobias" (Mikolajewski, Allan, Hart, Lonigan, & Taylor, 2012, p. 411). More recently, researchers have found that although internalizing and externalizing factors have primarily been viewed as two distinct entities, the two areas can also be correlated (Cosgrove et al., 2011). For purposes of this book, and clarity of presentation, the two systems are used in their most common form to provide increased structure to the discussions of the disorders normally clustered within these two broad categories.

The following three chapters focus on three disorder classifications that are most readily associated with the internalizing dimension, including disorders of anxiety, depression, and somatization. The disorders are discussed relative to child and adolescent psychopathology and address how these disorders appear developmentally, and any recent changes in the *DSM-5* that impact diagnostic criteria or how the disorders are conceptualized.

Seven

ANXIETY DISORDERS AND OBSESSIVE-COMPULSIVE AND RELATED DISORDERS

ANXIETY DISORDERS

Anxiety disorders are common in childhood and adolescence, with one-year prevalence rates estimated to be as high as 13% (Costello et al., 1996). Anxiety disorders share features of chronic worry about current or future events and can involve several common response patterns, including behavioral (escape and avoidance), cognitive (negative self-appraisals), and physiological (involuntary arousal: increased heart rate, rapid breathing, tremors, and muscle tension) symptoms.

Although the *DSM-III* recognized three anxiety disorders of childhood (separation anxiety disorder, avoidance disorder, and overanxious disorder), and the *DSM-IV-TR* (APA, 2000) placed separation anxiety disorder (SAD) within the category of Disorders First Evident in Infancy, Childhood and Adolescence, the *DSM-5* has revamped the category of Anxiety Disorders to include all disorders of anxiety regardless of the age of the individual to be diagnosed. The current list of *DSM-5* anxiety disorders can be found in Rapid Reference 7.1.

DON'T FORGET

Spence (1997) verified the existence of six separate but correlated forms of anxiety that can exist in children: panic-agoraphobia, social phobia, separation anxiety, obsessive-compulsive problems, generalized anxiety, and physical fears.

CAUTION

For those familiar with the *DSM-IV-TR* (APA, 2000), it is important to note that two types of disorders previously considered to be anxiety disorders—obsessive-compulsive disorder (OCD) and the stress disorders (PTSD and acute stress disorder)—have been removed from this category and placed in other categories. OCD can now be found in the category of Obsessive-Compulsive and Related Disorders, while the stress disorders have been relocated to a chapter titled Trauma- and Stressor-Related Disorders. However, for purposes of this text, OCD is discussed at the end of this chapter for the sake of continuity, while PTSD is discussed in Part VI: Special Topics.

Anxiety Disorders From a Developmental Perspective

Developmentally, separation anxiety disorder (SAD), selective mutism, and the specific phobias are the earliest-occurring anxiety disorders. Generalized anxiety disorder (GAD) is likely to have onset within the age range from 8 to 10 years of age, while onset in adolescence seems most likely for social anxiety disorder and panic disorder (see Saavedra & Silverman, 2002, for a review). The anxiety disorders are presented in this chapter, in the order that they appear in the *DSM-5*.

Rapid Reference 7.1

The Major *DSM-5* Categories of Anxiety Disorders

Separation anxiety disorder (SAD)	Excessive worry about separation from significant caregivers or home, lasting at least 4 weeks, and causing significant distress and impairment
Selective mutism	Failure to speak in certain situations, not attributed to language difficulties; marked by high levels of social anxiety
Specific phobia	Specific anxiety and fear elicited by an object or a situation, resulting in avoidant behaviors
Social anxiety disorder (social phobia)	Fear of anxiety regarding specific situations involving social or performance expectations

Panic attack	Intense, sudden onset of feelings of terror, fear, or apprehension accompanied by physical symptoms (shortness of breath, heart palpitations discomfort) and cognitive distortions (wanting to escape; fear of going crazy)
Panic disorder	Fear of having panic attacks
Agoraphobia	Fear of situations or places that might evoke a panic attack
Generalized anxiety disorder (GAD)	Pervasive, excessive worry and anxiety, e.g., "free-floating anxiety."

DON'T FORGET

High rates of comorbidity exist among the anxiety disorders. Children who are diagnosed with a primary anxiety disorder frequently present with other anxiety disorders.

SEPARATION ANXIETY DISORDER

Clinical Description and Associated Features

Children who have SAD experience intense feelings of distress that are developmentally inappropriate, lasting for at least four weeks. Occurrence of SAD prior to age 6 is considered early onset. The disorder manifests before 18 years of age (APA, 2013).

DON'T FORGET

The *DSM-5* (APA, 2013) diagnostic criteria for SAD require excessive worry about separation from the caregiver to be manifested in at least three of the following ways: fears of the caregiver succumbing to an accident or harm, excessive worry about an anticipated separation at some future time, school refusal, fear of being alone without the caregiver (or adult substitute), reluctance to sleep alone or sleep away from home, nightmares about separation, and repeated physical complaints (headaches, stomachaches) if separation occurs or is anticipated.

The need to remain in close proximity to the caregiver often results in significant impairment in social and academic functioning. Children with SAD may experience significant discomfort if asked to leave familiar territory. Symptoms of distress may be evident in physical and somatic complaints, such as pronounced stomachache and vomiting. Parents often find the child with SAD to be very demanding and intrusive.

SAD involves a number of potential symptoms emanating from the excessive fear and anxiety these children experience in consideration of any anticipated separation from the caregiver. The disorder causes significant distress and impairment in daily living. The *DSM-5* requires at least three symptoms from the following list, lasting at least four weeks:

- Excessive distress in anticipation of separation from the caregiver
- Excessive worry about potential harm to the caregiver
- Preoccupation with a future adverse event (being kidnapped) causing separation from the caregiver
- Reluctance to go away from familiar territory to attend work, school, etc.
- Reluctance to be alone or sleep away from home
- Nightmares about separation
- Repeated physical complaints (headache, stomachache) when separation is anticipated (APA, 2013)

Prevalence and Course

Although prevalence rates for SAD are relatively low in the general population (approximately 4%), rates can be as high as 10% in clinical populations. Separation anxiety disorder is more frequent in females than males and is often comorbid with GAD, depression, and somatic complaints (Last, Hersen, Kazdin, Orvaschel, & Perrin, 1991). Symptoms of SAD tend to reappear under stressful conditions. This disorder may be a precursor to increased risk for later depression and anxiety disorders and for the onset of panic attacks and agoraphobia for females in adulthood (Albano, Chorpita, & Barlow, 1996).

Etiology

The Role of Biological, Genetic, and Temperament Factors

At least one study found that more than 80% of children with SAD or GAD had mothers with a history of anxiety disorders (Last, Hersen, Kazdin, Finkelstein, & Strauss, 1987), and anxiety sensitivity has been associated with heritability (Stein, Jang, & Livesley, 1999).

Parenting and Behavioral Modeling

Overprotectiveness and reinforcement of the child's avoidance behaviors can influence the maintenance of SAD (Hudson & Rapee, 2000). In some families, maternal depression and family dysfunction may result in overparenting of the child who does not want to leave home for fear that he or she will not be able to protect the parent.

Assessment and Treatment/Interventions

Assessment instruments for all anxiety disorders are available in Rapid Reference 7.3.

Cognitive Behavioral Interventions

The use of cognitive-behavioral interventions can be successful in treating SAD (see Ollendick & King, 1998, for a review). The Coping Cat program (Kendall, 2000) has been demonstrated to be an effective way to reduce anxiety in children in randomized clinical trials of individual cognitive-behavioral training (Kendall, 1994) and more recently in group training (Flannery-Schroeder & Kendall, 2000). The program focuses on the development and practice of coping skills. The program also relies heavily on more behaviorally oriented components, such as imagined and in vivo exposure to the fear-producing situations using systematic desensitization.

DON'T FORGET

Seventy-five percent of children with SAD demonstrate school refusal; however, only one-third of children who refuse to attend school have SAD (Black, 1995). School refusal may occur for many reasons, including reluctance to attend school following a lengthy absence (e.g., period of illness), a change of schools, or fears of victimization and bullying.

DON'T FORGET

Parents who demonstrate warmth and structure produce the best child outcomes in terms of child self-confidence and self-reliance (Baumrind, 1991). Conversely, children of parents who are low on warmth and high on control (authoritarian parenting style) demonstrate more fearfulness, low self-esteem, and low initiative (Hudson & Rapee, 2000).

DON'T FORGET

Treatment of school refusal can be an important component of treating SAD in children. Structured contingency management programs with firm rules (expectations) that provide appropriate rewards for successful separation and remove reinforcement for avoidant behaviors can provide successful intervention for school refusal (Black, 1995).

SELECTIVE MUTISM

Clinical Description and Associated Features

Children who exhibit selective mutism demonstrate a reluctance to verbalize when expected, lasting at least one month, in specific situations, where speaking is anticipated (school-related activities, such as answering questions, interacting with classmates, etc.). This behavior is not a response to weak language skills or a speech problem, because the child seems quite capable of verbalizing when in more familiar territory (at home, or with close friends).

Prevalence and Course

According to the *DSM* (APA, 2013), little is known about the prevalence rates for selective mutism, since the disorder has not been widely studied. Prevalence rates have been estimated to be between .03% and 1%, with higher rates associated with clinic populations. There is little information as to the longevity of the disorder, however it is thought that most children "outgrow" the disorder, although symptoms may manifest as social anxiety disorder as the child ages.

Etiology

Onset is most likely associated with the advent of formal schooling (around 5 years of age) but may not surface until later if a child is homeschooled. There has been controversy as to how to best conceptualize the disorder, with some considering it as an early precursor to social anxiety disorder and others considering it a specialized form of language disorder or impairment, because 30% to 38% of children with the disorder also experience speech and language disorders (Steinhausen & Juzi, 1996). Children who are prone to negative affectivity or behavioral inhibition may be at increased risk for the disorder, as well as indicators of social anxiety, social isolation, or a parental history of shyness (APA, 2013).

Assessment and Treatment/Intervention

Assessment instruments for all anxiety disorders are available in Rapid Reference 7.3.

Due to the low prevalence rate for selective mutism, most of the research regarding treatment has involved individual case studies. Some of the more successful methods of treatment have involved behavioral methods, including shaping, systematic desensitization, and modeling (Pionek-Stone, Kratochwill, Sladezcek, & Serlin, 2002).

PHOBIAS AND FEARS

Clinical Description and Associated Features

Although fears are common in childhood, the nature and number of fears change with age. While fears concern "a danger or threat," worries relate more to a sense of "social or cognitive discomfort" (Laing, Fernyhough, Turner, & Freeston, 2009). Children can exhibit a wide range of fears based on the nature of different types of worries or stessors occurring at different developmental stages. The majority of studies report that the number of fears declines with age.

Some common fears are presented in Rapid Reference 7.2.

Rapid Reference 7.2

The Developmental Nature of Children's Common Fears

Developmental Age	Common Fears
Toddler stage	Strangers, toileting activities, personal injury
Preschool	Imaginary creatures, monsters, the dark, animals
Elementary school	Small animals, the dark, lightning and thunder, threats to personal safety
Middle school	Health (dental treatment), being sent to the principal's office
Adolescence	Physical illness, medical procedures, public speaking, sexual matters, political/economic conditions, and catastrophes (war)

Source: Adapted from Barrios and Hartmann, 1997.

Overall, while fears tend to decrease with age after 7 years old, worries continue to escalate in 80% of children (Muris, Luermans, Merckelbauch, & Mayer, 2000), and tend to relate mostly to concerns about performance or social issues (Laing et al., 2009). Girls tend to report more worries and fears than boys at all ages (Ollendick, 2001).

A specific phobia is a persistent, significant fear of an object or place that does not have a reasonable basis (APA, 2013). Adults and older children will be aware that this fear is unreasonable, although very young children may not. Avoidance of the feared object or event is frequent. Exposure to the feared object may elicit significant physiological responses, such as dizziness, shortness of breath, increased heart rate, and even fainting. Young children can respond to phobias by "crying, tantrums, freezing, or clinging" (APA, 2013, p. 197).

CAUTION

A diagnosis of specific phobia is not made unless the phobia interferes with functioning to a significant degree and is present for at least six months (APA, 2013).

The focus of the fear is anticipation of harm in some way (e.g., fear of dogs is a fear of being bitten). Responses of heightened anxiety increase as the child moves closer to the feared object. Often a strong desire to escape is imminent, and inability to escape may result in heightened arousal (panic). Having a specific phobia increases the likelihood of having another phobia, and specific phobias are often comorbid with other anxiety disorders and with mood disorders. The most common types of phobias include phobias involving animals (e.g., spiders, dogs), the natural environment (e.g., fear of heights, thunder), blood-injection-injury (needles), or situational causes (e.g., claustrophobia, fear of flying). Symptoms of phobias involve excessive reactions to encountering a feared object or situation and can include provoked responses involving the following:

- Immediate fear, anxiety
- Avoidance (*active avoidance*)
- Excessive responses, out of proportion to the danger assessed
- Persistence

CAUTION

Childhood is a time when many immunizations are needed. The most common phobic response to the sight of blood or receiving an injection is fainting. The *DSM-5* cautions that when a diagnosis of specific phobia is being considered for a child, the degree of impairment and duration of the fear/anxiety must be weighed relative to the child's stage of development (APA, 2013).

DON'T FORGET

The development of anxiety disorders in children can be associated with a wide range of influences, including genetic factors, temperament (behavioral inhibition), parent psychopathology, and other family factors, such as communication styles, parenting practices, and attachment history.

PUTTING IT INTO PRACTICE

Gloria is very fearful of thunderstorms. On one particular stormy night, an enormous clap of thunder roars through the house with such intensity that the furniture seems to shake. Just at that moment, the phone rings. Each ring is accompanied by another thunder clap. Now each time the phone rings, Gloria jumps, fearing that thunder will follow. Gloria has acquired a conditioned fear of telephone rings.

Prevalence and Course

Approximately 15% of children who are referred for anxiety have specific phobias, with girls reportedly being more fearful overall than boys (Silverman & Nelles, 2001). While prevalence rates for phobias in adolescence are approximately 16% (13- to 16-year-olds), for young children the rate is approximately 5% (APA, 2013).

In addition to specific phobias, two broader types of phobias have been associated with onset most likely in midadolescence: social anxiety disorder, panic disorder, and agoraphobia. The phobias (specific, social, and agoraphobia) elicit fears in response to an imminent threat, while GAD refers to a more free-floating and nonspecific worry.

Most phobias develop in childhood and adolescence, with the mean age of onset at 10 years and a median age of onset between 7 to 11 years. Although it is not always possible to isolate how a specific phobia develops, those with situation-specific phobias seem to acquire these at later ages than those who develop phobias related to natural environmental concerns or the blood-injection type (APA, 2013).

Etiology

The Role of Behavioral Factors and Conditioning

The etiology of specific phobias has most commonly been linked to individual conditioning experiences (Muris, Meesters, Merekelbach, Sermon, & Zwakhalen,

1998). *Classical conditioning* provides a framework for understanding how people develop phobic responses. For example, a very turbulent flight might result in future fear of flying. However, in addition to providing an explanation for how phobias might develop, classical conditioning can also provide the solution. Behavioral techniques can be applied to successfully decondition phobic responses. The nature of these systematic desensitization programs is discussed in the section on treatment.

In addition to classical conditioning, other behavioral explanations also exist, such as observation, modeling, and operant conditioning. Studies have linked anxious and fearful responses in some children to fearful maternal models (Pickersgill, Valentine, Pincus, & Foustok, 1999). Behaviorists also use *operant conditioning* to explain how fears can result in the development of a host of avoidant behaviors. In the example in the Putting It Into Practice box, if Gloria pulls the phone plug out of the wall, she will be able to avoid her acquired fear of phone ringing. However, avoidant behaviors can compromise adaptive behavior (Gloria will not get any phone calls), and fears can take on a life of their own as they generalize to other similar stimuli (e.g., phone ringing on the TV, alarm clock ring).

DON'T FORGET

Developmentally, phobias and separation anxiety are the earliest forms of anxiety.

CAUTION

Insecure attachment can develop from inconsistent or overprotective parenting responses to stressful situations. In both situations, the infant does not learn to internalize information on how to cope with distressing circumstances. Over time, the child may interpret many external cues as potentially threatening, setting the stage for the development of specific fears and generalized anxiety (Kendall & Ronan, 1990).

Parenting and Attachment Theory

Investigations of the influence of attachment on the development of anxiety in children have revealed that adolescents who were anxiously attached as infants (anxious-resistant attachment) were significantly more likely to develop anxiety disorders than their peers who were not anxiously attached (Warren, Huston, Egeland, & Sroufe, 1997).

Biological and Genetic Components

The etiology of specific phobias is probably best understood in terms of multiple pathways, including temperament, family characteristics, and exposure to conditioning experiences. Parents of children with anxiety disorders report that their children had more difficult temperaments as infants (crying and being fussy, irritable, and difficult to soothe), experienced more fears as toddlers, and experienced more problems adjusting to changes in routines than children without anxiety disorders (Rapee, 1997).

Assessment and Treatment/Interventions

Assessment instruments for all anxiety disorders are available in Rapid Reference 7.3.

Participant modeling and reinforced practice have been recognized as two empirically supported treatments for phobias in children (Ollendick & King, 1998). Models can be live or viewed in videotaped sessions and can be selected from a wide range of sources, including adults or peers. Research has supported the use of *in vivo participation* (live models) versus *covert or imaginal participation*. Reinforced practice is self-explanatory and relies on reinforcing successful practice in facing feared situations through the use of operant conditioning.

Several techniques can also be used to develop programs based on *systematic desensitization* methods initially developed by Wolpe (1958). Within this paradigm, individuals are taught relaxation techniques, and then with the assistance of their therapist, they develop a list of fears (a fear hierarchy, from the least to most feared aspect of a phobia). At each step of the hierarchy, the anxiety is paired with the relaxation response, until that step is mastered and no longer fearful.

SOCIAL ANXIETY DISORDER (SOCIAL PHOBIA)

Clinical Description and Associated Features

A pervasive fear of embarrassment or humiliation that often leads to avoidance of social or performance situations is at the center of social anxiety disorder. The anxiety can be evident in one or more social situations where an individual feels they are being evaluated or scrutinized, including social interactions (meeting and greeting people), being engaged in activities in public (eating, drinking), or performing (giving an oral presentation). In these situations, excessive fear and anxiety is:

- Exaggerated beyond any actual threat posed
- Persistent
- Causing significant distress or impairment.

Older children may realize that the fear is unreasonable but be unable to control it. Embarrassment may be associated with eating, drinking, or writing in public. Fears center around others' ability to detect their nervous tremors, blushing, or problems breathing. A diagnosis of social anxiety disorder in children requires that the anxiety occur when in the presence of their peers, not just adults, and must be evident for at least six months and interfere significantly with functioning.

Children and adolescents may respond to social anxiety with avoidant reactions (school attendance issues), escape behaviors (going to a library cubicle instead of the lunch room), negative self-appraisals, and increased physiological arousal (discomfort and somatic complaints). Understandably, their social skills are often poor.

DON'T FORGET

In younger children, symptoms may include tantrums, crying, freezing, or refusal to engage in social situations with unfamiliar people. The *DSM* also requires (1) evidence of normal social interaction with familiar people and (2) pervasive fear across adult and peer situations.

DON'T FORGET

As noted by Elkind, *personal fable* (tendencies to feel that no one has ever experienced what they are experiencing) and *imaginary audience* (everyone is looking at them) are two factors that may be particularly relevant to the development of a social anxiety disorder at this time.

Prevalence and Course

The lifetime prevalence for social anxiety disorder is estimated to be between 3% and 13%. However, prevalence rates for children have been estimated to be as low as 1% to 2% (Beidel, Turner, & Morris, 1999). One clinic study found that 27% of children with GAD and 5% of children with SAD had social anxiety disorder (Bernstein & Borchardt, 1991).

Social Anxiety and Younger Children

Compared to children with simple or specific phobias, children with social anxiety disorders tend to be older, have higher levels of severity, and are significantly more likely to become depressed later on (Last, Perrin, Hersen, & Kazdin, 1992). Despite this finding, there has been significant controversy regarding whether selective mutism (persistent failure to speak in certain social situations, as previously discussed) should be retained as a separate category of childhood disorders or conceptualized as an anxiety disorder, particularly a form of social anxiety. However, the *DSM-5* has retained the classification of selective mutism as a separate disorder. From a developmental perspective, children with behavioral inhibition (BI) demonstrate elevated reactions to novel stimuli (right brain activation) and, as toddlers, this response may be evident in being less assertive and in tendencies to withdraw from unfamiliar social situations (Fox & Pine, 2012).

Social Anxiety and Adolescence

It is not surprising that onset of social anxiety disorder has been most consistently linked with adolescence, given the nature of adolescent concerns regarding peer acceptance and social pressure (Beidel et al., 1999), with a median age of onset of 13 years. The vast majority of individuals with social anxiety, 75%, have onset between 8 and 15 years (APA, 2013). Prevalence rates for adolescence are similar to adult rates, at approximately 7%. Social anxiety disorder has been associated with increased risk for school dropout and decreased quality of life, yet only half of children with the disorder seek any treatment for the disorder (APA, 2013). Children who demonstrate BI can experience more social rejection over time, because of their tendencies to avoid social situations and stressors associated with social engagement. As a result, these children are at increased risk for developing avoidant coping mechanisms, which may be a precursor to social anxiety disorder in adolescence (Fox & Pine, 2012).

Individuals who only suffer from performance-based social anxiety typically are impaired in their occupation since these issues often impact their professional lives (e.g., musicians, athletes, dancers). Often individuals with performance-based issues do not experience social anxiety in situations that are not performance related (APA, 2013).

Etiology

Biederman and colleagues (1993) have found increased risk for anxiety disorders in general, and social anxiety in particular, in children who have a BI temperament. As discussed previously, parent communication, attachment, and parenting style have all been implicated in the development of fearfulness and phobic reactions in children. Genetically, there is an increased risk for social anxiety disorder in first-degree relatives who have the disorder (Fryer, Mannuzza, Chapman, Liebowitz, & Klein, 1993).

Assessment and Treatment/Interventions

Assessment instruments for all anxiety disorders are available in Rapid Reference 7.3.

In addition to techniques previously discussed for specific phobias, social skills training may also be a valuable component of any intervention program. Social skills interventions have been developed specifically to address concerns of children with social anxiety disorders (Francis & Ollendick, 1988; LeCroy, 1994) by focusing on skill awareness, situational awareness, practice and role play, and eventual in vivo application using participant modeling techniques.

PANIC ATTACKS AND PANIC DISORDER

Panic Attacks

Clinical Description and Associated Features

Panic attacks result from an intense, overwhelming, and inescapable fear that permeates thoughts, feelings, and sensations. Attacks are sudden and acute, lasting about 10 minutes. Because symptoms can include a number of somatic symptoms (palpitations, sweating, trembling, shortness of breath, feelings of smothering or dying, chest pain, dizziness), the attacks are often mistaken for heart attacks in adults. Cognitively, there can be a fear of losing control, depersonalization, or going crazy and a strong urge to escape. Attacks are accompanied by at least 4 and up to 13 somatic and cognitive symptoms. Panic attacks can be unexpected or triggered by situations (e.g., crowds, heights, confined spaces), and they can accompany any of the anxiety disorders. Although not a codable disorder in its own right, panic attacks can be extremely distressing and cause the individual intense discomfort, physically, emotionally, and cognitively. Panic attacks can include any of the following symptoms, the majority of which are physical in nature:

- Heart palpitations
- Sweating
- Trembling/ shaking
- Nausea and abdominal discomfort

- Chills or heat
- Feeling dizzy, lightheaded
- Numbness or tingling
- Feelings of loss of control
- Depersonalization
- Sensations of choking
- Chest pain
- Shortness of breath
- Fear of dying

Attacks can occur in response to expected (obvious cue or trigger) or unexpected causes. Although children can experience panic attacks, they are much more common in adolescents.

Because of its association with the anxiety disorders, the heightened arousal of a panic attack can be triggered by a specific phobia or can be the response of a severely distressed child with SAD who is not able to see his or her caregiver. Recently, studies have linked panic attacks to increased risk for developing other anxiety and depressive disorders, independent of comorbid internalizing psychopathology (Goodwin & Gotlib, 2004). The lifetime prevalence for panic attacks in youth ranges from 3.3% (Goodwin & Gotlib, 2004) to 11.6% (Craske, Kircanski, Epstein, Wittchen, & Pine, 2010), with lower prevalence rates reported in younger samples (9–17 years) relative to older youth (14–16 years). Onset for panic attacks is usually in late adolescence, with a peak time evident between the ages of 15 and 19 (Ollendick, Mattis, & King, 1994). Increased risk for the onset of panic attacks in adolescence has been associated with internalizing problems, such as anxiety, depression, negative affect, anxiety sensitivity, and separation anxiety (Hayward, Wilson, Lagle, Killen, & Taylor, 2004).

PUTTING IT INTO PRACTICE

The mall was very crowded, and Sara was becoming tired of shopping. All of a sudden, Sara felt like the floor was slipping out from under her. She was immediately overcome by a feeling of panic and dread. She felt like she was going to explode. Her heart started pounding, and her ears were ringing. She could see the ceiling start to spin, and she felt like she was going to faint. All of a sudden, she thought she was going crazy; it was as if the walls were going to close in on her and squeeze the life out of her. Someone tried to talk to her, but Sara ran out of the store into the parking lot in a frenzied attempt to escape. She needed some air. She felt like she was choking; she couldn't breathe. Five minutes later, everything seemed to come back into focus, as if she had just returned from another planet. Had she been abducted by aliens?

Panic Disorder

Clinical Description and Associated Features

If someone experiences repeated panic attacks and becomes preoccupied with the fear of having a panic attack, then a diagnosis of panic disorder may be appropriate. The *DSM-5* notes that in the month following a panic attack(s), an individual is considered to have developed a panic disorder if:

(a) There is persistent fear of having another panic attack (fear of losing control, or going crazy), and/ or
(b) The attack results in significant behavioral change resulting from attempts to avoid having another panic attack (avoidance maneuvers; reorganizing one's life to avoid attacks).

Kearney, Albano, Eisen, Allan, and Barlow (1997) found that in youth aged 8 to 17, some of the most common symptoms experienced were nausea, heart palpitations, shortness of breath, shaking, and extremes in temperature (hot or cold flashes). In addition, youth with panic disorder were also more likely to have symptoms of depression and heightened sensitivity to anxiety.

The frequency (weekly, monthly), duration, and severity (four symptoms to many symptoms) of panic attacks can vary widely and within the context of multiple anxiety disorders.

Prevalence and Course

Lifetime prevalence for panic disorder in community samples can be as high as 3.5%, with onset between late adolescence and the early thirties. The medium age of onset is about 20 to 24 years (APA, 2013). Women are twice as likely as men to have a panic disorder. In a study of more than 600 adolescents, King, Ollendick, Mattis, Yang, and Tonge (1997) found that 16% reported at least one panic attack (4 of 13 symptoms). In this study, females reported twice as many attacks (21.3%) as males (10.8%). When panic disorder onsets in adolescence, the course tends to be chronic and is often associated with comorbid disorders of depression, anxiety, and bipolar disorder (APA, 2013). In one longitudinal Dutch study of more than 1,500 youth, researchers found

DON'T FORGET

Studies have reported high rates of comorbidity between panic disorder and separation anxiety disorder. Although severe SAD in childhood may be a precursor to panic disorder later on, the risk is not consistent (APA, 2013).

that during the course of the study (baseline at age 10–12; data collection ages 18–20), 19.8% of cases experienced at least one panic attack, and 1.2% met the criteria for panic disorder (Mathyssek, Olino, Verhulst, & van Oort, 2012).

DON'T FORGET

Disorders often have multiple pathways and causes. Ollendick (2001) suggests that panic attacks result from interactions between temperament (high distress reactivity and behavioral inhibition) and attachment issues (separation distress), which may result in some children becoming more vulnerable to panic attacks.

Etiology

Biological, Genetic, and Neurotransmitter Function

Those in whom panic attacks occur before the age of 20 are 20 times more likely to have a first-degree relative who also has a panic disorder. Twin studies also suggest a genetic link (APA, 2000).

Irregular activity of the neurotransmitter norepinephrine has been implicated in the onset of panic attacks. The locus ceruleus, an area high in norepinephrine usage, which sends messages to the amygdala, which is known to trigger emotional reactions, has also been investigated (APA, 2013).

Cognitive Distortions

Cognitive theorists suggest that panic attacks can result from a misinterpretation of bodily sensations. Heightened awareness in panic-prone individuals is also often associated with *anxiety sensitivity*, which is evident in faulty assessments and a tendency to overreact to bodily sensations, which ultimately result in illogical conclusions.

Assessment and Treatment/Interventions

Assessment instruments for all anxiety disorders are available in Rapid Reference 7.3.

Pharmacological Treatment

Antidepressant drugs (most of which work to restore appropriate levels of norepinephrine) can be successful in alleviating panic attacks. At least one study has suggested that the selective serotonin reuptake inhibitors (SSRIs) can alleviate panic symptoms in children and youth (Renaud, Birmaher, Wassick, & Bridge, 1999).

Cognitive-Behavioral Treatment

One cognitive-behavioral treatment program, the Panic Control Treatment for Adolescents (PCT-A; Hoffman & Mattis, 2000), has been successful in helping adolescents develop coping skills to fend off future panic attacks, including cognitive appraisals, educational awareness, and situational exposure to reduce panic responses.

AGORAPHOBIA

Clinical Description and Associated Features

Although agoraphobia was not itself considered a codable disorder in the previous *DSM* (*DSM-IV-TR*; APA, 2000), the *DSM-5* now considers agropophobia as an anxiety disorder in its own right. Agoraphobia, which originates from the Greek language as "fear of the marketplace," is an intense fear and anxiety related to two or more possible situations:

- Use of public transportation (cars, ships, buses)
- Open spaces (bridges, parking lots)
- Enclosed spaces (elevators, cinemas)
- Standing in line
- Being out of the home, alone

Individuals with the disorder would avoid these situations (especially on their own) if they felt that they might not be able to escape, should panic symptoms occur. The situations provoke a sense of fear and anxiety, which is persistent and out of proportion to any actual threat. Individuals with agoraphobia may also meet criteria for panic disorder, in which case they would be diagnosed with both panic disorder and agoraphobia.

DON'T FORGET

In the previous *DSM-IV* (APA, 2000), panic disorder was thought to occur with or without agoraphobia, but was often accompanied by it, when fears of venturing out into open spaces resulted in many people becoming "house bound." Currently, the *DSM-5* recognizes both anxiety disorders, which can occur separately or as two comorbid disorders. Although there has been little research concerning the comorbid existence of panic disorder and agoraphobia in children and adolescents, family transmission of the disorders from parent to child is suspected (Last et al., 1991).

Prevalence and Course

Females are twice as likely as males to be diagnosed with agoraphobia, with approximately 1.7% of the population receiving a diagnosis annually. Although agoraphobia can be evident in childhood, the disorder is most likely to begin in late adolescence or early adulthood, with a mean onset of 17 years. The most likely scenario for reporting agoraphobia is after the occurrence of panic attacks or panic disorder, which occurs in approximately 30% of cases in community samples, to as high as 50% in clinic samples (APA, 2013).

Etiology

The Role of Biological, Genetic, and Temperament Factors

Of all the phobias, agoraphobia has the highest genetic factor of vulnerability to phobias and accounts for 61% of the variance (APA, 2013).

Parenting and Behavioral Modeling

Agoraphobia in childhood has been associated with experiencing negative life events (such as the loss of a parent through separation or death) or other stressful situations (kidnapping, mugging). The family situation is often described as lacking in warmth and high on parental overprotection.

Assessment and Treatment/Interventions

Assessment instruments for all anxiety disorders are available in Rapid Reference 7.3.

Treatment for agoraphobia would follow a similar course for treating other phobias, such as the use of systematic desensitization, participant modeling, and reinforced practice. The reader should review those treatment methods that appear under specific phobias.

GENERAL ANXIETY DISORDER

Clinical Description and Associated Features

Unlike the phobias and separation anxiety, children who experience GAD do not have a specific focus for their worries; instead, these children report pervasive worries that generalize across concerns about family, friends, school, health, and performance issues. Excessive worry and anxiety coupled with an inability to control the worry are the cardinal features of GAD.

The *DSM-5* does not distinguish between GAD in adults and children. However, while adults require three additional symptoms of excessive worry, children require only one additional symptom. The mood must be a pervasive mood (more days than not) over the course of 6 months. In addition, the disorder must be responsible for significant adaptive functioning deficits in the academic, social, or familial relationship areas.

Because of their overly conforming and hard-working nature, children with GAD are rarely referred for treatment by school personnel (Last et al., 1991). In addition to school- and peer-related problems, children with GAD may also worry about health-related issues or vague global concerns (Strauss, Lease, Last, & Francis, 1988).

CAUTION

Children with GAD may be overly conforming and hesitant to participate in activities. Perfectionistic tendencies may require excessive reassurance from others regarding their performance. Worries about the world at large may also be evident in their tendencies to ruminate regarding the potential for catastrophic events.

PUTTING IT INTO PRACTICE

During the interview, Jason seems unsettled and restless. When asked why he wasn't doing well in school, Jason said that it was hard to keep his mind on his work. He said he worried about a lot of things. He was worried that a robber might come and break into the house. He also worried that someone might steal his bike. He worried about whether he would make the baseball team this spring. He said it was like his head was always thinking of more things to worry about. Sometimes, before a test, he would actually get sick to his stomach because he was afraid he would not remember what he had studied.

DON'T FORGET

The *DSM* recognizes the physical or somatic nature of anxious symptoms in children and GAD in this population as excessive/pervasive worry plus one of the following symptoms: restlessness, easily fatigued, irritability, problems with concentration, muscle tension, or sleep disturbance (problems falling or staying asleep). Given these symptoms, it is not difficult to see why many children with GAD may be misdiagnosed as having ADHD.

Prevalence and Course

Between 2% and 5% of the population will be diagnosed with GAD in the course of their lifetime. Onset for GAD can be relatively early (8 to 10 years), with about one-third developing other anxiety or depressive disorders (Last, Perrin, Hersen, & Kazdin, 1996). Strauss and colleagues (1988) found that 70% of young children had comorbid GAD and SAD, while adolescents with GAD often had depression (47%) or specific phobia (41%).

Etiology

The Role of Biological, Genetic, and Temperament Factors

Twin studies suggest that as much as 30% to 40% of anxiety transmission may be caused by genetic factors (Eley, 1999). Although the neurotransmitter GABA (gamma-amniobutyric acid) may send messages to increase excitatory responses to threat, a malfunction may deter GABA's responsibility to send messages to inhibit responses (cease fire) when necessary. Continued firing and excitation may result (Lloyd, Fletcher, & Minchin, 1992).

Information Processing and Cognitive Biases for Emotional Information

According to cognitive theory, anxious individuals anticipate and interpret ambiguous events in a negative way. Compared to their peers, anxious children interpret events more negatively, tend to engage in self-blame more readily, and focus on the negative rather than positive aspects of events (Silverman & Ginsburg, 1995).

CAUTION

Although anxious children and children with ODD share tendencies to interpret ambiguous information in a negative and threatening way, children with ODD respond with aggression, while children with anxiety disorders respond with avoidance tactics (Barrett, Rappee, Dadds, & Ryan, 1996).

Parenting and Behavioral Modeling

Studies have shown that anxious parents may actually increase their children's tendencies to engage in anxious and avoidant behaviors (Barrett et al., 1996). Furthermore, children of anxious parents may not benefit from cognitive-behavioral training (CBT) to reduce anxiety unless parents are included in the CBT program as well (Cobham, Dadds, & Spence, 1998).

Assessment and Treatment/Intervention

The Coping Cat program, which has been successful for children who have SAD (see an explanation of the program in the section on SAD), has also assisted children with GAD.

DON'T FORGET

The Coping Cat program assists children to reduce anxiety by understanding and recognizing physical responses and developing problem-solving strategies to cope, using the following FEAR mnemonic:

F Feel frightened?
E Expect the worst?
A Attitude/Actions that can help
R Results and Rewards

PUTTING IT INTO PRACTICE

Esther had an overwhelming fear that her classmates would see her hand tremble as she copied notes from the board. She began to cover her hand with her left hand so that no one could see her taking notes. If anyone looked at her, Esther was sure they would notice the tremors. One day, filled with panic, Esther dropped her pen and ran out of the classroom. Her heart was pounding in her chest, and she felt that she would surely die. Esther called in sick the next day.

The Assessment of Childhood Anxiety Disorders

In their review of assessment and diagnostic instruments, Silverman and Saavedra (2004) review the main instruments used in evidence-based treatment studies. The authors stress the importance of using structured or semistructured interviews, rather than unstructured interviews, to ensure higher validity rates.

When assessing children for anxiety disorders, based on their review of kappa scores, the authors recommend using the Anxiety Disorders Interview Schedule for *DSM-IV*: Child and Parent Versions (ADIS for *DSM-IV*:C/P; Silverman &

Albano, 1996; Silverman et al., 2001). In their evaluation of parent rating scales, the authors recommend the Achenbach scales for internalizing disorders such as anxiety and mood.

A list of some of the more common measures for assessing anxiety in childhood and adolescence is presented in Rapid Reference 7.3. The list is not exhaustive but provides a general list of instruments that may be helpful in assessing the anxiety disorders. From this list, Silverman and Saavedra (2004) recommend three instruments for use in evidence-based practice: the Revised Children's Manifest Anxiety Scale (RCMAS), the State-Trait Anxiety Inventory for Children (STAIC), and the Fear Survey Schedule for Children—Revised (FSSC-R).

Treatments and Interventions

In their review of empirically supported treatments for children with phobic disorders, Ollendick and King (1998) suggest *participant modeling* and *reinforced practice* as two well-established treatment methods. Modeling as a treatment intervention is based on principles of observational learning (Bandura, 1977). Studies have demonstrated that participant modeling is superior to filmed models or participation alone. The technique of reinforced practice also has its roots in behavioral theory, specifically operant conditioning and contingency management. Studies have demonstrated that practice that is reinforced positively and practice plus self-instruction are superior to self-instruction alone or modeling plus practice. (See Ollendick & King, 1998, for a review.)

In their investigation, Ollendick and King (1998) also found several techniques that were in the "probably efficacious treatment methods" category, including imaginal desensitization, in vivo desensitization, filmed modeling, and cognitive-behavioral interventions using self-instruction training. The technique of *systematic desensitization* is often used to reduce an individual's fear by gradually exposing the person to the feared object or event and breaking the association between the event and the emotion (fear) by substituting an emotion that is incompatible with fear (relaxation). The technique and its variants can be very helpful tools to assist young children in overcoming irrational fears and phobias, such as school phobia. There are several variations to the systematic desensitization paradigm, distinguished by the way the feared stimulus and relaxation response can be paired. The pairing can occur *in vivo* (in reality) or be imagined. Studies have suggested that in vivo techniques are superior to merely imagining a situation, while imaginal desensitization has been found to be more effective than no treatment.

Rapid Reference 7.3

Some Common Assessment Instruments for the Evaluation of Anxiety in Children and Adolescents

Instrument	Ages	Brief Description
Revised Children's Manifest Anxiety Scale (RCMAS-2; Reynolds & Richmond, 2008)	6–17 years	Scales include Total Anxiety, Physiological Anxiety, Worry/Oversensitivity, Social Concerns/Concentration, and Lie Scale.
Anxiety Scale of the Beck Inventories for Youth (Beck, Beck, & Jolly, 2005)	7–12 years	One of five 20-item scales, measuring, self-concept, depression, anxiety, anger, and disruptive behavior.
The Multidimensional Anxiety Scale for Children (MASC; March, 1997)	8–19 years	Scales and subscales (in parentheses) include Physical Symptoms (Tense/Somatic), Harm Avoidance (Perfectionism/Anxious Coping), Social Anxiety, and Separation/Panic.
Fear Survey Schedule for Children—Revised (FSSC-R; Ollendick, 1983)	7–18 years	Five fear scales: Fear of Failure/Criticism, Fear of Unknown, Fear of Danger/Death, Fear of Injury, and Fear of Medical Situations.
State-Trait Anxiety Inventory for Children (STIAC; Spielberger, Edwards, Lushene, Montouri, & Platzek, 1973)	6–18 years	Two 20-item scales measuring state (situational) and trait (generalized) anxiety.
Social Phobia and Anxiety Inventory for Children (SPAI-C; Beidel, Turner, & Fink, 1996)	8–17 years	Scales include Assertiveness, General Conversation, Physical and Cognitive Symptoms, Avoidance, and Public Performance.
Anxiety Disorders Interview Schedule for *DSM-IV*: Child and Parent Versions (ADIS-IV; Silverman & Albano, 1997)	7–17 years	Available in parent and child versions. Assesses anxiety and related disorders.

Note: References for all instruments can be found in Appendix B.

DON'T FORGET

Wolpe (1958) developed procedures of systematic desensitization to progressively countercondition feared responses. Based on the underlying premise that relaxation and anxiety are incompatible responses, the program provides systematic steps to reduce anxiety.

Step 1: Clients are instructed in how to perform deep muscle relaxation.
Step 2: A fear hierarchy is constructed from the least to most feared aspect of a given situation (e.g., a hierarchy of fear-inducing thoughts regarding fear of flying might start with packing luggage and end with boarding the plane).
Step 3: The items from the fear hierarchy are gradually presented while the clients produce a deep muscle relaxation response.

OBSESSIVE-COMPULSIVE AND RELATED DISORDERS

Clinical Description and Associated Features

As was noted in the introductory comments to this section, the *DSM-5* has removed obsessive-compulsive disorder (OCD) from the category of anxiety disorders and has featured it in a section devoted to OCD and related disorders, which includes such disorders as OCD, body dysmorphic disorder, hoarding disorder, and body-focused repetitive behaviors such as hair pulling (trichotillomania) and skin picking (excoriation).

All disorders in this category share features of obsessive thoughts and repetitive compulsive behaviors. In the case of body dysmorphic disorder, the obsession is with thoughts of a flaw in appearance while in hoarding the compulsion is the need to preserve and not dispose of possessions even if these are of limited or no value. Trichotillomania and excoriation involve repetitive behaviors centered on the body. OCD often involves both obsessive thoughts (fears of contamination, need for symmetry, safety), which drive compulsive behaviors (cleaning, lining up, and repetitive checking of locks, stoves, etc.). The compulsive behaviors often are attempts to neutralize the anxiety caused by the obsessive thoughts. Behaviors are excessive (more than an hour per day) and can cause significant disruption to daily routines.

Prevalence and Course

Prevalence rates for OCD are estimated at approximately 1% of the population, with slightly more females than males meeting criteria, although males with the disorder tend to have earlier onset in childhood (APA, 2013). Prevalence rates for body dysmorphic disorder are around 2%, with very little differentiation between male and female rates. Rates among dermatology patients (9% to 15%) and cosmetic surgery patients (7% to 8%) are significantly higher. Hoarding symptoms are more common among older adults than children, although symptoms can appear in early adolescence (11–15 years). Trichotillomania and excoriation are significantly more common in females than males (10:1 for hair pulling; 75% female for excoriation), and both are evident in approximately 1% to 2% of the population.

DON'T FORGET

Although body dissatisfaction in adolescents is often linked to the potential for eating disorders in females, rates of body dissatisfaction in males have increased in the past 15 years (Youth Risk Behavior Survey; CDC, 2005). A specific form of body dysmorphic disorder, muscle dysmorphia (preoccupation with muscularity), also known as the Adonis complex, is increasingly evident in Western males (Pope, Phillips, & Olivardia, 2000b).

Etiology

Information about etiology comes primarily from research on OCD, with biological, behavioral, cognitive, and parenting theories all providing possible support for the development of OCD. From a genetic perspective, individuals with a family history of Tourette's disorder are at higher risk for childhood onset of OCD, especially for males (Tucker, Keckman, & Seahill, 1996). From a neurological perspective, OCD has been linked to low levels of serotonin, as well as the orbital region of the frontal cortex, including malfunction (overactivity) of the caudate nuclei (Saxena, Brody, & Maidment, 1999).

Assessment and Treatment/Interventions

Several of the pre-*DSM-5* scales for anxiety disorders have questions relating to OCD behaviors. One specific scale, the Children's Yale Brown Obsessive Compulsive Scale (CY:BOCS; Goodman, Rasmussen, & Price, 1988), provides a rating scale for children (6–18 years of age) on several dimensions of OCD, including severity, time spent, distress, and interference in daily functioning.

Treatments for OCD are primarily based on behavioral programs or medical management.

Medical Management

Selective serotonin reuptake inhibitors (SSRIs) have been effective in the treatment of OCD in children and adolescents (McClellan & Weery, 2003). Although clomipramine has also been successful, adverse side effects suggest caution in using this source in children and adolescents (Geller, Biederman, & Stewart, 2003).

Behavioral and Cognitive-Behavioral Methods

Several behavioral methods that have been successful in treating the anxiety disorders have also been very successful in the treatment of OCD. Exposure and Response Prevention (ERP) is a classic technique developed by Rachman (1993) that uses the paradigm of *exposure* to the anxiety-provoking situation (e.g., contamination), while *blocking the response* (e.g., cleaning). For example, the therapist would expose the client to the dreaded circumstance (throwing dirt on the floor) and restrain the client from cleaning up the mess. Over time, the client would develop tolerance and an increased ability to cope with similar circumstances. ERP has been proven effective in the relief of OCD symptoms in children and adolescents (March et al., 1997).

Other programs (Barrett, Heraly-Farrell, Piacentini, & March, 2004) have included family members in the program with excellent success rates, using cognitive and behavioral methods, such as a family-based cognitive behavioral treatment (CBFT) in a program known as the Focus Program (**F**reedom from **O**bsessons and **C**ompulsions **U**sing **S**pecial tools).

TEST YOURSELF

1. Which of the following is NOT considered one of the three primary internalizing disorders?

(a) Anxiety disorders
(b) Somatization disorders
(c) Eating disorders
(d) Depressive disorders

2. A 6-year-old child refuses to speak in public even though the child is quite capable of talking to her parents and siblings as soon as she gets home from school. This is most likely the result of an anxiety disorder known as

(a) Generalized anxiety disorder.
(b) Specific mutism.
(c) Selective mutism.
(d) Separation anxiety disorder.

3. **A therapist creates a fear hierarchy and presents selective images paired with instructions to engage in deep muscle relaxation. This technique is called**
   (a) Rachman's procedure.
   (b) systematic desensitization.
   (c) Coping Cat program.
   (d) in vivo sensitization.
4. **Fear of having repeated panic attacks can often lead to fear of venturing out into open places, which is known as**
   (a) free-floating anxiety.
   (b) arachnophobia.
   (c) Social phobia.
   (d) Agoraphobia.
5. **Which of the following is NOT an example of a symptom of a panic attack?**
   (a) heart palpitations
   (b) sweating
   (c) derealization
   (d) fear of contamination
6. **Which of the following anxiety disorders appears first, developmentally?**
   (a) Specific phobia
   (b) Panic disorder
   (c) Social phobia
   (d) General anxiety disorder
7. **Which is the most common symptom of separation anxiety disorder?**
   (a) Reluctance to sleep alone
   (b) Fear of the dark
   (c) School refusal
   (d) Eating problems
8. **Although most body dissatisfaction is related to females, males who demonstrate body dysmorphic disorder have been likened to having**
   (a) a preoccupation with body weight.
   (b) social phobia.
   (c) an Adonis complex, or muscle preoccupation.
   (d) a strong desire to be thin.

Answers: 1. c; 2. c; 3. b; 4. d; 5. d; 6. a; 7. c; 8. d

Eight

DISORDERS OF MOOD

Depression and Bipolar Disorder

It is not uncommon to feel irritable, unhappy, or upset at times, or to feel elated when we receive exciting news. However, for individuals suffering from depression and bipolar disorders, depressed or elated states can be extreme and long lasting, causing problems with day-to-day functioning.

There are two main mood states: depression, a state of low positive affectivity and the polar opposite, mania, a state of euphoria. The *DSM-5* (APA, 2013) has attempted to focus more on the continuum of mental illness based on severity of symptom presentation and developmental onset. With this in mind, there has been a concentrated effort to reorder the presentation of disorders in the *DSM* along these lines, with the result that bipolar disorder now precedes the depressive disorders in the manual. The rationale behind this reorganization is that the authors wanted to position bipolar disorder as separate from depression, yet midway between schizophrenia and depressive disorders. In this way, bipolar disorder is considered to be more severe than major depressive disorder, due to high rates of comorbidity with other disorders and often more enduring in terms of lifelong persistence (Angst, 2007). In addition, bipolar disorder is considered to have one of the "strongest links to family history" and genetic origin (APA, 2013, p. 123). The *DSM-5* has also separated the two disorders that were previously discussed in the same chapter on mood disorders.

However, for purposes of this book, the concept of mood disorders is a much better format for introducing readers to these disorders. For purposes of clarity, depressive disorders are discussed before the bipolar disorders, because knowledge and understanding of a major depressive episode (MDE) is necessary for comprehending both types of disorders, and this is more readily associated and understood when presented within the context of a major depressive disorder (MDD).

Several different disorders are contained within the *DSM-5* chapter on depressive disorders, including: major depressive disorder (MDD), persistent depressive disorder (PDD; previously known as dysthymia), depressive disorders that are medication/substance-induced or related to medical conditions, and a newly listed disorder called disruptive mood dysregulation disorder (DMDD).

Individuals who experience depressive disorders exhibit characteristics of unipolar depression, a pervasive negative mood state that is evident when one experiences symptoms of a major depressive episode (MDE), which can result in: low positive affect (which may appear as irritability in children); a loss of interest or pleasure; and a number of symptoms of *emotional* (guilt, sense of loss, apathy), *vegetative* (problems eating, sleeping, or maintaining normal weight), *behavioral* (loss of energy), or *cognitive* deficits (loss of concentration, attention, motivation).

Individuals who experience bipolar disorders fluctuate between depressed states and elated moods. They are considered to have bipolar disorder based on the existence of symptoms of a manic episode in addition to a MDE (prior to or after the manic episode). Symptoms of bipolar disorder can encompass a wide range of characteristics evident when one experiences a manic episode, depending on the severity and duration of the symptoms. As a result, there are a number of different types of bipolar disorder depending on the number of symptoms and duration. Symptoms are the opposite of those experienced during a MDE and can include feelings of grandiosity and elation, evident in *emotional* (expansive, elevated sense of self; irritability in children), *behavioral* (multi-tasking, engaging in high risk/pleasure-seeking behaviors), *vegetative* (little need for sleep) or *cognitive* excess (distractibility, concentration problems, racing thoughts, pressured speech).

DON'T FORGET

The depressive disorders are distinct from the bipolar disorders since the bipolar disorders include an elevated mood component (manic, hypomanic) as well as a depressed mood state, the combination of which is reflected in the prefix *bi*, meaning "dual states." The depressive disorders, in contrast, manifest a single (unipolar) emotional state of low positive affectivity.

PUTTING IT INTO PRACTICE

Christy was referred to the school social worker due to high absenteeism. When the social worker made a home visit, Christy's mother stated that her daughter's absences resulted from Christy's frequent complaints of feeling sick to her stomach. The mother disclosed that Christy had been involved in a bicycle accident more than two years ago, resulting in a separation of her cartilage from the rib cage when her chest hit the handle bars. Due to this painful condition, Christy missed more than a month of school and subsequently had to repeat the third grade. Christy's mother enrolled her in a private school for that year.

Christy re-enrolled at her home school this year; however, her friends are all in the next grade level. Since the accident, Christy often complains of not feeling well. She is very thin, and her teacher has noticed that her lunch is often left on her plate, barely touched. At home, Christy is often irritable and moody. She doesn't seem to have much interest in doing anything. The family is under considerable financial strain and lived with extended family until recently. Christy has had to share a bedroom with her younger sister, who is in the same grade as Christy. They do not get along.

Last week, after a brutal argument with her sister, Christy ran out of the house crying and saying she was going to kill herself. Her mother wondered if she was doing this just to get attention, because she did not believe that someone as young as Christy could actually be depressed. She was hoping Christy would just get over it.

MAJOR DEPRESSIVE DISORDER (MDD) AND PERSISTENT DEPRESSIVE DISORDER (PDD)

Clinical Description and Associated Features

With adults, a MDE requires that the mood be pervasive for a 2-week period. The average duration in adults and children is 4 months. A diagnosis of MDD requires either (a) a depressed mood state, evident in anhedonia (low positive affect) in adults or irritability in children, or (b) loss of interest or pleasure in day-to-day activities (APA, 2013). In addition to one of these criteria, the *DSM-5* stipulates four additional symptoms required for the diagnosis, from a list of seven potential symptoms: significant weight gain or loss (in children, failure to make expected gains), insomnia or hypersomnia, psychomotor retardation or agitation, fatigue, feelings of worthlessness, inability to concentrate, and recurrent suicidal ideation. The feeling is pervasive and symptoms are intense, with some symptoms often occurring on a daily level.

Persistent depressive disorder (PDD) is diagnosed if the following conditions hold:

1. A pervasive depressed mood (loss of interest, anhedonia) or irritability (in children) is evident for at least 2 years (at least 1 year in child populations).
2. Depression is accompanied by at least two of the seven symptoms previously noted from the symptom list for MDE.
3. During the course of the 2 years (adult) or 1 year (child), there has not been symptom relief for a period greater than 2 months.
4. There has been no evidence of a MDD during the 2 years (1 year for children).

Prevalence and Course

Approximately 5% of the general population of children and adolescents will suffer from depression; however, Costello and colleagues (2002) found that the rate doubles between childhood (2%) and adolescence (4% to 7%), with higher rates of the melancholic type of depression (anhedonic) prevalent at this stage of development. Studies have demonstrated that while boys and girls are equally likely to develop depression at younger ages, in adolescence, depression is almost twice as common in adolescent females than males (Fleming & Offord, 1990; Hankin & Abramson, 2001). Comorbidity is especially high between depression and the anxiety disorders, although many other comorbid relationships exist.

The course of depression can be long and enduring. Although only two weeks' duration is required for a MDE, the average length of a MDD is approximately four months. Kovacs, Akiskal, Gatsonis, and Parrone (1994) found that 76% of children with early-onset persistent depression develop MDD later on.

In addition to the long-term impact of the depressive disorders on future interpersonal and psychosocial problems, there is also an increased risk for developing other disorders. In one follow-up study of 6- to 12-year-olds with MDD, 30% developed bipolar disorder on follow-up (Geller et al., 1995).

CAUTION

He thought it was a light at the end of the tunnel, but it turned out to be another train coming at him: double depression. Often at the end of a lengthy bout of persistent depression, the cloud does not lift but becomes even darker. When persistent depressive disorder (PDD) develops into MDD, it is called *double depression*.

Developmental Adaptations

Although the core clinical features of MDD are similar in children, adolescents, and adults, these symptoms manifest in varied ways at different age levels. In addition, variations would also be expected in the nature of environmental stressors at different developmental stages (e.g., irritability is a common child symptom that substitutes for "sadness" in child populations).

The *DSM-5* recognizes different time requirements for symptom presentation in children (one year for PDD in children compared with two years for adults) and also provides a number of associated features of symptoms that might be typical at different developmental levels.

Symptoms and characteristics of depression can differ depending on the child's developmental level. Therefore, a discussion of characteristics that might be associated with depression in children and adolescents will follow a developmental focus.

DON'T FORGET

For diagnostic purposes, *irritability* is described as a cranky mood in children and may be evident in angry outbursts and low frustration tolerance.

DON'T FORGET

Spitz (1946) observed institutionalized infants who seemed to waste away in the absence of affectionate care despite having their physiological needs met (a condition called *marasmus*). Due to the extreme nature of their listlessness and chronic sobbing, Spitz called the reaction *anaclitic depression*.

Toddlers and Preschool Period

Recently, investigators have determined that preschool children as young as 3 years of age can demonstrate some classic symptoms and characteristics of MDD (anhedonia, sadness or irritability, neurovegetative signs). Toddlers can display symptoms of depression in loss of appetite, lack of sleep (vegetative symptoms), delays in the acquisition of developmental milestones (walking, talking, toilet training), and in their experiences of nightmares and night terrors. At this stage, more agitated expressions might include excessive head banging or rocking

DON'T FORGET

As a result of their investigations of MDD in preschool children, Luby and colleagues (2003, 2006) have advocated for modifications to the *DSM* criteria for MDD in very young children. Their findings suggest that the current criteria are too stringent for preschool children, leading to underdiagnosis at this age level.

behaviors. Investigators have also found that thematic play can provide useful information regarding the nature of depressive symptoms in children at this age level (Luby et al., 2003, 2006).

Childhood

Although genetic transmission may be a strong factor in adolescent depression, childhood (prepubertal) depression may be more environmental than genetic (Thapar, Harold, & McGuffin, 1998). Environmental stressors at this age level might include family conflict, problematic parenting style, and peer rejection. In childhood, symptoms of depression might be evident in somatic complaints, irritability, and social withdrawal. Common comorbid clusters within this age range include behavior disorders, ADHD, and anxiety disorders (APA, 2013). Depressed children often have low self-esteem and can be very self-critical. At this stage, depression will probably manifest in poor academic achievement and poor social relationships. Behaviors may vacillate between acting out (anger) and withdrawal (sadness). Low frustration tolerance is likely.

Adolescence

In adolescents, there is a higher rate of the endogenous/melancholic subtype of depression, and there are higher rates of suicide attempts and fatalities than in prepubertal children (Ryan et al., 1987). Adolescent depression is continuous with adult depression (Ryan et al., 1987), and as with adult depression, there is stronger evidence of a genetic component. Some of the more common symptoms in adolescence include psychomotor retardation/hypersomnia and delusions (especially auditory hallucinations). Common comorbid clusters at this age range include behavior disorders, ADHD, anxiety disorders, substance disorders, and eating disorders (APA, 2013).

CAUTION

Given the high level of sensitivity to body image at this age level, negative thoughts may turn to negative self-appraisals based on physical features that are considered ugly or unattractive and body type (the adolescent may consider him- or herself overweight). Negative thought patterns may generalize to low self-esteem, poor school achievement, social withdrawal, or heightened risk taking evident in delinquent behavior, sexual acting out, or substance abuse. Youth with MDD have higher rates of pregnancy and increased risk of suicide (Ryan et al., 1987).

CAUTION

Suicide was the third leading cause of death in youth and young adults (10 to 19 years of age) in 1997 (Shaffer & Craft, 1999). Between 1979 and 1997, the suicide rate for 10- to 14-year-olds doubled, while the rate for adolescents in the 15- to 19-year range increased by 13% (Guyer, MacDorman, Martin, Peters, & Strobino, 1998).

Risks and Protective Factors

A number of risk factors have been linked to the development of depressive disorders in childhood and adolescence: abuse or neglect, stress, loss of a parent or loved one, comorbid disorders (ADHD or conduct or learning disorders), breakup of a romantic relationship, having a chronic illness (e.g., diabetes), and other trauma, such as a natural disaster (NIMH, 2000b).

Family Risk Factors

A high prevalence rate for alcoholism among first-degree relatives of prepubertal children and adolescents with mood disorders has been reported (Puig-Antich, Geotz, & Davies, 1989). Family poverty and conflict between parents have also been cited as increasing the risk for depression in children as well as their parents (Hammen, 1991).

DON'T FORGET

McDermott and Palmer (2002) found that younger children responded to the trauma of a natural disaster (an Australian bushfire) with depressed symptoms, whereas older (middle-school) children responded with emotional distress more similar to symptoms of PTSD.

DON'T FORGET

Children of depressed mothers are twice as likely to be depressed over their lifetime than their peers whose mothers are not depressed. Over 40% of children whose mothers are depressed are diagnosed with childhood depression.

In their study of the parenting style of depressed mothers, Malphurs and colleagues (1996) found that depressed mothers were more withdrawn (emotionally unavailable for their children) and intrusive (controlling, irritable, and impatient). Other studies have demonstrated that infants and young children of depressed mothers are at higher risk for developing insecure attachments and poor emotion regulation and that their daughters are at increased risk for becoming depressed (Cicchetti & Toth, 1998).

Peer Influence

Lack of social competence, low peer support, and rejection or peer neglect are all risk factors for child and adolescent depression (Harter & Marold, 1994). Children who are depressed are often irritable, have fewer acquired social skills, and are more likely to engage in negative or aggressive interactions.

Depressive Syndromes and Symptoms

Not everyone who experiences a depressed mood will meet the clinical criteria for a depressive disorder, as indicated in the *DSM*. Children, adolescents, and adults can all experience depressed moods or feel depressed on occasion. Sometimes these feelings are reactive to particular stressors, at other times, nostalgia or melancholy might trigger feelings of sadness, while on other occasions mood can be influenced by physiological (hormonal) changes or changes that are substance induced (e.g., alcohol is a depressant). However, a depressed mood is often temporary and transitory in nature. Depressed syndromes are clusters of symptoms, such as those that have been identified by Achenbach and Rescorla (2001), as evident in *anxious/depressed syndrome* (primarily characterized by negative emotions) and *depressed withdrawn syndrome* (low positive affect and social withdrawal).

DON'T FORGET

While both genetic and environmental influences have been implicated in the development of MDD, environmental influences are likely to be more instrumental in childhood depression, while genetic factors are more prominent in the development of MDD in adolescence.

Etiology

Genetic Background and Neurotransmitter Functions

Children, adolescents, and adults who have a family history of depression are at higher risk for depression. However, other factors that also operate in the home, such as parenting style, may be as significant as genetic transmission. Results from twin studies suggest that a genetic link is stronger for adults and adolescents than for children, who are better accounted for by environmental factors.

Neurotransmitter functions. Although evidence for neuroendocrine imbalance (hormone cortisol) has been related to depression in adults, this has not been substantiated in children. Antidepressants that have been instrumental in increasing low levels of the neurotransmitter serotonin in adult depression have had mixed results with children. Some studies have found antidepressants not to be effective in reducing symptoms of depression in children (Fischer & Fischer, 1996).

CAUTION

The FDA issued a public health advisory (March 22, 2004) and asked manufacturers of several antidepressant drugs to include warnings on the label regarding the recommendation to closely monitor adults, children, and adolescents for a potential worsening of depression and suicidality in patients being treated with antidepressant medications.

Cognitive-Behavioral Model

Theorists who support a cognitive model link the cause of unipolar depression to maladaptive thought processes, which interpret events in negative ways. The two most influential cognitive explanations are the models of *negative thinking* and *learned helplessness.*

Negative thinking. According to Beck (1997), negative thinking colors our perceptions of the world. Negative thoughts are pessimistic, viewing the glass as half empty rather than half full. Negative schemas eventually develop into what Beck refers to as the *negative triad,* whereby individuals interpret their experiences, their self-hood, and their future in negative ways.

Several errors of thinking can occur as a result of negative schemas that perpetuate the negative thought process, including minimizing the positive and magnifying or overgeneralizing the negative.

DON'T FORGET

The cognitive triad comprises the three pervasive thoughts of hopelessness, helplessness, and worthlessness.

Learned helplessness. Seligman (1975) originally articulated the concept of *learned helplessness* to describe the reactions of experimental animals that were repeatedly shocked on one day and then provided with a barrier they could jump over to reach safety on the following day. However, most of the dogs did not flee; they gave up. Seligman reasoned that the dogs had learned that the shocks were not within their control, and they did not engage in problem-solving behaviors because they felt helpless to influence the outcome.

PUTTING IT INTO PRACTICE

Sally and Jenna take the same psychology quiz. Sally does well, but Jenna fails the quiz. According to attribution theory, Sally can make a positive attribution (i.e., pat herself on the back and say "I did well because I am smart" [internal or global attribution] and "I always expect to get good grades because I study hard" [stable]). However, Jenna might need to save face, so she might reason that the test was unfair (external attribution) and that furthermore this professor always gives unfair tests (stable), or that something must have distracted this professor because she usually gives fair tests (unstable).

In this scenario, Sally has responded positively, while Jenna has developed a defensive maneuver to protect herself from thinking negatively about herself: Jenna writes her failure off as a bad test.

More recently, *attribution theory* (linking of thoughts to outcomes) has added a new twist on learned helplessness to help explain why only some people respond to stressors with defeat.

Family and Peer Influence Models

The role of family processes on depression. In their analysis of the role of family processes in adolescent depression, Sheeber, Hops, and Davis (2001) suggest four potential areas in which family dynamics may influence their adolescent's vulnerability to developing depression: the adversarial family climate (high stress or low support), the negative reinforcement model, the self-fulfilling prophecy, and poor modeling for emotion regulation.

CAUTION

Aggression can become depression. In their model, Patterson and Capaldi (1990) suggest that the children who tend to be verbally or physically aggressive ultimately seal their own fate as they are increasingly rejected by their peers. Other children respond to rejection with increased oppositional behaviors and heightened rejection, which leads to low self-esteem and ultimately depression.

Peer influences in mediating depression. While Sheeber and colleagues (2001) looked at the influence of family processes on adolescent depression, Patterson and Capaldi (1990) developed a model that looks at much earlier influences. The authors suggest that children who are reared in a negative family environment enter the social arena with low self-esteem, poor interpersonal skills, tendencies to respond aggressively (verbally or physically), and a negative cognitive style.

An Ecological Transactional Model

In discussing their model, Cicchetti and Toth (1998) emphasize the need to consider the concepts of *multifinality* and *equifinality* in discussing the potential course and outcomes of depression in children and adolescents. The authors discuss the need to consider the "potentiating and compensatory" processes across all levels of influence from early ontogenic development (early development of physiological systems of regulatory arousal and attachment relationships) through the micro-, exo-, and macrosystem influences on the development of depression. It is within such a model, the authors suggest, that interventions can be developed to target stage-specific needs and family influences as well as social contextual influences.

Assessment and Treatment/Intervention for Depressive Disorders

The use of structured and semistructured interview schedules in the assessment of internalizing disorders has been previously discussed (see Chapter 3 for a review). In addition, many of the general behavioral rating scales and individual personality scales also include measures of depression. Several common instruments for measuring depression are listed in Rapid Reference 8.1.

Medication

The role of medication in the treatment of depression has previously been discussed, as well as the recent warnings issued, and will not be reviewed again at this time.

Empirically Supported Treatments

In their review of clinical treatments for depression in children and adolescents, Kaslow and Thompson (1998) discussed child and adolescent programs that met criteria for probably efficacious treatments as outlined by the American Psychological Association. The programs, which both use CBT, were a child-based program developed by Stark, Swearer, Jurkowski, Sommer, and Bowen (1996) and an adolescent program developed by Lewinsohn, Clarke, Rhode, Hops, and Seeley (1996).

Cognitive-Behavioral Treatment

The use of CBT for the reduction of depressive symptoms in adults has met with significant success. Beck (1997) has developed a structured 20-session program that is aimed at gradually increasing activities and elevating mood through challenging automatic thoughts, identifying negative thinking, and restructuring thoughts from maladaptive to adaptive thinking. Lewinsohn and colleagues (1996) have developed a CBT program for adolescents that was adapted from Beck's program and includes a parent component.

Rapid Reference 8.1

Common Assessment Instruments for Evaluation of Depression in Children and Adolescents

Instrument	Ages	Brief Description
The Depression Scale of Beck Youth Inventories 2nd Edition (Beck, Beck & Jolly, 2005)	7 to 14	20-item scale assesses depression based on *DSM-IV* criteria. Four-choice format measures negative thoughts related to self, life, and future expectations.
The Hopelessness Scale for Children (Kazdin, 1986)	6 to 13	True/false response format 17 questions assess hopelessness, which correlates highly with depression and suicide ideation.
Child Depression Inventory-2 (Kovacs, 2003)	6 to 17	Score for Total Depression, as well as five subscales: Negative Mood, Interpersonal Problems, Ineffectiveness, Anhedonia, and Negative Self-Esteem.
Depression and Anxiety in Youth Scale (Newcomer et al., 1994)	6 to 18	Identification of MDD and over-anxious disorder based on the *DSM-III-R* classification. Self-report, parent, and teacher versions, available.
Reynolds Adolescent Depression Scale-2 (Reynolds, 2002)	13 to 18	Self-report measure based on four-choice format yields a score for Total Depression.
Reynolds Child Depression Scale-2 (Reynolds, 1989)	Grades 3 to 6	Self-report measure provides graphic choice format (five faces ranging from happy to sad) for young children. Score for Total Depression.

Note: References for all instruments can be found in Appendix B.

CAUTION

Remember that, as an internalizing disorder, depression may be more difficult to assess on the basis of observational reports and measures. Youth may also not be aware that what they are feeling is depression, or they may not be able to articulate their feelings adequately. It is also very important to remember that depression in children is often expressed as irritability, which may manifest in verbal and physically aggressive responses and may be misdiagnosed as problems of conduct.

Stark and colleagues (1996) have developed a CBT program for depressed children and their parents. Initially, the program was used as a school-based treatment approach, but Stark has modified the program to include individual and group formats. The program initially focuses on the development of positive mood and ultimately seeks to teach children to reframe their negative thought patterns.

DISRUPTIVE MOOD DYSREGULATION DISORDER

Clinical Description and Associated Features

The *DSM-5* has introduced a new classification for depressive disorders in children, which has met with considerable controversy. The rationale for adding this new classification was to reduce the rates of diagnosis of pediatric bipolar disorder, which have escalated in the past 10 years. The diagnosis of bipolar disorder (BD) in children and youth has been a challenge due to symptom presentations of other disorders that have considerable overlap with BD, such as attention-deficit/hyperactivity disorder (ADHD), posttraumatic stress disorder (PTSD), and anxiety disorders, and share many of the features of symptoms of bipolar disorder. The new classification of disruptive mood dysregulation disorder (DMDD) was established to distinguish between children who evidenced symptoms of "severe and persistent irritability" (APA, 2013, p. 157) from those who exhibited more classic episodic symptoms of bipolar disorder.

DMDD, also briefly known as temper dysregulation disorder with dysphoria, is characterized by frequent and severe temper outbursts (three or more times per week), across multiple settings, and is accompanied by persistent negative mood states. DMDD is diagnosed if the behaviors are present for at least 12 months. The disorder most likely has onset after 6 years of age and prior to 10 years of age.

In addition to the criteria needed to establish the presence of the disorder, the *DSM-5* also includes a number of exclusionary criteria. For example, clinicians need to rule out the existence of manic symptoms, and if a child meets criteria for DMDD and oppositional defiant disorder (ODD), then the child should be diagnosed with DMDD.

CAUTION

Studies tracking the prevalence rates for bipolar disorder (BD) in children and youth have found that while rates for adults diagnosed with the disorder increased by 3.5% between 1996 and 2004, prevalence rates for children and adolescents increased by 53.2% (children) to 58.5% (adolescents) during this same time period (Brotman et al., 2007).

DON'T FORGET

Growing concern about the escalating rates of diagnoses of bipolar disorder in children and youth has been the impetus for several debates, one of which is whether symptoms of the disorder should be more narrowly defined (prevalence rates for bipolar I are approximately .5%), or if symptoms should be considered to be part of the wider bipolar spectrum, which could conceivably increase prevalence rates 10-fold (Hirschfeld et al., 2003).

The introduction of DMDD into the *DSM-5* has resulted in researchers posing several important questions, including: "Will disruptive mood dysregulation disorder reduce false diagnosis of bipolar in children?" (Margulies, Weintraub, Basile, Grover, & Carson, 2012) or will the new diagnosis "add further to the overuse of antipsychotics in kids, not solve it" (Frances, 2011), while others question the introduction of a disorder that lacks an empirical basis (Stingaris, 2011). Some of the problems facing clinicians in diagnosing DMDD or bipolar disorder in children is the tendency for symptoms to overlap with other disorders, and the fact that several disorders have irritability as a symptom for children. Leibenluft (2011) found that youth with irritability who were designated as having severe mood dysregulation were at lower risk for developing bipolar disorder than youth with bipolar who had manic or hypomanic symptoms, providing support for the existence of two separate disorders.

DON'T FORGET

Although irritability is a symptom that is referred to frequently in diagnostic categories of the *DSM* pertaining to children (depression, posttraumatic stress disorder, ODD), the mood is not often clearly defined, other than referring to it as a negative mood state. In their study of youth with severe irritability, Deveney and colleagues (2013) defined *irritability* as a lower threshold for experiencing negative feelings in response to a frustrating experience (blocked goal).

Prevalence and Course

In a recent study, Copeland, Angold, Costello, and Egger (2013) investigated the prevalence, comorbidity, and correlates of the disorder in a community sample of 3,258 children from 2 to 17 years of age. Results revealed that DMDD was relatively uncommon after early childhood, with three-month prevalence rates ranging from .8% to 3.3%.

Comorbidity rates with other disorders ranged from 62% to 92%, with depressive disorders and oppositional defiant disorder (ODD) among the most common. The chances of DMDD occurring with both an emotional and behavioral disorder ranged from 32% to 68%. The researchers concluded that DMDD is a category that "identifies a group of children with severe emotional and behavioral dysregulation" (p. 178), and that future efforts should investigate which symptoms are unique to DMDD and which aspects are shared with other individual emotional and behavioral disorders.

Etiology/Treatment and Intervention

Although little is known about the etiology and treatment of DMDD, a recent investigation by Deveney and colleagues (2013) suggests that increased research into brain-related patterns could provide much-needed insight. Deveney and colleagues compared responses of 19 youth with severe irritability (severe mood dysregulation) to 23 controls, using functional MRI to record brain-related responses to a frustration-evoking task. Results revealed a marked decrease in activation of the parietal, parahippocampal, and thalamic/cingulated/strata regions of the brain in the youth with severe irritability compared to controls. This decreased activation was noted only on trials where negative feedback was given. Although the researchers had hypothesized differences in the frontal areas as well, this was not supported; however, they suggest that sample size may have reduced statistical sensitivity to this effect. Given the lack of information and complex nature of the underlying processes involved, further investigation of brain-related responses may be instrumental in informing future practices in the identification, treatment, and intervention for DMDD.

BIPOLAR DISORDERS

Clinical Description and Associated Features

The *DSM-5* provides criteria for manic, mixed, and hypomanic episodes of a bipolar disorder. A manic episode is described as a "distinct period" of abnormally elevated, expansive, or irritable mood, lasting for at least a week, causing significant impairment, and accompanied by at least three of the following seven symptoms:

1. Heightened sense of self-esteem or grandiosity
2. Little need for sleep
3. Pressured speech
4. Flight of ideas
5. Distractibility
6. Heightened goal-directed activity (psychomotor agitation, sexualized behaviors, social contacts)
7. Excessive involvement in risky behaviors (spending spree, theft, sexual behavior)

Bipolar I is diagnosed if one or more manic or mixed episodes (both major depressive episode and a manic episode overlapping within a one-week period) are evident.

Cyclothymic Disorder, a chronic fluctuating mood disturbance, is diagnosed when the prevailing mood for the past 2 years has involved hypomanic symptoms and depressive symptoms (not meeting criteria for MDD).

DON'T FORGET

In addition to the low positive affect associated with unipolar depression, children and adolescents who have bipolar disorder also experience the highs of manic states.

CAUTION

The difference between a *manic episode* (one week) and a *hypermanic episode* (four days) is in the duration and severity. A hypermanic episode is a less severe episode (which does not cause significant impaired functioning) of heightened and expansive mood lasting for at least four days. Both episodes require three symptoms from the list. Bipolar II is diagnosed in cases of major depressive episodes with a hypermanic episode.

In their review of literature over the previous 10 years concerning child and adolescent bipolar disorder (BD), Geller and Luby (1997) suggest that childhood-onset BD may be more severe, chronic, and have rapid-cycling features similar to the more severe types and often treatment-resistant forms of adult BD. The mixed manic and rapid-cycling patterns may manifest as brief and multiple episodes, which may cycle numerous times within a single day (Geller et al., 1995).

In their literature review, Geller and Luby (1997) provide examples of how the core features of a manic episode might be evident in childhood and adolescence. The following summary is based on their review.

In childhood, rather than discrete episodes, there are more likely to be rapid mood shifts between elation and irritability. A sense of childhood grandiosity or inflated self-esteem that defies logic may result in children's believing that they are being taught incorrectly or that they are above the law. Some students may have grandiose aspirations in manic periods of being a famous athlete or musician while having minimal talent, or becoming an astronaut while failing in school. Problems with sleep may be evident: Younger children may watch television all night in their rooms or rearrange their furniture instead of sleeping, and adolescents may engage in late-night partying. Pressured speech and flight of ideas are similar to adult symptoms but with content specific to child or adolescent interests.

Children and adolescents may also get caught up in high levels of motor and goal-directed activity and multitasking (making telephone calls while making illustrations, sorting card collections, etc.). Dangerous and risk-taking behaviors may be evident in sexual promiscuity, fast driving, spending sprees, and theft.

CAUTION

Although the *DSM* has added many associated and symptom features for childhood depressive disorders (MDD, PDD), there is virtually no mention of how the bipolar disorders might manifest differently in children. However, one specifier for BD that may be particularly relevant to childhood-onset bipolar is the *rapid cycling* specifier, used when four or more mood episodes occur within a 12-month period. Although this specifier is seen in approximately 10% to 20% of adult populations, current literature suggests that this may be a predominant feature of BD in children. The *DSM-5* has increased the number of specifiers for BD to assist in better clarifying the nature of the disorder, such as those accompanied by symptoms of anxious distress (keyed up), rapid cycling, or melancholic features (loss of pleasure and emotional reactivity, guilt, weight loss, depression).

PUTTING IT INTO PRACTICE

Arthur was giggling wildly and running down the hall when his fifth-grade teacher cited him for breaking a school rule. When Arthur got to his desk, he immediately threw his books on the floor and stamped his feet in protest. A time-out did little to change his mood, and Arthur glared at the other students while he huffed in the corner. During this time-out, unknown to the teacher, Arthur managed to stab himself in the arm with a pencil. Two minutes later, Arthur asked if he could rejoin the class activity and began laughing hysterically at an animated picture the teacher was showing on the overhead projector. Arthur could not resist making remarks about the lesson and challenged the teacher on her interpretation of the facts. When he was sent to the principal's office because of his disruptive and disrespectful attitude, Arthur openly confronted the principal for hiring a teacher who couldn't teach and stated furthermore that he could teach the class better himself.

In this scenario, Arthur displays many of the symptoms typical of childhood-onset BD.

Prevalence and Course

Prevalence rates are relatively unknown in child populations, however, adolescent prevalence has been suggested to be around 1% of the population. One of the difficulties in obtaining accurate prevalence rates is the fact that bipolar disorders are difficult to diagnose in children and adolescents, since the disorder shares features of other common child and adolescent disorders (e.g., ADHD, ODD). In addition, identification of "elation, grandiosity, and/or increased goal activity" may be very difficult to separate from age-appropriate behaviors, because youth at times will be "overly happy, silly, and goofy," while grandiosity may be difficult to distinguish from children's tendencies to overestimate their capabilities (Birmaher, 2013).

Etiology

Biological and Genetic Background

Family history is strongly associated with bipolar disorder.

DON'T FORGET

Aggressive behavior can be a common characteristic of BD. According to Steiner (2000), aggression associated with BD is often of the escalating type.

DON'T FORGET

Heredity is strongly associated with BD. Studies have found a 30% to 40% risk of inheriting BD in those with one bipolar parent and as high as a 50% to 70% risk if both parents have a major affective disorder (Levine, 1999).

Assessment and Treatment/Interventions

Differential Diagnosis

Bipolar disorder can often be confused with ADHD and CD due to the existence of overlapping symptoms. Children or adolescents who seem depressed and also demonstrate symptoms that resemble those of ADHD but are more severe (excessive temper outbursts, rapid mood swings) should be evaluated for the existence of BD, especially if family history is positive for the disorder (NIMH, 2000a).

According to Geller (2001), the biggest problem in the diagnosis of BD in children is how to tell a child with mania from a child with ADHD (p. 4).

When one reviews the diagnostic criteria for mania, it is readily apparent that almost half of the criteria (decreased need for sleep, excessive talking, distractibility, irritable mood) are symptoms shared by ADHD. Geller and colleagues (2001) have responded to the challenge by going back and focusing on the *DSM* definition of mania and finding the two cardinal features of mania (elation and grandiosity), then combining these two features into one necessary criterion. Geller and colleagues believed that using this criteria would assist in distinguishing between BD and ADHD. Additionally, the manic symptom of hypersexuality was found in 43% of the bipolar sample in the absence of any reported history of sexual abuse.

Treatment Alternatives

Due to the complex nature of BD in children and adolescents, a multimodal treatment plan that combines medications and psychotherapeutic interventions and emphasizes relapse prevention has been recommended (AACAP, 1997). In their review of lithium, a mood stabilizer that has been used in the treatment of BD in children and youth, Tueth, Murphy, and Evans (1998) suggest that lithium is well tolerated by children and adolescents. However, there are a number of reported side effects that may make compliance difficult to maintain in adolescent populations: stomach upset, nausea, overeating, weight gain, tremor, enuresis, and acne. In studies of adolescent noncompliance, 90% of youth who were noncompliant with lithium relapsed in an 18-month time span (Strober, Morrell, Lanpert, & Burroughs, 1990).

DON'T FORGET

Mania, unlike the euphoric states of adult bipolar symptoms, may present as irritable and destructive outbursts in children. Early-onset BD (prior to puberty) is often characterized by rapid cycling and irritability and may often co-occur with CD and ADHD or have symptoms that closely mimic these two disorders. Later-onset (adolescence) BD tends to have a sudden and acute onset, often starting with a manic episode and showing less cormorbidity with ADHD and CD (NIMH, 2000).

CAUTION

The use of antidepressants to treat depression in an individual with BD may precipitate manic symptoms if taken without a mood stabilizer. Furthermore, stimulant medication for ADHD-like symptoms in a child with BD can exacerbate manic symptoms (NIMH, 2000).

Suicide: Clinical Description and Associated Features

Children and adolescents with suicidal ideation experience intense feelings of depression, anger, hopelessness, anxiety, and worthlessness. They often feel helpless and ineffective to change circumstances that cause them overwhelming psychological pain. Children and adolescents who contemplate suicide have suicidal thoughts, or what is called *suicidal ideation*. Not all children who have thoughts of suicide will engage in a suicide attempt, however, and fortunately not all attempts will result in a completed suicide. While females are more likely than males to attempt suicide, males are more likely to succeed in completed suicides.

DON'T FORGET

Three times as many females attempt suicide, but four times as many males succeed in completed suicides.

The reason for the disparity between attempts and completions is in the lethality of the methods used. Females tend to attempt suicide through drug overdose, whereas males use guns (60% of males die of self-inflicted gunshot wounds), hanging, and other more violent means (Garland & Zigler, 1993).

Risk Factors for Suicide

Substance abuse, aggressive or disruptive behaviors, and depression have all been cited as the strongest predictors of suicide attempts in children and youth.

Since substance abuse and alcohol are implicated in approximately 50% of suicides, it has been suggested that increasing rates of suicide among adolescents may be related to increased rates of alcohol abuse (Brent, 1995). Lewinsohn, Clarke, Seeley, and Rohde (1994) found that youth with previous suicide attempts were 18 times more likely to attempt suicide again than youth who had not attempted suicide.

CAUTION

Having depression or BD are major risk factors for suicide. As many as 7% of adolescents who develop a MDD will commit suicide prior to reaching middle adulthood (Weissman et al., 1999).

Further information from Shaffer and colleagues (1996) revealed that 66% of those who completed suicides had at least one of three main risk factors: prior suicide attempt, substance or alcohol abuse, and evidence of a

CAUTION

One of the strongest predictors of a future suicide attempt is a previous suicide attempt. Shaffer and colleagues (1996) found that 30% of adolescents who committed suicide had at least one previous attempt.

mood disorder. In addition, the authors found that a life stressor usually precipitated the suicide attempt.

CAUTION

Common precipitating life stressors for suicide attempts in adolescents include loss of a relationship, teen pregnancy, physical or sexual abuse, disciplinary crisis or trouble with school or the law, conflict with parents or conflict in the home between parents, exposure to suicide (which can cause a contagion effect), and a recent move (Shaffer et al., 1996).

Suicide and Protective Factors

Borowsky, Ireland, and Resnick (2001) investigated protective factors that might guard against suicide attempts in black, Hispanic, and white adolescents. Results revealed that common protective factors that cut across all ethnic groups were academic achievement and connectedness to parents, family, and school. Additionally, emotional well-being (for all females) and high grade-point average (for all males) were also safeguards. Further analysis revealed that the presence of three protective factors reduced suicide risk by 70% to 80%. Based on their findings, Borowsky and colleagues suggest the need to evaluate the role of suicide prevention programs using multisystemic therapy (MST) to focus on improving parenting skills, decreasing negative and coercive parenting practices, and strengthening family cohesion and connectedness.

Suicide Prevention Programs

Although school-based screening for suicide risk and prevention programs are common, few have met with positive outcomes, and some even increase the risk, known as an *iatrogenic effect* (when treatments harm). Overholser, Hemstreet, Spirito, and Vyse (1989) reported that in their study, students who were most in need of protection responded that they felt even more distressed and hopeless after participating in the program.

One empirically supported program that has been very successful is the Signs of Suicide (SOS) Prevention Program, which noted a 40% reduction in suicide attempts in students participating in the program (Aseltine, 2003; Aseltine & DiMartino, 2004; Aseltine, James, Schilling, & Glanovsky, 2007). The secondary school program treats suicidal ideation as a medical emergency, and students are trained to recognize the warning signs and to respond according to the principles inherent in ACT: **A**cknowledge the signs; let them know you **C**are; and **T**ell a responsible adult. During the 2004–2005 academic year, the program had been launched in more than 650 schools nationwide.

TEST YOURSELF

1. **Depressed mood in children is often expressed as**
   (a) crying.
   (b) irritability.
   (c) pervasive sadness.
   (d) fatigue.
2. **Double depression refers to**
   (a) having depression for twice as long as normal.
   (b) persistent depressive disorder developing into major depression.
   (c) two bipolar episodes back to back.
   (d) a unipolar episode followed by a bipolar episode.
3. **According to *DSM persistend depressive disorder* in children requires symptoms to be present for**
   (a) 2 months.
   (b) 2 years.
   (c) 1 month.
   (d) 1 year.
4. **Currently, it is believed that childhood depression is caused by______ and adolescent depression is due to______.**
   (a) situational influences, genetic influences
   (b) genetic influences, situation influences
   (c) situational influences, situation influences
   (d) genetic influences, genetic influences
5. **Although more ______ attempt suicide, more ______ are successful.**
   (a) males, females
   (b) females, males
   (c) children, adolescents
   (d) males, males
6. **Cognitive theorists attribute depression to the cognitive triad. Which of the following components is not part of the triad?**
   (a) Hopelessness
   (b) Helplessness
   (c) Uselessness
   (d) Worthlessness

7. **Cicchetti and Toth developed a model of depression based on the**
   (a) cognitive attributions model.
   (b) ecological transactional model.
   (c) psychodynamic model.
   (d) internalizing-externalizing model.
8. **Compared to adults, children with bipolar disorder tend to have cycles that are**
   (a) longer and less intense.
   (b) shorter and less intense.
   (c) brief, intense, and rapid cycling.
   (d) the same as adult bipolar disorder.

Answers: 1. b; 2. b; 3. d; 4. a; 5. b; 6. c; 7. b; 8. c

Nine

SOMATIC SYMPTOM AND RELATED DISORDERS

It is not uncommon for children to complain of aches and pains that do not have a medical basis. In fact, functional somatic complaints, with medically unexplained symptoms, account for approximately 20% of child visits to pediatric clinics (Robinson, Greene, & Walker, 1988). Whereas children and youth with serious physical illness often demonstrate a progressive decline in school performance, health, and physical well-being, children who are somatizers often have a more rapid onset, tend to have families with similar symptom presentations, and have no physical basis for the somatic complaints.

SOMATIC SYMPTOM DISORDER

Clinical Description and Associated Features

Somatic symptom disorder and other related disorders is a new category for the *DSM-5*. Previously known as the somatoform disorders, disorders in this category share features of predominant somatic symptoms that manifest in the presence of significant distress and impairment. Some of the disorders contained in this category include somatic symptom disorder, illness anxiety disorder, conversion disorder, and factitious disorder. (See Rapid Reference 9.1.) In the *DSM-5*, the emphasis has shifted from concentrating on symptom presentation without any physical cause or medical explanation to the abnormal thoughts, feelings, and behaviors that accompany these symptoms. To this end, the criteria required for a diagnosis of somatic symptom disorder include the following:

1. The presence of somatic symptoms (one or more) causing significant distress or dysfunction, lasting for 6 months

2. Thoughts, feelings, or behaviors surrounding these symptoms, which are either:
   (a) In excess of the seriousness of the presentation
   (b) Accompanied by excessive anxiety
   (c) Behavioral preoccupation (time, effort) surrounding symptoms or health (p. 311)

Specifiers can be added to distinguish if the symptoms include pain (with predominant pain) or persistence (in excess of six months).

The new classification is more appropriate than somatization disorder for diagnostic purposes related to child problems, since somatization disorder required the inclusion of one symptom of sexual dysfunction, which was not developmentally appropriate.

In their investigation of child and youth somatization, Garber and colleagues (1991) collected responses to the Children's Somatization Inventory (CSI) from 540 school-aged children and adolescents in Tennessee. Responses indicated that 50% of children and youth surveyed reported at least one somatic complaint, 15% reported four or more symptoms, and 1% had 12 or more symptoms. There was increased reporting of multiple symptoms with increasing age. In this survey, approximately 11% of adolescent boys and 15% of adolescent girls reported multiple somatic complaints.

CAUTION

Although the majority of somatic complaints precipitated by environmental stressors are transient and usually dissipate as the stress subsides, for some children somatization can become a recurrent and debilitating condition that may eventually manifest as a disorder, if somatic symptoms become the focal point and interfere with relationships (at home and school) and academic performance.

Disorders in this category collectively represent physical and somatic complaints that *do not* have a medical or organic basis, and emotional distress is experienced as physical or somatic discomfort and/or pain. Most often, a relationship can be established between the onset of the somatic complaint and the introduction of a psychosocial stressor. Although most individuals with these disorders do not pretend to be ill or fake illness, those with factitious disorder imposed on self do feign illness in themselves or others (factitious disorder imposed on another), but unlike malingering, they do not feign illness for material reward, rather the deception is motivated by a desire to be seen as "ill" or "injured" and may develop after actually being hospitalized for a medical illness or injury. Although the majority of those with somatic symptom disorders have complaints that are distressing to them and interfere with daily functioning, the pain and distress that these individuals feel is not under their voluntary control, and responses occur at a subconscious level. However, those with factitious disorders are distressed if the symptom presentations are not believed by others, and they may actually engage in self-harm to create an illness that requires medical attention.

The *DSM-IV-TR* (APA, 2000) recognized six different subtypes of somatic disorders, in two categories: (1) the hysterical disorders (somatization disorder, undifferentiated somatization disorder, conversion disorder, and pain disorder), and (2) the preoccupation disorders (hypochondriasis and body dysmorphic disorder). The *DSM-5* has eliminated the subcategory of hysterical disorders, reduced the number of different types of symptom disorders, and relocated body dysmorphic disorder within the chapter on obsessive-compulsive and related disorders (see Chapter 7). The classification of hypochondriasis has been dropped, and individuals who are preoccupied with a fear of having a serious illness can be classified as having either a somatic symptom disorder or illness anxiety disorder, depending on the nature and severity of the preoccupation with having a severe illness, in the absence of medical evidence to support a medical diagnosis.

Rapid Reference 9.1

Somatic Symptom and Related Disorders

Disorders	Actual Loss or Change in Physical Functioning
Somatic symptom disorder	Presence of one or more symptoms causing significant distress or dysfunction Excessive preoccupation in thoughts, feelings, and behaviors associated with the symptoms
Illness anxiety disorder	Preoccupation with fear of having a serious disease now or at some future time Excessive anxiety related to potential health issues Behavioral tasks related to illness (repeated checking/avoidance)
Conversion disorder	Loss of function (motor/sensory) without medical basis and incompatible with recognized conditions; causes significant distress and impairment
Factitious disorder imposed on self	Individual presents as if ill, feigning symptoms of illness or injury, but is not malingering for material gain
Factitious disorder imposed on another	An individual induces signs of illness, injury in another (e.g., a parent can induce illness in a child), but motives are not for material gain

Somatic Symptoms From a Developmental Perspective

In a study of the use of healthcare services by children and youth, Schor (1986) found that children's responsiveness to stressful life events peaked at two transition periods: transition to elementary school and entry into middle/junior high school. Furthermore, physical complaints resulted in an increased use of healthcare services during these times to investigate the nature and causes of somatic complaints. Studies have demonstrated that stress can impact on emotional well-being in children, resulting in numerous somatic complaints (Garber et al., 1991).

Somatic complaints have also been associated with depression and anxiety in children and youth, but because many of the measurements developed to assess anxiety and depression also include items with somatic content (headaches, stomachaches, nausea, etc.), the nature of the association is not clear. The situation is further complicated by the fact that depression in young children is more likely to be precipitated by stressful environmental determinants than by genetic factors (Thapar et al., 1998). Somatic complaints (e.g., not feeling well, headaches, stomachaches) can be the presenting symptoms or comorbid symptoms of depression and anxiety in children. Somatic symptoms are often precipitated by environmental stressors. Children undergoing stressful situations report higher rates of somatic symptoms than do children who are not experiencing stressful circumstances (Campo & Fritsch, 1994).

> **DON'T FORGET**
>
> The association between symptoms of anxiety, depression, and somatic complaints has been well established in the literature, as symptoms from these syndromes all cluster under the dimension of internalizing problems (Achenbach & Rescorla, 2001).

Garber and colleagues (1991) found many common somatic complaints in their pediatric population, including headaches, fatigue, sore muscles, abdominal and back pain, and blurred vision. The most frequently reported symptoms were headaches, low energy, sore muscles, nausea or stomach upset, and back and stomach pain. Children who were high somatizers (i.e., who responded with the most symptoms) tended to endorse the following somatic categories: headaches (25%), low energy (21%), sore muscles (21%), and abdominal discomfort (17%). Factor analysis of the CSI responses revealed a four-factor solution: pseudoneurologic, cardiovascular, gastrointestinal, and pain/weakness.

A review of studies on pain symptoms in children reveals a developmental course that can predict the nature of children's somatic complaints. Initially, children present with a *predominant symptom* (rather than multiple symptoms).

The most commonly reported somatic complaints in prepubertal children are headaches and abdominal pain (Garber et al., 1991).

Studies have also demonstrated a continuity between these unexplained symptoms in childhood and symptoms experienced in adulthood (Hotopf, 2002). Later-occurring symptoms (adolescence) include pain in the extremities, muscle aches, fatigue, and neurological symptoms (Walker, Garber, & Greene, 1991).

Although children often translate symptoms of stress into physical complaints, it is important to differentiate between feigning illness to avoid a laborious task (homework, school tests) and symptoms of "true" somatization. If a child is intentionally producing symptoms of illness to assume a "sick role," then the disorder is more appropriately categorized as a factitious disorder imposed on self. If illness is feigned to avoid a task, then the label is more appropriately one of malingering. Individuals with factitious disorders often are reinforced by unconscious secondary gain (i.e., attention provided because they appear ill). However, malingering is motivated by primary gain: There is an ulterior motive to appearing ill.

Although children commonly respond to psychosocial stressors with reported physical and somatic complaints, a diagnosis of somatization disorder in children was rare in the past, because (a) criteria were developed for adult populations; (b) onset was late due to a usual history of several years' duration (doctor shopping); and (c) eight different symptoms, including one sexual symptom, were required. As a result, the newly formed category of somatic symptom disorder is a much better fit for developmental populations.

DON'T FORGET

Developmentally, abdominal pain seems to precede complaints of headaches. Studies have found that recurrent abdominal pain (RAP) is frequently related to emotional symptoms in children and their parents (Garber, Zeman, & Walker, 1990).

DON'T FORGET

Developmentally, young children usually present with one symptom (*monosymptomatic*) and with increasing age report multiple symptoms (*polysymptomatic*).

CAUTION

The difference between factitious disorder and malingering is one of motivation. Although both conditions involve an intention to appear ill, in factitious disorder the intent is to assume a sick role, with no primary gain. In malingering, although illness may also be feigned, the motivation would be for primary gain.

DON'T FORGET

The symptoms of somatic disorder must have no medical basis, or if there is a medical problem, symptoms must be in excess of that which would be expected.

Reviewing the literature concerning the nature and history of somatic complaints in children, Fritz, Fritsch, and Hagino (1997) suggest that the rarity of diagnosis of somatization disorder in children and youth most likely reflected the "developmentally inappropriate" nature of the criteria rather than the disorder's having an adult onset. Support for this suggestion can be found in reports of adult patients who have presented with severe forms of somatic disorder. These patients often disclosed a history of illness beginning in childhood (Hotopf, 2002).

PUTTING IT INTO PRACTICE

Sara was very difficult to manage at home. In fact, Sara was so demanding that her mother, Grace, sent Sara to live with her grandparents in New York when Grace returned to Georgia with her new husband. Sara missed a lot of school because of illness, which never could be diagnosed (headaches, stomachaches, body aches, and fatigue). Her grandparents ultimately could not handle the constant doctor appointments and medical bills, and eventually they returned Sara to her mother. Despite being very bright and an A student until middle school, Sara had spent the past 2 years in special education programs because she was too emotionally distracted and had missed too much school. Diagnosed with anxiety and depression, Sara was taking several different medications. The school was calling Grace on a daily basis, saying that Sara was falling asleep in class and complaining of fatigue, headaches, and stomach problems. Sara spent most afternoons sleeping in the nurse's office, because she was "too tired" to lift her head. Despite numerous trips to the doctor and numerous medical tests, the doctors could find no physical cause for Sara's somatic complaints.

Specifier: With Predominant Pain

When somatic symptom disorder is accompanied by a marked level of pain that causes distress and a functional impairment, the specifier "with predominant pain" may be added. The disorder is thought to be precipitated by psychosocial factors, and the pain is not due to malingering. Pain is a difficult condition to measure due to its subjective nature. In children, the situation of measurement becomes even more complex because of limitations in the use of self-report at younger ages. Although very young children can demonstrate awareness of pain or hurting initially in themselves and eventually in others, it is not until school age that children can articulate the intensity (level) of pain and associated feelings.

Recurrent Abdominal Pain

Recurrent abdominal pain (RAP) is clinically defined as having three or more episodes of reported pain over a 3-month period, with the pain being severe enough to interfere with normal functioning. Although the etiology is unknown, medical review often is unable to determine an organic cause for the pain in the majority of RAP cases.

In pediatric populations, RAP is a high-incidence and potentially seriously disabling condition. Garber and colleagues (1991) found that between 10% and 30% of children and adolescents present with RAP. Studies have also suggested that RAP can be a durable and long-term condition. Children who reported RAP at 4 years of age were likely to continue patterns and were three times more likely than their peers to demonstrate RAP 6 years later (Borge, Nordhagen, Botten, & Bakketeig, 1994).

Prevalence and Course

Given the difficulties associated with previous diagnostic criteria, little is known about the prevalence rates for somatic disorder in childhood and adolescence (Fritz et al., 1997). However, in their study of somatization complaints, Offord and colleagues (1987) found that between 11% of females and 4% of males (12 to 16 years) were identified as having recurrent and distressing somatic complaints. Available data concerning adolescent populations suggest that symptoms associated with somatic complaints, such as headaches, stomachache, dizziness, and pain, are a relatively frequent occurrence (Taylor, Szatmari, Boyle, & Offord, 1996). In their study of 1,035 adolescents (12 to 17 years of age) residing in Bremen, Germany, researchers Essau, Conradt, and Petermann (2000) found that 11% of their sample reported criteria that matched undifferentiated somatoform disorder, which had less stringent requirements more closely resembling current criteria for somatic symptom disorder.

In their study, Essau and colleagues found that at least two-thirds of their sample reported having one symptom, which lasted for six months. The most commonly reported symptoms were headaches (15.5%), lump in the throat (14.4%), and abdominal pain (12.4%). They also found gender differences, which supported other findings. Boys report more headaches at a younger age, whereas girls report more headaches as teens (Abu-Arefeh & Russell, 1994). The disorder seems to have a familial and gender course, with up to 10% to 20% of females developing the disorder in families in which a close relative also had the disorder (APA, 2000). Females tend to endorse more somatic complaints than males (Garber et al., 1991).

Barkmann, Braehler, Schulte-Markwort, and Richterich (2011) found that psychosocial stress was the single highest predictor for chronic somatic complaints (CSC) in their population of 1,027 German children and youth, 11 to 18 years of age. In this sample, the most frequent complaints were related to skin problems, cold hands, and fatigue. CSC were also overrepresented in females in this sample. In addition, the researchers found that parents significantly underestimated CSC, especially in males. Zolog and colleagues (2011) found that among their population of fourth- to sixth-grade children in Spain, the most prevalent symptom was abdominal pain (11.2%), followed by headaches (10.1%). In this population, children with the lightest level of physical complaints had more symptoms of anxiety and depression and overall impairment at home, school, and with peers.

DON'T FORGET

Females with somatic complaints also tend to have either anxiety or depression, while males with the disorder are also at risk for substance problems (Essau et al., 1999). There are high rates of association between reporting somatic complaints, anxiety, and depression (Zolog et al., 2011).

Etiology

Studies have investigated several risk factors associated with somatic symptoms, including parental divorce (Zoccolillo & Cloniger, 1985), parent illness (Hotopf, 2002), and child sexual abuse (Kinzl, Trawegert, & Biebl, 1995). Children can respond to stress in various ways based on their temperament and the extent and nature of family support systems. Children often convert stress into physical symptoms. Some precipitating situations that can be particularly stressful in childhood include transitions to new school programs, parent divorce, a relocation or move, and being overwhelmed academically. Somatization can become a child's way of attempting to cope with life's stresses, which can have maladaptive consequences.

Biological and Genetic Factors

Wender and Klein (1981) found that higher risk for somatic disorders occurred in families with antisocial personality disorder, ADHD, alcoholism, and other somatic disorders. Twin studies have been inconclusive. Studies of temperament have increased our understanding of how inhibited (shy or wary) children may be less able to cope with severe environmental demands. These children may be more sensitive emotionally and prone to internalizing disorders due to their low threshold for uncertainty and their poor coping mechanisms.

Psychodynamic Perspective

Psychodynamic theorists discuss hysteria in terms of primary and secondary gain. In psychodynamic terms, somatic complaints can represent unconscious conflicts, so that physical pain represents psychic pain. Being unable to deal with someone who is a pain in the neck might literally translate into neck stiffness, while being sick to the stomach might reflect being unable to stomach a situation any longer. Primary and secondary gain can be explained in the following way: At a primary level, hysterical or physical symptoms keep conflicts out of conscious awareness. The person is able to focus on the physical problem rather than the psychic pain. On a secondary level, the debilitation caused by the physical problem usually removes the person from the responsibility of having to confront a distasteful task.

CAUTION

Out of psychic awareness, out of mind. A supervisor who did not want to fire his best friend had developed a paralysis in the hand when he awoke the next morning. As a result, he was unable to sign the termination papers (conversion disorder).

PUTTING IT INTO PRACTICE

Wanda is having a great afternoon chatting with an old college roommate whom she hasn't seen for years. The conversation has gone on for quite some time, and 5-year-old Amy, Wanda's daughter, has had enough of this boring afternoon tea party. After several unsuccessful attempts to get her mother's attention, Amy does the inevitable. She complains to her mother that she is "not feeling well." Her stomach hurts, she says, and she asks if they can please go home now.

DON'T FORGET

The measurement and monitoring of intensity of pain can be accomplished successfully in children as young as 5 years of age by having children select intensity levels using graduated scaling techniques presented in graphic form: for example, a series of facial expressions or rising thermometer (Biere, Reeve, Champion, & Addicoat, 1990).

CAUTION

There has been some speculation that children with RAP may have heightened somatic awareness or hypersensitivity. Absenteeism is high in children and adolescents with RAP and has been reported to be as high as 10% of the academic year (Liebman, 1978).

DON'T FORGET

Similar to results of investigations of other somatic disorders, family factors seem to play a key role in the presence of RAP in children. Investigators have found increased rates of depression and anxiety in children with RAP and in their mothers (Garber et al., 1990). Walker, Garber, and Greene (1991) found that, compared to controls, child characteristics for RAP included significantly more emotional and somatic complaints, while family characteristics included increased emphasis on family illness.

Behavioral Perspective

A behavioral explanation for the development of a somatic disorder would be linked to reinforcements received for being ill and/or learned behaviors through modeling a family member who was also chronically ill. Some of the secondary gains for being ill might be increased attention and reduced expectations.

Cognitive Perspective

The cognitive perspective would explore how maladaptive thoughts might translate into physical symptoms. Clinical practice suggests that children often express their desire for attention by communicating with parents through physical symptoms.

Family and Parenting

Having a parent who has a chronic physical illness may predispose children to somatic disorders later in life (Garber et al., 1990; Hotopf, 2002). Furthermore, family systems theory might predict that having a child with an apparent illness could help deflect the family focus from other family problems. Within this framework, family members can redefine their roles to focus on the sick child while averting emphasis from other potentially conflicted areas of family or marital life. Children who somaticize often have families that also share anxious and depressive features (Garber et al., 1990).

Culture

Adult populations worldwide reveal many differences in the types and rates of somatic symptoms (APA, 2000). For example, the *DSM-IV-TR* (APA, 2000) mentions symptoms specific to Africa and South Asia, including burning sensations in the hands and feet and the sensation of "worms crawling in the head or ants crawling under the skin" (p. 487). Although research is definitely lacking concerning child and adolescent cross-cultural comparisons, with children cultural differences have been reported in the rates (but not necessarily types) of somatic complaints (Bird, 1996). One cross-cultural study revealed that Russian children had higher scores than American children on the Somatic Complaint scale of the Achenbach Child Behavior Checklist (Carter, Grigorenko, & Pauls, 1995). However, regardless of differential rates of reporting across cultures, several studies have reported that strong associations between somatic complaints and symptoms of anxiety and depression are universal (Carter et al., 1995; Garber et al., 1991).

CONVERSION DISORDER

Clinical Description and Associated Features

Of all the somatic disorders, conversion disorder is the most frequently and commonly researched area in children (Regan & Regan, 1989). Conversion disorder was initially called Hysterical Neurosis (Conversion Type) in the second revision of the *DSM* (APA, 1968) and is referred to as dissociative (conversion) disorder in the 10th revision of the *International Classification of Diseases* (*ICD-10*; WHO, 1993). Conversion disorder is a condition that usually consists of a single somatic symptom that impacts on normal motor or sensory function, and occurs when psychological conflicts manifest dramatically in physical symptoms that cause debilitating results but have no medical or organic basis. Symptoms suggest a medical or neurological basis (pseudoneurological), but upon investigation results are negative. The disorder may appear immediately after the stressful event or after a delay.

CAUTION

Although the individual may claim paralysis, as in hand paralysis (glove anesthesia) or foot paralysis (foot anesthesia), symptoms will not follow the normal neurological pathway (e.g., paralysis will stop at the wrist or ankle, which is anatomically impossible). Conversion symptoms are also inconsistent, with the patient being able to move the purportedly paralyzed limb if distracted.

The symptom or deficit is not intentionally produced but is induced by stressors or psychosocial conflicts that can initiate and exacerbate the condition. Some of the manifestations of the disorder include problems with balance or localized weakness, paralysis, difficulty swallowing (lump in the throat), loss of sensitivity (touch), double vision, blindness or deafness, convulsions (seizures), and hallucinations.

There are several associated features that represent extreme variations of an individual's reaction to the loss of function, ranging from *la belle indifférence* (lack of concern about the symptoms) to displaying symptoms in a dramatic or histrionic manner. In children under 10 years of age, conversion symptoms are most likely to be expressed as seizures or problems of gait (*DSM-5*; APA, 2013). Symptoms that have been reported more frequently by children and adolescents include pseudoseizures, disturbances of gait, and paralysis (Leslie, 1988).

Prevalence and Course

Conversion disorder is rarely diagnosed prior to 10 years of age and is generally diagnosed in late childhood to early adulthood (APA, 2000). In children and youth, the disorder may peak in the middle school years. One common preschool-aged phenomenon is a tendency for young children to develop a pseudoparesis or limp after a minor injury. The limp may last for a few hours or continue for days (Fritz et al., 1997). The most likely explanation for prolonging this behavior seems to be the attention received as secondary gain. The most common form of conversion disorder is pseudoseizures, which represent between 15% and 50% of all conversion disorders (Fritz et al., 1997). Although pseudoseizures look very much like real seizures, electroencephalograms (EEGs) reveal no actual seizure activity.

Etiology

Based on limited data, research seems to indicate that risk for conversion disorder might be familial; however, support has been limited to monozygotic but not dizygotic twins (APA, 2000). Although there is limited support for genetic transmission, environmental risk factors, such as family factors, have been implicated in contributing to how the disorder is expressed and maintained.

DON'T FORGET

Investigations of possible etiological factors have focused on the types of stressors and conditions that might place children at greater risk for conversion disorders.

Risks and Protective Factors

Stressors

Although it would be assumed that the vast majority of children with conversion disorder have experienced stressful circumstances, Siegel and Barthel (1986) found that as many as 90% of children with conversion disorder had encountered a recent and significant stressor at home or school. Some of the most common stressors identified are peer relationship difficulties, family discord or marital problems, academic difficulties, and economic hardship or unemployment in the family (Lehmkuhl, Blanz, Lehmkuhl, & Braun-Scharm, 1989).

> **DON'T FORGET**
>
> Families of children with conversion disorders often share many of the same characteristics: preoccupation with illness, communication focused on disease and loss, and hyperawareness of and sensitivity to bodily functions or dysfunction.

Family Characteristics

Studies have shown that children whose family members have a chronic illness are more likely to model similar symptoms themselves (Siegel & Barthel, 1986). Seltzer (1985) outlines several possible family types as determined by their response to having a child with conversion disorder: anxious families (preoccupied with illness), chaotic families (in which somatization is a source of nurturance and attention), and compensating families, who, according to the family systems model, use the sick child to deflect family problems.

Previous Illness

Investigators report that conversion disorder develops in some children following a legitimate illness. Fritz and colleagues (1997) report that between 10% and 60% of children who have a conversion disorder had a previous illness.

ILLNESS ANXIETY DISORDER

Clinical Description and Associated Features

Individuals who suffer from illness anxiety disorder believe, erroneously, that they have a serious medical illness. Lacking physical evidence to substantiate the multiple symptoms that they present, these individuals will often engage in so-called doctor shopping, seeking out someone to support their claims. The belief that they are seriously ill is not within their control, nor are they malingering.

Illness anxiety disorder replaces hypochondriasis disorder and is used to classify a disorder characterized by a preoccupation with having a disease now or at some point in the future. The disorder is marked by thoughts, feelings (anxiety), and behaviors (repeatedly checking health status, avoiding precarious situations) that evolve around excessive health concerns. If an individual has a health issue, the preoccupation, distress, and concern is well beyond that attributed to the health problem. The disorder causes significant distress and dysfunction.

CAUTION

The preoccupation and obsession with their pseudo-serious medical disease may have the same underlying dynamics as the symptoms of individuals with OCD. The comorbidity between these two disorders has been rated as high as 8% (Barsky, 1992). However, while people with OCD are often painfully aware of the unreasonableness of their obsessions and compulsions, individuals with anxiety illness disorder truly are convinced that they are seriously ill.

DON'T FORGET

Elkind and Bowen (1979) described two common adolescent preoccupations: *imaginary fable* (thoughts about one's own uniqueness) and *imaginary audience* (preoccupation with being the center of scrutiny and others' observations).

Assessment and Treatment of Somatic and Related Disorders

Due to the nature of somatic and related disorders, assessment will often require considerable medical input to rule out organic causes. In addition, because somatizers believe the pain is related to medical reasons, they may not be willing or able to understand the need for therapeutic intervention. Due to high rates of comorbidity among the child and adolescent disorders, and because investigations have reported comorbid associations between somatizing and depression, anxiety, and OCD, differential diagnosis should be undertaken whenever somatoform disorders are suspected.

Very little has been documented regarding assessment and intervention of somatic disorders in children and adolescents. Clinical experience would suggest the use of the structured and semistructured interviews as a start. Also, several rating scales and personality inventories include a somatic scale as a component. A list of these instruments can be found in Rapid Reference 9.2.

In the absence of empirically based findings regarding treatment for somatoform disorders in children and adolescents, once again clinical experience would suggest the use of behavioral or cognitive-behavioral methods that integrate components of systematic desensitization and educational awareness of the disorder.

Rapid Reference 9.2

Some Common Instruments That Contain Scales That Measure Somatic Complaints

Instrument	Ages	Scale
Personality Inventory for Youth (PIY; Lachar & Gruber, 1995)	7 to 17	The PIY Somatic Concerns scale has three subscales: Psychosomatic Syndrome, Muscular Tension and Anxiety, and Preoccupation with Disease.
ASEBA (Achenbach & Rescorla, 2001)	6 to 18	The Somatic Complaints Syndrome scale and the Somatic Problems (*DSM*-oriented scales) are available on all three versions of the ASEBA (parent, teacher, and self-report).
CPRS-R:L (Conners, 1998)	3 to 17	Parent rating scale contains a Psychosomatic subscale.
BASC-2 (Reynolds & Kamphaus, 2004)	3 to 17	All three versions of the BASC2 (parent, teacher, self-report) contain a Somatization scale.

Note: References for all instruments can be found in Appendix B.

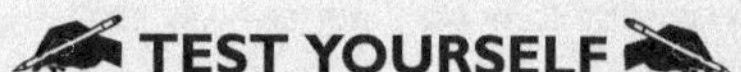

TEST YOURSELF

1. Diagnosis of somatization disorder was rare in childhood because

(a) children do not experience somatic symptoms.
(b) children cannot articulate their somatic symptoms.
(c) children do not recognize somatic concerns at a conscious level.
(d) the *DSM* criteria were developmentally inappropriate.

2. Illness anxiety disorder replaces the previous category of

(a) hysteria nervosa.
(b) Briquet's syndrome.
(c) hypochondriasis.
(d) pseudopsychoillness.

3. Which of the following is TRUE regarding somatic disorders (SD)?

(a) Males with SD are at greater risk for substance problems.
(b) Females with SD report greater memory problems.
(c) SD is linked to anxiety but not depression.
(d) Family links to SD have not been investigated or substantiated.

4. The new category of somatic disorders differs from the previous category of somatization disorder in that

(a) it only requires half as many symptoms.
(b) only five generalized symptoms are required.
(c) it requires only one physical complaint for at least 6 months.
(d) only one physical complaint for at least 1 year.

5. Somatic symptoms in children and adolescents differ. Which of the following statements is TRUE?

(a) Younger children present with multiple symptoms, while adolescents present with one primary symptom.
(b) Teens usually have fewer somatic complaints than younger children.
(c) The most commonly reported symptoms in younger children are headaches and stomach pain.
(d) Recurrent abdominal pain (RAP) in children has no relationship to parent or family medical symptoms.

6. Intentionally producing symptoms of illness in order to gain secondary rewards, such as increased attention, would be referred to as

(a) Malingering.
(b) Factitious disorder.
(c) Conversion disorder.
(d) illness by proxy.

7. John is planning to run in a marathon when he discovers that one of the competitors is a former lover, whom he cannot face or run against. When he wakes up on the morning of the race he cannot move his foot below the ankle. John would likely be diagnosed with

(a) neurasthenia.
(b) pseudopedia.
(c) Conversion disorder.
(d) Body dysmorphic disorder.

8. Which of the following is TRUE regarding recurrent abdominal pain (RAP)?

(a) RAP represents a low incidence condition in pediatric populations.
(b) Between 5% and 10% of children and teens present with RAP.
(c) Absenteeism has been reported as high as 10% in those with RAP.
(d) Family factors do not influence RAP in children.

Answers: 1. d; 2. c; 3. a; 4. c; 5. c; 6. b; 7. c; 8. c

Part IV

Disruptive Behavior Disorders

Whereas internalizing disorders are often difficult to diagnose and assess due to their covert and internal nature, externalizing problems are often intrusive, disruptive, and frequently involve aggressive responses that can be physically and verbally intimidating. By the time that parents or teachers appeal for help from professionals in managing these very difficult behaviors, the situation is often one in which the child is *out of control—and in control.*

Longitudinal studies (Tremblay et al., 1999) have demonstrated that, normally, overt acts of aggression peak in the second year and diminish with age as children become more socialized. However, not all children follow this preferred developmental path. For some children, overt aggression is a stable pattern of behavior lasting from middle school well into adolescence. This pattern or developmental trajectory of increased aggressive responses seems particularly durable for early starters (Aguilar, Sroufe, Egeland, & Carlson, 2000). In the first three years of development, Aguilar and colleagues found that the following family characteristics placed children at the greatest risk for developing disruptive behavior disorders: avoidant attachment, caregiver depression, stress, low SES, caregiver sensitivity, and quality of caregiving.

The *DSM-5* lists several disorders in this category, all sharing features of problems in an individual's ability to control the expression of his or her emotions or behaviors, which can result in the violations of the rights of others (personal or property violation) and can place the individual at odds with authority figures and societal norms. Disorders in this chapter that are relevant to child and adolescent psychopathology include oppositional defiant disorder, intermittent explosive disorder, conduct disorder, pyromania, and kleptomania. Although antisocial personality disorder is dually situated in this and the chapter on personality disorders, it will not be discussed here, since diagnostic criteria place onset for the disorder outside of the developmental period. New to the category of conduct disorder is the inclusion of specifiers for "limited prosocial emotions," including lack of remorse or guilt, callous lack of empathy, unconcerned about performance, and shallow or deficient affect. Specifiers are also available to subtypes of conduct disorder based on age of onset (childhood, adolescent, or unspecified).

Ten

DISRUPTIVE BEHAVIOR DISORDERS

OPPOSITIONAL DEFIANT DISORDER (ODD)

Clinical Description and Associated Features

The cardinal features of ODD evolve around symptoms of three persistent and negative behavior patterns (of at least 6 months' duration), directed toward authority figures, including "angry irritable mood," "argumentative and defiant behaviors," and "vindictiveness" (APA, 2013). Given this constellation of behaviors, it is not surprising that children with ODD create significant stress in any environment where compliance and rule-governed behavior are expected.

PUTTING IT INTO PRACTICE

David has always been difficult to manage. From the earliest of times, David would rather take the path of most resistance. Before he could even talk, David would just stubbornly sit on the ground, rather than follow his mother's lead. With the advent of language, David evolved from "No, I won't" into a pattern of constant arguing and defending himself. However, despite his great vocabulary, compliance was not a word that David *ever* learned. Every request resulted in a losing battle for his mother, and every battle ended in a war of the wills.

The oppositional behavior pattern is persistent, relentless, and durable. Children with ODD display a number of behavioral symptoms that make them extremely difficult to manage because of their confrontational nature.

A diagnosis of ODD (APA, 2013) requires four symptoms, from the following list of eight symptoms, occurring on a frequent basis:

Anger/irritability:
- Loss of temper
- Touchy and easily irritated
- Angry and resentful

Argumentative/defiant:
- Argumentative with adults/confrontational
- Defiant/refuses to comply with requests
- Deliberately annoying
- Blames others for mistakes or problems

Vindictive
- Spiteful and vindictive (APA, 2013, p. 462)

The behaviors must occur more frequently and in excess of what would be expected given the child's age and developmental level. As would be anticipated, given the types of behaviors demonstrated and the frequency and intensity with which they are expressed, significant impairment would be expected at home (family relationships), school (social and academic), and employment (part-time work, etc.).

In the initial case study, David demonstrates many of the clinical and associated features of ODD. Children with ODD are often stubborn and noncompliant. They can be very contrary and argumentative with others; however, they are quick to shift the blame to other people, defending their actions as necessary given others' unreasonable demands. These children may also appear to be passively aggressive, as they systematically ignore repeated requests to follow directions. They will not compromise, refusing to bend even a little, and they often adhere stubbornly to a refusal to negotiate.

DON'T FORGET

A diagnosis of ODD must occur before age 18, and symptoms must not be better accounted for by either conduct disorder (CD), to be discussed shortly, or antisocial personality disorder. In other words, the clinician is required to make a *differential diagnosis* between ODD and CD. Because CD is the more severe disorder, it would take precedence over ODD in the pecking order in making a differential diagnosis if symptoms met criteria for CD.

ODD behaviors initiate in the home and often carry over to familiar adults with whom they will push the boundaries and test the limits. These children may deliberately annoy others, especially well-known peers and siblings, who may also be a constant source for intimidation and verbal aggression.

Children with ODD may present with either a low self-concept or a sense of inflated self-esteem. Like David, children with ODD often engage their parents in battles that escalate into a high level of emotional turmoil on both sides. Parents often ultimately employ a coercive and negative parenting style in response to their children's aggressive and defiant behaviors. However, it has been well documented that these negative and coercive practices often perpetuate the problem (Patterson, Capaldi, & Bank, 1991).

CAUTION

It is always important to consider the influence of age and developmental stage when making a diagnosis. Remember that oppositional behavior is normal at some stages of development. Therefore, transient oppositional behavior, as is often demonstrated by toddlers and teenagers (the two terrible Ts), would not warrant a diagnosis of ODD unless the intensity and duration were atypical (APA, 2013).

CAUTION

ODD behaviors may not be evident in the school or community and are not likely to be evident in the clinical interview. These children seem to be most comfortable with pushing the boundaries in *familiar territory*. ODD behaviors may extend into the school situation if they are very ingrained or automatic and if reinforced by teachers or peers.

Prevalence and Course

Prevalence rates have been estimated between 1% to 11% of the population, with an average of 3.3% (APA, 2013), depending on whether estimates include clinical or community samples. Prior to puberty, more males than females are diagnosed with ODD; however, the rates equalize in adolescence. High rates of comorbidity have been established for ODD with CD, learning disorders, and ADHD. More than 80% of children diagnosed with ODD have comorbid ADHD, while 65% of children with ADHD will have ODD.

Path analysis suggests a sequence of maladaptive behaviors that begins with ADHD, progresses to ODD, and ultimately culminates in CD (Loeber, Green, Lahey, Christ, & Frick, 1992). However, there is also evidence that discontinuity can exist (behaviors dissipate with age) in the milder forms of the maladaptive behaviors (Loeber & Stouthamer-Loeber, 1998).

CAUTION

Coercion theory (Patterson et al., 1991) would predict that parents who engage in highly charged hostile and negative interchanges with their children actually escalate their child's aggressive and defiant behaviors. Patterns of hostile and negative interactions actually reinforce and maintain increasing levels of aggressive and defiant behaviors.

CONDUCT PROBLEMS AND CONDUCT DISORDER

Literature often uses the term *conduct problems* (CP) to refer to behaviors associated with the more serious end of the disruptive behavior spectrum. The diagnostic category used by the *DSM-5* for the more severe disruptive behavior disorder is conduct disorder (CD).

Clinical Description and Associated Features

According to the *DSM-5* (APA, 2013), the main clinical feature of CD is "a repetitive and persistent behavioral pattern" that involves the violation of social norms or the rights of others. Criteria for CD are based on symptoms that fall into four categories of aggressive behaviors and violations of rules and age-appropriate norms. A diagnosis of CD is made if an individual demonstrates at least three of the following symptoms, within the previous 12 months, and at least one in the past 6 months:

- Acts of aggression toward others and animals
  - Bullying, threatening
  - Initiating fights
  - Use of a weapon to cause harm
  - Cruelty to others
  - Cruelty to animals
  - Theft while confronting (e.g., mugging)
  - Forced sexual activity
- Destruction of property
  - Fire setting with intent to harm
  - Property destruction

- Deceit or theft
  - Committing break-ins (e.g., house, car)
  - Conning others
  - Theft (e.g., shoplifting, forgery)
- Rule violations
  - Staying out all night*
  - Running away
  - Frequently playing truant*

If the youth is older than 18 years, then CD can only be diagnosed if antisocial personality disorder is not the more appropriate diagnosis. For items with the asterisk, behaviors should have evidence of occurring before 13 years of age.

Youth with CD often initiate aggressive acts and often engage in physical altercations or threaten, bully, and intimidate others. These youth can manipulate others through their skillful ability to con others by lying, deceit, and a failure to follow through on promises and obligations. Rule violations begin at an early age (before 13 years of age). Youth may run away from home (at least twice) for a lengthy duration.

> **DON'T FORGET**
>
> According to diagnostic criteria of the *DSM*, in order of severity, the most severe disorder takes precedence in diagnosis. From the least to most severe, the disorders are ODD, CD, and antisocial personality disorder (APD). However, APD cannot be given as a diagnosis to persons under 18 years of age.

Youth with CD may show little remorse or empathy and demonstrate minimal concern for the feelings and thoughts of others. Aggressive tendencies may be heightened in situations that are more ambiguous, as they may have a bias toward reading hostile intent into the motives of others and react accordingly.

Youth with CD may feign feelings of guilt or remorse in order to avert a harsher punishment or to divert blame to their companions. Other associated features include engaging in high-risk behaviors, which may include increased risk of accidents, substance use or abuse, sexually transmitted diseases, and teen pregnancy (APA, 2013).

There are three subtypes of the disorder based on age of onset (childhood onset, adolescent onset, or unspecified onset), as well as specifiers for the disorder severity (*mild*: few criteria and minor harm; *moderate;* and *severe*: many criteria causing significant harm to others), and those relating to "limited prosocial emotions."

Limited Prosocial Emotions

The specifier of "limited prosocial emotions" is new to the *DSM-5* and is used to indicate a persistent pattern of of interaction (over at least 12 months) characterized by at least two of the following attributes:

- Lack of remorse or guilt
- Callous/lack of empathy
- Lack of concern about performance
- Shallow or deficient affect (APA, 2013, p. 471)

Studies have demonstrated that children who exhibit callous-unemotional (CU) and aggressive traits process emotionally based information in a way that is less responsive physiologically. They are also less likely to respond to harsh parenting practices, more likely to engage in high-risk behaviors, and show less response in the amygdale which is responsible for monitoring emotional control and the fear response (Jones, Laurens, Herba, Barker, & Viding, 2009; Marsh, Gerber & Peterson, 2008). In addition, those children with disruptive behaviors who also display CU traits tend to have significantly higher levels of genetic influence, whereas those without CU traits tend to be more influenced by environmental factors (Viding, Jones, Frick, Moffitt, & Plomin, 2008).

DON'T FORGET

Social cognitive theorists suggest that aggressive acts in some children may be activated by a *hostile attribution bias*: a tendency to interpret ambiguous actions or expression as having a hostile intent and then responding to the perception of threat.

CAUTION

CD with *childhood-onset type* applies if at least one criterion symptom was present prior to 10 years of age, while CD with *adolescent-onset type* is used if no symptoms were evident prior to 10 years of age.

Prevalence and Course

Prevalence rates for CD have been estimated to be between 2% and 10%. There are indications that the prevalence rate for CD has increased over the past (APA, 2000). Conduct disorder is one of the most frequent presenting concerns of youth who are referred to mental health settings. Males outnumber females; however, gender differences have been reported for different behavioral outcomes. Males tend to exhibit symptoms of vandalism, physical altercations, and theft, and they have more school discipline issues. Females with CD manifest symptoms in running away, substance use, truancy, and prostitution (APA, 2013).

As with ODD, high rates of comorbidity exist for CD. Due to the increasing age of the population, in addition to those areas of comorbidity already mentioned for ODD, youth with CD also have high comorbid associations with substance abuse and depression. Half of youth with CD have substance abuse problems (Reebye, Moretti, & Gulliver, 1995).

CAUTION

Aggregating youth with severe behavior problems into groups for treatment purposes can have adverse effects. It has also been noted that children on this developmental path tend to have poor social relationships and tend to gravitate toward other youth with similar developmental trajectories and engage in deviancy training among disordered peers (Dishion, Spracklen, Andrews, & Patterson, 1996).

Within the realm of disruptive behavior disorders, conduct problems represent the most serious, complex, and problematic behaviors. Considerable research focus has been placed on the major pathways delineated by the onset of conduct problems: childhood onset, also called *early starters*, and adolescent onset, also referred to as *late starters*.

Early-Onset Pathway: Early Starters

Longitudinal studies suggest that overt aggression should desist in a downward progression after the age of 2. However, young children who evidence conduct problems at a very early age often persist and develop more serious conduct behaviors over time that generalize across situations, reaching further out into the community at large (Patterson & Yeorger, 2002).

Outcomes for children and youth in this category are poor, and ingrained behaviors can be highly resistant to intervention.

Late-Onset Pathway: Late Starters

Less research information is available about this subgroup, who seem to have less deviance and end up getting into trouble by association with the more deviant peer group, often because of inadequate parental monitoring (Patterson et al., 1991). This group may be more resilient, because they have developed more adequate coping skills (socially and behaviorally) at earlier levels.

DON'T FORGET

In a factor analysis of criteria associated with ODD and CD, Frick and colleagues (1993) found four quadrants of potential responses based on overt/covert and destructive/nondestructive behaviors. A table of these behaviors can be seen in Rapid Reference 10.1.

More Data on Subtypes of CD

Using the clusters of overt/covert and destructive/nondestructive behaviors and information from their longitudinal study of problem behaviors in children and youth, Loeber and Keenan (1994) suggest a number of potential subtypes of CD:

- *Authority conflict pathway.* As with ODD, behaviors are defiant and involve rule violations. Defiance does not result in harm to others (e.g., truancy, running away).
- *Covert pathway.* Violations include rule violations (e.g., shoplifting, vandalism) but do not include acts of violence toward others.
- *Overt pathway.* Youth are aggressive at a young age and continue to engage in more serious acts of aggression and violence toward others.
- *Dual overt/covert (combination of two previous pathways).* Youth engage in rule violations and aggressive acts.
- *Triple pathway.* Youth demonstrate behaviors from all three clusters.

Results of their study revealed the following outcomes: the triple-pathway youth had the worst overall future outcomes, while the dual overt/covert youth were most likely to engage in delinquent behaviors. For youth on the overt pathways, unless intervention was successful, aggression led to increasing violence, crimes, and increasingly poor adolescent outcomes. Those youth on an exclusive authority conflict pathway continued to engage in battles with authority figures; however, they had the best overall outcomes of all subtypes.

Oppositional Defiant Disorder and Conduct Disorder: Two Unique Disorders or One?

Initially, there was much debate regarding whether ODD and CD represented a continuum of severity, with ODD being a milder form or precursor to CD. More recently, several arguments have been raised in support of retaining the two disorders as distinct. One reason is that age of onset for ODD (typically 4- to 8-year range) is earlier than for CD (childhood onset, one symptom prior to age 10; adolescent onset, no conduct problems prior to age 10). Another reason is that 75% of children with ODD do not develop CD. Although ODD and CD share

DON'T FORGET

While ODD is associated with overt and nondestructive behaviors, CD is linked with covert behaviors that can be destructive and violate the rights of others.

aggressive features, studies have revealed that these two disorders present with qualitatively distinct forms of aggressive behavior.

In their meta-analysis of 60 factor-analytic studies, Frick and colleagues (1993) identified four quadrants of behaviors aligned along two dimensions: overt versus covert behaviors and destructive versus nondestructive behaviors. The four resulting behavior subtypes can be viewed in Rapid Reference 10.1.

The study was important because it revealed that items that distinguished between ODD and CD clustered along overt (ODD: aggressive and oppositional) versus covert (CD: status and property violations) dimensions.

DON'T FORGET

Arguments in favor of retaining separate categories for ODD and CD include age of onset (ODD earlier than CD); discontinuity rather than continuity (majority of children with ODD do not develop CD); and qualitatively distinct forms of aggressive behavior (ODD aggressive/nondestructive; CD destructive and rule violations).

DON'T FORGET

The behavioral items in the study by Frick and colleagues (1991) map onto the two syndromes that make up the Externalizing scale on the Achenbach scales (Achenbach, 1991): Aggressive scale behaviors fitting best with ODD and the Delinquent scale fitting behaviors of CD.

Rapid Reference 10.1

Four Quadrants of Aggressive Behaviors

Conduct Disorder	Oppositional Defiant Disorder
Covert Nondestructive	**Overt Nondestructive**
Status violations: Truancy, running away, rule violations, swearing	Oppositional: Touchy, stubborn, argumentative, defiant, annoying
Covert Destructive	**Overt Destructive**
Property violations: Vandalism, theft, fire setting	Aggression: Bullies, fights, blames others, is cruel or spiteful

Source: Frick et al., 1993.

THE CATEGORY OF DISRUPTIVE BEHAVIOR DISORDERS

As previously discussed, research supports the existence of ODD and CD as two unique disorders (Frick et al., 1993). However, as disruptive behavior disorders, ODD and CD *share many common features*, such as defiance, aggression, and rule-breaking behaviors, and have much in common regarding etiology, assessment, and treatment. Furthermore, although 75% of children with ODD will not be diagnosed with CD, 90% of youth with CD had an initial diagnosis of ODD (Rey, 1993). The following sections (Etiology, Assessment, and Treatment) apply to both ODD and CD unless otherwise specified.

Etiology

Biological, Neurological, and Genetic Factors

Neurological investigations have found less frontal lobe activity in the brains of youth with CD (Moffit & Henry, 1989). Twin and adoption studies have also indicated that CD can be influenced by both genetic and environmental factors. Increased risk for disruptive behavior disorders (DBD) has been noted in families where the biological or adoptive parent has APD or when biological parents suffer from alcohol dependence, mood disorders, schizophrenia, or a history of ADHD (APA, 2000).

Based on findings from studies conducted with adult populations, elevated levels of the hormone testosterone (Dabbs & Morris, 1990) may be implicated in the genetic transmission of aggressive impulses. In addition, low levels of DBH (which converts dopamine to noradrenaline) may produce higher thresholds for sensation-seeking behaviors in some children (Quay, 1986).

Psychodynamic Theories

A *psychodynamically* oriented therapist might interpret aggressive and defiant behaviors as a manifestation of deep-seated feelings of lack of parental love, absence of empathy, and an inability to trust (Gabbard, 1990).

Behavioral Theories

Within a behavioral framework, noncompliant and aggressive behaviors would develop in response to a prescribed set of learning principles. A clinician from a *behaviorist perspective* would attempt to isolate the factors in the environment responsible for reinforcing and sustaining the behavior. Within the family context, *coercion theory* (Patterson et al., 1991) might be used to explain how patterns of noncompliance and aggression have been sustained by the parents' repeated giving in to demands.

Cognitive Theories

Looking at hostile and aggressive behaviors from the vantage point of the *cognitive perspective*, emphasis would be placed on determining how maladaptive thoughts influence hostile and defiant behaviors. Studies by Dodge and colleagues (Dodge, 1991) have revealed that aggressive children often have a *hostile attribution bias* and misread ambivalent cues as being inherently hostile (e.g., a half-smile is interpreted as a sneer) or rejecting. In these instances, children may respond in a hostile and defensive manner, because they attribute hostile or rejection intentions to others.

DON'T FORGET

Decreased activity in frontal lobe functioning has been associated with a poor ability to inhibit behavioral responses and weaknesses in planning ability. This association may help explain why there are such high rates of comorbidity between ADHD and the disruptive behavior disorders.

DON'T FORGET

Child noncompliance can be an effective means of avoidance or escape from doing undesirable tasks, such as in requests to comply (e.g., picking up toys or cleaning a bedroom). Coercion theory would predict that, in these situations, the parent will often respond with escalating and coercive responses (yelling, screaming, hitting) likely due to their occasional success.

Family Patterns, Attachment, and Parenting

A *family systems* clinician might focus on the parent–child relationship, and childhood aggression may be interpreted as the child's attempt to shift the balance of power resulting from inconsistent or extreme boundaries and/or limit setting by parents. With respect to theories of attachment and parenting, research evidence has linked insecure attachment to aggressive preschool behaviors (Greenberg, 1999), while Baumrind (1991) would suggest that an *authoritarian parenting style* could set the stage for latent aggression giving way to expression in the adolescent years.

Assessment and Treatment

In addition to the general structured and semistructured interview schedules, the general behavioral rating scales discussed previously provide several scales devoted to conduct problems. The behavioral scales also provide information regarding possible comorbid relationships among the various behaviors sampled.

The following specific scales would be anticipated to have clinical or borderline clinical elevations for ODD and CD populations. On the ASEBA (Achenbach & Rescorla, 2001), children with ODD and CD will likely have elevated scores on the following syndrome scales: Social Problems, Rule-Breaking Behavior, Aggressive Behavior, Externalizing Problems, and Total Problems. The *DSM*-oriented scales of the ASEBA will likely show elevations on ODD and CD. Conners parent and teacher scales (CPSR, CTSR, 1998) would have elevations on the Oppositional and Social Problem scales, while the Conners-Wells Adolescent Self-Report Scale (CASS, 1997) would likely indicate Family Problems, Conduct Problems, and problems with Anger Control. On the Behavior Assessment System for Children (BASC-2; Reynolds & Kamphaus, 2004), the Aggression, Conduct Problems, and Composite Externalizing Problems scales would likely be elevated.

Empirically Supported Treatments for Disruptive Behavior Disorders

One of the problems in finding evidence-based treatments specifically for ODD or CD has been that many findings are grouped under the broad category of disruptive behavior disorders. Brestan and Eyberg (1998) reviewed and evaluated 82 studies involving more than 5,000 youth (with disruptive behavior disorders: ODD and/or CD) according to criteria established by the APA Task Force of the American Psychiatric Association (1995) on evidence-based treatments. The authors found that the majority of programs reviewed were based on cognitive-behavioral methods, with or without a parent component. The authors found two parent training programs that met the higher criteria: a parent training program developed to reduce behavior problems in young children (Webster-Stratton, 1984) and a behavioral parent training program based on a manual called *Living with Children: New Methods for Parents and Teachers* produced by Patterson and Gullion (1968). The manual provides lesson plans for parents directed toward improving skills in areas of prioritizing and targeting behaviors for intervention and developing reinforcement programs to reduce unwanted and increase desirable behaviors.

Brestan and Eyberg (1998) highlighted two programs as probably efficacious: a children's problem-solving skills program (Kazdin, Esveldt-Dawson, French, & Unis, 1987) and a program targeting anger control (Lochman, Burch, Curry, & Lampton, 1984). Both programs focus on skill training over a relatively large number of sessions. The Problem-Solving–Skills-Training (PSST; Kazdin, 1996) program is a 20-session program developed to teach children how to solve problems in a highly predictable and logical manner. The Coping Power (Larson & Lochman, 2002) program is a 33-session program developed to promote anger control.

Specific Interventions for ODD

Intervention programs for ODD have met with difficulties because of the highly resistant nature of the disorder (Rey, 1993) and have been highly critized for not considering contextual factors that impact on high-risk families (Kazdin, 1996). However, programs specific to ODD have recently begun to attract increased attention.

In their review of existing interventions for ODD, Greene, Ablon, Goring, Fazio, and Morse (2003) criticize the majority of existing programs for targeting interventions almost exclusively at parenting practices in families that are often highly stressed and who drop out of programs at high rates. The authors suggest that the results of many of these studies present a biased picture of only the most-motivated families who completed the program. The authors suggest the need to target cognitive distortions and deficiencies evident in children with ODD. Greene and colleagues (2003) have developed an alternative intervention program, called Collaborative Problem Solving (CPS; Greene & Ablon, 2004), to address deficiencies in the ODD child's processing in areas of emotion regulation, frustration tolerance, problem solving, and flexibility. The CPS program is designed to increase parent awareness of the underlying parent–child characteristics that propel the ODD behavior through the development of three strategies to manage behaviors. Empirical investigations comparing the CPS program to parent training (PT) using Barkley's defiant-youth program (Barkley, 1997) revealed superior short-term and long-term improvement for ODD children, which was statistically and clinically significant.

Specific Interventions for CD

Children and youth with serious emotional and behavioral disorders have been serviced by a continuum of care from the least-restrictive (outpatient) to most-restrictive (residential treatment centers [RTC]) alternatives. Until recently, the majority of empirical support for treatment effectiveness has come mainly from clinic-based studies. Despite the extensive use of RTC placements for the most severely disordered youth, empirical evidence has been minimal and lacking in experimental controls (U.S. Department of Health and Human Services, 1999).

Home-based alternatives, such as family preservation programs, also have suffered from a lack of empirical support or have demonstrated inconsistent outcomes (Meezan & McCroskey, 1996). Yet studies of the effectiveness of multisystemic therapy (MST) have demonstrated that providing services in the community can be successful for juvenile offenders (Henggeler &

Borduin, 1990), compared to hospitalization as an alternative (Schoenwald et al., 2000). Success of the MST approach, which focuses on multiple determinants of deviant behavior, has been attributed to ecological validity (community outreach) and cognitive-behavioral methods.

Other community-based alternatives that have been supported empirically include comparisons by Chamberlain and Reid (1991, 1998) of the success of juveniles placed in specialized foster care programs (SFC) using methods developed by Patterson, Reid, Jones, and Conger (1975), compared to juveniles assigned to RTCs. In another study, Wilmshurst (2002) found that youth with severe emotional and behavioral disorders (EBD) who were randomly assigned to a community-based family preservation program (using cognitive-behavioral methods) made significant gains (statistically and clinically) compared to peers assigned to a five-day residential alternative.

In their review of treatment programs for youth with conduct problems, McMahon and Kotler (2004) stress the need to include family in the assessment and intervention process due to the significant influence of the family in precipitating and maintaining the conduct problems. The authors select several programs for discussion, including programs in Oregon designed by Patterson and colleagues: functional family therapy and MST. (For a more extensive review, see McMahon & Kotler, 2004.)

Oregon Social Learning Center (OSLC) PT Programs

The program developed by Gerald Patterson and colleagues (Patterson et al., 1975) was one of the *well-established programs* identified by Brestan and Eyberg's (1998) extensive review. The program has been extensively researched and replicated and found to be successfully modified as an intervention for families with younger children (2.5- to 6.5-year-olds), older children (6.5- to 12.5-year-olds), and adolescents and in conditions that reduced family treatment time from 31 hours to 13 to 16 hours. The program focuses on assisting parents to target and track specific behaviors and then develop reinforcement systems (point systems, contingency plans) to increase positive and decrease negative behaviors. Parents are trained to improve problem-solving and negotiation strategies.

Multisystemic Therapy (MST)

Henggeler and colleagues (1998) have developed a manualized multidimensional program for working with juveniles in their community, involving family, schools, and peers. The multimodal program is a strengths-based approach to family empowerment and uses a wide variety of techniques: family therapy and cognitive and behavioral approaches (contingency management, anger management, etc.). The MST approach has been researched extensively, and there is wide empirical support for the use of MST across a wide variety of serious juvenile problems: sexual offenders, chronic offenders, violent offenders, and youth with comorbid substance use and abuse (Henggeler & Borduin, 1990; Schoenwald et al., 2000).

TEST YOURSELF

1. Regarding conduct disorder (CD) and oppositional defiant disorder (ODD), which of the following statements is FALSE?

(a) Developmentally, ODD usually occurs before CD.
(b) The majority of children with ODD usually develop CD.
(c) ODD behaviors can include defiance and loss of temper.
(d) CD behaviors involve acts of serious aggression toward others.

2. Frick and colleagues (1991) found that ODD and CD behaviors clustered into four quadrants. Which of the following statements is FALSE?

(a) ODD behaviors involve status violations.
(b) CD behaviors involve property violations.
(c) ODD behaviors are defiant.
(d) CD behaviors involve truancy and rule violations.

3. According to Patterson and colleagues, coercion theory would predict which of the following relationships between parents and children with conduct problems (CP)?

(a) Parents of children with CP are coerced into aiding and abetting.
(b) There is a lack of interaction between parents and children with CP.
(c) Hostile parent reactions escalate CP behaviors.
(d) Parents of children with CP are too passive.

4. Jason interprets an ambiguous facial expression as an angry face, and he retaliates with an aggressive response. This is an example of

(a) an early-starter response.
(b) a late-starter response.
(c) learned helplessness.
(d) hostile attribution bias.

5. Studies suggest that aggregating youth with severe behavior problems for the purposes of treatment can result in

(a) significant positive outcomes.
(b) increased opportunities to develop social skills.
(c) increased empathic awareness.
(d) deviancy training.

6. **Greene and colleagues (2003) criticize the majority of treatment programs for ODD because most programs**
   (a) do not include a parent training component.
   (b) do not retain parents for the entire program.
   (c) do not motivate parents.
   (d) fail to target cognitive distortions and deficits in the children.
7. **Studies concerning the effectiveness of residential treatment centers (RTC) compared with community-based treatment (CBT) programs for youth with severe conduct problems have found that**
   (a) CBT alternatives are often superior to RTCs.
   (b) RTCs are superior to CBTs.
   (c) there is no difference in treatment effectiveness between the programs.
   (d) no research has compared alternative programs.

Answers: 1. b; 2. a; 3. c; 4. d; 5. d; 6. d; 7. a

Part V

Later-Onset Disorders

Although adolescence was once thought of as the period of *sturm und drang* (storm and stress), marking the transition from childhood to adulthood (Hall, 1904), we now know that only a minority of youth will encounter significant problems during this period of development (Arnett, 1999). However, significant neurological, physical, social, emotional, and cognitive changes that take place during this time period can set the stage for increased risk of developing problems in several areas, including eating disorders, substance use problems, delinquent behaviors, social anxiety, depression, and suicide (Cicchetti & Rogosh, 2002). This section focuses primarily on youth during the preadolescent and adolescent years, at a time when they can be particularly vulnerable to developing eating disorders or substance use problems.

Although the majority of eating disorders have onset within the adolescent years, the *DSM-5* has included feeding disorders (previously housed in the chapter on Disorders Usually First Diagnosed in Infancy, Childhood, or Adolescence) within the chapter on eating disorders, so feeding disorders will be briefly discussed in this section, as well as restrictive food intake disorder, which may be a precursor to the development of later-onset eating disorders, such as anorexia nervosa or bulimia nervosa. Given the adolescent focus on identity and group affiliation, body dissatisfaction can result from tendencies to match the thin ideal portrayed in the media, placing adolescent girls at increased risk for the development of anorexia nervosa or bulimia nervosa, the third leading cause of chronic illness reported for young females in late adolescence (Rosen, 2003). New to the eating disorder category is binge-eating disorder, which was previously housed in the Appendix of the *DSM-IV-TR* (APA, 2000), awaiting sufficient research to support its inclusion in the *DSM* proper.

It is not uncommon for youth to engage in risky behaviors or experiment with substances, however, the vast majority abandon the practice in young adulthood (Kouzis & Labouvie, 1992). Several hypotheses have been put forward to distinguish between experimental and more serious users, including tendencies for some drugs to serve as a gateway (the gateway hypothesis) or stepping stone (stepping stone theory) to more serious drug usage. The stepping stone theory suggests a direct causal link from marijuana to heroin, while the gateway hypothesis suggests that certain drugs increase the risk for other drugs (Kandel, 2002). However, these theories have been criticized, because they do not distinguish between experimenters and heavy users, and they do not address different patterns of substance usage in heavy users (Golub & Johnson, 1994).

The main substances used by adolescents include alcohol, tobacco, marijuana, and inhalants. The *DSM-5* has changed the way that substance disorders are conceptualized, and it no longer distinguishes between substance dependence and substance abuse. Currently, the *DSM-5* recognizes two sets of criteria: one set of criteria for substance use disorders and one set of criteria for substance-induced disorders (intoxication, withdrawal, and related behaviors). There are 10 different categories of substances (alcohol, caffeine, cannabis, hallucinogens, inhalants, opiods, sedatives, stimulants, tobacco, and other). There is a common set of criteria for substance use disorder, which is applied to each of the 10 substance categories, and there is a symptom-specific set of criteria for intoxication and withdrawal for each of the substance categories based on the nature of the substances and symptoms associated with that particular substance.

Eleven

FEEDING AND EATING DISORDERS

Although the previous *DSM* separated discussions of feeding disorders and eating disorders based on age of onset, the *DSM-5* (APA, 2013) presents feeding and eating disorders within the same chapter, based on the rationale that all of the disorders contained within the chapter share similar outcomes of "altered consumption or absorption of food," resulting in impaired physical health and psychological well-being (p. 329). There are six disorders contained within this section, including pica, rumination disorder, avoidant/restrictive food intake disorder, anorexia nervosa, bulimia nervosa, and binge-eating disorder. With the exception of pica, all eating and feeding disorders are considered to be mutually exclusive. The following discussion presents the disorders in the same order in which they are discussed in the *DSM-5*.

PICA

Clinical Description and Associated Features

Infants initially explore their world by mouthing objects, and they can commonly injest nonnutritive substances, especially if they are not well supervised. The cardinal feature of pica, however, is consumption of one or more nonnutritive substances on a regular and persistent basis over a period of at least one month. Other criteria for the condition include ruling out that the behavior is not part of a cultural or socially normative practice and determining that the behavior is not developmentally appropriate. Some of the more common substances that are injested include "paper, soap, cloth, hair, string, wool, soil, chalk, talcum powder, paint, gum, metal, pebbles, charcoal or coal, ash, clay, starch, or ice" (APA, 2013, p. 330).

The topic of pica has not been widely studied, and as a result, there have been different views on the nature of the phenomenon, historically. As a result, literature on pica has described the practice in many ways, ranging from "a socially acceptable practice to a life-threatening behavior" (Carter, Wheeler, & Mayton, 2004, p. 346). Pica has also been seen to accompany other disorders, such as intellectual disabilities and developmental disorders, including autism spectrum disorder.

Prevalence and Course

Depending on the population sampled (clinical or community-based), prevalence rates for pica can range from 3% to 22% (Swift, Paquette, Davison, & Saeed, 1999). Prevalence rates are difficult to determine accurately, because pica has commonly been included as a symptom of other eating and feeding disorders, such as anorexia nervosa, bulimia, and rumination, all of which share deviations in the ingestion of foods that can be considered atypical.

Etiology

The origins of pica are not clear, and explanations of etiology have ranged from deficiencies in diet to the acquisition of learned behaviors. Most researchers recognize the multifactorial nature of the disorder and include elements from medical derivations (e.g., parasite infestation, levels of digestive enzymes or acid levels in stomach, and iron deficiency), as well as those related to cognitive and behavioral sources (Parry-Jones & Parry-Jones, 1992).

Assessment and Treatment

In their review of assessment and treatment for pica, Donnelly and Olczak (1990) cited the use of time-out, restraint, and overcorrection as the most frequently reported interventions for pica, with more contemporary trends favoring approaches that were least restrictive. Functional behavioral assessments and behavior intervention plans have been the most recent and frequent methods of assessment and treatment. For example, Hagopian and Adelinis (2001) used a combined paradigm of response prevention and redirection to reduce pica in a 26-year-old man who had been diagnosed with moderate mental retardation and bipolar disorder. Although the response blocking resulted in elevated aggression initially, redirection to a more preferred food (popcorn) was eventually successful. Using a similar technique, Goh and colleagues (1995) developed a pica exchange program (i.e., pica could be exchanged for highly desired foods) that was successful in reducing pica in three out of four individuals with intellectual disabilities.

RUMINATION DISORDER

Clinical Description and Associated Features

The characteristic feature of this disorder is the repeated regurgitation and rechewing of food, occurring over the course of at least one month. Regurgitation is not the result of a medical condition and is not a symptom of another eating disorder. The disorder is common in infants and those with intellectual disability. Because the food is regurgitated and not ingested, weight loss, failure to thrive, and even death can result. As many as 25% of infants with rumination disorder will die. Precipitating factors associated with the disorder include stressful conditions, lack of stimulation or neglect, and a strained parent–child relationship. In older children and adults, intellectual disability is the predisposing factor (APA, 2000). Onset is usually between 3 and 12 months; however, in cases with intellectual disability, onset may be later.

Prevalence and Course

Prevalence rates for pica are difficult to determine, due to the limited research in the area. However, one study found that rumination is a self-induced, purposeful, and pleasurable behavior, with an incidence rate five times greater in male than in female subjects (Mayes, Humphrey, Handford, & Mitchell, 1988). Other research in the area of intellectual disabilities suggests a prevalence rate between 5% to 10% among individuals with intellectual disability, which is higher among those with more severe/profound levels of ID, males, and those with autism (Gravenstock, 2000).

Etiology

The exact cause of rumination disorder is unknown, but several possible conditions that may trigger the disorder have been suggested, including onset after a physical illness, severe stress or neglect, or other circumstances that may disrupt the normal course of attachment to the caregiver, causing the child to engage in rumination, as a source of self-comfort. The behavior may also be reinforced by increased attention.

Assessment and Treatment

Gravenstock (2000) suggests the need to closely observe the behaviors in order to "avoid diagnostic confusion with, for example, secondary cyclical vomiting caused by affective disorder or epilepsy" (p. 631). Gravenstock also advocates that early intervention and treatment are important to avoid the negative social (withdrawal, self-stimulation, exclusion) and physical (dehydration, malnutrition, dental erosion) outcomes. Some suggested treatment programs include enhancing positivie stimulation in the environment, providing attention for positive behaviors (contingency management programs), and medical intervention when needed.

AVOIDANT/RESTRICTIVE FOOD INTAKE DISORDER

Clinical Description and Associated Features

The *DSM-5* (APA, 2013) has replaced feeding disorder of infancy or early childhood with avoidant/restrictive food intake disorder, which emphasizes the child's motivation to avoid or restrict the intake of food, resulting in at least one of the following significant negative physical consequences:

- Significant weight loss or failure to meet growth expectations
- Significant loss in quality of nutrition (physical exam, lab tests)
- The need to rely on tube feeding or oral supplements
- Diminished capacity for psychosocial functioning (APA, 2013, p. 334).

The disorder is mutually exclusive with the other eating disorders, except pica. Other conditions that might be associated with the disorder include avoidance based on sensory characteristics of a given food type (e.g., brand, texture) or avoidance due to anticipated negative consequences based on prior history (e.g., choking, vomiting).

Prevalence and Course

Although the *DSM-5* does not report a prevalence rate for avoidant/restrictive food intake disorder, food refusal can result in failure to thrive (FTT), which can account for 1% to 5% of all infant hospital admissions (Douglas, 2002). Nicholls, Chater, and Lask (2000) compared rates for eating disorders in 81 children aged 7 to 16 years according to three different scales: the *DSM* (APA, 2000), the *International Code of Diseases* (WHO, 1993), and the Great Ormond Street classification system developed specifically for children (GOS; Bryant-Waugh &

Lask, 1995). In addition to anorexia and bulimia, the GOS identifies three other eating disorders: food avoidance emotional disorder, selective eating, and pervasive refusal. According to the GOS, 26% of children met criteria for food avoidance with emotional disorder, and 13.7% met criteria for selective eating. The *DSM-5* outlines several features that can be associated with the category of avoidant/restrictive eating and suggests that in older children and adolescents, the behavior might be associated with more generalized emotional difficulties that do not meet criteria for anxiety, depression, or bipolar disorder, where they exhibit a general malaise "sometimes called food avoidance emotional disorder" (p. 335).

Etiology

Increased risk for avoidant/restrictive food intake is associated with having a history positive for gastrointestinal conditions or medical problems associated with eating behaviors, having a parent (mother) with an eating disorder, or family anxiety. Children with anxiety disorders, OCD, ASD, or ADHD are also at increased risk for the disorder.

Assessment and Treatment

As with any eating or feeding problem, it is important to rule out any potential organic cause (Douglas, 2002). The causes of avoidant/restrictive food intake can be multifactoral in nature. Eating can be conditioned to be an aversive activity if associated with being forced to eat, gagging, choking, or experiencing food poisoning or becoming ill after eating certain foods. Attachment theory has also been used to explain why some children develop different types of eating disorders, since children with eating and feeding disorders often demonstrate more attachment problems and difficulties in parent–child relationships than their peers without eating or feeding problems (Drotar, Stein, & Perrin, 1995).

Based on the theoretical model used, several treatment programs could be developed to address eating or feeding concerns based on different contingency-based models (behavioral) or in enhancing the parent–child relationship through parent training or conjoint parent and child play therapy.

For example, Fonagy and Target (1996) have provided empirical support for psychodynamic developmental therapy for children (PDTC), a therapeutic approach that integrates concepts and techniques from a psychodynamic perspective within a developmental framework. Using play as the medium, therapists work with children to strengthen their skills in self-regulation, awareness of others, and capacity to relate to others through play. It would seem that this type of approach could be applied to problems in the areas of avoidant/restrictive food intake.

PUTTING IT INTO PRACTICE

At 16 years of age, Sara is 5 feet, 4 inches tall, and she weighs 125 pounds today. Last week, Sara weighed 130 pounds, and next week she will probably weigh 120 pounds. Although her weight is approximately where it should be on the height and weight chart, Sara compares herself to models in the magazines, and she is convinced that she looks fat.

Sara is constantly dieting, but she is not good at it. She has starved herself for the past 2 days. Today, she is irritable and upset. That is usually the feeling that starts the cycle. Now she will binge to ease the tension. In a two-hour period, Sara will consume an entire cheesecake, a large Coke, a cheeseburger, a large helping of fries, a box of chocolate chip cookies, and a half-quart of ice cream. After the binge, Sara will feel guilty, depressed, upset, and angry with herself until she purges the food through self-induced vomiting. In a few days, the entire bulimic cycle will begin again. Sara has bulimia nervosa.

Anorexia Nervosa and Bulimia Nervosa

Individuals with anorexia nervosa and bulimia nervosa share several common features. Onset of the eating disorder often occurs after a period of intense dieting. People with both disorders are most likely females (90%) who are preoccupied with being thin and are concurrently preoccupied with food. Both share a fear of becoming obese and have a distorted sense of body shape and weight.

Despite these common features, individuals with anorexia nervosa and bulimia nervosa have personality differences. The major defining feature that separates individuals with anorexia nervosa from individuals with bulimia nervosa is that those who have anorexia nervosa will ultimately be successful in their refusal to maintain a normal body weight. As a result, anorexics will register a body mass index (BMI) score of less than 17.5 kg/m^2 (APA, 2013).

DON'T FORGET

The news media often reports stories of celebrities who have disclosed having an eating disorder, such as Princess Diana. In the early 1980s, when few people knew about the prevalence of eating disorders, the country was shocked to find out that Karen Carpenter, a famous singer and entertainer, had died from medical complications resulting from anorexia nervosa.

CAUTION

Young girls in the 11- to 13-year-old range become increasingly weight conscious and try to lose weight, at the same time when weight gain resulting from puberty is normal. Early-maturing girls are at greater risk than later-maturing girls for developing eating disorders (Swarr & Richards, 1996).

DON'T FORGET

Despite the term *anorexia*, which means "loss of appetite," the anorexic is preoccupied with food and is constantly hungry because of her self-induced starvation.

ANOREXIA NERVOSA

Clinical Description and Associated Features

The diagnostic feature of anorexia nervosa is the refusal to maintain a minimally acceptable weight. Individuals with the disorder will maintain their weight approximately 15% below what is considered normal (based on one of several available versions of the Metropolitan Life Insurance tables or pediatric growth chart). The *DSM-5* (APA, 2013) suggests a body mass index (BMI) equal to or lower than 17.5 kg/m^2 (equivalent to 85% of the normal weight for an individual's height). Anorexics' intense fear of gaining weight is the focal point of their motivation to monitor their food intake to the extent that the disorder can be fatal.

PUTTING IT INTO PRACTICE

Tracy finally felt good about herself. She had been weighing herself three times a day, and today she finally found that she had lost over 20 pounds in the previous three months. Tracy had learned to curb her appetite by cooking for others and then rushing off, not having time to eat. She was obsessed with food but was even more obsessed with having the willpower to stop herself from eating. Tracy finally knew she had won the battle when her period stopped. That was her benchmark. Now she knew she had lost enough weight. Now if she could only lose a little more from her buttocks, she would be happy.

Driven by a fear of gaining weight and a distorted perception of their body size and shape, individuals with anorexia nervosa usually begin to lose weight initially through restricting higher-calorie foods. Ultimately, with increased restrictions, their diet becomes limited to a few low-calorie foods, such as celery. The *DSM* (APA, 2013) diagnostic criteria for anorexia nervosa include the following symptoms: (a) "maintaining of weight less than minimally normal given or for children and adolescents less than minimally expected" (APA, 2013, p. 338); (b) intense fear of gaining weight or becoming fat; and (c) a distorted sense of body shape. The *DSM* provides guidelines for severity ratings based on BMI: Mild (less than or equal to 17 kg/m^2), Moderate (BMI 16–16.99 kg/m^2), Severe (BMI 15–15.99 kg/m^2), Extreme (BMI less than 15 kg/m^2). To determine the severity of the disorder in children and adolescents, the *DSM* recommends use of the Center for Disease Control (CDC) BMI percentile calculator. The CDC calculator for adults, teens, and children can be found at www.cdc.gov/healthyweight/assessing/bmi.

Individuals with anorexia often feel a sense of power in being able to control their desire to eat. Other associated features include feelings of ineffectiveness, perfectionism, inhibited emotional expression and spontaneity, rigid thinking patterns, and a strong need to control environmental influences.

Inherently, for individuals with anorexia nervosa, self-concept and self-esteem are virtually synonymous with body image. They view weight loss as an achievement and self-starvation as strength of character. Their distorted sense of body proportion does not allow them to perceive how their bones might protrude from their bodies or that their malnutrition has caused them to appear like walking skeletons. Physiologically, their restricted diets can cause significant health problems. Refusal to eat may result in the necessity for medical interventions, such as tube feeding, in order to avert a fatality.

Subtypes of Anorexia Nervosa

There are two subtypes of anorexia nervosa. When most people think about anorexia nervosa, they think about the *restricting subtype*. The restricting subtype maintains the low weight by restrictive dieting, fasting, or excess exercise. Individuals of this subtype do not normally engage in the binge-and-purge process. Individuals with the *binge-eating/purging subtype* of anorexia nervosa may engage in the binge-and-purge process by eating more than they typically would eat and then follow eating with a purge activity (self-induced vomiting, laxatives). Some individuals with this subtype may not binge in the true sense of the word, but even if they eat a small amount, they will follow eating with a purge activity to rid the body of the food. Usually binge-and-purge activities take place on a regular (weekly) basis.

DON'T FORGET

The anorexic cycle begins with fear of obesity and a distorted body image. This leads to self-starvation. Starvation leads to preoccupation with food. Ultimately, anxiety and depression are woven into the cycle at each stage.

DON'T FORGET

Rosen, McKeag, Hough, and Curley (1986) surveyed female athletes and found that many were at high risk for eating disorders. In their survey of college gymnasts, approximately 62% admitted to engaging in self-destructive weight-control techniques, such as diet pills (24%), self-induced vomiting (26%), laxatives (7%), and diuretics (12%).

Prevalence and Course

According to the *DSM-5*, the 12-month prevalence rate for anorexia is 0.4%, and approximately 1% of the population will be diagnosed with anorexia nervosa in a lifetime, although there is concern that this rate is increasing. The disorder is found primarily in females (approximately 90%). The disorder is most pronounced in female adolescents from middle- to upper-class Caucasian families (Pate, Pumariega, Hester, & Gaarner, 1992). However, a preoccupation with thinness has not only resulted in overall increased prevalence rates but also has seen the disorder become more pervasive across all social strata and ethnic groups. The typical age of onset is between 14 to 18 years of age. Better prognosis is associated with earlier adolescent onset. Recovery rates are low, with only approximately 10% fully recovering from the disorder, while almost 50% achieve partial recovery (Herzog et al., 1993). Approximately half of females who are anorexic go on to develop bulimia at some later stage.

The course of anorexia nervosa is somewhat unpredictable, however, the disorder can be precipitated by a stressful event. Although some individuals succumb to a single episode, others will follow a more chronic course evident in fluctuating weight loss and gain, relapse, and increasing health problems. Within the first five years, many individuals with the restricting subtype of anorexia nervosa will

CAUTION

According to the *DSM*, anorexia nervosa is far more prevalent in industrial societies. The disorder is most frequently found in the United States, Canada, Europe, Australia, Japan, New Zealand, and South Africa. The incidence of eating disorders is considerably lower in countries where women have fewer decision-making roles (Miller & Pumariega, 1999).

develop an eating pattern that is more typical of the binge-eating/purging subtype. If this shift is accompanied by sufficient weight gain, then the diagnosis may also change from anorexia nervosa to bulimia nervosa. Unchecked, chronic starvation and weight loss can result in severe dehydration and electrolyte imbalance that may require hospitalization. Of those requiring hospitalization, the mortality rate is high (10%) due to either suicide, starvation, electrolyte imbalance, or other medical complications (APA, 2013).

Anorexia nervosa is associated with depression, irritability, anxiety, social withdrawal, and insomnia. Obsessive-compulsive characteristics are also common, as anorexics are preoccupied with food (APA, 2013). Lack of impulse control is common in the binge-eating/purging subtype, which may also be evident in comorbid disorders of substance abuse. Anxiety (75%), depression (73%), and personality disorders (74%) are also highly comorbid disorders (Deep, Nagy, Weltzin, Rao, & Kaye, 1995; Herzog, Schellberg, & Deter, 1997).

BULIMIA NERVOSA

Clinical Description and Associated Features

The cardinal feature of bulimia nervosa is the bulimic cycle that involves binge eating followed by compensatory methods designed to prevent weight gain. The diagnostic criteria for bulimia nervosa include recurrent episodes of binge eating and recurrent use of compensatory strategies to prevent weight gain. The binge and compensatory behaviors occur at least twice a week for at least three months, and self-worth is evaluated through weight and body proportion.

DON'T FORGET

According to the *DSM-5* (APA, 2013) a *binge* is defined as consuming an excessive amount of food (within a discrete amount of time) than would normally be eaten given similar circumstances. A *binge-eating episode* includes both of the following: (a) consuming an excessive amount of food during a discrete period of time (e.g., 2 hours) and (b) a feeling of loss of control resulting from overeating (p. 345).

Subtypes of Bulimia Nervosa

There are two subtypes of bulimia nervosa based on the compensatory methods used: the *purging type* (self-induced vomiting, laxatives, diuretics, enemas) and the *nonpurging type* (fasting, excessive exercise).

Because of the guilt and shame associated with eating and purging, individuals with bulimia can go undetected for some time. Binges are usually done in private, and food is often consumed at a rapid pace. Precipitating circumstances surrounding a binge episode might include feelings of depression, environmental stressors, irritability, tension, and hunger (fasting).

DON'T FORGET

There are two subtypes for each eating disorder. Anorexia nervosa has subtypes based on how weight is kept to the minimum (restricting types and binge-eating/purging type). Subtypes of bulimia nervosa are classified on the nature of the compensatory strategy used to eliminate what has been consumed (purging and nonpurging types). Among the subtypes, similarities exist between the binge-eating/purging type of anorexia and the purging type of bulimia. Similarities are also evident in the restricting type of anorexia and nonpurging type of bulimia in the use of fasting and excessive exercise to control weight gain.

Although bulimics engage in compensatory behaviors to remove calories from their bodies, the practice of repeated vomiting has several adverse side effects. Physically, acids from the stomach can cause deterioration of the esophagus over time and erode enamel on teeth. Studies have also determined that repeated vomiting results in people feeling more hungry and less satiated than if they had not engaged in bouts of vomiting (Wooley & Wooley, 1985). Therefore, bulimics are often caught in cycles that produce more intense feelings of hunger, and they are at higher risk for repeat binge-purge episodes.

The *DSM-5* includes specifiers to indicate the severity of the disorder based on the average number of weekly episodes: Mild (1–3 episodes), Moderate (4–7 episodes), Severe (8–13 episodes) and Extreme (14 or more episodes).

DON'T FORGET

The bulimic cycle begins with a feeling of tension or irritability that produces a strong desire to eat. The urge leads to a loss of control and a binge episode. Following the binge episode, the bulimic feels guilty, depressed, uncomfortably full, and compensates by getting rid of the food (purging or nonpurging). Following the compensatory behaviors, the bulimic feels in control once again.

Prevalence and Course

The 12-month prevalence rate is 1% to 1.5%, with a lifetime prevalence of approximately 1% to 3%. The male-to-female ratio is 1 male for 10 females. Onset is later than for anorexia nervosa, and bulimia usually begins in late adolescence or early adulthood. The course is often chronic, with high rates of relapse. Most individuals with bulimia nervosa have fluctuating weight loss but primarily remain within the average weight range for their height. Of those diagnosed with bulimia nervosa, approximately 10% to 15% will meet criteria for anorexia nervosa at some point in their lifetime. The majority of those who do cross over will revert back to bulimia nervosa or vascillate between the two disorders. In addition, some who initially meet criteria for bulimia nervosa will ultimately engage in binge episodes without compensatory measures and eventually meet criteria for binge-eating disorder (discussed at the end of this chapter).

Throughout the course of development, many adolescent girls engage in experimental diets and compensatory weight loss behaviors. One survey of college students found that 50% engaged in binges on a periodic basis, while some students reported using compensatory behaviors of vomiting (6%) or laxatives (8%) at least once (Mitchell, Pyle, & Miner, 1982). Attie and Brooks-Gunn (1995) suggest that eating disorders tend to develop in response to two stressful life transitions: onset of adolescence and onset of young adulthood.

ETIOLOGY OF EATING DISORDERS

Several possible explanations have been suggested concerning the development of eating disorders. In all likelihood, etiology is a complex interaction between biological, psychological, and environmental (family and peer stressors) factors. Similarities and differences between anorexia nervosa and bulimia nervosa have been highlighted throughout this chapter.

Although the two eating disorders share many of the same features, and as discussed, there may be cross-over between the two, there are also important differences between anorexia nervosa and bulimia nervosa, especially when the classic examples of each are compared. A summary of the classic differences can be found in Rapid Reference 11.1.

Onset of anorexia occurs earlier than bulimia, and studies have shown that family characteristics and personality characteristics seem to differ in females with anorexia and bulimia, especially when comparing the two more contrasting and unique types of these disorders, for example, anorexia nervosa (restricting type) and bulimia nervosa (binge-eating/purging type). While individuals with

Rapid Reference 11.1

Differences Between Anorexia Nervosa (Restricting Type) and Bulimia Nervosa

Anorexia Nervosa (Restricting Type)	Bulimia Nervosa
Earlier age of onset: 14 to 18 years	Later age of onset: 15 to 21 years
Amenorrhea (absence of menstrual cycle) as a consequence of low body weight	Amenorrhea less likely; irregularities in menstrual cycle more common
Greater denial of parent–child conflict; less demonstration of open conflict	Greater tendencies for more intense, hostile, and open parent–child conflict
Less family history of obesity	Greater family history of obesity
Tendencies toward introverted behaviors such as social withdrawal and decreased interest in sex over time	Tendencies toward extroverted behaviors manifested in substance abuse and promiscuity or heightened interest in sex
High tendencies of comorbidity with depression and obsessive-compulsive personality disorder or traits	High tendencies of comorbidity with anxiety, as well as depression, substance abuse, obsessive-compulsive traits, and borderline personality disorder

anorexia (restricting type) tend to be more rigid, perfectionistic, and obsessive in their quest for thinness, those with the binge-eating/purging type of bulimia tend to be more outgoing and sociable. However, while anorexics are more likely to be sexually immature, bulimics tend to have greater difficulties with impulse control and can be more sexually active (Halmi, 1995).

Studies of family characteristics have also noted differences in these two eating disorder groups, with more pathology evident in families of those suffering from bulimia.

DON'T FORGET

Similarities between the two eating disorders include the following:

- Onset after intense dieting
- Fear of obesity
- Preoccupation with thinness and food
- Distorted sense of body shape and weight

Biological, Genetic, and Neurotransmitter Functions

The risk for developing an eating disorder is six times as great if the person has a relative with an eating disorder (Strober, Freeman, Lampert, Diamond, & Kaye, 2000). At least one twin study found that if one monozygotic twin has bulimia, then there is a 23% chance that the other twin will develop the disorder (Walters & Kendler, 1995). Low levels of serotonin (Carrasco, Diaz-Marsa, Hollander, Cesar, & Saiz-Ruiz, 2000) have also been associated with eating disorders, similar to other disorders previously discussed.

> **DON'T FORGET**
>
> Low serotonin levels have also been linked to depression and obsessive-compulsive disorder.

Garner, Garfinkel, and O'Shaughnessy (1985) suggest that early eating patterns and inheritance combine to define an individual's *weight set point*. The authors use the theory of weight set point to explain why dieting in isolation does not work. In order to lose weight, restricted eating must also be accompanied by increasing the metabolic rate (exercise) to offset the internal regulating functions. Genetically, there seems to be a history of maternal obesity in families of bulimics.

> **DON'T FORGET**
>
> The authors suggest that the weight set point is the body's internal weight regulator that responds to messages sent by the hypothalamus. When activated, the lateral hypothalamus (LH) sends a message of increased hunger; stimulation of the ventromedial hypothalamus (VH) sends a message of decreased hunger. If weight drops below the ideal set point, the LH is activated to increase hunger, and the metabolic rate is lowered to preserve the set point; if weight is above the set point, the VH is stimulated to depress appetite, and the metabolic rate is raised.

Temperament and Personality

Approximately half of anorexics will be restrictive, while the other half will demonstrate characteristics of the binge-eating/purging type. Personalities among these two types differ, with the binge-eating/purging type sharing many features of bulimia. The restrictive subtype tend to be more inhibited, perfectionistic, insecure, conforming, and capable of high levels of self-control. By comparison, those with the binge-eating/purging type tend to be more outgoing, extroverted, and have problems with impulse control (Casper, Hedeker, & McClough, 1992).

Family Influences

Family dynamics can play a major role in the precipitation and maintenance of eating disorders. Mothers of females with eating disorders tend to be perfectionistic and also prone to dieting themselves. Bruch (1991) maintains that while *effective parents* are sensitive to their child's needs and respond appropriately to biological (hunger) and emotional (nurturing) needs, *ineffective parents* respond inappropriately by providing comfort food at times when their children are not hungry but when they are anxious or irritable. In this case, inappropriate responses serve two functions: They preempt the child's establishment of her or his own set of internal signals to activate hunger, and they link food to comfort.

Minuchin, Rosman, and Baker (1978) described four characteristics of *anorexic families*, including enmeshment, overprotectiveness, rigidity, and denial of conflict. They saw these families as overly concerned about outward appearances and very controlling in their influence. Given little room to develop independence within this controlling and enmeshed environment, anorexia provides these girls with the ability to control their own food intake, while delaying their maturation (lack of onset of womanhood) and remaining dependent.

In contrast, *bulimic families* tend to have more psychopathology (depression and substance abuse) compared to controls. Fairburn, Welch, Doll, Davies, and O'Connor (1997) found that compared to families of anorexics where open confrontation is avoided, families of bulimics engage in more open hostility, parent–child conflict, and confrontation. Families of bulimics also tended to engage in more relational aggression intent on blaming and attempting to control each other.

DON'T FORGET

Families of anorexics tend to be characterized by rigidity, enmeshment, and control, whereas families of bulimics demonstrate more overt hostility and are less nurturing and cohesive.

Socioenvironmental Influences

Surveys regarding how people perceive their body image, relative to the ideal image, reveal that dissatisfaction with body image has increased significantly in the past 25 years. Compared to responses collected in 1972, women's dissatisfaction ratings for their overall body image obtained in 1997 doubled the number dissatisfied (from 25% to 56%). Although women were less content than men about their body image, males also increased their sense of dissatisfaction about their body image substantially in the interim, from 15% to 43% (Garner, Cooke, & Marano, 1997). In one study of 9- and 10-year-old girls, researchers found that between 31% to 81% of 9-year-old girls and between 46% to 81% of 10-year-old girls expressed fears of being fat and had engaged in dieting and binge-eating episodes (Mellin, Irwin, & Scully, 1992).

Cognitive and Behavioral Theories

Cognitive distortions are evident in the thought processes of individuals with eating disorders. Tendencies toward negative self-appraisals and obsessional preoccupation with food are the prominent features of this pattern of maladaptive thinking. Behaviorally, the anorexic cycle and the bulimic cycle are negatively reinforcing and self-perpetuating.

ASSESSMENT AND TREATMENT OF EATING DISORDERS

In addition to the broad assessment instruments discussed previously, the Eating Disorder Inventory-2 (EDI-2; Garner, 1991) is a self-report instrument that assesses common psychological and behavioral traits associated with bulimia and anorexia. There are eight subscales: Drive for Thinness, Bulimia, Body Dissatisfaction, Ineffectiveness Scale, Perfectionism, Interpersonal Distrust, Interoceptive Awareness, and Maturity Fears.

Intervention and Treatment of Anorexia Nervosa

Medical Intervention

Close contact with the primary care physician is very important in cases of eating disorders because of the seriousness of the physical complications that can develop. In anorexia, three goals of treatment are monitored very closely: (1) weight gain; (2) resolution of underlying maladaptive thoughts, behaviors, and interpersonal relationships; and (3) maintenance of weight gain.

Behavioral Interventions

Behavioral interventions target positive behaviors to replace and intervene in the anorexic cycle. Within the hospital setting, anorexics are often placed on behavioral plans that offer tangible rewards (e.g., access to telephone, television, makeup, etc.) in exchange for eating.

Cognitive-Behavioral Therapy

Several cognitive-behavioral programs have been developed to assist anorexics. One program that combined cognitive therapy and family therapy obtained a 64% success rate (reached ideal weight) at the end of a 16-month treatment program. Follow-up revealed that 82% maintained gains one year later (Robin, Bedway, Diegel, & Gilroy, 1996). Components of a cognitive-based program would be promoting eating disorder awareness, developing appropriate weight goals and attitudes, linking privileges to goal attainment, monitoring of eating behaviors by an adult (to avoid purging), fostering awareness of maladaptive thought patterns (perfectionism, negative thinking), developing relaxation techniques, and focusing on relapse prevention. In addition, individual therapeutic sessions would address psychosocial stressors (family, peers) and therapy directed toward any comorbid problems (e.g., anxiety and depression). Cognitive-behavioral programs can be provided on an individual or group basis and frequently involve the family.

Family Interventions

Minuchin and colleagues (1978) developed several techniques for working with anorexic families. Observation of family dynamics for eating disorders provided the most salient information when the session was conducted during a meal. Family systems interventions focus on issues of enmeshment and the family's tendencies to avoid issues of marital or family conflict by focusing energy on the anorexic child.

Intervention and Treatment of Bulimia Nervosa

Medical Interventions

Although bulimia does not pose the medical threat that anorexia does, there is still a need to monitor medical side effects. In addition, antidepressants (SSRIs) such as fluoxetine (Prozac) may be an effective adjunct to treatment of bulimia in reducing depressive symptoms, elevating mood, and decreasing the need to engage in binge episodes (Bezchlibnyk-Butler & Jeffries, 1997).

Cognitive-Behavioral Therapy

Maladaptive thinking such as linking self-esteem to body image can be reframed using cognitive-behavioral methods, which were outlined earlier for anorexia nervosa. With the binge-eating/purging type, monitoring would require restricted access to binge-type, high-calorie foods (e.g., cake, ice cream). Group therapies often combine anorexics and bulimics in the same eating disorder groups.

Family Interventions

Because bulimic families are typically much more volatile than anorexic families, therapy would likely be directed at developing more appropriate methods of communication, achieving appropriate conflict resolution, and reestablishing appropriate boundaries.

BINGE-EATING DISORDER (BED)

Clinical Description and Associated Features

In the previous version of the *DSM* (APA, 2000), binge-eating disorder (BED) was relegated to Appendix B for consideration of future status. Since that time, growing evidence of the disorder, which represents an impaired ability to control excessive eating episodes that cause significant distress, has resulted in the inclusion of BED as an eating disorder in the *DSM-5*. A BED episode occurs when (a) there is consumption of a significantly large amount of food within a two-hour period, (b) accompanied by a feeling of loss of control. In addition to these criteria, the episode must involve three or more of the following eating traits and/or feelings:

- Consumption of more than normal
- Feeling uncomfortably full
- Consuming large amounts of food, in the absence of physical hunger
- Solitary eating due to embarrassment
- Feelings of disgust, self-loathing, and guilt

Unlike anorexia or bulimia, BED is not followed by compensatory strategies (such as self-induced vomiting, laxatives, fasting, or excessive exercise); however, similar to anorexia or bulimia, overindulgence is followed by feelings of guilt, embarrassment, disgust, and depression. There was controversy as to whether any compensatory behaviors (e.g., purge on occasion) should be included or excluded from the defining criteria. The *DSM-5* (APA, 2013) has opted that the disorder is "not associated with the recurrent use of inappropriate compensatory behavior" (p. 350). As might be anticipated, frequent binge-eating episodes in the absence of purge behaviors may result in fluctuating weight problems, including being overweight or obese. Onset is usually in late adolescence or early adulthood, and BED is often comorbid with depression. The *DSM-5* includes specifiers of severity based on the number of weekly binge-eating episodes: Mild (1–3 episodes), Moderate (4–7 episodes), Severe (8–13 episodes), Extreme, 14 or more episodes).

Prevalence and Course

The 12-month prevalence rate for BED among adults is 1.6% for females and .8% for males (APA, 2013). The disorder is as prevalent among racial and ethnic minority groups as it is among white females. According to the *DSM-5*, BED typically begins in adolescence or young adulthood (p. 352). Decaluwe and Braet

(2003) studied the prevalence of BED among 196 obese children and adolescents (between 10 and 16 years of age) and found that only 1% of the sample met the criteria for BED, although 9% exhibited objective bulimic episodes (OBE is defined as overeating with loss of control), but did not meet all *DSM* criteria for BED. The authors concluded that OBEs are more common in females than males and that episodic overeating was more common than binge eating. Children who experienced OBEs had a greater tendency to be overweight and demonstrated more psychopathology related to eating behaviors than their peers without OBEs. Developmentally, overweight was seen to precede binge eating, and the average age for the first encounter with OBE was 10.8 years.

Etiology

BED tends to run in families and can occur in normal or overweight and obese individuals; the disorder can be common among those seeking treatment for being overweight or obese. In contrast to those with anorexia nervosa or bulimia nervosa, who may develop the disorder after engaging in diets to lose weight, those with BED tend to engage in dieting and weight loss activities after onset of the disorder. However, compared to those who are overweight or obese without BED, those who experience BED consume more calories in binges and suffer from more impairment in functioning as a result of elevated levels of distress and associated psychiatric comorbidity. Individuals who are diagnosed with BED are at increased risk for bipolar disorder, depression, and anxiety disorders.

Assessment and Treatment

In their study of obese children and adolescents seeking treatment for obesity, Decaluwe and Braet (2003) found a subgroup of girls and boys who demonstrated significant eating problems, such as engaging in OBEs. The researchers emphasize the importance of assessing binge-eating symptoms when devising treatment programs for children and adolescents suffering from obesity.

Several programs for eating disorders already discussed could have application to BED, including behavioral, cognitive-behavioral, and psychoeducational programs designed to improve eating habits. Telch, Agras, and Linehan (2003) adapted the use of dialectical behavior therapy (DBT) and applied the technique as a treatment for a group of women diagnosed with BED. Women in the study, treated with DBT, evidenced significant improvement on measures of binge eating and eating pathology compared with controls. By the end of the study, 89% of the women receiving DBT had stopped binge eating. Abstinence rates were reduced to 56% at the six-month follow-up. The researchers conclude that results suggest that DBT warrants further investigation as a potential treatment for BED.

DON'T FORGET

Dialectical behavior therapy (DBT) was initially developed by Linehan and colleagues (2001) and has been a successful therapeutic method used primarily to treat adults who suffer from borderline personality disorder, which features significant problems with emotion regulation and self-control. DBT is an integrated program that combines cognitive-behavioral methods (group work focusing on social skills and practice in coping with stressful situations) and psychodynamic sessions (individual client-therapist) focusing on mindfulness, acceptance, and change.

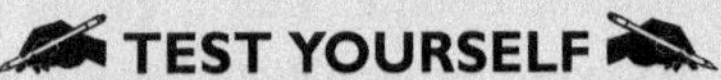

TEST YOURSELF

1. The word *anorexia* means

(a) to waste away.
(b) to do without.
(c) loss of appetite.
(d) loss of desire.

2. According to the *DSM*, a diagnosis of anorexia nervosa requires a weight maintenance of

(a) 75% of the minimum expected.
(b) 85% of the minimum expected.
(c) 90% of the minimum expected.
(d) 95% of the minimum expected.

3. Which of the following is TRUE regarding anorexia nervosa and bulimia nervosa?

(a) Onset of anorexia is usually earlier than bulimia.
(b) Bulimia is often associated with the restricting type of diet.
(c) Anorexics rarely become bulimic.
(d) Lack of impulse control is often a characteristic of anorexia.

4. According to the *DSM-5*, a binge-eating episode must include

(a) consuming an excessive amount of food in a discrete period of time.
(b) ritualistic eating habits.
(c) a feeling of loss of control resulting from overeating.
(d) both a and c.

5. **Anorexia nervosa is**
   (a) universal.
   (b) evident only in the United States.
   (c) more prevalent in industrial societies.
   (d) more prevalent in low SES populations.
6. **Which of the following is NOT an example of a nonpurging type of bulimia?**
   (a) Fasting
   (b) Excessive exercise
   (c) Diuretics
   (d) Restrictive dieting
7. **Which of the following is NOT a similarity between anorexia and bulimia?**
   (a) Fear of obesity
   (b) Sexual inhibition
   (c) Distorted sense of body shape
   (d) Onset after intense dieting
8. **Which of the following is NOT a part of the *anorexic family* described by Salvador Minuchin and colleagues (1978)?**
   (a) Open hostility
   (b) Enmeshment
   (c) Overprotectiveness
   (d) Rigidity

Answers: 1. c; 2. b; 3. a; 4. d; 5. c; 6. c; 7. b; 8. a

Twelve

SUBSTANCE-RELATED DISORDERS

In a survey of more than 10,000 teenagers enrolled in grades 7 through 12 in the United States conducted in 2000, more than 9% stated that they had used a weapon in the past year, 25% had smoked cigarettes in the past 30 days, and one in seven 7th- and 8th-graders had already experienced sex (Blum et al., 2000). Although these results demonstrated improvements in some areas over previous findings, the report suggests that many teens continue to engage in high-risk behaviors. Blum and associates (2000) found that the three factors that contributed most to high-risk behaviors in teens included school failure, percentage of unstructured free time, and nature of peer activities.

There has been a significant change in the way the *DSM-5* conceptualizes disorders contained in the chapter on Substance-Related and Addictive Disorders. In this chapter, the *DSM* clusters disorders related to excessive drug use, which have a common outcome relating to the activation of reward centers in the brain. The chapter also includes addictive behaviors such as gambling and Internet gaming, which are also responsible for activating similar reward centers in the brain.

The *DSM* no longer distinguishes between substance dependence and substance abuse, and instead discusses two groups of criteria, one for substance use disorders and the other for substance-induced disorders (intoxication, withdrawal, and related behaviors) that are associated with each of the 10 different categories of substances, including alcohol, caffeine, cannabis, hallucinogens, inhalants, opioids, sedatives, stimulants, tobacco, and other.

SUBSTANCE USE DISORDER

Clinical Description and Associated Features

The diagnostic criteria for substance use disorder apply to all classes of substances, except caffeine, and relate to specific behavior patterns resulting from substance use that cause clinically significant impairment in four areas: loss of control over substance use, social impairament, use despite the risks, and pharmacological/physical changes:

Lack of control over substance use

- Increased amounts, or usage extending longer than intended
- Unsuccessful efforts to cut down
- Excess time spent in procuring or using
- Cravings, strong urges to use

Social impairment

- Use results in failure to fulfill major role
- Continued use despite adverse consequences (social, interpersonal)
- Reduced opportunities (social, work) due to substance use

Substance use despite the risks involved

- Recurrent use in hazardous situations
- Persistent use despite knowledge of negative consequences

Physiological responses of increased tolerance and withdrawal

- Tolerance (increased amounts are needed to achieve the desired effect; lessened effect of same amount used)
- Withdrawal (symptoms of withdrawal; substance taken to relieve withdrawal) (APA, 2013, pp. 483–484)

Severity is determined based on the number of symptoms evident, ranging from mild (two to three symptoms) to severe (six or more symptoms).

DON'T FORGET

Tolerance refers to either needing more of a substance to achieve the desired effect or experiencing less of an effect from continued use of the same amount. *Withdrawal* symptoms are specific physiological or psychological reactions causing discomfort in response to abstinence from the substance. Often those experiencing withdrawal symptoms will reestablish contact with the substance, or a similar substance, to alleviate the symptoms.

DON'T FORGET

Caffeine is the only substance of the 10 substance categories that does not have diagnostic criteria for substance use, since the *DSM-5* notes that "data are not available at this time to determine the clinical significance of a caffeine use disorder or its prevalence" (p. 504). The *DSM-5* does, however, recognize symptoms of substance-induced disorders for caffeine, for intoxication and withdrawal.

SUBSTANCE-INDUCED DISORDERS

Clinical Description and Associated Features

The *DSM-5* discusses 10 categories of substances, including alcohol, caffeine, cannabis, hallucinogens (phencyclidine and other hallucinogens), inhalants, opiods, sedatives, hypnotics or anxiolytics, stimulants, and tobacco. For each class of substance, different symptoms are presented for intoxication and withdrawal. In addition to these classes of substances, the *DSM* also notes that many over-the-counter medications and prescription medications can also cause substance-related disorders. Symptoms of intoxication and withdrawal will differ depending on the nature of the substance used. For example, alcohol intoxication is related to problem behaviors (physical or psychological changes) that might manifest in aggressive behavior, mood swings, or impaired judgment. One or more of the following indicators of alcohol use may be evident: slurred speech, lack of coordination, unsteady gait, nystagmus, impaired attention/memory, and stupor or coma. Cannabis intoxication can cause a wide variety of symptoms, including impaired motor coordination, euphoria, anxiety, and social withdrawal, often accompanied by two or more of the following symptoms: headache, increased appetite, dry mouth, and tachycardia.

Substance Intoxication

An individual becomes intoxicated when ingestion of a substance results in a specific set of symptoms (substance-specific syndrome). Each substance has its own set of syndrome-specific symptoms. The syndrome is considered reversible, because once the effect of the substance wears off, then the intoxicated behaviors revert to preintoxication levels. Some examples of intoxicated behaviors include belligerence, mood lability, cognitive impairment, and impaired judgement.

Intoxication can impact several sensory functions, including perception, psychomotor behavior (reflexes), concentration and attention, and cognitive processing. Intoxication can also influence personality and interpersonal behaviors.

Although alcohol use may initially be associated with less-inhibited social behaviors and an apparent facade of social ease, repeated use may result in social withdrawal. According to the *DSM*, responses to intoxication are similar among some substances (e.g., amphetamines and cocaine both produce grandiosity and hyperactivity, while alcohol intoxication shares similar features with the sedative, hypnotic, and anxiolytic substances). Common substances used by adolescents and youth are presented in Rapid Reference 12.1. Some of the more common presenting features of intoxication are outlined in the chart.

DON'T FORGET

Intoxication results from the substance's effect on central nervous system (CNS) functioning. Different substances affect the CNS in different ways in different individuals and at different times. For example, alcohol might make one person argumentative and another giddy.

Rapid Reference 12.1

Common Drugs Used by Adolescents and Youth and Their Symptoms

Drug Name	How Used	Slang Terms	Symptoms of Intoxication
Marijuana	Most common method is smoking the dried grass rolled into marijuana cigarettes (joints)	Weed, pot, bud, herb, grass, reefer, ganja, green, Mary Jane, cheeba, dope, smoke	The high generally wears off in about 2–3 hours.
Marijuana + embalming fluid	Usually really marijuana + PCP	Loveboat: symptoms of paranoia, difficulty concentrating, agitation, and suspicions	Common experiences of intoxication: mood elevation; increased awareness of senses; increased appetite; sleepiness; dizziness; anxiety and paranoia; short-term memory problems

(Continued)

Drug Name	How Used	Slang Terms	Symptoms of Intoxication
GHB (gamma-hydroxybutyrate)	A clear, odorless substance that can be mixed with drinks	GHB, gamma oh, goop, jib, liquid ecstacy, sleep, soap, booster, Somatomax	Disinhibition, disorientation, and confusion; also known as *date rape drug* Withdrawal: anxiety, tremors, delirium, hallucinations
LSD (D-lysergic acid diethylamide)	Pills, blotter tabs	Acid, dots, hits, blotter, purple haze, barrels, sugar cube, Elvis, blue cheer, electric Kool-Aid, Zen	Dilated pupils; tremors; flushing; chills; distorted sense of time; depersonalization Negative bad trip effects: paranoia, delusions, anxiety, and mood swings
PCP (phencyclidine)	Often used to "lace" other drugs (e.g., sold as many other drugs). Snorted, ingested orally, smoked, or injected	*PCP*: angel dust, amoeba, sherms, STP, embalming fluid, peace pills, animal tank *PCP + Marijuana:* wet, greens, killer weed, leak, dippers *PCP + Ecstacy:* elephant flipping, pikachu	Low dose: drowsy; constricted pupils; impaired motor skills Higher dose: erratic behavior

Source: Information adapted from www.justfacts.org, a website provided by The Center for Substance Abuse Research (CESAR), University of Maryland, College Park, MD. http://www.cesar.umd.edu/cesar/drug_info.asp, Accessed 01/18/2014

Substance Withdrawal

Substance withdrawal refers to a specific set of behaviors (substance-specific syndrome) resulting from abstinence from a substance that has been taken on a chronic, repeated, and prolonged basis. The resulting syndrome impacts significantly to cause distress and impairment in day-to-day functioning in areas of importance. Withdrawal is often accompanied by a high level of discomfort and distress and impacts on physiological and psychological functioning. The user often has a craving for the substance to relieve the symptoms of withdrawal. Substances that are likely to cause withdrawal symptoms include alcohol, cocaine, nicotine, opioids, and sedatives. Most symptoms of withdrawal are the opposite of symptoms noted for intoxication.

Prevalence and Course

Prevalence rates based on age level and substance are available in Rapid Reference 12.2 and are reported as lifetime prevalence rates. The course of substance use has been investigated across development. Age of onset has been declining, with most recent estimates suggesting indoctrination into drug use at about 11 to 12 years of age (Fitzgerald, Davies, Zucker, & Klinger, 1994). Retrospective interviews with adolescents who engage in excessive use of substances have revealed that earlier substance use (prior to age 15) is more likely to result in later excess usage, and that as the number of conduct problems increases, the corresponding risk for excessive substance use increases accordingly (Robins & McEvoy, 1990).

Prevalence rates for substance use vary depending on the nature of the substance. For example, alcohol use is common among youth and adults in the United States, with a 4.6% prevalence rate among 12- to 17-year-olds and an 8.5% rate among adults. Cannabis use is prevalent among approximately 3.4% of youth 12 to 17 years of age and around 1.5% of adults (APA, 2013).

Other than the *DSM* criteria that were established primarily for adults, there is no clear agreement on how to define when alcohol or drug use becomes problematic or criteria that might be used to more appropriately define substance use in adolescents and youth (Winters, Latimer, & Stinchfield, 2001).

Since 1975, the University of Michigan, under a grant from the National Institute on Drug Abuse (NIDA), has collected data on use of illicit drugs in adolescents and youth. Initially, the Monitoring the Future Study (MTF; Johnston, O'Malley, Bachman, & Schulenberg, 2013) surveyed substance use in 12th graders only; however, since 1991 survey responses have been collected from 12th graders, 10th graders, and 8th graders. The most recent survey, collected in 2013, involved approximately 50,000 students in public and private schools across the nation. A comparison of results from 2010 and 2013 can be found in Rapid Reference 12.2. The survey provides significant information regarding current trends in drug use. Although the data reveal a steady decline in reported usage over the years, the rates are still alarmingly high in some areas. In 2013, there was a steady increase in reported usage of any illicit drug with increasing age: 20% of 8th graders, 38% of 10th graders, and 50% of 12th graders. Alcohol use was the most prominent substance reported at all grade levels, with 23% of 8th graders having used alcohol in the past year and 11% within the past 30 days. At the high school level, almost half (47%) of 10th graders and almost two-thirds of 12th graders (62%) had used alcohol within the past year, while 25% of 10th graders and 39% of 12th graders reported use in the past 30 days. Cigarette smoking and marijuana/hashish usage were also among the heaviest drug use reported. Inhalant use was one of the few areas that noted a decline, rather than an increase, with age.

Rapid Reference 12.2

Monitoring the Future Study: A comparison of lifetime prevalence rates for substance use in adolescents and youth in 8th, 10th, and 12th graders in 2010 and 2013

	8th Grade		10th Grade		12th Grade	
Drug	2010	2013	2010	2013	2010	2013
Any illicit drug	21.4	20.3	37.0	38.8	48.2	50.4
Marijuana	17.3	16.5	33.4	35.8	43.8	45.5
Inhalants	14.5	10.8	12.0	8.7	9.0	6.9
LSD	1.8	1.4	3.0	2.7	4.0	3.9
Cocaine	2.6	1.7	3.7	3.3	5.5	4.5
Crack	1.5	1.2	1.8	1.5	2.4	1.8
Heroin	1.3	1.0	1.3	1.0	1.6	1.0
Tranquilizer	4.4	2.9	7.3	5.5	8.5	7.7
Alcohol	35.8	27.8	58.2	52.1	71.0	68.2
30 day*	13.8	10.2	28.9	25.7	41.2	39.2
Cigarettes	20.0	14.8	33.0	25.7	42.2	38.1
1/2 pack+ per day**	.9	.7	2.4	1.5	4.7	3.4
Steroids	1.1	1.1	1.6	1.3	5.5	3.4
MDMA	3.3	1.8	6.4	5.7	7.3	7.1

Source: Reprinted from the National Institute on Drug Abuse website at www.drugabuse.gov.
*Consumed alcohol within the past 30 days.
**Use of cigarettes, at least half a pack daily.

In their summary of the most recent findings, Johnson and colleagues (2013) report that cigarette smoking continues to drop, and current rates represent the lowest rates in the history of the survey. Other positive trends include significant decreases in alcohol use among all grades and declining use of illicit drugs, especially the use of synthetic marijuana (known as K2 or "Spice") among high school seniors, which dropped from 11.3% in 2012 to 7.9% in 2013. The perception of risk for the synthetic stimulant drug, *bath salts*, which was added to the survey in 2012, also demonstrated an increased awareness among seniors of the harmfulness of that drug, with 59.5% now admitting that the drug is harmful, compared to 33.2% the previous year. Other positive trends included the drop in nonmedical usage of prescription medications, such as Vicodin and Oxycontin, and a decline in the use of inhalants. However, the study also pointed out some disturbing trends, especially significant increases in the use of marijuana (past-year and past-month rates) among all users and significant increases in daily marijuana use among 10th graders, in the wake of less perceived risk of harm from usage. Amphetamine use for nonmedical reasons also increased among 12th graders in their past-year and current usage.

The majority of drug experimentation in adolescence does not amount to a significant and lifelong addiction. In fact, the majority of youth abandon the practice once they enter young adulthood (Kouzis & Labouvie, 1992). However, for some, the developmental pathway is not so positive. Youth who rely on heavy and repeated usage over time develop poor outcomes and are at higher risk for juvenile delinquency, teen pregnancy, and academic failure (Newcomb & Felix-Ortiz, 1992).

Studies of ethnic differences in substance use have compared use of alcohol, barbiturates, amphetamines, and hallucingoens and found that usage of these drugs is more prominent among Caucasian males, while abuse of heroin, crack, and cocaine is more prevalent in Hispanic youth. Native American youth tend to abuse alcohol (Vik, Brown, & Myers, 1997).

DON'T FORGET

Cultural differences in substance use are evident when results from surveys generated in the United States are compared with surveys conducted in Europe. Comparing rates from the 2007 version of *Monitoring the Future* (MTF; Johnston, O'Malley, Bachman, & Schulenberg, 2008), with results from the *European School Survey Project on Alcohol and Other Drugs* (ESPAD; Hibell et al., 2009) revealed that when rates for substance use were compared among 15- and 16-year-olds in the United States and Europe, the highest lifetime prevalence rates reported in the United States were for alcohol (61.7%), tobacco (34.6%), cannabis (31%), any other illicit drugs (18.2%), and inhalants (13.6%), compared to European youth reports for prevalence of use for alcohol (66%), tobacco (58%), cannabis (19%), and inhalants (9%).

Etiology

Biological, Genetic, and Neurotransmitter Function

From a biological perspective, genetic influences contribute to the development of substance use, accounting for 40% to 60% of the variance in risk for alcohol use and 30% to 80% of the variance in risk for cannabis use (APA, 2013). Early investigations of alcohol abuse among twins determined that if one twin abused alcohol, the likelihood of the second twin to also abuse alcohol was 54% (Kaij, 1960). Further support is also available from studies of children of alcoholics who were adopted at birth. These children show a higher rate of alcohol abuse than children who did not have biological parents who were alcoholics (Cadoret, Yates, Troughton, Woodworth, & Stewart, 1993).

Studies of neurotransmitter function and genetic transmission have found that an abnormal dopamine receptor (D2) can be found in the majority of individuals who have alcohol dependence and in at least half of those addicted to cocaine (Lawford et al., 1997). One of the most popular theories of addiction suggests that recurrent substance use mimics the effect of naturally occurring neurotransmitters and that the body reduces production as a result (Goldstein, 1994). For example, taking alcohol to relax simulates the neurotransmitter GABA's effect of reducing anxiety. Taking alcohol on a repeated basis, the brain has less need for GABA and production declines. As tolerance is increased, the person requires more and more alcohol to achieve the same effect.

Behavioral Perspective

From a behaviorist perspective, the altered states (reduction of tension or elevation of mood) produced by drugs can be a rewarding alternative for those who are taking them, because substance use is related to activating reward centers in the brain. Individuals who become addicted to substances, and demonstrate physiological symptoms of tolerance and withdrawal, often continue to indulge in the substance because it is a way to alleviate tension and is self-rewarding, which increases the risk for increased use. Reduction of tension is an initial side effect of several drugs, including alcohol and marijuana. Given a high level of stress and tension, many people may *self-medicate* to reduce tension. Support for this suggestion can be found in studies that have found high levels of depression and anxiety among those who abuse substances.

> **DON'T FORGET**
>
> Increased usage and decreased production of GABA creates a dependency on the drug to simulate what would have been a natural GABA function.

Sociocultural Perspective

Youth whose families and peers sanction drinking are much more likely to become problem drinkers than those whose families are unsupportive. In a longitudinal study that tracked approximately 100 youth from preschool to high school, Shedler and Block (1990) found that substance use (marijuana) could be clustered into three categories: *frequent users* (used at least once weekly, plus had tried another drug), *abstainers* (had not tried any drugs), and *experimenters* (tried a few times, plus tried one other drug). Results revealed that teens who experimented with marijuana (which was a relatively commonly used drug at that time) were normal, well-adjusted teenagers. Frequent users had the worst profiles; starting out as insecure and distressed in elementary school, these troubled teenagers continued to experience problems socially and emotionally, evident in their hostile and antisocial behaviors. Abstainers were also maladjusted and tended to be overcontrolled, timid, and withdrawn.

Dishion, McCord, and Poulin (1999), at the University of Oregon, developed a 12-week intervention program focused on 11- to 14-year-old youth who were considered high risk for drug abuse and increasingly more serious delinquent behaviors. The program, called the Adolescent Transitions Program (ATP), involved 158 at-risk youth (83 boys and 75 girls) who were enrolled in grades 6 through 8. Youth were randomly assigned to one of four groups: peer group, peer plus parent group, parent-only group, and control group (no intervention). The ATP focused on improving skills in the following areas: emotion management, relationship building, and limit setting and saying no to drugs. Parent groups focused on communication skills and problem management.

The study provided a dramatic demonstration of how negative peer influences, *deviancy training*, can encourage rule-breaking behaviors and drug use at a time when peer influence is at a peak and the likelihood of experimentation with drugs is the most pronounced. Within this context, adolescents with low self-esteem or those who are alienated may be most vulnerable to drug use to enhance their acceptability and peer status.

CAUTION

At the end of the 12-week program, all three groups revealed improved skills and parent–child relationships relative to the control group. However, follow-up 3 years later revealed that those who were aggregated with peers during the 12-week period reported two times the tobacco use compared to nongrouped peers, and 75% reported more delinquent behaviors. Furthermore, those youth who had the least amount of delinquent behaviors initially showed the greatest amount of change but in a negative direction.

Diathesis-Stress Model

Given the nature of drug use and abuse, it is highly likely that etiology results from a combination of multiple factors. One model that attempts to incorporate several factors into an explanation of the development of drug abuse is the *diathesis-stress model* (Windle & Tubman, 1999). The model looks at how some individuals might be more vulnerable to drug-related attempts to cope with stress based on individual characteristics (familial alcoholism, genetic transmission, personality/temperament). At the best of times, coping skills might be adequate. However, when environmental factors (family, school, peers, economics) are adverse, resulting stress may make some individuals more likely to respond using drugs to self-medicate and buffer stress.

Risks and Protective Factors

Several factors can place youth at risk for substance use and abuse that operate at all levels of influence. At a personal level, genetic links to an alcoholic parent may increase their risk to substance use when environmental pressures increase. Poor self-esteem, depression, anxiety, and attentional problems have all been linked with increased risk for substance use. Association with peers who use substances and living in a neighborhood where drugs are readily accessible also place youth at risk. Conversely, having a supportive family, feeling a sense of belonging to school and community, and doing well academically are all protective factors that buffer youth from engaging in frequent substance use.

The National Institute on Drug Abuse (NIDA, 2003a) has recently published the second edition of *Preventing Drug Use Among Children and Adolescents: A Research-Based Guide for Parents, Educators, and Community Leaders*. The document is also available on the NIDA website at www.drugabuse.gov. The guide introduces 16 principles of prevention, addressing issues of risks and protective factors, prevention planning, and prevention-program delivery based on the existing research. The first four principles address the importance of addressing issues of risks and protective factors in prevention such that programs enhance protective factors and reduce risks. The principles acknowledge several facts concerning risks and protective factors, including age-related changes and family influences having greater impact in the earlier years, while associating with substance-abusive peers may be an important risk later on (Dishion et al., 1999). Domains of influence are also an important factor when considering the influences of risks and protective factors that can cut across individual, family, peer, school, and community settings.

CAUTION

Frequency of use is not always reported in surveys of substance use. In this survey, it is an important component, as experimentation can be high in adolescence, especially for alcohol, cigarettes, and marijuana. For the sake of brevity, only the lifetime prevalence is reported in Rapid Reference 12.2 for the majority of drugs. The reader is encouraged to review the published results, which include annual, 30-day, and, at times, daily usage rates.

CAUTION

The term *binge drinking* is used to refer to heavy consumption on a single occasion (e.g., five or more drinks during the same drinking session). Prevalence rates for drug usage often refer to frequency of taking drugs rather than quantity of drug consumed. One survey reported that approximately 33% of high school seniors and 25% of sophomores engage in binge drinking at least twice a month (Johnson & Pandina, 2000).

Researchers have also investigated the types of drugs taken relative to increasing severity. Results suggest that the most common progression in drug taking begins with alcohol and cigarettes and then progresses to marijuana. Entry into the hard-drug market, such as the market for cocaine and heroin, is at the later stages of drug use. Investigations of the *gateway phenomenon* (how early drug use sets the stage for later and harder drugs) reveal that the majority of youth who experiment with drugs, such as alcohol, cigarettes, and marijuana, do not go on to take harder drugs (Waldron, 1998). Youth who are at risk for progressing from experimentation to the development of a habitual and compulsive pattern of drug use often have other comorbid disorders and associated risk factors (which are discussed shortly).

Many children and youth who use substances have comorbid disorders. Several other disorders have been linked to excess substance use, including depression, anxiety, disruptive behavior disorders, eating disorders, and ADHD. Many have ADHD, plus depression, plus substance use problems (Kaplan, 1998). Information from the National Comorbidity Study revealed that individuals with anxiety disorders are two to three times more likely to engage in substance use compared to their nonanxious peers (Kendler, Gallagher, Abelson, & Kessler, 1996).

ADHD and Substance Abuse

In their eight-year follow-up of ADHD children in adolescence, Barkley and colleagues (1990) found that hyperactive teens with ADHD were significantly more likely than their nonhyperactive peers to use cigarettes and alcohol. However, a recent study that followed ADHD children into adolescence revealed higher levels of substance use (alcohol, tobacco, and illicit drug use) than their non-ADHD peers (Molina & Pelham, 2003). Furthermore, the authors suggest that a diagnosis of ADHD in childhood seems to be as strong a predictor for substance use as having a family history of substance use and that this risk is not substance specific but cuts across alcohol, tobacco, marijuana, and other drugs.

The authors suggest that results may point to a developmental pathway from inattention to substance abuse mediated by academic impairment and suggest that executive functioning deficits may be at the basis of this link to substance use.

CAUTION

In the study by Molina and Pelham (2003), the remarkable finding was that it was not the severity of hyperactive-impulsive symptoms or ODD/CD symptoms but the *severity of inattention* that predicted the vulnerable population.

CAUTION

A general concern regarding the treatment of children with ADHD through the use of stimulant medication has been the underlying fear that this will lead to an increased rate of substance use later on. However, research does not support this concern. In fact, successful treatment of ADHD actually serves as a protective factor for later substance use, as adults who were not treated for ADHD are associated with much higher rates of substance use problems (Biederman et al., 1999).

Treatment

In recent years, there has been increasing recognition of the unique features of drug abuse in youth compared to adults and the need to incorporate these features into programs designed specifically for adolescents (Deas, Riggs, Langenbuncher, Goldman, & Brown, 2000).

Twelve-Step Models

The 12-step models have as their origin the 12-step orientation developed by Alcoholics Anonymous (AA) and Narcotics Anonymous (NA), which were founded on the beliefs that addiction is a progressive disease and that treatment requires abstinence (Kassel & Jackson, 2001). Traditionally, 12-step programs involve community-based meetings that are frequented by recovering members who support each other's abstinence through confessions, sharing stories, and often by providing opportunities for connecting with a lifeline buddy for crisis purposes. Because of the anonymity of the individuals involved in the programs, empirical evidence is lacking concerning the outcomes of the majority of 12-step programs. However, Brown (1993) revealed that 12-step groups, such as AA, NA, and Cocaine Anonymous, are supported and widely attended by recovered youth, while investigations of the 12-step Minnesota Model found that youth who attended the program had better outcomes than untreated youth (Kassel & Jackson, 2001).

Cognitive-Behavioral Therapy (CBT)

Substance programs that use cognitive-behavioral therapy (CBT) focus on several targets to reframe maladaptive thinking patterns that have developed as conditioned responses to environmental triggers. The underlying premise is based on learning theory and hypothesizes that substance use develops as a response to environmental cues or triggers and consequences (socially reinforcing events, physiological arousal) that precipitate and maintain abusive habits (Waldron & Kern-Jones, 2004).

DON'T FORGET

Waldron and Kern-Jones (2004) discuss how framing a cognitive perspective within a social learning model (Bandura, 1977) allows for greater consideration of multiple factors in the acquisition and maintenance of substance use through mechanisms of observation and imitation learning (parents and peers) in such areas as social reinforcement, self-efficacy, and the development of associated belief systems.

Programs that use CBT mainly focus on enhancing skills in self-management through awareness of triggers and developing adaptive ways of responding to these triggers. Important components of these programs include self-monitoring, assertiveness/refusal skills, avoidance of specific triggers, problem solving, relaxation training, and other approaches to adaptive coping (Monti, Abrams, Kadden, & Cooney, 1989). A key component of the program is a built-in relapse-prevention component. Empirical investigations of CBT programs have studied the efficacy of these programs delivered individually, in groups, or with family.

In their investigations, Liddle and Hogue (2001) found that youth assigned to individual CBT or family therapy had significant declines in internalizing and externalizing problems and a reduction in drug use. Liddle and Hogue (2001) and Waldron and Kern-Jones (2004) both found a delay factor operating in CBT programs for youth alone. Liddle and Hogue suggested that perhaps time is required to consolidate the CBT skills that were not evident at posttreatment but emerged as delayed positive outcomes on later follow-up. Initial findings from these and other studies of CBT suggest that CBT programs delivered individually, in groups, or with families can be an effective method of treating substance use problems in youth. However, as Waldron and Kern-Jones (2004) suggest, investigation of how these programs can be successful must also address the iatrogenic effects found in other studies that aggregated high-risk youth (Azrin, Donohue, Besalel, Kogan, & Acierno, 1994; Dishion et al., 1999). Ultimately, a greater understanding will be obtained regarding how to best deliver treatment that is supportive and not detrimental.

Family-Based Treatment

Investigations including the family in treatment alternatives for substance problems have used CBT (see preceding section), multisystemic therapy (MST; Henggeler et al., 1998), functional behavioral family therapy (Emery, 2001), and multidimensional family therapy (MDFT; Liddle, 2009) approaches. The inclusion of a family component in the treatment program has been demonstrated to increase participant engagement in the process and increase program effectiveness (Stanton & Shadish, 1997). In a study comparing behavioral family therapy to a treatment alternative (process-oriented treatment), Azrin and colleagues (1994) found family therapy to have a 50% success rate for reduction of alcohol and drug use compared to increased usage in the process-oriented group. In another comparison study, Donohue and Azrin (2001) found family behavioral therapy superior to a program using a problem-solving method.

Liddle, Rowe, Dakof, Henderson, and Greenbaum (2009) have applied MDFT successfully in multiple settings (office-based, in-home, brief-intensive outpatient, day treatment, residential) and in a variety of ways, depending on the nature of the problem and the level of severity (3 to 6 months' duration, or one to three times weekly). Therapists gather data from multiple sources (adolescent, parents, family, extrafamilial systems) and focus on how to enhance positive feelings and emotional connectivity to support the adolescent's success in achieving their goals. The program has been successful in reducing substance use (success rates vary between 41% and 66%) and demonstrate greater symptom reduction (30% to 85%) compared with other treatment programs (Liddle et al., 2009).

Prevention

In the United States, federal funds have been available since 1994 to assist in the provision of education programs to prevent drug abuse. However, since 1998, due to amendments to the Safe and Drug-Free Schools and Communities Act (SDFSCA), federal grant requirements have included the need to use empirically based programs (evidence-based curriculum). Several programs exist that incorporate features that have been proven effective through research to reduce drug use and abuse, including awareness of the harmful effects of illicit drugs, nicotine, and alcohol and information regarding how to be more assertive and effective in refusing drugs when offered. Empirically based drug abuse prevention programs targeted at middle school students have been successful in significantly reducing early use of tobacco, alcohol, and other drugs.

Despite the availability of funds and the mandate to include evidence-based programs, a survey conducted by Ringwalt and colleagues (2002) found that 75% of middle schools were using programs that were not supported by research. In fact, the curriculum used by the majority of middle schools, the Drug Abuse Resistance Education program (DARE), has been researched extensively and found to be ineffective in the prevention of drug use and abuse. Other than DARE, the two most popular programs used in public and private schools that have research support are Project Alert and Life Skills Training.

The Life Skills Training program (LST) has been demonstrated to be effective in significantly reducing drug use and abuse in minority students who are at risk for drug use because of poor academic performance and association with substance-abusing peers (Botvin, Griffin, Diaz, & Ifill-Williams, 2001; Griffin, Botvin, Nichols, & Doyle, 2003). Although the LST program was initially tested on white students in suburban schools, this school-based prevention program has since demonstrated effectiveness across minority ethnic populations (African American, and Hispanic) and socioeconomic levels. The portability of the LST program was demonstrated in a controlled investigation of the program's effectiveness in 29 inner-city New York schools. The LST program was delivered to seventh graders by regular education teachers in 15 sessions (45-minute duration). Sessions provided information about social skills, drug refusal, and personal management. Compared to students who received the standard New York City school drug education program, students enrolled in the LST program demonstrated lower rates of alcohol, cigarette, and inhalant abuse than their peers who were not enrolled in the LST program.

DON'T FORGET

The prevention guidelines (NIDA, 2003a) suggest that school programs should focus on age-appropriate behaviors and intervene to reduce risk factors associated with later maladaptive behaviors such as aggression and self-control (preschool). In elementary school, targets should include emotional awareness, social problem solving, increased communication, and academic support. Improved study habits, academic support, drug resistance skills, self-efficacy, and antidrug attitudes are important areas of focus in middle and high school.

DON'T FORGET

One of the most common programs used in schools throughout the United States for the "prevention" of substance use is the DARE program, although research has shown that the program is ineffective in reducing substance use (West and O'Neal, 2004).

Principles of prevention planning (NIDA, 2003a) outline several important research-supported areas to target in the family, school, and community. Family programs should include drug awareness, parent skills training, increased monitoring and supervision, and the need for consistent discipline and limit setting.

Combined family and school programs enhance a community's efficacy in promoting cohesiveness and a sense of belonging.

TEST YOURSELF

1. The most common substance used by youth worldwide, is

(a) cannabis.
(b) alcohol.
(c) tobacco.
(d) inhalants.

2. There was a time when John could have one drink and feel the effects of decreased anxiety and increased sociability. Now it takes three drinks to get half the effect. It is likely that John has developed

(a) dependence.
(b) tolerance.

(c) withdrawal.
(d) increased sensitivity to the substance.

3. **According to the DSM an individual can match criteria for a substance use disorder without exhibiting either tolerance or withdrawal.**

   True or False?

4. **According to the latest results of the MFT (Monitoring the Future) Study collected in 2013, which is FALSE?**
   (a) Cigarette smoking continues to drop and is at its lowest rate ever.
   (b) There is a decrease in reported usage across all substances with increasing age.
   (c) Attitudes toward harm of cannabis use have been softening.
   (d) Cigarette smoking and marijuana were among the heaviest drugs used.

5. **One survey reported that up to one third of high school seniors engage in binge drinking (at least five drinks a session) at least once a month.**

   True or False?

6. **Studies that have investigated the comorbidity of ADHD and substance use have found that**
   (a) hyperactive teens are more likely to use cigarettes and alcohol than non-hyperactive peers.
   (b) severity of inattentive symptoms predicts risk to substance use.
   (c) ADHD is as strong a predictor of substance use as family history.
   (d) investigators have found all of the above.

7. **Although 12-step programs seem to be a viable treatment alternative for adolescents who have substance use problems, obtaining empirical support has been difficult due to**
   (a) high dropout rates in these programs.
   (b) anonymity associated with the programs.
   (c) lack of systematic approach.
   (d) lack of interest.

8. **Recent investigations of treatment alternatives for youth with substance use problems have found that including the family in treatment**
   (a) can increase participation and program effectiveness.
   (b) can undermine program success.
   (c) is inferior to individual process-oriented treatment.
   (d) is virtually impossible.

Answers: 1. b; 2. b; 3. true; 4. b; 5. true; 6. d; 7. b; 8. a

Part VI

Special Topics in Child and Adolescent Psychopathology

This final section includes information on two areas that have not yet been addressed: trauma- and stressor-related disorders and the impact of cultural diversity on child and adolescent psychopathology.

The *DSM-5* has reorganized the presentation of disorders related to stress and currently discusses all relevant disorders in the same chapter, which contains a wide range of disorders from the temporary response to a known stressor (adjustment disorders) to the long-term and profound impact of trauma caused by severe deprivation in early child-rearing (reactive attachment disorder and disinhibited social engagement disorder), or the impact of experiencing or witnessing a traumatic event (posttraumatic stress disorder and acute stress disorder). Previously, the disorders were found in various chapters entitled Anxiety Disorders (PTSD and acute stress disorder), Disorders Usually First Diagnosed in Infancy, Childhood, or Adolescence (attachment disorders) and Adjustment Disorders. New to the *DSM-5* is the separation of the attachment disorders into two separate disorders (previously reactive attachment disorder was considered to be one disorder with two possible presentations: inhibited or disinhibited type) and the development of a new set of criteria for the diagnosis of PTSD in preschool children (prior to 6 years of age).

The importance of understanding the role of culture in shaping our beliefs of mental illness, influencing symptom presentations and conceptualizations of distress, has been an area of growing concern among mental health professionals. After an initial discussion of culture, race, and ethnicity, the chapter focuses on risks and prevalence rates facing children and youth from minority populations. This chapter provides an overview of the impact of culture on child and adolescent psychopathology and a brief look at demographics, common parenting practices, and prevalence of mental health issues among four populations: African Americans, Latino/Hispanic Americans, Asian Americans and Pacific Islanders, and Native American Indians.

Thirteen

TRAUMA- AND STRESSOR-RELATED DISORDERS

Environmental stressors can occur on a daily basis. Some stressors are more intense and prolonged than others and, as a result, can cause more severe emotional repercussions. When stress results in a temporary state of distress, the disorder is described as an adjustment disorder. However, when the stressor is of a catastrophic nature, then posttraumatic stress disorder (PTSD) or acute stress disorder may develop in the aftermath. Some children experience severe forms of early trauma as a result of exposure to caregiving practices that are minimally supportive on a social, emotional, or physical level. In these cases, children may develop reactive attachment disorder (RAD) or disinhibited social engagement disorder (DSED). Given that these disorders all share features of exposure to a stressor that results in significant distress, the *DSM-5* has grouped all of them within the chapter on Trauma- and Stressor-Related Disorders and removed them from previous *DSM-IV* chapters on Anxiety Disorders (PTSD, acute stress disorder), Adjustment Disorders (adjustment disorders), and Disorders Usually First Diagnosed in Infancy, Childhood, or Adolescence (attachment disorders).

ADJUSTMENT DISORDERS

Clinical Description and Associated Features

Adjustment disorder is defined by the *DSM-5* (APA, 2013) as a psychological response to an identifiable stressor (or stressors) that results in significantly distressing emotional and behavioral reactions. The response is notably more intense than would be expected, given the circumstances, and causes significant impairment in functioning. Wenar and Kerig (2000) categorize adjustment disorders as a bridge between normal behavior and psychopathology. The reaction occurs

DON'T FORGET

When our capacity to cope with existing demands exceeds our ability to cope, then stress becomes distress.

within three months of the stressful situation and does not last longer than 6 months after the stressor is removed. The stressor may be an isolated event or incident (e.g., loss of job, termination of relationship), recurrent (yearly income tax crisis), or chronic (poverty), and can affect an individual or an entire group (family).

Prevalance and Course

The prevalence of adjustment disorders is between 5% and 20% in a community mental health setting, and as high as 50% in a psychiatric facility (APA, 2013).

Difficulties coping with stressors may result in the development of an adjustment disorder, which can be accompanied by a number of different symptoms. The *DSM-5* provides specifiers that indicate whether the disorder is accompanied by *anxiety* (fears, doubts, restlessness, separation anxiety), *depression* (irritability, moodiness, sadness, withdrawal), *a mixture of anxiety and depressed mood, disruptive behaviors* (aggression, rule violations, truancy), or *a mixture of disturbed emotions and conduct.* Awareness of adjustment problems is important to provide interventions that can prevent the disorder from escalating into another, more serious disorder.

How an individual responds to a stressor varies depending on his or her cultural background, developmental stage, temperament, and gender. Although women are twice as likely as men to be diagnosed with adjustment disorder, boys and girls have an equal likelihood of being diagnosed. Prevalence rates for children and adolescents vary between 2% and 8%, with those living in high-stress environments being vulnerable to increased risk. For children, headache and stomachache are the most common somatic symptoms (Alfven, 2001), while feeling "mad" is the most common cognitive/emotional response to a stressor (Sharrer & Ryan-Wenger, 1995).

PUTTING IT INTO PRACTICE

When Eric's father was transferred, Eric did not want to move. When his parents put the house up for sale, Eric wrote a message on the bulletin board in his bedroom telling prospective buyers that the house was haunted. Eventually, his parents caught on to Eric's plan, and the house did sell. As a result, the family moved from Chicago to Boston, and Eric settled into a period of intense withdrawal. He refused to make friends with his new classmates. Entering middle school was bad enough, but starting in a new school was even worse. Eric blamed his parents continually for his problems with peers, academics, and teachers. However, when basketball season started, Eric, who was a star performer, quickly made the team and developed a set of friendships that changed his circumstances drastically, as the old Eric was revitalized.

In this example, although a school move and relocation are normal stressful events for children, Eric's response is extreme, debilitating, and causing severe impairment in his family, social, and academic functioning. However, true to its name, Eric's *period of adjustment* to his new circumstances did eventually resolve, and Eric ultimately was able to engage in his new surroundings.

DON'T FORGET

One of the most important factors of temperament that determine a child's ability to cope with a stressor is the self-regulatory system of *effortful control* (Rothbart, 2003; Rothbart & Bates, 2006). Effortful control is the voluntary ability to regulate emotions and inhibit behavioral responses to stressors when necessary (behavioral inhibition) by suppressing a dominant (prepotent) response in favor of a more adaptive response.

In their meta-analysis of coping styles involving 63 studies, Compas, Conner-Smith, Saltzman, Thomsen, and Wadsworth (2001) found that children and adolescents engaged in four potential coping styles evolving around themes of *engaged coping*, such as active coping (cognitive decision making, problem solving) and seeking social support (emotion-focused support), and *disengaged coping*, such as distraction and avoidance (avoidance of negative emotions). The researchers concluded that children who use problem-focused and engaged coping styles tend to be better adjusted than those who use patterns of disengaged coping.

Some of the most stressful events in early childhood, middle childhood, and adolescence that can trigger an adjustment reaction include adjustments to stressors in school, family, and the environment:

- *Adjustment to stressors in school.* The transitions to elementary school (6 years of age) and junior high school (12 years of age) have been linked to increased access to public health services because of children's complaints of headaches, stomachaches, and body pains (Schor, 1986). Stress may be related to changes in the school setting and expectations that accompany transitions related to shifting from smaller class sizes and close teacher supervision to larger classes, multiple teachers, higher expectations, and less guidance and supervision (Seidman, Aber, & French, 2004).

- *Adjustment to stressors in the family.* Family conditions that can contribute to stress for children include unpredictability and lack of structure. These conditions can impact motivation, feelings of self-worth, and influence negative outcomes for children in several areas, including behavior regulation (attention, working memory), reading, and parent verbal responsiveness (Evans, Gonnella, Marcynyszyn, Gentile, & Salpekar, 2005). Adolescents living in stressful family situations marked by conflict are prone to chronic emotional arousal and increased reactivity to other stressful events (Repetti, Taylor, & Seeman, 2002).
- *Adjustment to stressors in the environment.* Stressful life transitions and exposure to neighborhood violence at an early age can increase a child's risk for developing aggressive behaviors in later years (Attar, Guerra, & Tolan, 1994). Stress and experiencing stressful life events have been demonstrated to impact child and adolescent mental health in negative ways (Grant, Compas, Thurm, & McMahon, 2004).

ATTACHMENT DISORDERS

Clinical Description and Associated Features

Children who are reared in environments that are significantly deprived, such that their basic affective and emotional needs have not been met, or who have experienced repeated changes in caregivers, or who have been reared in an environment that provides minimal opportunity to form attachments can develop one of two forms of emotional disturbance in their ability to form relationships with others: (a) reactive attachment disorder (RAD), which is characterized by extremely withdrawn and inhibited responses to adult caregivers, or (b) disinhibited social engagement disorder (DSED), which is characterized by indiscriminate attempts to engage in relationships with unfamiliar adults. Both disorders require that the child is at least 9 months of age for a diagnosis to be made.

In the *DSM-IV* (APA, 2000), there was only one attachment disorder, RAD, which was considered to have two different types of presentations: the inhibited type or the disinhibited type. The *DSM-5* now conceptualizes these types as two separate disorders, in keeping with how the disorder was conceptualized in the *International Classification of Diseases* (WHO, 1993). Children who are diagnosed with RAD or DSED have been identified in maltreated, institutionalized, or previously institutionalized populations (Rutter et al., 2007; Zeanah, Smyke, & Dumitrescu, 2002).

REACTIVE ATTACHMENT DISORDER (RAD)

Clinical Description and Associated Features

Children who are diagnosed with reactive attachment disorder (RAD) demonstrate significantly inhibited and withdrawn behaviors toward caregivers in two important ways: (1) They do not seek comfort from caregivers when they are distressed; and (2) they are unable to be comforted when they are distressed. Behavior patterns illustrate at least two of the following: minimal ability to respond appropriately to others; minimal positive affect; or behavior patterns characterized by fearfulness, irritability, and sadness (APA, 2013, p. 265). A diagnosis of RAD requires that symptoms of RAD be evident before 5 years of age, and the characteristics are not better accounted for by symptoms of autism spectrum disorder (ASD).

DISINHIBITED SOCIAL ENGAGEMENT DISORDER (DSED)

Clinical Description and Associated Features

Children diagnosed with DSED demonstrate indiscriminate behaviors to unfamiliar adults that are characterized by at least two of the following behaviors: minimal discretion in approaching or interacting with strangers; attempts to be overly familiar (verbally or physically) with others; minimal checking back with caregivers in unfamiliar settings; or tendencies to wander off with an unfamiliar adult. The behaviors are considered to be evident for more than 12 months and are not better accounted for by the impulsivity associated with attention-deficit/hyperactivity disorder.

PREVALENCE AND COURSE OF THE ATTACHMENT DISORDERS

Based on their longitudinal investigation of children who were adopted from institutions, Gleason and colleagues (2011) support the need to conceptualize two separate types of attachment disorders. The researchers found that 17.6% of children in the institutions exhibited characteristics of DSED, while 4.1% exhibited the characteristics associated with RAD. According to the *DSM-5*, RAD is rare, with less than 10% of children exposed to severe deprivation developing the disorder. Prevalence for DSED is somewhat more elevated, with about a 20% prevalence rate in populations that have been exposed to severe deprivation.

Given that attachment disorders result from pathogenic care involving severe conditions of emotional or physical maltreatment or some form of institutionalized care, it is not surprising to see that many children meet criteria for both an attachment disorder and PTSD (Hinshaw-Fuselier, Boris, & Zeanah, 1999).

POSTTRAUMATIC STRESS DISORDER

Posttraumatic stress disorder (PTSD) and acute stress disorder are triggered by a stressor, the nature of which is so extreme that the trauma can impact an individual's life in many profound ways. Acute stress disorder features the same criteria as PTSD in describing the type of traumatic event that qualifies (see criteria A in the following section); however, the duration of acute stress disorder does not last longer than 1 month.

Clinical Description and Associated Features

The *DSM-5* conceptualizes PTSD in several new ways. There are now two sets of criteria for a diagnosis of PTSD: a set of criteria for adults, youth, and children 6 years or older (the *standard criteria*) and a set of criteria for children younger than 6 years (the *criteria for preschool children*). This discussion begins by describing criteria in the standard version and then how criteria have been modified for preschool children. The presence of symptoms from the following categories must be evident for more than one month and may have the specifier "with delayed expression," if diagnostic criteria are not fully met until six months after the event. The standard version has five criteria clusters: Cluster A provides criteria for determining whether the event meets standards for a traumatic event, while Clusters B–E describe the symptoms contained within four symptom clusters:

- *Criteria A: The traumatic event.* The *DSM-5* continues to describe a traumatic event as one that exposes an individual to "actual or threatened death, serious injury, or sexual violence," which meets criteria for one of the following: direct experiencing of the event; witnessing the event; learning of the event involving a close family member or friend; or having repeated exposure (such as in first responders).
- *Criteria B: Experiencing of intrusive symptoms.* One symptom is required from this category that lists several examples, such as recurrent dreams, memories, flashbacks, or repetitive play or trauma play in children.
- *Criteria C: Avoidance behaviors.* One symptom required from avoiding memories or thoughts, or avoiding people/places/events that trigger memories.

- *Criteria D: Negative thoughts or mood.* This is a new category, and two symptoms are required that refer to loss of memory about the event, negative beliefs, self-blame, negative emotional states, detachment, and so on.
- *Criteria E: Symptoms of arousal and reactivity.* At least two symptom of heightened arousal/reactivity must be present, such as irritable or angry outbursts, engagement in self-destructive or risk-taking activities, exaggerated startle response, sleep disturbances, and problems with concentration. (APA, 2013, pp. 272–273).

The preschool version of the PTSD criteria modify the standard version in the following important ways:

- *Criteria A: Traumatic event.* The event is described in the same way and manner as it is in the standard version, except that the reference to first responders is excluded.
- *Criteria B: Experiencing of intrusive symptoms.* One symptom is required, and symptoms are described in more developmentally appropriate ways (e.g., trauma play enactment).
- *Criteria C: Avoidance or negative thoughts.* The two adult criteria are combined into one category for preschool children. Only one symptom is required from this category.
- *Criteria D: Heightened arousal and reactivity.* Two or more symptoms are required.

Symptom duration is the same as for the standard criteria and must be evident for at least 1 month.

PUTTING IT INTO PRACTICE

Juan, a 17-year-old Hispanic youth, was referred to the school psychologist at the end of the first school term because of apparent academic and emotional concerns. His grades were slipping, and it looked like he might not get any credits his first term. The counselor has also explained that Juan was the driver in a fatal car wreck at the end of the previous academic year, in which his best friend was killed. Although Juan was hospitalized, the counselor said that he insisted on going to the funeral, even though he could barely move, having suffered several broken ribs.

When the psychologist met with Juan, he was initially reluctant to discuss the accident, but as rapport was established, he admitted to feeling helpless, feeling fatigued because of lack of sleep, and having problems concentrating on his school work. He

(*continued*)

(*Continued*)

wanted to quit school, because he did not want to be in the same class with students who blamed him for his friend's death, and furthermore he did not see why he should plan for a future. He admitted to having vivid dreams of his friend, seeing him as if he were alive. Often he would wake up, startled. He had no recollection of how the accident happened, as he could not remember the details, even though a witness had said that another car was involved.

Although he has a girlfriend, Juan rarely feels like doing anything, and in the past few months he has preferred to be alone. Although he was very close to his deceased friend's family (they were inseparable), he has not seen them since the funeral.

In this case, Juan is faced with the aftermath of a traumatic experience in which he was seriously injured and his friend was killed. He feels helpless because of the accidental nature of the wreck. Undoubtedly, Juan has significant survivor guilt. Faced with traumatic events of this nature, individuals react with fear, horror, or helplessness. In younger children, these feelings are often expressed in disorganized and agitated behaviors.

DON'T FORGET

Children may exhibit reexperiencing developmentally through such actions as trauma reenactment through play or dreams that feature themes of monsters or rescue, and distress may be evident in somatic complaints, such as headaches and stomachaches (Carrion, Weems, Ray, & Reiss, 2002).

CAUTION

The *DSM-5* modified criteria of PTSD symptoms for preschool children to better match child characteristics in this developmental period. Before this revision, there was much discontent with existing criteria, because almost half of the criteria (8 out of 18 symptoms) required verbal descriptions of experiences of internal states, which were not suitable for preschool children with limited verbal skills (Scheeringa, Zeanah, Myers, & Putnam, 2005).

Other associated features of the disorder may include a sense of increased guilt or survivor guilt. Of particular importance in working with children and adolescents are several associated features that are mentioned throughout the chapters on PTSD (APA, 2000, 2013). A summary of this list can be found in Rapid Reference 13.1.

Rapid Reference 13.1

Associated Features of PTSD in Children and Adolescents

Symptoms that might be evident in survivors of sexual or physical abuse or in children who are a witness to violence include the following:

- Difficulties with affect regulation
- Behaviors that are impulsive and self-destructive
- Somatic complaints
- Feelings of shame
- Feelings of hopelessness or despair
- Social withdrawal
- Hostility
- Constantly being on guard, feeling threatened
- Change in personality
- Impaired social relationships
- Feelings of permanent damage
- Dissociative symptoms

PUTTING IT INTO PRACTICE

Although *emotional numbing* is not typically the most prevalent symptom in children with PTSD (Carrion et al., 2002), it has been observed at all levels. Several studies suggest that *reexperiencing* is the most prevalent symptom in school-age children (Carrion et al., 2002; LaGreca, Silverman, Vernberg, & Prinstein, 1996).

In a recent study of child symptoms of PTSD, Weems, Saltzman, Reiss, and Carrion (2003) addressed the underlying relationship between emotional numbing and hyperarousal. The authors were particularly interested in whether theories of the relationship between these two symptom clusters for adult populations (Litz, 1992) would apply to children. The hypothesis is that emotional numbing may result from emotional exhaustion resulting from hyperarousal. In a sample of 59 children who were victims of interpersonal trauma (mean age 10 years, 6 months), the authors found preliminary evidence that the direction of effects between emotional numbing and hyperarousal was in the predicted direction, suggesting that emotional numbing in children may result from emotional exhaustion caused by a depletion of cognitive and emotional resources (hyperarousal).

Prevalence and Course

It is difficult to obtain consistent estimates of prevalence rates of PTSD for children and adolescents because of wide variability in the nature of the trauma experienced, whether the trauma was a single episode (natural disaster) or repeated episodes (child victimization) and whether the sample was from a community or clinical population. The rate for adults was estimated to be 8%, and the rate for at least one adolescent population (average age 17 years) was reported to be 6.3% (Giaconia et al., 1994). A more recent study of a population of younger adolescents (12 to 17 years of age) found prevalence rates at 3.7% for males and 6.3% for females (Kilpatrick et al., 2003). Rates from clinical populations tend to be considerably higher. For example, in their study of sexually abused children (3 to 16 years of age), McLeer, Deblinger, Henry, and Orvaschel (1992) found that 43.9% met criteria for PTSD.

Preschool children may manifest symptoms of trauma in hyperarousal, fear and aggressive responses, separation anxiety, increased irritability, tantrums, nightmares, and sleeping problems (Graham-Bermann et al., 2008). In school-aged children, sleep problems are also a common symptom, noted in increased tendencies to have nightmares, night terrors, sleepwalking, or bed wetting (Amaya-Jackson & March, 1995b). Attention and concentration problems at this age may be evident in poor school achievement, while numbing and avoidance may be manifest in behaviors that appear restless and having problems concentrating (Malmquist, 1986). Children may overreact to school drills and fire alarms, which could trigger the startle response (March, Amaya-Jackson, & Pynoos, 1994).

DON'T FORGET

Responses to trauma can vary depending on the child's age, developmental level, and cognitive capacity or limitations. In addition, responses can also depend on the degree of exposure and the proximity to the event, with closer proximity to the actual trauma having more enduring and severe symptoms (Pynoos, 1994).

It has also been noted that, for some children, numbing and avoidance may take the form of restlessness, poor concentration, hypervigilance, and behavioral problems (Malmquist, 1986).

Children may avoid thoughts, locations, play themes, and concrete items that may remind them of the event. Traumatic exposure may also lead to a temporary elevation in increased risk-taking behaviors (Pynoos, 1990). With young children, problems may surface particularly around bedtime and can be expressed as fear of the dark or fear of sleeping alone in anticipation of nightmares. Adolescents with PTSD may engage in more risk-taking behavior, have more aggressive impulses, and demonstrate more survivor guilt (Pynoos & Nader, 1993).

CAUTION

There are several reasons why PTSD may go undiagnosed in childhood. Those involved with the child (parents, teachers, counselors) may minimize the impact of the trauma to reassure themselves that the child is still intact or rationalize that, given the child's age, the trauma impact will be temporary. Some parentified children from chronically traumatic environments may try to protect the caregiver by minimizing the impact of the trauma. In addition, children with PTSD might alternate long periods of reexperiencing with equally long periods of avoidance and numbing, which might be misinterpreted as having resolved PTSD issues (AACAP, 1998a).

PUTTING IT INTO PRACTICE

Ricky is *hyperactive, distractible,* and *impulsive.* His teacher is certain that he has ADHD. However, Ricky's teacher is unaware that he is a witness to severe bouts of domestic violence on a recurrent basis and that being hyperactive, distractible, and impulsive can indicate anxiety and even PTSD in children. There is a high comorbidity rate between PTSD and ADHD, and some children with PTSD present with ADHD symptoms (Cuffe, McCullough, & Pumariega, 1994; McLeer et al., 1992).

DON'T FORGET

Pynoos and Nader (1993) suggest that adolescents may be particularly vulnerable to the effects of trauma exposure. Developmentally, as children get older, there is increased interaction with the environment, which can lead to increased exposure to potential stressors. In addition, adolescents tend to react to trauma through risk-taking behaviors, which can increase the chances of experiencing more stressful consequences. According to Pynoos (1994), the impact of severe trauma at adolescence can be particularly devastating and life altering, as it can disrupt the trajectory of positive growth and sever the opportunity of integrating past experiences with future expectations.

DON'T FORGET

Comorbidity is a common occurrence with PTSD, and increased risk has been noted for depression, anxiety, and substance abuse (Pfefferbaum, 1997). Some authors have speculated that PTSD might predispose children to the development of depressive disorders (Yehuda & McFarlane, 1995). Based on the results of their study, McDermott and Palmer (2002) suggest that in the aftermath of a trauma, younger children may be more vulnerable to symptoms of depression, while middle school children may be vulnerable to the full-blown emotionally distressing symptoms of PTSD.

CAUTION

Pynoos (1994) discusses how trauma could impact on development in two important ways: proximal and distal. In the more immediate or proximal sense, the trauma can impact on newly acquired skills and competencies. In this way, the trauma could interrupt the solidification process and actually result in regressive behaviors. The more long-term or distal impact could be a future influence on overall personality formation with respect to increased risk taking, heightened threat appraisals, and inappropriate self-attributions.

CAUTION

Reports suggest that females are at higher risk for PTSD and can be up to five times more likely than males to develop PTSD symptoms when exposed to trauma (Breslau, Davis, Andreski, & Peterson, 1991). There has been a suggestion that boys may not manifest symptoms that would be recognized as clearly as girls, and boys may act out rather than present with internalizing symptoms, such as anxiety or depression, which are often tapped by PTSD instruments and interviews (Ostrov, Offer, & Howard, 1989).

Like the initial case study of Juan, PTSD victims often experience significant survivor guilt, which in Juan's case was particularly strong because he was also responsible for the accident that caused the trauma. As Pynoos and Nader (1993) suggest, if the trauma results in the death of a family member or friend, then the situation becomes even more complex. The interaction between trauma and grief reactions often results in continued focus on the traumatic circumstances surrounding the death and blocks the grieving process and subsequent adaptation.

DON'T FORGET

Attachment research has found that traumatized infants who respond with disorganized/disoriented responses to their parent's return in Ainsworth's Strange Situation studies (Ainsworth, Blehar, Waters, & Wall, 1978) demonstrated elevated levels of cortisol at the reunion (Spangler & Grossmann, 1999). On the other hand, mothers of securely attached infants actually moderate stress by lowering the cortisol responses in their vulnerable (behaviorally inhibited) infants (Nachmias, Gunnar, Mangelsdorf, Parritz, & Buss, 1996).

Etiology

Biological, Genetic, and Neurological Correlates

There is evidence that highly stressful events produce physical changes in the body and brain. Abnormal activity of the neurotransmitter *norepinephrine* and elevated levels of the hormone *cortisol* have both been implicated in the process (Baker et al., 1999). There is also evidence that enduring heightened arousal over time may alter the ability of the *hippocampus* (the portion of the brain that regulates stress hormones) to manage future stressful situations (Bremner, 1999).

Specific factors that tend to *increase vulnerability* for PTSD are a past history of childhood sexual or physical trauma, low self-esteem, separation from parents before age 10, prior psychiatric disorder, psychiatric disorder in a first-degree relative, being female (Davidson, 1993), and preexisting anxiety or depression (Breslau et al., 1991). The development of chronic PTSD in childhood has been related to personality variables of locus of control and lack of personal efficacy (Joseph, Brewin, Yule, & Williams,

DON'T FORGET

Environmental conditions such as poverty, parental mental illness, and teen parenthood are known to be high-risk conditions for the development of poor child outcomes (Zeanah, Boris, & Larrieu, 1997). Understandably, parents who are overwhelmed and distressed can often be less supportive to their children's needs.

DON'T FORGET

Factors have also been identified that increase the *risk for exposure to traumatic events*. Having a low education, being male, extraversion, early conduct problems, and family history of psychiatric problems all increased the chances of exposure to traumatic events (Breslau et al., 1991).

1993), while preexisting (trait anxiety) or negative emotionality are predictive of the development of more severe PTSD symptoms (Lonigan et al., 1994).

Subtypes of PTSD

It has also been suggested that a subtyping distinction should be made based on the type of trauma to which an individual has been exposed. According to Terr (1991), there should be a distinction between singular *Type I traumas* (major traumatic event, e.g., vehicle accident, bridge collapse) and repeated *Type II traumas* (such as multiple and long-term physical or sexual abuse). According to Terr, while Type I trauma would be expected to elicit patterns of responses that demonstrate the classic reexperiencing, avoidance, and hyperarousal, Type II traumas might elicit more pervasive symptoms of denial, numbing or dissociation, and rage.

CAUTION

Exposure to violence or abuse at an early age sets the stage for an increased incidence of high-risk behaviors in adolescents, such as teen pregnancy, early sexual activity, eating disorders, substance use, anxiety disorders and depressive disorders, suicide attempts, and emotional disorders (Horowitz, Weine, & Jekel, 1995).

Horowitz and colleagues (1995) found that 67% of adolescent girls (aged 12 to 21) attending an urban mental health clinic met criteria for PTSD, while one study found that the risk for PTSD in children with a history of sexual abuse was 21% (Deblinger, McLeer, Atkins, Ralphe, & Foa, 1989). Young girls who have been abused sexually are two to three times more likely to experience repeated victimization in adulthood and to be victims of family violence (Cloitre, Tardiff, Marzuk, Leon, & Potera, 1996). Furthermore, Deblinger and colleagues (1989) suggest that the PTSD symptom profile of sexually abused children may differ from other forms of abuse, with more symptoms of reexperiencing and inappropriate sexual behaviors.

CAUTION

Pynoos (1994) has also noted that parent reaction to the child's trauma can have a positive or negative influence: acting to soothe and calm the child or exacerbate the emotional responsiveness by inducing the contagion effect.

Witness to violence. Exposure to violence and abuse in homes and the surrounding community can result in significant PTSD responses to violent trauma and set the stage for future psychopathology. Children who witness domestic violence, even if they were not victimized, reported significantly higher PTSD scores than children who did not witness violence

(Kilpatrick & Williams, 1997). Berton and Stabb (1996) found that 29% of high school juniors surveyed in a major metropolitan area had sufficient symptoms to predispose them to PTSD as a result of witnessing community violence. Consequences of childhood exposure to violence and abuse include social avoidance, foreshortened future, and lack of life opportunities.

DON'T FORGET

The long-term impact of PTSD has been studied by various researchers, and the results suggest that, for some children, the influence can be devastating. Greene and Ablon (2004) followed children who were exposed to the Buffalo Creek Dam collapse. Of the initial 37% who demonstrated PTSD symptoms two years after the incident, follow-up 17 years later revealed that 7% continued to meet criteria for PTSD.

Behavioral and Cognitive Models of *PTSD*

Proponents of cognitive-behavioral models interpret the child's response to the traumatic event from a learning theory perspective. Within this framework, reexperiencing a traumatic event can be equated to a conditioned fear response. Although the trauma is not likely to be repeated, extinction does not occur, because the fear is continually reenergizing through stimulus generalization and increased connections. Emotional processing can alter how future threat is appraised, turning relatively innocuous events into signals of potential threat (Foa & Kozak, 1986). Other cognitive theorists stress the maladaptive cognitive assumptions and appraisals resulting in dysfunctional beliefs about the future (Ehlers & Clark, 2000).

CAUTION

Brewin, Dagleish, and Joseph (1996) suggest that traumatic memories may become activated as situationally accessible memories (SAMs) that are distinct from other memories, because they are not readily accessed by conscious effort but are triggered by environmental cues.

DON'T FORGET

Caregivers can influence their child's PTSD by being too attentive or not attentive enough. McFarlane (1987) found that *maternal overprotectiveness* of children with PTSD led to the worst child outcomes, while *parent avoidance* of PTSD resulted in elevation of PTSD. Interventions that target improved parent–child relationships and handling stressful experiences significantly improved child outcomes regarding PTSD (Olds et al., 1998).

Models of Attachment and Parenting

Studies have determined that parent variables can influence the outcome for PTSD children in several ways. Scheeringa and Zeanah (2001) reviewed 17 studies that simultaneously assessed parent and child responses to trauma using *DSM-IV* criteria. In all but one study, the researchers found a significant post-trauma association between less-adaptive parent functioning and less-adaptive child functioning. Based on their results, the authors have developed a model of the *relational context of PTSD*, which has at its core the belief that the primary caregiving relationship is central to expression of PTSD symptoms throughout development. Scheeringa and Zeanah (2001) use the concept of *relational PTSD* to refer to the "compound effect" resulting from the "co-occurrence of post-traumatic symptomatology in an adult caregiver and a young child, when the symptomatology of one partner, usually the adult, exacerbates the symptomatology of the other" (p. 809). Although parent and child may not necessarily experience trauma from the same event, the trauma response influences the other's symptoms in a negative way. The three patterns are summarized in Rapid Reference 13.2.

The model of relational PTSD proposed by Scheeringa and Zeanah (2001) gains additional support when viewed within the context of the attachment literature relating to trauma-exposed adults. From an attachment perspective, studies of disorganized attachment in infants have linked this type of attachment to caregivers who have not resolved a previous trauma or who are preoccupied or overwhelmed with their trauma history, resulting in a caregiver who is frightened or frightening to the infant or young child.

Rapid Reference 13.2

Relational PTSD: Response Patterns and Child Outcomes

Parent Response Pattern	Description/Rationale	Child Outcomes
Withdrawn/ Unresponsive/ Unavailable	The parent is emotionally unavailable for the child: Parent's unresolved past trauma, which is reawakened by the child's symptoms, probably leads to the parent's attempts to avoid the child's symptoms.	Worsening of the child's PTSD symptoms

Parent Response Pattern	Description/Rationale	Child Outcomes
Overprotective/ Constricting pattern	Parent is prone to reexperiencing the trauma intrusively: even if the parent was not exposed to the trauma, the parent feels a sense of guilt about not having protected the child from the trauma.	Worsening of the child's PTSD symptoms
Reenacting/ Endangering/ Frightening pattern	Parent preoccupation with trauma: parent floods the distressed child with questions and comments specific to the event.	Child may use increased avoidance; caregivers may unconsciously place their children at risk for future trauma.

Source: Scheering and Zeanah (2001).

Even if the attachment relationships are adequate, Lyons-Ruth and Jacobvitz (1999) suggest that if a trauma is severe enough (as would be in cases of PTSD), the potential impact on caregiving could be to impair the process to the extent that it could disorganize the attachment strategy of the child or adult. Caregivers with unresolved trauma may also have a significantly lower threshold for triggers that might reawaken unresolved fears, leading to a perpetuation of disorganized attachment responses, and set the stage for intergenerational transmission of disorganization to occur. Within this "stress-relational-diathesis model," the authors suggest that the impact of early maternal deprivation may remain a latent factor until sufficient stress is introduced and at which time atypical and maladaptive behaviors will again resurface.

DON'T FORGET

Main and Solomon (1986) used the term *disorganized/disoriented attachment pattern* for the odd behaviors (apprehension, crying, freezing, conflicting movements, trance-like expressions) displayed by some infants upon their parent's return during Ainsworth's Strange Situation procedure. Although normally the need for attachment is elevated at times of stress, for disorganized/disoriented infants, the parent is simultaneously a source of comfort and a source of fear that elicits contradictory attempts to approach and flee the caregiver. This approach/flee response pattern has been linked to *parents who are feared* (victims of abuse) or parents with their own abuse history (Lyons-Ruth & Jacobvitz, 1999), or *parents who are frightened*, as in cases where parents have unresolved loss or trauma (Main & Hesse, 1990).

DON'T FORGET

Stress can impact on all levels of functioning, including the following:

Cognitive: Maladaptive thoughts, memory problems, concentration problems, hypervigilance, poor recall for details, foreshortened sense of future

Affective: Anxiety, irritability, labile affects, restricted affect, traumatic dreams, fear and avoidance, phobias

Behavioral: Trauma play, hyperactivity, regressive behaviors, anger outbursts, impulsivity, distractibility

Somatic-Physiological: Startle response, headaches, stomachaches, fatigue, sleep deprivation

Assessment

Richards and Bates (1997) discuss the symptoms of PTSD that are evident in cognitive, affective, behavioral, and somatic responses. The authors suggest that targeting specific treatment strategies to enhance coping in these areas may be an effective approach to managing stress in children with PTSD.

In addition to participation in one of the clinically structured or semistructured interviews, measures of generalized anxiety, depression, and mental status can be obtained using the more general child behavior rating scales discussed earlier. The Personality Inventory for Youth (PIY; Lachar & Gruber, 1995) contains several scales assessing emotional and behavioral adjustment in the home and school environments that would be helpful, including a somatic scale to evaluate vegetative symptoms. The Trauma Symptom Checklist for Children (TSCC; Briere, 1996) is specifically designed to evaluate the impact of traumatic events in children 8 to 16 years of age. Children rate their responses on a four-point scale that yields five clinical subscales: Anxiety, Depression, Anger, Posttraumatic Stress, and Dissociation. An alternate form contains a sixth scale measuring Sexual Concerns. In addition to the clinical subscales, the instrument also provides measures of avoidance or symptom denial (under-response) and heightened responding (hyper-response).

Treatment

Trauma-Focused Cognitve-Behavioral Therapy (TF-CBT)

In their recent report, the AACAP (2010) recognizes the need to develop a comprehensive plan for the treatment of PTSD in children. Treatment plans should involve consultations with the child's school support team and physicians and include trauma-focused therapy. The importance of including trauma-focused cognitive-behavioral therapy (TF-CBT), as opposed to more generic forms of CBT programs, is that trauma-focused therapy has been proven superior, because it challenges the child or adolescent's reluctance to talk about and avoidance of issues related to the trauma (Cohen, Deblinger, Mannarino, & Steer, 2004). Inclusion of parents in the therapy has also been successful in further reducing trauma-related symptoms (Deblinger, Lippmann, & Steer, 1999). The AACAP (2010) also acknowledges that the use of SSRI treatments may be beneficial for some children with symptoms of depression, anxiety, or obsessive-compulsive disorder. They do suggest that best practice should be to begin with TF-CBT alone, and then switch to combined SSRI and TF-CBT treatment if warranted.

Cohen and colleagues (2004) evaluated a multisite, randomized controlled trial of TF-CBT for 224 children (ages 8 to 14 years) with PTSD resulting from sexual abuse. The cognitive-behavioral program, TF-CBT, and a therapeutic treatment alternative (child-centered therapy [CCT]) were manualized and delivered in 12 weekly sessions to parent and child dyads. The TF-CBT program emphasized skills in feeling expression, emotional management, and cognitive abuse processing. The CCT program was an ego-supportive alternative that focused on trust building and empowerment of the parent–child dyad in processing the abuse. Children who participated in the TF-CBT program demonstrated significantly greater improvement of PTSD abuse-associated areas (behavior problems, social problems, shame, depression, and abuse attributions) compared to children in the CCT program. Furthermore, parents also reported less depression and more support of their child as a result of their involvement in the TF-CBT program. The authors conclude that TF-CBT is an effective treatment intervention for children who have experienced sexual abuse.

Trauma Accommodation Syndrome

Velkamp and Miller (1994) have developed a five-stage model for conceptualizing how children process stressful responses from inception to resolution. The model provides a good framework for targeting interventions and monitoring progress and is presented in the following box.

TRAUMA ACCOMMODATION SYNDROME

Stage 1: Traumatic or life-threatening event
Stage 2: Fear, helplessness, horror
Stage 3: Reenactment: repetitious play, frightening dreams, and/or avoidance that leads to a recurrence of intrusive thoughts or images, resulting in disorganized and agitated behavior
Stage 4: Reevaluation and reexperiencing
Stage 5: Cognitive reappraisal, resolution, accommodation, and adaptation

Source: Adapted from Velkamp and Miller (1994).

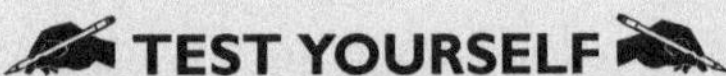

1. According to the *DSM-5*, criteria for PTS *must* include

(a) experiencing of intrusive symptoms.
(b) negative thoughts or mood.
(c) avoidance behaviors and symptoms of arousal and reactivity.
(d) all of the above.

2. In children, repetitive images may take the form of repetitive play.

True or False?

3. Which of the following is NOT a typical symptom of PTSD?

(a) Recurrent need to revisit the site of the PTSD event
(b) Interrupted sleep/nightmares
(c) Emotional numbing
(d) Anger or irritation

4. All of the following are probable symptoms of PTSD in children, *except*

(a) disorganized and agitated behaviors.
(b) clinging.
(c) crying.
(d) flashbacks.

5. PTSD was one of the first disorders ever included in the original *DSM*.

True or False?

6. According to Scheeringa and colleagues (1995), use of *DSM-IV* criteria for PTSD in very young children was

(a) inappropriate because almost half of the criteria required verbal descriptions.
(b) appropriate because criteria can be observed.

(c) inappropriate because very young children do not experience PTSD.
(d) appropriate for children 4 years of age and up.

7. Which of the following findings did McDermott and Palmer (2002) reveal as a result of their investigation of children's responses to the bushfire disaster?

(a) Middle school children (grades 7 to 9) reported the most emotional distress.
(b) Younger children (grades 4 to 6) reported the most emotional distress.
(c) Adolescents reported the most emotional distress.
(d) There were no significant age-related findings.

8. Which of the following is a risk factor for developing PTSD, posttrauma?

(a) Being female
(b) A history of sexual abuse
(c) Exposure to violence and abuse in the home
(d) All of the above

Answers: 1. d; 2. true; 3. a; 4. d; 5. false; 6. a; 7. a; 8. d

Fourteen

CHILDREN OF DIVERSE CULTURES

INTRODUCTION

The importance of understanding how behavioral and developmental expectations may differ across and within various cultures is fundamental to an appreciation of whether behaviors that are seen as deviant in some cultures are also viewed as deviant in other cultures. Within this framework, Bronfenbrenner's (1979, 1989; Bronfenbrenner & Morris, 1998) biological transactional ecological model is well suited to providing an increased understanding of how systems (i.e., family, social, economic, political) interact with culture to provide opportunities or barriers for youth at various stages of development. The ecological/developmental framework provides an excellent vantage point for assessing the impact of poverty, immigration, and ethnicity on psychosocial development and adjustment.

DON'T FORGET

Bronfenbrenner's (1979) ecological framework portrays the contexts of development as concentric circles emanating out from the child, who represents the innermost circle of *individual characteristics* (biological and neurological context, e.g., genetic makeup, intelligence, temperament). In Bronfenbrenner's model, *culture* is the outermost circle and represents the *attitudes, beliefs, values, guidelines,* and *activities* that interact with all other contexts to influence behavior.

Culture, Race, and Ethnicity

The changing demographics within the United States have placed a growing emphasis on the need to develop an increased awareness and understanding of (a) the role of culture, race, and ethnicity on how individuals and groups define what is normal or atypical; (b) variations in affective, behavioral, cognitive, or linguistic expressions of distress; and (c) the attitudes toward mental health services and interventions.

Although the terms *culture, race*, and *ethnicity* are often used interchangeably, it is important to distinguish important factors associated with each of these terms. The term *race* is most often used to refer to physical and biological characteristics attributed to genetic inheritance. Because race can carry implications of social reference and politics, it is most likely to fall victim to stereotyping and discrimination. *Ethnicity* refers to shared characteristics of social and cultural backgrounds that are passed on from generation to generation (Brems, 2008). The distinction between race and ethnicity is that while race refers to biology, ethnicity refers to social context. This term is most likely to be used when differences are reported among minority groups. *Culture* is the term with the broadest meaning referring to the greater social construct. Matsumoto (2000) defines *culture* as a dynamic system of rules (attitudes, values, beliefs, norms, behaviors) developed by a group to ensure a group's survival. Although relatively stable (communicated from generation to generation), culture must remain flexible to adapt to changes across time. Although it is important to recognize the impact of values and beliefs on subsequent practices and behaviors, it is equally, if not more, important to recognize the potential role of individual differences within that grouping to avoid stereotyping.

DON'T FORGET

Culture is defined as the *values, beliefs*, and *practices* that represent a given ethnocultural group.

CAUTION

There can be a fine line between being culturally sensitive and cultural stereotyping. Stuart (2004) cautions that focusing too intensely on an individual's group membership may result in loss of the individual apart from that group (p. 6).

DON'T FORGET

High rates of somatization in African American males and high rates of depression in Asian women may be illustrations of unique aspects of how *distress* is expressed by these diverse cultures.

Cultural attitudes and beliefs influence how mental illness is accepted and understood, coping strategies used, inclinations to access services and service utilization, as well as responses to intervention and treatment programs. In the past several years, there have been several movements to increase awareness of cultural influences in psychopathology.

Gibbs and Huang (2003) outline three broad areas in which ethnicity can influence mental health in children and adolescents. Ethnicity can:

1. Shape beliefs about what constitutes mental illness
2. Influence different symptom presentations, reactive patterns, and defensive styles
3. Influence whether it is acceptable to seek assistance for mental health issues outside of the family and who to consult (elder, priest, minister, herbalist, etc.)

Multicultural Guidelines

It has been estimated that by the year 2020, children from ethnic minorities will account for the majority of school-aged children in the United States (Lee, 1997). It is well known that children living in low-socioeconomic conditions are at increased risk for social, emotional, behavioral, and academic problems. It is important to recognize that although higher percentages of ethnic minorities live in conditions of low-socioeconomic status (Patterson, Kupersmidt, & Vaden, 1990), children from ethnic minorities who live in these conditions are at increased risk of continuing to live in these conditions (Wilson & Aponte, 1985). Given the high risk for negative outcomes, it is important for practitioners to have preparation and training in working with diverse populations, especially working with child and adolescent populations. Mental health organizations have recognized the need for culturally responsive practices to meet the needs of this growing area of concern. As a result, guidelines for training, research, and improved practices for working with diverse populations have been integrated into standards developed to address these issues by all of the major mental health organizations, including the American Psychological Association, American Counseling Association, American School Counselor Association, and the National Association of School Psychologists.

The *DSM-5* continues to expand on earlier efforts to address cultural issues with the goal of increased understanding of how cultural context can influence the assessment, diagnosis, and treatment of mental illness. Within the manual, information regarding cultural variations in prevalence rates and symptom presentation are introduced and discussed throughout the *DSM-5* in sections devoted to *culture-related diagnostic issues*. In the section on Cultural Formulation, the *DSM* discusses how an understanding of culture, race, and ethnicity is integral to developing a case formulation from a cultural perspective. Within this context, the *DSM-5* addresses five key areas of emphasis:

- The cultural identity of the individual (racial, ethnic, or cultural identity)
- Cultural conceptualizations of distress

- Psychosocial stressors and concepts of vulnerability and resilience
- Recognition of differences and similarities resulting from cultural influence between the individual and the therapist
- The influence of culture on issues of assessment (APA, 2013, p. 750)

The *DSM-5* emphasizes the need to recognize that different cultures may have varying perspectives and concepts of distress that can influence how different individuals "communicate suffering, behavioral problems or troubling thoughts or emotions" (p. 758).

The *DSM-IV* (APA, 2000) added 25 culture-bound syndromes to refer to maladaptive and aberrant behavior patterns that apply to different minority groups. However, the *DSM-5* distinguishes between cultural syndromes, idioms of distress, and culture-bound syndromes in the following way: Idioms represent ways of expressing distress that may differ between cultures, whereas cultural syndromes tend to focus more on unique variants of disorders associated with different cultures. Within this context, cultural explanations refer to how different cultures may attribute different etiology to causing the distress. As a result, the *DSM-5* now includes a Glossary of Cultural Concepts of Distress, providing examples of how distress is represented in different cultures.

A very brief description of cultural concepts of distress relating to the four major cultures discussed in this book is presented in Rapid Reference 14.1.

Rapid Reference 14.1

Examples of Some Cultural Concepts of Distress

Culture-Bound Syndrome/Culture	Description	DSM-Related Conditions
Ataque de nervios: Precipitated by stressful life events	Being out of control: trembling, crying, shouting, verbal/physical aggression	Panic attack, panic disorder, trauma- or stressor-related disorder
Latino	Dissociative experiences: seizure-like or fainting spells	
Susto: Precipitated by frightening event	Fright or soul loss, unhappiness and sickness	Resembles PTSD, depression, and somatization

(Continued)

Culture-Bound Syndrome/Culture	Description	*DSM*-Related Conditions
Nervios: Precipitated by stressful life events Latino	Wide range of vague symptoms of stress: headaches, tearfulness, irritability, sleep and eating disturbances, trembling, somatic disturbance, etc.	Depression, anxiety, somatization
Taijin kyofusho Japanese	Phobia regarding body (appearance, odor, expression) causing intense fear of humiliation	Social anxiety disorder, body dysmorphic disorder

Source: DSM-5 (APA, 2013).

This discussion provides a brief look at demographics, most common parenting practices/style, types and prevalence of mental health issues, and the implications for treatment and intervention. Although information has been provided by several different sources, the majority of the information presented here regarding demographics comes from *Mental Health: Culture, Race, and Ethnicity—A Supplement to Mental Health: A Report of the Surgeon General* (USDHSS, 2001).

DON'T FORGET

The Surgeon General's report reveals that, compared to Whites, minorities:

- Have less access and availability of services
- Are less likely to receive services
- Receive poorer quality of care
- Have less representation in mental health research

CAUTION

Although prevalence rates for mental health disorders may be similar for Whites and minorities, the outcomes are not. Minorities experience the greater burden of having a disorder in the aftermath of poor quality of care. Disproportionate numbers of minorities do not recover from mental illness and experience continued downturn in economic disadvantage.

THE IMPACT OF CULTURE ON CHILD PSYCHOPATHOLOGY

Adult Perceptions of Mental Illness and Behavior Problems

Reluctance of parents to accept a mental health explanation for their child's behavior may be based on unique cultural explanations (physical or spiritual cause) and/or fears that labeling may result in further discrimination based on ethnicity and race (Walker, 2002). As a result, differences in religious, cultural, social, and moral values may cause significant misunderstandings between parent and teacher or clinician. Although there has been increased awareness of the poor quality of mental health services available for minorities in the past 10 years, recognition of mental health issues of children and adolescents from diverse cultures has received less attention (Walker, 2002).

Children and Adolescents of Minority Populations: An Overview

Understanding the underlying attitudes, practices, and values of a given culture also requires an understanding that variations in cultural features exist within a given culture. Without this premise, the danger of stereotyping is imminent. Therefore, although the remainder of this chapter is devoted to discussing four minority groups in greater detail, it is important to stress the need to balance knowledge of common cultural practices with an appreciation of within-culture diversity.

Prevalence and Risks

It has been predicted that non-White and Hispanic-speaking youth under 18 years of age will constitute more than 45% of the population of youth in the United States by the year 2020 (U.S. Census Bureau, 1996). A more recent census report (U.S. Census Bureau, 2009) indicates that nearly half of children under 5 years old are minorities and that for all children under 18 years of age, 44 percent were a minority and 22 percent were Hispanic. Low-income minority children and adolescents are at greater risk for mental health and behavioral disorders because of their low socioeconomic status (SES), stressful family environments, and poor access to supportive services.

With the advent of globalization, migration, and greater immigration, increased focus has been placed on determining the risks of children in diverse populations. The following overview of risk factors for children from diverse backgrounds follows Bronfenbrenner's model (1979, 1989) as a framework for discussion. Following the overview, the discussion focuses on four minority groups in greater detail.

Individual Child (Birth/Health Issues)

Poor prenatal attention and healthcare in early childhood have placed minority and poor children at a disadvantage relative to their peers living in more financially secure environments. African American children are twice as likely as White children to be born to teen mothers, placing them at risk for later delinquency, and twice as likely to be low-birthweight babies, placing them at risk for later educational problems (Breslau, Paneth, & Lucia, 2004). In 1978, there was a nationwide ban on the use of lead-based paint. However, many children living in poverty continue to be exposed to the dangerously high levels of lead poisoning that can damage the developing brain, resulting in learning disabilities, problem behaviors, and stunted growth and headaches (U.S. Environmental Protection Agency, 2014). Children in poverty and African American children are also at increased risk for asthma, resulting in increased days of restricted activity and poor school attendance (Newacheck & Halfon, 2000).

Immediate Environment (Family, Peers, Neighborhoods, and Schools)

Family and parenting practices. Parenting practices can vary widely among different cultures, which can impact child outcomes (Forehand & Kotchick, 1996). Although *authoritative parenting styles*, which are high in structure and nurturing, have been associated with positive outcomes in middle-class families (Baumrind, 1991), for families living in conditions of lower SES and inner-city neighborhoods, research by McLoyd (1998) suggests that an *authoritarian parenting style*, which emphasizes strict adherence to rules and obedience, may serve a protective function, especially in environments that can expose children to risk or danger, and be associated with more positive outcomes for both males and females (Baumrind, 1971; Deater-Deckard, Dodge, Bates, & Pettit, 1996).

Neighborhood and schools. Attending quality schools and engaging in positive social experiences can contribute enhanced learning opportunities and development of emotion regulation, resulting in an improved ability to cope with stress and develop increased behavioral control. Yet, when early intervention or prevention practices can have the most profound impact, those in greatest need may be the least likely to be able to access services for a variety of reasons (e.g., transportation, financial problems, etc.), including *expulsion* from preschool. A study of randomly selected Massachusetts preschool programs revealed that 27.42 preschoolers were expelled per 1,000 students enrolled in preschool programs (Gilliam & Shabar, 2006), a rate that was more than 34 times the state rate for K–12 children and 13 times the national rate for K–12 children. Prevalence of exposure to violence is highest among African American and Latino-Latina youth, especially those living in lower-SES neighborhoods (Buka, Stichick, Birdthistle, & Earls, 2001). At least one study reported that 27% of African American youth with chronic exposure to violence reported symptoms of PTSD (Fitzpatrick & Boldizar, 1993).

Socioeconomic Status

Rates of minority children living in poverty have been staggering, with ethnic minority children being overrepresented. Between 2000 and 2004, reported rates for living in poverty by ethnic group were 1 out of 3 African Americans, 1 out of 10 Latinos, and 1 out of 10 Caucasians. However, when rates were examined for living in circumstances of "extreme poverty" (living below one-half the poverty level), percentage rates for minorities were reported as 33% of African American children, 31% of Native American children, 27% of Hispanic children, and 16.5% of Caucasian children (CDC, 2005).

Cultural Diversity: Children and Adolescents From Minority Populations

Keeping in mind that wide variability exists between and within cultures, the following discussions provide the best attempt to be culturally sensitive while avoiding cultural stereotypes. As such, the next section provides an overview of four minority cultures within the United States: African Americans, Latino/Hispanic Americans, Asian Americans/Pacific Islanders, and American Indians.

CAUTION

The impact of culture and ethnicity on prevailing or presenting problems must always be considered within the greater context of other environmental influences, including the degree to which this child or family adheres to the practices, attitudes, and values of the minority culture.

DON'T FORGET

Minority youth often experience feelings of alienation, cultural conflicts with their families, academic failure, and peer victimization (USDHSS, 2001). In their report on youth suicide prevention with culturally and linguistically diverse populations, Lazear, Doan, and Roggenbaum (2003) report the following:

- Approximately 64% of all American Indian suicides were committed by youth 15 to 24 years of age.
- Asian Pacific Islander females aged 15 to 24 years have the highest suicide rate in the country.
- Suicide rates by African American youth (10 to 14 years) increased 233% between 1980 and 1995.
- Rates for depression reported among girls in grades 5 to 12 vary according to ethnicity: Asian American (30%), Hispanic (27%), non-Hispanic White (22%), and African American (17%).
- Reports of suicide attempts within the previous 12 months were highest for Hispanic males (12.8%) and females (18.9%), compared with all other youth.

Risk of suicide among all teenagers has been increasing. The suicide rate for Caucasian teens 10 to 14 years of age increased 120% between 1980 and 1995 (Lazear et al., 2003). However, among minority youth, the trend toward suicide and depression is even more pronounced.

On an average day, 109,000 teens are housed in juvenile detention. More than 60% of all youth who are incarcerated in juvenile justice facilities are racial or ethnic minorities from low-income families. Teplin, Abram, McClelland, Dulcan, and Mericle (2002) found that 66% of males and 75% of females in juvenile detention had at least one psychiatric disorder: half of males and almost half of females had substance abuse disorders, more than 40% had disruptive behavior disorders, and 20% of females met criteria for major depressive disorder. Results of this and other surveys on minority youth and the juvenile justice system suggest that minority youth are overrepresented in the justice system and underrepresented in the mental health system.

DON'T FORGET

A probable outcome of chronic exposure to violence is the development of PTSD. In one study, as many as 27% of African American youth had PTSD (Fitzpatrick & Boldizar, 1993).

The influence of cultural diversity on family attitudes and parenting practices has received increasing interest in the literature (see Kotchick & Forehand, 2002, for review). According to Ogbu (1981), parenting practices are driven by cultural forces that exist by necessity to ensure survival and success of the family and preservation of cultural attitudes, values, and practices. Within this framework, parenting practices are developed based on the availability of resources within the community to develop competencies in keeping with prescribed cultural values. Ogbu (1981) also states that, in these circumstances, childrearing is often guided by folk theories that have been developed to foster behavior in children that is culturally valued.

The following discussion focuses on four major minority groups: African Americans, Latino/Hispanic Americans, Asian Americans/Pacific Islanders, and American Indians. Unless otherwise cited, demographics reported have been obtained from *Mental Health: Culture, Race and Ethnicity: A Supplement to Mental Health: A Report of the Surgeon General* (USDHSS, 2001).

AFRICAN AMERICANS

Demographics and Sociocultural Background

Although approximately 12% of the U.S. population is African American, it is important to understand that the Black population is also increasing in its own diversity as immigrants continue to arrive from as far away as Africa and as close as the neighboring Caribbean Islands. In addition, there is considerable disparity among African Americans who are at higher economic and educational advantage compared with the majority who are disadvantaged (McAdoo, 1997). The majority (53%) of African Americans reside in the southern United States and represent 57% of the population living in large, urban, inner-city areas that are noted for high crime, poor housing, poor employment opportunities, and access to fewer support services.

A disproportionate number of African Americans are living in poverty (22%) compared to the U.S. population at large (13%). Infant mortality of Black infants is twice that of White infants, and Black preschoolers are three times more likely than their White peers to have HIV/AIDS (Willis, 2004).

DON'T FORGET

Inner-city living is associated with increased risk of homicide, which is the leading cause of death among young African American adult males. Risk for homicide is 6 to 10 times higher for Black compared to White males, with an increase in murder rate among 15- to 19-year-olds rising from less than 600 in 1984 to more than 1,200 in 1987.

Familial Influences and Parenting Practices

Despite what seems like overwhelming odds and a history marked with racism and oppression, African Americans have demonstrated a remarkable ability to survive. Over the years, investigators have come to appreciate the role of family and culture in building a foundation for coping based on a supportive network of extended family and kin through sharing resources, housing, and tasks. In addition to extended family networks, survival has also been attributed to flexibility of male and female roles and non-gender-specific role functions. Within the African American community, in addition to religious practices, the church often occupies a central focus for social, civic, and educational activities (Allen & Majidi-Ahi, 2001).

The impact of the kinship network, however, may take its toll on those who are ultimately supported by the system. McAdoo (1997) explains that the family often collectively works together (older children leaving school to help financially) so that the youngest member of the family (often a female) can have the benefits of a higher education and escape the poverty level. However, the burden of the family sacrifice continues to weigh heavily on the recipient, who may be conflicted to either return the resources to the family or isolate herself in self-preservation.

One important value that is stressed by African Americans is the value of independence. By achieving independence, family members are able to be self-sufficient, as well as being able to provide temporary assistance to other family members as needed (Willis, 2004). The role of the family and extended family in preserving a sense of cultural heritage can also be seen in the oral tradition, as communication of expression often takes verbal or musical form.

Looking at African American parenting practices from the perspective suggested by Ogbu's model (1981), it becomes increasingly clear how these practices are geared toward survival of heritage and culture and preservation of the family based on limited resources and high-risk environments. The common thread that unites these families is the desire to instill pride in their cultural heritage while recognizing racial discrimination and a history of oppression of people of color (Willis, 2004).

Although initial investigations of parenting practices focused on cross-cultural comparisons, more recent studies have begun to concentrate on how various parenting practices within cultures relate to different child outcomes. Recent studies of *authoritative* parenting practices (high warmth, negotiated control) versus *authoritarian* parenting style (low warmth, high control) have revealed that use of authoritarian practices by African Americans can have a positive effect for minority youth. In this case, use of more punitive physical discipline may protect children from engaging in high-risk behaviors in an environment that is fraught with opportunities for deviant behavior and actually may increase their chances of survival and success (Kelley, Power, & Wimbush, 1992).

CAUTION

Baumrind's (1971) model has been widely cited in research on parenting practices, with most positive outcomes for children attributed to parent use of an *authoritative* rather than *authoritarian* parenting style. However, far fewer studies have considered how well these models fit ethnic minority youth.

CAUTION

In their review of psychiatric disorders and service usage, Angold and colleagues (2002) found that overall usage rates of services were well below prevalence rates for disorders in African American youth.

CAUTION

It is also important to note that because symptoms of suicidal behavior in African American youth may be more evident in acting out and aggressive and high-risk behaviors, detection of suicide intent may be misdiagnosed (Weddle & McKenry, 1995).

African American families are less likely to seek psychiatric help for their children and more likely to approach family doctors, ministers, or friends for advice (Willis, 2004).

Prevalence Rates of Psychological and Behavioral Disorders

Although they are less likely to suffer from depression, African Americans are more likely than non-Hispanic Whites to experience phobias. Among the mental disorders, somatization disorder (15%) and schizophrenia (Black males) have disproportionately higher prevalence rates and poorer outcomes in African American populations. There is a significantly higher prevalence rate reported for schizophrenia in second-generation African Caribbeans living in the United Kingdom (APA, 2000). The *DSM-5* cautions that there is evidence of overdiagnosis of schizophrenia in African American and Hispanic populations (APA, 2013, p. 109).

Although African Americans represent only 12% of the population of the United States, they are overrepresented in 40% of the homeless population. They constitute almost 40% of all juveniles in legal custody, and they constitute 45% of all children in public foster care. Exposure to violence is high, with more than 25% of African American youth meeting diagnostic criteria for PTSD.

Psychiatric hospitalization rates for severe disorders, such as schizophrenia, have been reported to be two to three times higher than for White youth. African American youth are also more likely to be referred to juvenile justice rather than a treatment facility.

Although alcohol consumption is lower than that of White youth, drug use among lower-income African American youth is often related to a drug culture of delinquency, selling drugs, and the use of cocaine and heroin. High rates of teen pregnancy among African American girls is associated with high dropout rates, unemployment, and future welfare use (Rosenheim & Testa, 1992).

DON'T FORGET

Pittman and Chase-Lansdale (2001) studied the role of parenting style on adolescent outcomes for African American girls living in impoverished environments. They found that parenting style was significantly related to multiple negative outcomes, including externalizing and internalizing behaviors, academic achievement, work orientation, sexual experience, and pregnancy history. Girls whose mothers were disengaged (low on both parental warmth and supervision/monitoring) had the most negative outcomes in all domains.

LATINO/HISPANIC AMERICANS

Demographics and Sociocultural Background

There are approximately 35 million Hispanic Americans living in the United States, with the vast majority (two-thirds) represented by Mexican Americans. The remaining Hispanic Americans have Puerto Rican, Cuban, South American, Central American, Dominican, and Spanish roots. The majority of Latinos live in California, Arizona, New Mexico, Colorado, and Texas.

Education varies among the subgroups, however, with a little over half of young adults having completed a high school education. Poverty rates range from a low of 14% (Cuban Americans) to highs between 31% (Puerto Ricans) and 37% (Mexican Americans). As a comparison, 13.5% of the American population at large live at or below the poverty line.

Familial Influences and Parenting Practices

Although the Hispanic population is very diverse, the following summary outlines some of the common underlying values and beliefs. At the foundation of the Mexican American family is the kinship network, promoting a mixture of traditional and more contemporary approaches. The extended family system, including *compadres* (godparents), provides for each other in terms of emotional, social, and financial support. The collective nature of the family network fosters an attitude of cooperation, affiliation, and interdependence, as opposed to more individualistic values of independence, competition, and confrontation (Ramirez, 2001).

Mexican American parents may seem less intent on children achieving milestones in the required time frame and more accepting of a child's individual limitations. Although young children are usually treated with permissiveness and indulgences, in later years they are expected to help out with family duties such as cleaning, cooking, and child care. Gender roles are traditional, with female children expected to be more homebound, while males are given more latitude and encouragement to explore their environment. Both roles are seen as preparatory for their future roles as mothers and fathers (Ramirez, 2001).

DON'T FORGET

The Surgeon General's report (USDHSS, 2001) suggests that use of mental health services by Hispanics and Latinos is poor, with fewer than 20% contacting healthcare providers. Families may be more inclined to seek assistance from natural healers than from medical professionals.

Prevalence Rates of Psychological and Behavioral Disorders

Compared to White youth, Latino youth demonstrate more anxiety-related and delinquency-related behavior problems, depression, and drug abuse. In their study of minority youth in the California system of care, Mak and Rosenblatt (2002) found that Hispanic youth were more likely to have been diagnosed initially with disruptive behavior disorder and substance use problems, despite later indications (parent and clinician rating scales) that this was not the case. As a result, the authors suggest that clinicians may make misdiagnoses at admission based on preconceived notions and that these errors could seriously undermine treatment effectiveness.

ASIAN AMERICANS AND PACIFIC ISLANDERS

Demographics and Sociocultural Background

Asian Americans or Pacific Islanders (AA/PIs) represent approximately 4% of the U.S. population. Approximately half of the AA/PI population is located in the West, most notably in California and Hawaii. Asian Pacific Americans are the fastest growing ethnic minority in the United States, having doubled their population each decade since 1970. The terms *Asian American* and *Pacific Islander* are used to refer to more than 60 different ethnic groups that have emigrated to the United States from Asia, the Pacific Rim, and the Pacific Islands. Asian Americans are often referred to as the *model minority* because of their visible success, but they have also been subjected to anti-immigration sentiment, and distinctions among ethnic groups are often blurred (Chan & Lee, 2004). In this chapter, discussion is limited to Chinese and Japanese Americans.

Chinese Americans

Some Chinese Americans have been in the United States for six generations, while others are recent immigrants. The beliefs, attitudes, and values of the Asian culture are highly influenced by the philosophies contained in the teachings of Confucianism, Taoism, and Buddhism. At the basis of Confucianism is family piety found in respect for one's parents and elders. Taoism speaks to the individual character rather than the family and focuses on living in tune with nature (yin and yang) and building inner strength through meditation, asceticism, and self-discipline. Buddhism teaches that life's suffering can be avoided by eliminating earthly desires.

Although the majority of Chinese speak Mandarin, the remainder speak multiple variations or dialects that have evolved into distinct languages.

Newer immigrant communities are often formed around Chinatowns that provide employment for the unskilled working class and the more wealthy entrepreneurs. This situation often results in two distinct classes (Wong, 1995).

Japanese Americans

The Japanese use different words to categorize immigrant generations. The *Issei* were the first generation to arrive in the United States in the early 1900s, and their children born in the United States are referred to as *Nisei*. Third-generation Japanese are called *Sansei*, while fourth and fifth generations are called *Yonsei* and *Gosei*, respectively. The majority of Japanese Americans settled in Hawaii and California. Japanese Americans in Hawaii are more closely aligned with other Asian Americans and, as such, have maintained a greater extent of their culture than those who remained on the mainland (Nagata, 2001).

Educationally, more than half of Japanese American young adult males and almost half of young adult females have their bachelor's degree or higher. While other Asian groups are increasing in size, Japanese Americans have registered an increasing decline in population.

Familial Influences and Parenting Practices

Adolescence is a period of transition in most cultures; however, in a North American climate, the period is marked by goals of increased independence from family and forging of a unique identity. For Asian American youth, this period can be fraught with extreme pressure resulting from a divided sense of self that straddles two different cultural frameworks. Studies have demonstrated that Asian minority youth can experience culture shock, evident in disappointment, depression, and anger, which is often intense and complicated by conflicted relationships with families who prioritize dependency and submission rather than independence and confrontation (Yeh & Huang, 2000).

DON'T FORGET

Cultural differences along the dimension of *individualism* and *collectivism* (I/C) predict the extent to which a given culture fosters the goals of the *individual* (autonomous, independent) versus the *group* (connection and cooperation) (Hofstede, 1980). Although families in North America encourage development of the individual (competition, independence), Asian families traditionally have been motivated by goals to support the group (cooperation and dependency).

Traditionally, Asian families have functioned along prescribed guidelines, with privileges assigned to specific roles. The male head of household had unchallenged authority and was responsible for the family's economic status and respect within the community. The mother was responsible for nurturing the children, and working outside of the home was not encouraged. The firstborn male was given preferential treatment, and male children were esteemed relative to females.

DON'T FORGET

Contemporary forces have softened rigid adherence to prescribed roles of the past, as have increases in marriages to non-Asian partners. However, there continues to be strong cultural emphasis on emotional restraint, and not expressing emotions continues to be a valued trait. Piety to family continues to be a significant factor, with shame and loss of face as the ultimate punishment for not maintaining appropriate conduct that might reflect badly on one's family (Nagata, 2001).

Prevalence Rates of Psychological and Behavioral Disorders

Historically, knowledge of the mental health needs of Asian Americans and Pacific Islanders has been limited. In addition to language barriers, the apparent shame and stigma attached to seeking mental health resources may also be an important contributor to the extremely low utilization rates of mental health services. According to the Surgeon General's supplementary report (USDHSS, 2001), only 17% of those with mental health issues seek assistance, and then usually only when the symptoms reach crisis proportions.

CAUTION

It has been reported that one-year prevalence rates for depression among Chinese Americans is between 3% and 7%. In addition, Chinese Americans are more likely to demonstrate depressive symptoms as somatic complaints to a greater extent than African Americans or non-Hispanic Whites.

Although suicide rates for Chinese, Japanese, and Filipino Americans are lower than for White Americans, rates for Native Hawaiian adolescents are higher than any other adolescent group in Hawaii (USDHSS, 2001), while rates for Asian Pacific Islander females (ages 15 to 24) are consistently the highest in that age group (Lazear et al., 2003).

In their review of racial/ethnic literature, McCabe and colleagues (1999) found few studies that have investigated Asian/Pacific Islander American youth in juvenile justice or mental health and no studies reporting on these youth in educational classes for the severely emotionally disturbed (SED). Although Asian/Pacific Islander Americans have been underrepresented, McCabe and colleagues (1999) found that Asian/Pacific Islander Americans were present at rates comparable to other minority groups in alcohol and drug treatment sectors and juvenile justice. The authors suggest that because these youth primarily were from Southeast Asia, a history of refugee-related traumas might account for the vulnerability of this population compared to other Asian/Pacific youth studied previously.

AMERICAN INDIANS

Demographics and Sociocultural Background

The American Indian population (including Alaska natives) is approximately 1.5% of the total U.S. population. The population is extremely diverse, with more than 561 officially recognized tribes. As might be expected, linguistic diversity is also high, with more than 200 different languages spoken.

Historically, the majority of American Indians lived on reservations (80%), but because of reductions in federal funding, only 20% of the population can be found on reservations today. American Indians suffer from chronic unemployment. Mortality rates are high and are attributed to alcoholism, cirrhosis of the liver, homicide, and suicide.

The national average for high school graduation is 75%, however, the American Indian average is 66%. Twice as many American Indians are unemployed compared to White Americans. Approximately 26% of the population lives in poverty. American Indians constitute 8% of the total population of homeless. In the criminal justice system, 4% of all inmates are American Indians.

Familial Influences and Parenting Practices

American Indian families support a collective rather than individualistic perspective. However, in sharp contrast to values placed on dependence versus independence in Asian cultures, the American Indian culture values independence and autonomy over dependence. A wide range of acculturation exists within American Indian communities, with some communities assimilating to the dominant American culture, whereas others focus on preserving their traditional heritage (Joe & Malach, 2004). As a collective society, their involvement can often extend outside of the family to the tribe at large. Roles and responsibilities of family members differ among the various tribes. Elders are often seen as the purveyors of wisdom and pass down the tradition through storytelling in the oral tradition (LaFramboise & Graff Low, 2001).

DON'T FORGET

Although children's early accomplishments are often a reason for celebration, parents do not share the White American urgency or pressure regarding the timing of meeting important milestones, believing more in readiness being the master of performance. In addition, time settings aligned to a present-time orientation or an event-timed orientation (first laugh, first smile) may also prove problematic (Joe & Malach, 2004).

Communication is indirect rather than direct and is designed to protect the immediate family members from being directly involved in punishment for misdeeds (protects family bonds) or rewards for accomplishments (ensures family humility). Messages are often navigated through a chain of family and kin until ultimately being delivered to the source. Messages designated to guide the youth's development or provide guidance in determining restitution for wrongdoing are delivered to the designated source, while behaviors worthy of accolade are routed to the community town crier, who will announce the event (LaFramboise & Graff Low, 2001).

Prevalence Rates of Psychological and Behavioral Disorders

Indian Health Service (IHS) clinics are mainly located on reservations, where only 20% of the American Indian population resides. The Surgeon General's supplementary report (USDHSS, 2001) states that little is known about usage rates of services in this population. However, the report does state the following: 50% of adolescents in a juvenile justice facility of a Northern Plains reservation had a substance abuse or mental health disorder, and many had multiple disorders (USDHSS, 2001). Prevalence rates for substance/drug abuse were estimated to be as high as 70% in some populations sampled, while exposure to trauma/violent victimization was reported to be as high as twice the national average.

Substance abuse is a predominant cause for concern, especially among 13-year-old American Indian children. In addition, as high as 70% of American Indians among Northern Plains and Southwestern Vietnam veterans admitted to alcohol- or drug-related problems. Violent victimization among this population is more than twice the national average, with a rate of 22% of the population experiencing symptoms of PTSD, compared to 8% in the general population (USDHSS, 2001).

ASSESSMENT

Cultural Competence

Within the past 10 years, there has been increasing recognition that professionals and communities need to work together toward greater understanding of the needs of diverse cultural populations. Culturally competent service delivery should be pervasive and include legal and ethical issues, school culture and educational policy, psychoeducational assessment, and working with interpreters and research (Rogers et al., 1999). With respect to assessment, several key areas are highlighted for consideration when working with culturally and linguistically diverse (CLD) students, including prior educational history, SES, racism, acculturation, and language acquisition.

It is also important to consider whether normed tests are valid for use with CLD students based on fairness of content, educational background, and product versus process orientation. In many areas, children are deemed to be language competent and eligible for formal assessment using IQ and other standard measures once they have been in the country for 2 years. However, evidence suggests that at least 5 to 7 years are required for academically oriented language development. The situation is further complicated if tests are not available in bilingual versions, as the use of an interpreter to administer an English version of a test would invalidate the results.

CAUTION

Cummins (1984) suggests that English language proficiency is initially acquired through basic interpersonal communication skills (BICS). The expected timeline in developing BICS, which is roughly equivalent to social communication, is approximately two to three years. However, in the classroom, academic learning requires the development of cognitive academic language proficiency skills (CALPS), which involve reading, writing, and curriculum content. Learning adequate CALPS requires anywhere from five to seven years.

Lynch (2004) suggests several cautions and guidelines for working with interpreters and translators. It is important that the interpreter not only be language proficient (including dialect) but also have an understanding of the available resources. Ideally, the interpreter not only provides a medium for verbal communication but also interprets the underlying cultural message in order to bridge the two cultures. Given the professional requirements of the interpreter, Lynch (2004) cautions against the use of family members as interpreters. Given many of the family dynamics discussed throughout this chapter, parents may be very reluctant to discuss private issues with extended family members present. The use of older children as family interpreters can be especially problematic, placing a psychological burden on these children to act as pseudoparents in their role as interpreter with professionals serving the family.

TREATMENT

Several papers have been developed to provide guidelines for professionals in developing greater cultural competence (National Mental Health Information Center [NMHIC, 1996]; *American Psychological Association (APA) Guidelines for Providers of Psychological Services to Ethnic, Linguistic, and Culturally Diverse Populations*). In discussing a training guideline for psychiatric residences working with children and adolescents, Kim (1995) highlights five essential components of a culturally competent service delivery:

- Recognition and acceptance of cultural differences
- Cultural self-awareness
- Appreciation of the dynamic nature of cultural differences
- Commitment to acquiring a basic understanding of the child's cultural background
- Modification and adaptation of practice skills to address the cultural context of the child and family

TEST YOURSELF

1. Compared to Whites, minorities have

(a) greater access to services.
(b) more representation in mental health research.
(c) higher-quality services.
(d) less access to services.

2. The highest rate of suicide among adolescents is held by which minority group?
(a) Native American females
(b) African American males
(c) Asian Pacific Islander females
(d) Hispanic males

3. Which of the following ethnic minorities values the quality of dependence in their children?
(a) Native American
(b) Asian American
(c) African American
(d) Hispanic American

4. The term *model minority* has been used to describe which minority group?
(a) Asian American
(b) African American
(c) Native American
(d) Hispanic American

5. Which of the following minority youth would be MOST likely to suffer from PTSD?
(a) Asian American
(b) African American
(c) Native American
(d) Hispanic American

6. Which of the following results from the Supplement to the Surgeon General's Report on Culture, Race, and Ethnicity (USDHSS, 2001) is FALSE?
(a) Approximately 21% of children and adults in the United States have a mental disorder.
(b) Prevalence rates of disorders did not differ appreciably between Whites and minorities living in the community.
(c) African American males had the highest rates of schizophrenia.
(d) Outcomes for having a mental disorder are similar for Whites and minorities.

7. Buka and colleagues' (2001) report on exposure to violence (ETV) revealed that
(a) ETV is higher among minority youth.
(b) ETV is highest in inner-city neighborhoods.
(c) chronic ETV is associated with higher risk for PTSD.
(d) all of the above are true.

8. **According to research, which of the following parenting styles would be MOST appropriate for ethnic minority youth living in low SES environments?**
   (a) Authoritative
   (b) Authoritarian
   (c) Permissive
   (d) Independent
9. **Which of the following youth would be expected to experience the MOST difficult transition from adolescence to adulthood based on bridging their two cultures?**
   (a) African American
   (b) Asian American
   (c) Hispanic
   (d) Native American
10. **According to studies of English language proficiency, how many years does it normally take to acquire English proficiency for academic subjects?**
   (a) 2 to 3 years
   (b) 1 to 3 years
   (c) 4 to 5 years
   (d) 5 to 7 years

Answers: 1. d; 2. c; 3. b; 4. a; 5. b; 6. d; 7. d; 8. b; 9. b; 10. d

Appendix A

CODES OF ETHICAL CONDUCT

American Counseling Association. (2005).
The American Counseling Association code of ethics

The American Counseling Association (ACA) was founded in 1952 and has more than 52,000 members. The ACA Code of Ethics defines principles of ethical behavior to serve as guidelines and standards of practice for its members. The ethics code is available on the ACA website at http://www.counseling.org/Resources/aca-code-of-ethics.pdf.

American Psychological Association. (2002, 2010).
Ethical principles of psychologists and code of conduct

The newly adopted ethics code went into effect June 1, 2003, and represents the ninth revision since 1953. The American Psychological Association has more than 150,000 members and is the largest association of psychologists in the world, with 53 professional divisions currently. The ethics code provides a common set of principles and standards to guide psychologists in their professional and scientific work. The ethics code was published in the December 2002 edition of *American Psychologist* (vol. 57, no. 12) and is available on the association website at http://www.apa.org/ethics/code/principles.pdf. This is the latest version, which includes the 2010 Amendments.

American School Counselors Association. (2010).
Ethical standards for school counselors

The American School Counselors Association (ACSA) formed in 1952 and currently has 15,000 members. The Ethical Standards provide principles of ethical behavior required in the provision of school counseling services. The latest revision of the ethics code (2010) is available on the ASCA website at http://www.schoolcounselor.org/asca/media/asca/home/EthicalStandards2010.pdf.

National Association of School Psychologists. (2010). Professional conduct manual and principles for professional ethics: Guidelines for the provision of school psychological services

The National Association of School Psychologists (NASP) was founded in 1969 and is the largest association of school psychologists worldwide. NASP has developed a comprehensive set of standards to guide school psychologists in their professional conduct in the provision of school psychological services practice. Copies of the standards are available through NASP Publications, 4340 East West Highway, Suite 402, Bethesda, MD, 20814 or on the NASP website: http://www.nasponline.org/standards/2010standards/1_%20Ethical%20Principles.pdf.

Appendix B

REFERENCES FOR ASSESSMENT INSTRUMENTS AND RESOURCES

STRUCTURED AND SEMISTRUCTURED CLINICAL INTERVIEWS

Ambrosini, P. J. (2000). Historical development and present status of the Schedule for Affective Disorders and Schizophrenia for School-Age Children (K-SADS). *Journal of the American Academy of Child & Adolescent Psychiatry, 39*, 49–58.

Reich, W., Welner, Z., Herjanic, B., & MHS Staff. (1997). *Diagnostic Interview for Children and Adolescents computer program (DICA-IV)*. North Tonawanda, NY: Multi-Health System.

Shaffer, D., Fisher, P., Lucas, C., Dulcan, M. K., & Schwab-Stone, M. E. (2000). NIMH Diagnostic Interview Schedule for Children, Version IV (NIMH DISC-IV): Description, differences from previous versions, and reliability of some common diagnoses. *Journal of the American Academy of Child & Adolescent Psychiatry, 39*, 28–38.

Silverman, W. K., & Albano, A. M. (1996). *Anxiety Disorders Interview Schedule for Children for DSM-IV (child and parent versions)*. San Antonio, TX: The Psychological Corporation.

RATING SCALES AND SELF-REPORT MEASURES

Achenbach, T. M. (1991). *Manual for the Child Behavior Checklist 4–8 and the 1991 Profile*. Burlington: University of Vermont, Department of Psychiatry.

Achenbach, T. M., & Rescorla, L. A. (2001). *Manual for the ASEBA school-age forms and profiles*. Burlington, VT: ASEBA.

Beck, A., Beck, J., & Jolly, J. (2005). *The Beck Youth Inventories of Emotional and Social Impairment (BYI)*. San Antonio, TX: The Psychological Corporation.

Beidel, D., Turner, S. M., & Fink, C. M. (1996). Assessment of childhood social phobia: Construct, convergent and discriminative validity of the Social Phobia and Anxiety Inventory for Children (SPAI-C). *Psychological Assessment, 8*, 235–240.

Briere, J. (1996). *Trauma Symptom Checklist for Children: Professional manual*. Odessa, FL: Psychological Assessment Resources.

Brown, T. E. (2001). *Brown Attention-Deficit Disorder Scales manual*. San Antonio, TX: The Psychological Corporation.

Conners, C. K. (1998). *Conners Rating Scales—Revised technical manual*. North Tonawanda, NY: Multi-Health Systems.

Conners, C. K. (2008). *Conners* (3rd ed.; Conners 3). North Tonawanda, NY: Multi-Health Systems.

Garner, D. M. (1991). *The Eating Disorder Inventory—2*. Odessa, FL: Psychological Assessment Resources.

Gioia, G. A., Isquith, P. K., Guy, S. C., & Kenworthy, L. (2000). *Behavior Rating Inventory of Executive Function (BRIEF) professional manual*. Odessa, FL: Psychological Assessment Resources.

Gilliam, J. E. (1995). *Gilliam Autism Rating Scale (GARS)*. Austin, TX: Pro-Ed.

Goodman, W., Rasmussen, S., & Price, L. (1988). *The Children's Yale Brown Obsessive-Compulsive Scale (CY-BOCS)*. New Haven: Connecticut Mental Health Center, Clinical Neuroscience Research Unit.

Kazdin, A. E., Rodgers, A., & Colbus, D. (1986). The Hopelessness Scale for Children: Psychometric characteristics and concurrent validity. *Journal of Consulting and Clinical Psychology, 54*, 241–245.

Kovacs, M. (2003). *Child Depression Inventory*. North Tonawanda, NY: Multi-Health Systems.

Lachar, D., & Gruber, C. P. (1995). *Personality Inventory for Youth (PIY) manual*. Los Angeles, CA: Western Psychological Services.

March, J. S. (1997). *The Multidimensional Anxiety Scale for Children (MASC)*. North Tonawanda, NY: Multi-Health Systems.

Myles, B. S., Bock, S. J., & Simpson, R. L. (2001). *Asperger Syndrome Diagnostic Scale (ASDS) examiner's manual*. Austin, TX: Pro-Ed.

Newcomer, P. L., Barenbaum, E. M., & Bryant, B. R. (1994). *DAYS: Depression and Anxiety in Youth Scale*. Austin, TX: Pro-Ed.

Ollendick, T. H. (1983). Reliability and validity of the Revised Fear Survey Schedule for Children (FSSC-R). *Behavior Research and Therapy, 21*, 234–245.

Reynolds, C. R., & Kamphaus, R. W. (2004). *Behavior Assessment System for Children: BASC2 manual*. Circle Pines, MN: American Guidance Service.

Reynolds, C. R., & Richmond, B. O. (2008). *Revised Child Manifest Anxiety Scale—2*. Los Angeles, CA: Western Psychological Services.

Reynolds, W. M. (2002). *Reynolds Adolescent Depression Scale (RADS)*. Odessa, FL: Psychological Assessment Resources.

Reynolds, W. M. (1989). *Reynolds Child Depression Scale (RCDS)*. Odessa, FL: Psychological Assessment Resources.

Reynolds, W. M. (1998). *Adolescent Mental Health Questionnaire (APS)*. Odessa, FL: Psychological Assessment Resources.

Schopler, E., Reichler, R., & Renner, B. R. (1993). *Childhood Autism Rating Scale (CARS)*. Los Angeles, CA: Western Psychological Services.

Spielberger, C. D., Edwards, C. D., Lushene, R. E., Montouri, J., & Platzek, D. (1973). *Manual for the State-Trait Anxiety Inventory for Children (STAIC)*. Palo Alto, CA: Consulting Psychologists Press.

INTELLECTUAL/COGNITIVE FUNCTIONING AND ADAPTIVE BEHAVIOR

Elliott, C. D. (2007). *Differential Ability Scales* (2nd ed.). San Antonio, TX: The Psychological Corporation.

Harrison, P., & Oakland, T. (2003). *Adaptive Behavior Assessment System (ABAS) and the ABAS—Second edition with downward extension*. San Antonio, TX: The Psychological Corporation.

Lambert, N., Nihira, K., & Leland, H. (1993). *ABS-S2: The Adaptive Behavior Scale—School* (2nd ed.). Austin, TX: Pro-Ed.

Roid, G. H. (2003). *Manual for the Stanford Binet Intelligence Scales* (5th ed.). Itasca, IL: Riverside.

Sparrow, S. S., Balla, D. A., & Cicchetti, D. V. (1984). *Vineland Adaptive Behavior Scales.* Circle Pines, MN: American Guidance Service.

Wechsler, D. (2002). *Manual for the Wechsler Preschool and Primary Scale of Intelligence,* (3rd ed.; WPPSI-III). San Antonio, TX: The Psychological Corporation.

Wechsler, D. (2003). *Manual for the Wechsler Intelligence Scale for Children* (4th ed.; WISC-IV). San Antonio, TX: The Psychological Corporation.

RESOURCES

Sattler, J. M. (2008). *Assessment of children: Cognitive foundations* (5th ed.). La Mesa, CA: Jerome M. Sattler.

Sattler, J. M. (2014). *Foundations of behavioral, social, & clinical assessment of children.* San Diego, CA: Jerome M. Sattler.

Appendix C

INDIVIDUALS WITH DISABILITIES EDUCATION IMPROVEMENT ACT OF 2004 (IDEA 04)

Children with disabilities were initially granted opportunities for federally funded special education programs under Public Law 94-142, which was passed in 1975 as the Education of All Handicapped Children Act (EHA). The law was renamed the Individuals with Disabilities Education Act (IDEA) in 1990 and has been amended several times over the years. In November 2004, Congress passed the Individuals with Disabilities Education Improvement Act of 2004, which President George W. Bush signed into law on December 3, 2004. The law went into effect in July 2005. The entire congressional report can be accessed on the web from the *Federal Register* at http://idea.ed.gov/download/finalregulations.pdf. It can also be accessed in its entirety at http://www.nichcy.org/wp-content/uploads/docs/PL108-446.pdf. Parts of the law reproduced in this Appendix were accessed from these websites.

IDEA 2004 mandates special education and related services for children with disabilities who may qualify for services under one of the 13 specific categories of disabilities listed, including intellectual disability, hearing impairments (including deafness), speech or language impairments, visual impairments (including blindness), serious emotional disturbance, orthopedic impairments, autism, traumatic brain injury, other health impairments, and specific learning disabilities. An exhaustive review of the changes in the law is not the intention of this discussion, which will focus on how the law impacts on the identification of children and youth with specific learning disabilities.

Among the several changes to the law, which has aligned itself more closely with No Child Left Behind (NCLB), is that the law has redefined how states may determine whether a child has a specific learning disability. This represents a dramatic shift in how specific learning disabilities may be determined compared with IQ-achievement discrepancy formulas that have been used for the past 30 years.

It is important to note that the law has not changed how a learning disability is defined, which remains virtually unchanged from the 1997 version of IDEA. According to IDEA 04, the definition for a specific learning disability, which can be found in Section 602 (29) of the law, is stated as follows (changes to the new version are presented in italics with replaced word in brackets):

> 602(29) SPECIFIC LEARNING DISABILITY—
>
> (A) IN GENERAL—The term "specific learning disability" means a disorder in one or more of the basic psychological processes involved in understanding or in using language, spoken or written, which disorder may manifest itself in an imperfect ability to listen, think, speak, read, write, spell, or do mathematical calculations.
>
> (B) DISORDERS INCLUDED—Such term includes such conditions as perceptual disabilities, brain injury, minimal brain dysfunction, dyslexia, and developmental aphasia.
>
> (C) DISORDERS NOT INCLUDED—Such term does not include a learning problem that is primarily the result of visual, hearing, or motor disabilities, of intellectual disability, of emotional disturbance, or of environmental, cultural, or economic disadvantage.

As was discussed in Chapter 6, there has been considerable controversy in the past concerning the use of the IQ-achievement discrepancy formula for determining whether a child has a specific learning disability, under IDEA. Among the criticisms: 1) are the length of time required to substantiate a 2-year lag between IQ and achievement, and 2) the potential for cultural bias using the IQ-achievement discrepancy model. IDEA 04 has made a significant change to the law by addressing how to identify children with specific learning disabilities.

In Section 614 of the law, IDEA 04 has added sections on eligibility determination that include the following:

> 5) SPECIAL RULE FOR ELIGIBILITY DETERMINATION—In making a determination of eligibility under paragraph (4)(A), a child shall not be determined to be a child with a disability if the determinant factor for such determination is—
>
> (A) lack of scientifically based instruction in reading;
>
> (B) lack of instruction in mathematics; or

(C) limited English proficiency.

(6) SPECIFIC LEARNING DISABILITIES—

(A) IN GENERAL—Notwithstanding section 607(b), when determining whether a child has a specific learning disability as defined in section 602(29), a local educational agency shall not be required to take into consideration whether a child has a severe discrepancy between achievement and intellectual ability in oral expression, listening comprehension, written expression, basic reading skill, reading comprehension, mathematical calculation, or mathematical reasoning.

(B) ADDITIONAL AUTHORITY—In determining whether a child has a specific learning disability, a local educational agency may use a process that determines if the child responds to scientific, research-based intervention as a part of the evaluation procedures described in paragraphs (2) and (3).

As was discussed in Chapter 6, the vast majority (80%) of individuals with specific learning disabilities (SLDs) have problems primarily in reading. Research also suggests that compared to their fluent-reading peers, poor readers can have lifelong learning deficits caused by the cumulative impact of reading fluency on accessing information, vocabulary development, and higher-order learning (*Matthew effects* discussed in Chapter 6).

IDEA 04 has addressed controversies regarding the use of the IQ-achievement discrepancy model to identify children with learning disabilities by encouraging the use of the response to intervention (RTI) model, in place of the discrepancy model. This model allows for the use of empirically based interventions to combat reading difficulties, while serving as a benchmark for identification of those who do not respond to the intervention as children with SLDs.

Those who support the changes to IDEA 04 argue that the majority of students with SLDs are readily identifiable because of their obvious problems with reading and that the RTI model will be the most efficient and effective way of addressing these problems. They feel that children will obtain more immediate and appropriate interventions without having to wait for a formal evaluation, while those who benefit from the interventions can avoid further involvement in the identification process.

Those who oppose the changes in law voice their concerns about the loss of distinction between children who do not make adequate academic progress due to lower ability, compared to those who struggle academically as a result of neurological impairments associated with SLDs.

REFERENCES

Abu-Arefeh, I., & Russell, G. (1994). Prevalence of headache and migraine in school children. *British Medical Journal, 309*, 765–769.

Achenbach, T. M. (1966). The classification of children's psychiatric symptoms: A factor analytic study. *Psychological Monographs, 80* (7, whole no. 609).

Achenbach, T. M. (1991). *Manual for the Child Behavior Checklist/4–18 and 1991 profile.* Burlington: University of Vermont, Department of Psychiatry.

Achenbach, T. M., McConaughy, S. H., & Howell, C. T. (1987). Child and adolescent behavioral and emotional problems: Implications of cross-informant correlations for situational specificity. *Psychological Bulletin, 101*, 213–232.

Achenbach, T. M., & Rescorla, L. A. (2001). *Manual for the ASEBA School-Age Forms and Profiles.* Burlington: University of Vermont, Research Center for Children, Youth, and Families.

Aguilar, B., Sroufe, L. A., Egeland, B., & Carlson, E. (2000). Distinguishing the early-onset/persistent and adolescent-onset antisocial behavior types: From birth to 16 years. *Development and Psychopathology, 12*, 109–132.

Ainsworth, M. D., Blehar, M. S., Waters, E., & Wall, S. (1978). *Patterns of attachment: A psychological study of the strange situation.* Hillsdale, NJ: Erlbaum.

Albano, A. M., Chorpita, B. F., & Barlow, D. H. (1996). Childhood anxiety disorders. In E. J. Mash & R. A. Barkley (Eds.), *Child psychopathology* (pp. 279–329). New York, NY: Guilford Press.

Alfven, G. (2001). Understanding the nature of multiple pains in children. *Journal of Pediatrics, 138*(2), 156–158.

Allen, L., & Majidi-Ahi, S. (2001). African American children. In J. T. Gibbs & L. N. Huang (Eds.), *Children of color* (pp. 143–170). San Francisco, CA: Jossey-Bass.

Aman, M. G., Hammer, D., & Rohahn, J. (1993). Mental retardation. In T. H. Ollendick & M. Hersen (Eds.), *Handbook of child and adolescent assessment* (pp. 321–345). Needham Heights, MA: Allyn & Bacon.

Amaya-Jackson, L., & March, J. (1995). Posttraumatic stress disorder. In J. S. March (Ed.), *Anxiety disorders in children and adolescents* (pp. 276–300). New York, NY: Guilford Press.

American Academy of Child and Adolescent Psychiatry (AACAP). (1997). Official Action. Practice parameters for the assessment and treatment of children and adolescents with bipolar disorder. *Journal of the American Academy of Child and Adolescent Psychiatry, 36*, 138–157.

American Academy of Child and Adolescent Psychiatry (AACAP). (1998a). Practice parameters for the assessment and treatment of children and adolescents with depressive disorders. *Journal of the American Academy of Child and Adolescent Psychiatry*, 10(Suppl.), 63S–83S.

American Academy of Child and Adolescent Psychiatry (AACAP). (2010). Practice parameters for the assessment and treatment of children and adolescents with posttraumatic stress disorder. *Journal of the American Academy of Child and Adolescent Psychiatry, 49*, 414–430.

American Association on Intellectual and Developmental Disabilities. (2009a). *Intellectual disability: Definition, classification and systems of support* (11th ed.). Washington, DC: Author.

American Association on Intellectual and Developmental Disabilities. (2009b). *Intellectual disability*. Retrieved from www.aaidd.org/intellectualdisabilitybook/content_2348.cfm?navID=267

American Association on Mental Retardation (AAMR). (2002). *Mental retardation: Definition, classification, and systems of support* (10th ed.). Washington, DC: Author.

American Psychiatric Association (APA). (1952). *Diagnostic and statistical manual of mental disorders*. Washington, DC: Author.

American Psychiatric Association (APA). (1968). *Diagnostic and statistical manual of mental disorders* (2nd ed.). Washington, DC: Author.

American Psychiatric Association (APA). (1980). *Diagnostic and statistical manual of mental disorders* (3rd ed.). Washington, DC: Author.

American Psychiatric Association (APA). (1987). *Diagnostic and statistical manual of mental disorders* (3rd rev. ed.). Washington, DC: Author.

American Psychiatric Association (APA). (1994). *Diagnostic and statistical manual of mental disorders* (4th ed.). Washington, DC: Author.

American Psychiatric Association (APA). (2000). *Diagnostic and statistical manual of mental disorders* (4th ed., text revision). Washington, DC: Author.

American Psychiatric Association (APA). (2013). *Diagnostic and statistical manual of mental disorders* (5th ed.). Arlington, VA: American Psychiatric Publishing.

American Psychological Association (APA). (1996). *APA guidelines for providers of psychological services to ethnic, linguistic, and culturally diverse populations*. Retrieved from www.apa.org/divisions/div45/resources.html

American Psychological Association, Task Force on Psychological Intervention Guidelines. (1995). *Template for developing guidelines: Interventions for mental disorders and psychological aspects of physical disorders*. Washington, DC: Author.

Andrews, G., Pine, D. S., Hobbs, M. J., Anderson, T. M., & Sunderland, M. (2009). Neurodevelopmental disorders: Cluster 2 of the proposed meta-structure for DSM-V and ICD-11. *Psychological Medicine, 39*(12), 2013–2023.

Angold, A., Erkanli, A., Farmer, E. M. Z., Fairbank, J. A., Burns, B. A., Keeler, G. S., & Costello, E. J. (2002). Psychiatric disorder, impairment, and service use in rural African American and White youth. *Archives of General Psychiatry, 59*, 893–901.

Angold, A. E., Costello, E. J., & Erkanli, A. (1999). Comorbidity. *Journal of Child Psychology and Psychiatry, 40*, 57–87.

Angst, J. (2007). The bipolar spectrum. *British Journal of Psychiatry, 190*, 189–191.

Arnett, J. J. (1999). Adolescent storm and stress, reconsidered. *American Psychologist, 54*, 317–326.

Aseltine, R. H. (2003). Evaluation of a school-based suicide prevention program. *Adolescent and Family Health, 3*, 81–88.

Aseltine, R. H., & DiMartino, R. (2004). An outcome evaluation of the SOS suicide prevention program. *American Journal of Public Health, 94*, 446–451.

Aseltine, R. H., James, A., Schilling, E. A., & Glanovsky, J. (2007). Evaluating the SOS suicide prevention program: A replication and extension. *BMC Public Health*. Retrieved from http://www.biomedcentral.com/1471-2458/7/161

Attar, B. K., Guerra, N. G., & Tolan, P. H. (1994). Neighborhood disadvantage, stressful life events and adjustments in urban elementary-school children. *Journal of Clinical Child & Adolescent Psychology, 23*, 391–400.

Attie, I., & Brooks-Gunn, J. (1995). The development of eating regulation across the life span. In D. Cicchetti & D. J. Cohen (Eds.), *Developmental psychopathology: Vol. 2. Risk disorder and adaptation* (pp. 332–368). New York, NY: Wiley.

Azrin, N. H., Donohue, B., Besalel, V. A., Kogan, E. S., & Acierno, R. (1994). Youth drug abuse treatment: A controlled outcome study. *Journal of Child and Adolescent Substance Abuse, 3*, 1–16.

Bailey, A., Phillips, W., & Rutter, M. (1996). Autism: Toward an integration of clinical, genetic, neuropsychological, and neurobiological perspectives. *Journal of Child Psychology and Psychiatry, 37*, 89–126.

Baker, D. G., West, S. A., Nicholson, W. E., Ekhator, N., Kasckow, J., Hill, K. K., … Geracioti, T. D. (1999). Serial CSF corticotropin-releasing hormone levels and adreno-cortical activity in combat veterans with posttraumatic stress disorder. *American Journal of Psychiatry, 156*, 585–588.

Bandura, A. (1977). *Social learning theory*. Englewood Cliffs, NJ: Prentice Hall.

Bandura, A. (1985). A model of causality in social learning theory. In M. Mahony & A. Freeman (Eds.), *Cognition and therapy* (pp. 81–99). New York, NY: Plenum Press.

Bandura, A. (1986). *Social foundations of thought and action: A social cognitive theory*. Englewood Cliffs, NJ: Prentice Hall.

Barbaresi, W. J., Katusic, S. K., Collagin, R. C., Weaver, A. L., & Jacobsen, S. J. (2005). Math learning disorder: Incidence in a population-based birth cohort, 1976–82. Rochester, Minn. *Ambulatory Pediatrics, 5*, 281–289.

Barkley, R. A. (1997). Behavior inhibition, sustained attention, and executive function. *Psychological Bulletin, 121*, 65–94.

Barkley, R. A. (1998). *Attention-deficit hyperactivity disorder: A handbook for diagnosis and treatment* (2nd ed.). New York, NY: Guilford Press.

Barkley, R. A. (2006a). Primary symptoms, diagnostic criteria, prevalence, and gender differences. In R. A. Barkley (Ed.), *Attention-deficit hyperactivity disorder: A handbook for diagnosis and treatment* (3rd ed., pp. 76–121). New York, NY: Guilford Press.

Barkley, R. A. (2006b). Associated cognitive, developmental, and health problems. In R. A. Barkley (Ed.), *Attention-deficit hyperactivity disorder: A handbook for diagnosis and treatment* (3rd ed., pp. 122–183). New York, NY: Guilford Press.

Barkley, R. A. (2006c). Comorbid disorders, social and family adjustment, and subtyping. In R. A. Barkley (Ed.), *Attention-deficit hyperactivity disorder: A handbook for diagnosis and treatment* (3rd ed., pp. 184–218). New York, NY: Guilford Press.

Barkley, R. A., & Cunningham, C. E. (1978). Do stimulant drugs improve the academic performance of hyperkinetic children? A review of outcome research. *Clinical Pediatrics, 17*, 85–92.

Barkley, R. A., Fischer, M., Edelbrock, C. S., & Smallish, L. (1990). The adolescent outcome of hyperactive children diagnosed by research criteria: 1. An 8-year perspective follow-up study. *Journal of the American Academy of Child and Adolescent Psychiatry, 32*, 233–256.

Barkley, R. A., & Gordon, M. (2002). Research on comorbidity, adaptive functioning, and cognitive impairments in adults with ADHD: Implications for a clinical practice. In S. Goldstein & A. T. Ellison (Eds.), *Clinician's guide to adult ADHD: Assessment and intervention* (pp. 43–69). San Diego, CA: Academic Press.

Barkmann, C., Braehler, E., Schulte-Markwort, M., & Richterich, A. (2011). Chronic somatic complaints in adolescents: Prevalence, predictive validity of the parent reports, and associations with social class, health status and psychosocial distress. *Social Psychiatry & Psychiatric Epidemiology, 46*, 1003–1011.

Barlow, D. H. (2002). *Anxiety and its disorders: The nature and treatment of anxiety and panic* (2nd ed.). New York, NY: Guilford Press.

Barnett, A. L. (2008). Motor assessment in DCD: From identification to intervention. *International Journal of Disability Development and Education, 55* (2), 113–129.

Barrett, P. M., Healey-Farrell, I., Piacentini, J., & March, J. S. (2004). Obsessive-compulsive disorder in childhood and adolescence: Description and treatment. In P. M. Barrett & T. H. Ollendick (Eds.), *Handbook of interventions that work with children and adolescents* (pp. 187–216). West Sussex, UK: Wiley.

Barrett, P. M., Rappee, R. M., Dadds, M. M., & Ryan, S. M. (1996). Family enhancement of cognitive style in anxious and aggressive children. *Journal of the American Academy of Child and Adolescent Psychiatry, 24*, 187–203.

Barrios, B. A., & Hartmann, D. P. (1997). Fears and anxieties. In E. J. Mash & R. A. Barkley (Eds.), *Treatment of childhood disorders* (pp. 249–337). New York, NY: Guilford Press.

Batsche, G. M., & Knoff, H. M. (1995). Linking assessment to intervention. In A. Thomas & J. Grimes (Eds.), *Best practices in school psychology III* (pp. 569–586). Washington, DC: National Association of School Psychologists.

Baumrind, D. (1971). Current pattern of parental authority. *Developmental Psychology Monographs, 4*(1, part 2).

Baumrind, D. (1991). The influences of parenting style on adolescent competence and substance use. *Journal of Early Adolescence, 11*, 56–95.

Beck, A. T. (1976). *Cognitive therapy and emotional disorders*. New York, NY: International University Press.

Beck, A. T. (1997). Cognitive therapy: Reflections. In J. K. Zeig (Ed.), *The evolution of psychotherapy: The third conference* (pp. 55–68). New York, NY: Brunner/Mazel.

Beidel, D. C., Turner, S. M., & Morris, T. L. (1999). Psychopathology of childhood social phobia. *Journal of the American Academy of Child and Adolescent Psychiatry, 38*, 643–650.

Bellugi, U., Jarvinen-Pasley, A., Doyle, T., Reilly, J., Reiss, A., & Korenberg, J. (2007). Affect, social behavior and the brain in Williams syndrome. *Current Directions in Psychological Science, 10*, 99–104.

Berninger, V. W., & Hart, T. M. (1992). A developmental neuropsychological perspective for reading and writing acquisition. *Educational Psychologist, 27*(4), 415–434.

Bernstein, G. A., & Borchardt, C. M. (1991). Anxiety disorders of childhood and adolescence: A critical review. *Journal of the American Academy of Child and Adolescent Psychiatry, 30*, 519–532.

Berton, M. W., & Stabb, D. D. (1996). Exposure to violence and post-traumatic stress disorder in urban adolescents. *Adolescence, 31*, 489–498.

Bezchlibnyk-Butler, K. Z., & Jeffries, J. J. (1997). *Clinical handbook of psychotropic drugs*. Toronto, Canada: Hogrefe & Huber.

Biederman, J., Faraone, S., & Lapey, K. (1992). Comorbidity of diagnosis in attention-deficit hyperactivity disorder. In G. Weiss (Ed.), *Child and adolescent psychiatry clinics in North America: Attention deficit disorder* (pp. 335–360). Philadelphia, PA: W. B. Saunders.

Biederman, J., Mick, E., & Farone, S. V. (2002). Influence of gender on attention deficit hyperactivity disorder in children referred to a psychiatric clinic. *American Journal of Psychiatry, 159*, 36–42.

Biederman, J., Rosenbaum, J. F., Boldue-Murphy, E. A., Faraone, S. V., Chaloff, J., Hirshfeld, D. R., & Kagan, J. (1993). A 3-year follow-up of children with and without behavioral inhibition. *Journal of the American Academy of Child and Adolescent Psychiatry, 32*, 814–821.

Biederman, J., Wilens, T., Mick, E., Spencer, T., & Faraone, S. V. (1999). Pharmacotherapy of attention-deficit/hyperactivity disorder reduces risk for substance use disorder. *Pediatrics, 104*, e20.

Biederman, J., Wozniak, J., Kiely, K., Ablon, S., Faraone, S., Mick E., … Kraus, I. (1995). CBCL clinical scales discriminate prepubertal children with structured interview-derived diagnosis of mania from those with ADHD. *Journal of the American Academy of Child and Adolescent Psychiatry, 34*, 464–471.

Biere, D. F., Reeve, R. A., Champion, G. D., & Addicoat, L. (1990). The Faces Pain Scale for the self-assessment of the severity of pain experienced by children: Development, initial validation, and preliminary investigation for ration scale properties. *Pain, 4*, 139–150.

Bird, H. (1996). Epidemiology of childhood disorders in a cross-cultural context. *Journal of Child Psychology and Psychiatry, 37*, 35–49.

Bird, H. R., Gould, M. S., & Staghezza, B. (1992). Aggregating data from multiple informants in child psychiatry epidemiological research. *Journal of the American Academy of Child and Adolescent Psychiatry, 31*, 78–85.

Birmaher, B. (2013). Bipolar disorder in children and adolescents. *Child and Adolescent Mental Health, 18*(3), 140–148.

Black, B. (1995). Separation anxiety disorder and panic disorder. In J. S. March (Ed.), *Anxiety disorders in children and adolescents*. New York, NY: Guilford Press.

Bloomquist, M. L. (1996). *Skills training for children with behavior disorders: A parent and therapist guidebook*. New York, NY: Guilford Press.

Blum, R. W., Beuhring, T., Shew, M., Bearinger, L., Sieving, R., & Resnick, M. D. (2000). The effects of race/ethnicity, income, and family structure on adolescent risk behaviors. *American Journal of Public Health, 90*, 1885–1891.

Bonanno, G., Papa, A., Lalande, K., Westphal, M., & Coifman, K. (2004). The importance of being flexible: The ability to both enhance and suppress emotional expression predicts long-term adjustment. *Psychological Science, 15*, 482–487.

Borge, A., Nordhagen, B., Botten, G., & Bakketeig, L. S. (1994). Prevalence and persistence of stomach ache and headache among children: Follow-up of a cohort of Norwegian children from 4 to 10 years of age. *Acta Pediatrics, 83*, 433–437.

Borowsky, I. W., Ireland, M., & Resnick, M. D. (2001). Adolescent suicide attempts: Risks and protectors. *Pediatrics, 107*, 485–495.

Botvin, G. J., Griffin, K. W., Diaz, T., & Ifill-Williams, M. (2001). Preventing binge drinking during early adolescence: One- and two-year follow-up of a school-based preventive intervention. *Psychology of Addictive Behaviors, 15*, 360–365.

Bremner, J. D. (1999). Does stress damage the brain? *Biological Psychiatry, 45*, 797–805.

Brems, C. (2008). *A comprehensive guide to child psychotherapy and counseling*. Long Grove, IL: Waveland Press.

Brent, D. S. (1995). Risk factors for adolescent suicide and suicidal behavior: Mental and substance abuse disorders, family environmental factors, and life stress. *Suicide Life-Threatening Behaviors, 25*, 52–63.

Breslau, N., Davis, G., Andreski, P., & Peterson, E. (1991). Traumatic events and posttraumatic stress disorder in an urban population of young adults. *Archives of General Psychiatry, 48*, 218–222.

Breslau, N., Paneth, N. S., & Lucia, V. (2004). The lingering academic deficits of low birth weight children. *Pediatrics, 114*(4), 1035–1040.

Brestan, E. V., & Eyberg, S. M. (1998). Effective psychosocial treatments of conduct-disordered children and adolescents: 29 years, 82 studies, and 5,272 kids. *Journal of Clinical Child Psychology, 27*, 180–189.

Brewin, C. R., Dagleish, T., & Joseph, S. (1996). A dual representation theory of posttraumatic stress disorder. *Psychological Review, 103*, 670–686.

Bronfenbrenner, U. (1979). *The ecology of human development*. Cambridge, MA: Harvard University Press.

Bronfenbrenner, U. (1989). Ecological systems theory. *Annals of Child Development, 6*, 187–249.

Bronfenbrenner, U., & Morris, P. A. (1998). The ecology of developmental process. In R. M. Lerner (Ed.), *Handbook of child psychology: Vol. 1. Theoretical models of human development* (5th ed., pp. 535–584). New York, NY: Wiley.

Brooke J. S., & Pelham, W. E. (2003). Childhood predictors of adolescent substance use in a longitudinal study of children with ADHD. *Journal of Abnormal Psychology, 112*, 497–508.

Brotman, M. A., Rich, B. A., Schmajuk, M., Reising, M., Monk, C. S., & Dickstein, D. P. (2007). Attention bias to threat faces in children with bipolar disorder and comorbid lifetime anxiety disorders. *Biological Psychiatry, 61*, 819–821.

Brown, S. A. (1993). Recovery patterns in adolescent substance abusers. In J. S. Baer, G. A. Marlatt, & R. J. McMahon (Eds.), *Addictive behaviors across the lifespan: Prevention, treatment, and policy issues* (pp. 161–183). Newbury Park, CA: Sage.

Brown, T. E. (2005). *Attention deficit disorder: The unfocused mind in children and adults.* New Haven, CT: Yale University Press.

Bruch, H. (1991). The sleeping beauty: Escape from change. In S. I. Greenspan & H. L. Pollock (Eds.), *The course of life, Vol. 4: Adolescence*. Madison, CT: International Universities Press.

Bryant, D. P., Bryant, B. R., Gersten, R., Scammacca, N., Funk, C., Winter, A., ... & Pool, C. (2008). The effects of Tier 2 intervention on first-grade mathematics performance of first-grade students who are at risk for mathematics difficulties. *Learning Disability Quarterly, 31*, 47–63.

Bryant-Waugh, R., & Lask, B. (1995). Eating disorders in children. *Journal of Child Psychology and Psychiatry, 36*, 191–202.

Buka, S. L., Stichick, T. L., Birdthistle, I., & Earls, F. (2001). Youth exposure to violence: Prevalence, risks, and consequences. *American Journal of Orthopsychiatry, 71*, 298–310.

Cadoret, R., Yates, W. R., Troughton, E., Woodworth, G., & Stewart, M. A. (1995). Adoption study demonstrating two genetic pathways to drug abuse. *Archives of General Psychiatry, 52*, 42–52.

Campbell, S. B., March, C. L., Pierce, E. W., Ewing, L. J., & Szumowski, E. K. (1991). Hard-to-manage preschool boys: Family context and the stability of externalizing behavior. *Journal of Abnormal Child Psychology, 19*, 301–318.

Campo, J. V., & Fritsch, S. L. (1994). Somatization in children and adolescents. *Journal of the American Academy of Child and Adolescent Psychiatry, 33*, 1223–1235.

Cantwell, D. P. (1994). *Therapeutic management of attention deficit disorder: Participant workbook*. New York, NY: SCP Communications.

Carlberg, C., & Kavale, K. (1980). The efficacy of special versus regular class placement for exceptional children: A meta-analysis. *The Journal of Special Education, 14*, 295–308.

Carroll, L. (1865/1992). *Alice's adventures in wonderland*. Toronto, Canada: Tor Books.

Carrasco, J. L., Diaz-Marsa, M., Hollander, E., Cesar, J., & Saiz-Ruiz, J. (2000). Decreased platelet monoamine oxidase activity in female bulimia nervosa. *European Neuropsychopharmacology, 10*(2), 113–117.

Carrion, V. G., Weems, C. F., Ray, R., & Reiss, A. L. (2002). Towards an empirical definition of pediatric PTSD: The phenomenology of PTSD symptoms in youth. *Journal of the American Academy of Child and Adolescent Psychiatry, 41*, 166–173.

Carter, A. S., Grigorenko, E. L., & Pauls, D. L. (1995). A Russian adaptation of the Child Behavior Checklist: Psychometric properties and associations with child and maternal affective symptomatology and family functioning. *Journal of Abnormal Child Psychology, 23*, 661–684.

Carter, S. L., Wheeler, J. J., & Mayton, M. (2004). Pica: A review of recent assessment and treatment procedures. *Education and Training in Developmental Disabilities, 39*(4), 346–358.

Casper, R. C., Hedeker, D., & McClough, J. F. (1992). Personality dimensions in eating disorders and their relevance for subtyping. *Journal of the American Academy of Child and Adolescent Psychiatry, 31*, 830–840.

Centers for Disease Control (CDC; 2005). Youth Risk Behavior Surveillance (YRBS, 2005). *Morbidity and Mortality Weekly Report 55*(SS55).

Centers for Disease Control and Prevention (CDC). (2009). Prevalence of autism spectrum disorders—Autism and Developmental Disabilities Monitoring Network, United States, 2006. *Morbidity and Mortality Weekly Report, 58*(SS10) 1–20.

Chamberlain, P., & Reid, J. (1991). Using a specialized foster care community treatment model for children and adolescents leaving the state mental hospital. *Journal of Community Psychology, 19*, 266–276.

Chamberlain, P., & Reid, J. (1998). Comparison of two community alternatives to incarceration for chronic juvenile offenders. *Journal of Consulting and Clinical Psychology, 66*, 624–633.

Chan, S., & Lee, E. (2004). Families with Asian roots. In E. W. Lynch & M. J. Hanson (Eds.), *Developing cross-cultural competence* (3rd ed., pp. 219–298). Baltimore, MD: Paul H. Brookes.

Chorpita, B. F. (2002). The tripartite model and dimensions of anxiety and depression: An examination of structure in a large school sample. *Journal of Abnormal Child Psychology, 30*, 177–190.

Chorpita, B. F., Plummer, C. P., & Moffitt, C. (2000). Relations of tripartite dimensions of emotion to childhood anxiety and mood disorders. *Journal of Abnormal Child Psychology, 28*, 299–310.

Cicchetti, D., & Rogosch, F. (2002). A developmental psychopathology perspective on adolescence. *Journal of Consulting and Clinical Psychology, 70*, 6–20.

Cicchetti, D., & Toth, S. L. (1991). A developmental perspective on internalizing and externalizing disorders. In D. Cicchetti & L. Toth (Eds.), *Internalizing and externalizing expressions of dysfunction* (pp. 1–19). Hillsdale, NJ: Erlbaum.

Cicchetti, D., & Toth, S. L. (1998). The development of depression in children and adolescence. *American Psychologist, 53*(2), 221–241.

Clark, D. B., & Baker, B. L. (1983). Predicting outcome in parent training. *Journal of Consulting and Clinical Psychology, 51*, 309–311.

Cloitre, M., Tardiff, K., Marzuk, P. M., Leon, A. C., & Potera, L. (1996). Childhood abuse and subsequent sexual assault among female inpatients. *Journal of Traumatic Stress, 9*, 473–482.

Cobham, V. E., Dadds, M. R., & Spence, S. H. (1998). The role of parental anxiety in the treatment of childhood anxiety. *Journal of Consulting and Clinical Psychology, 66*, 893–905.

Coghill, D., & Sonuga-Barke, E. J. (2012). Annual research review: Categories versus dimensions in the classification and conceptualization of child and adolescent mental disorders—Implications of recent empirical study. *Journal of Child Psychology and Psychiatry, 53*, 469–489.

Cohen, J. A., Deblinger, E., Mannarino, A. P., & Steer, R. A. (2004). A multisite, randomized controlled trial for children with sexual abuse–related PTSD symptoms. *Journal of the American Academy of Child and Adolescent Psychiatry, 43*, 393–402.

Coie, J. D., Dodge, K., & Coppotelli, H. (1982). Dimensions and types of social status: A cross-age perspective. *Developmental Psychology, 18*, 557–570.

Comer, R. J. (2013). *Abnormal psychology* (8th ed.). New York, NY: Worth.

Compas, B. E., Connor-Smith, J. K., Saltzman, H., Thomsen, A., & Wadsworth, M. E. (2001). Coping with stress during childhood and adolescence: Problems, progress and potential in theory and research. *Psychological Bulletin, 127*, 87–127.

Copeland, W. E., Angold, A., Costello, E. J., & Egger, H. (2013). Prevalence, comorbidity and correlates of DSM-5 proposed disruptive mood dysregulation disorder. *American Journal of Psychiatry, 170*, 173–179.

Cornoldi, C., Venneri, A., Marconato, R., Molin, A., & Montinari, C. (2003). A rapid screening measure for the identification of visuospatial learning disability in schools. *Journal of Learning Disabilities, 36*, 299–306.

Cosgrove, V. E., Rhee, S. H., Gelhorn, H. L., Boeldt, D., Corley, R. C., & Ehringer, M. A. (2011). Structure and etiology of co-occurring internalizing and externalizing disorders in adolescence. *Journal of Abnormal Child Psychology, 39*(1), 109–123.

Costello, E. J., Angold, A., Burns, B. J., Stangel, D. K., Tweed, D. L., Erkanli, A., & Worthman, C. M. (1996). The Great Smoky Mountains Study of Youth: Goals, design, methods, and the prevalence of *DSM-III-R* disorders. *Archives of General Psychiatry, 53*, 1129–1136.

Costello, J., Pine, D., Hammen, C., March, J., Plotsky, P. M., & Weissman, M. (2002). Development and natural history of mood disorders. *Biological Psychiatry, 52*(6), 529–542.

Craske, M. G., Kircanski, K., Epstein, A., Wittchen, H. U., & Pine, D. S. (2010). Panic disorder: A review of DSM-IV panic disorder and proposals for DSM-V. *Depression and Anxiety, 27*, 93–112.

Cuffe, S. P., McCullough, E. L., & Pumariega, A. J. (1994). Comorbidity of attention-deficit/hyperactivity disorder and posttraumatic stress disorder. *Journal of Child and Family Studies, 3*, 327–336.

Cummins, J. (1984). *Bilingual special education: Issues in assessment and pedagogy*. San Diego, CA: College-Hill.

Dabbs, J., & Morris, R. (1990). Testosterone, social class, and antisocial behavior in a sample of 4,462 men. *Psychological Science, 1*, 209–211.

Davidson, J. (1993). Issues in the diagnosis of post-traumatic stress disorder. In R. S. Pynoos (Ed.), *Posttraumatic stress disorder: A clinical review* (pp. 1–15). Lutherville, MD: Sidran Press.

Dawson, G., & Osterling, J. (1996). Early intervention in autism: Effectiveness and common elements of current approaches. In M. J. Guralnick (Ed.), *The effectiveness of early interventions: Second-generation research* (pp. 307–326). Baltimore, MD: Paul H. Brookes.

Deas, D., Riggs, P., Langenbuncher, J., Goldman, M., & Brown, S. (2000). Adolescents are not adults: Developmental considerations in alcohol users. *Alcoholism: Clinical and Experimental Research, 24*, 232–237.

Deater-Deckard, K., Dodge, K., Bates, K. A., & Pettit, G. S. (1996). Physical discipline among African-American and European-American mothers: Links to children's externalizing behaviors. *Developmental Psychology, 32*, 1065–1072.

Deblinger, E., Lippmann, J., & Steer, R. (1999). Sexually abused children suffering post-traumatic stress symptoms: Initial treatment outcome findings. *Child Maltreatment, 1*(4), 310–321.

Deblinger, E., McLeer, S. V., Atkins, M. S., Ralphe, D., & Foa, E. (1989). Posttraumatic stress in sexually abused, physically abused, and nonabused children. *Child Abuse and Neglect, 13*, 403–408.

Decaluwe, V., & Braet, C. (2003). Prevalence of binge-eating disorder in obese children and adolescents seeking weight-loss treatment. *International Journal of Obesity, 27*, 404–409.

Deep, A. L., Nagy, L. M., Weltzin, T. E., Rao, R., & Kaye, W. H. (1995). Premorbid onset of psychopathology in long-term recovered anorexia nervosa. *International Journal of Eating Disorders, 17*, 291–297.

DeFries, J. C., & Alarcon, M. (1996). Genetics of specific reading disability. *Mental Retardation & Developmental Disabilities Research Reviews, 2*, 39–48.

Demonet, J., Taylor, M. J., & Chaix, Y. (2004). Developmental dyslexia. *Lancet*, *363*, 1451–1460.

Deveney, D. M., Connolly, M., Haring, C. T., Bones, B. L., Reynolds, R. C., Kim, P., … Leibenluft, E. (2013). Neural mechanisms of frustration in chronically irritable children. *American Journal of Psychiatry*, *170*, 1186–1194.

Diller, L. H. (1996). The run on Ritalin: Attention deficit disorder and stimulant treatments in the 1990's. *Hastings Center Report*, *26*, 12–18.

Dishion, T. J., McCord, J., & Poulin, F. (1999). When interventions harm: Peer groups and problem behavior. *American Psychologist*, *54*, 755–764.

Dishion, T. J., Spracklen, K. M., Andrews, D. W., & Patterson, G. R. (1996). Deviancy training in male adolescent friendships. *Behavior Therapy*, *27*, 373–390.

Dodge, K. A. (1991). The structure and function of reactive and proactive aggression. In D. J. Pepler & K. H. Rubin (Eds.), *The development and treatment of childhood aggression* (pp. 201–218). Hillsdale, NJ: Erlbaum.

Dodge, K., Bates, J., & Pettit, G. (1990). Mechanisms in the cycle of violence. *Science*, *250*, 1678–1683.

Donahue, B., & Azrin, N. (2001). Family behaviour therapy. In E. F. Wagner & H. B. Waldron (Eds.), *Innovations in adolescent substance abuse interventions* (pp. 205–227). Oxford, UK: Elsevier Science.

Donnelly, D. R., & Olczak, P. V. (1990). The effect of differential reinforcement of incompatible behaviors (DRI) on pica for cigarettes in persons with intellectual disability. *Behavior Modification*, *14*, 81–96.

Douglas, J. (2002). Psychological treatment of food refusal in young children. *Child and Adolescent Mental Health*, *7*(4), 173–180.

Drotar, D., Stein, R., & Perrin, E. (1995). Methodological issues in using the Child Behavior Checklist and its related instruments in clinical child psychology research. *Journal of Clinical Child Psychology*, *21*(2), 184–192.

Dunston, P. J. (1992). A critique of graphic organizer research. *Reading Research and Instruction*, *31*, 57–65.

Durlak, J. (1998). Common risk and protective factors in successful prevention programs. *American Journal of Orthopsychiatry*, *68*, 512–520.

Dykman, R. A., & Ackerman, P. T. (1992). Attention deficit disorder and specific reading disability: Separate but often overlapping disorders. In S. Shaywitz & B. Shaywitz (Eds.), *Attention deficit disorder comes of age: Toward the twenty-first century* (pp. 165–184). Austin, TX: Pro-Ed.

Ebesutani, C., Smith, A., Bernstein, A., & Chorpita, B. F. (2011). A bifactor model of negative affectivity: Fear and distress components among younger and older youth. *Psychological Assessment*, *23*, 679–691.

Edelbrock, C. S., & Costello, A. J. (1988). Structured psychiatric interviews for children. In M. Rutteer, A. H. Tuma, & I. Lann (Eds.), *Assessment diagnosis in child psychopathology* (pp. 87–112). New York, NY: Guilford Press.

Ehlers, A., & Clark, D. M. (2000). A cognitive model of posttraumatic stress disorder. *Behavior Research and Therapy*, *38*, 319–345.

Eisenmajer, R., Prior, M., Leekam, S., Wing, L., Gould, J., Welham, M., & Ong, B. (1996). Comparison of clinical symptoms in autism and Asperger's disorder. *Journal of the American Academy of Child and Adolescent Psychiatry*, *35*, 1523–1531.

Eley, T. C. (1999). Behavioral genetics as a tool for developmental psychology: Anxiety and depression in children and adolescents. *Clinical Child and Family Psychology Review*, *2*, 21–36.

Elia, J., & Rapoport, J. L. (1991). Ritalin versus dextroamphetamine in ADHD: Both should be tried. In L. L. Greenhill & B. B. Osmon (Eds.), *Ritalin: Theory and patient management* (pp. 69–74). New York, NY: Mary Ann Liebert.

Elkind, D., & Bowen, R. (1979). Imaginary audience behavior in children and adolescents. *Developmental Psychology, 15*, 38–44.

Emery, R. E. (2001). Behavioral family intervention: Less "behavior" and more "family." In A. Booth, A. C. Crouter, & M. Clements (Eds.), *Couples in conflict* (pp. 241–249). Mahwah, NJ: Erlbaum.

Eminson, M., Benjamin, S., Shortall, A., Woods, T., & Faragher, B. (1996). Physical symptoms and illness attitudes in adolescents: An epidemiological study. *Journal of Child Psychological and Psychiatry, 37*, 519–528.

Essau, C. A., Conradt, J., & Petermann, F. (1999). Prevalence, comorbidity, and psychosocial impairment of somatoform disorders in adolescents. *Psychology, Health, and Medicine, 4*, 169–180.

Essau, C. A., Conradt, J., & Petermann, F. (2000). Frequency, comorbidity, and psychosocial impairment of specific phobia in adolescents. *Journal of Clinical Child Psychology, 29*, 221–232.

Evans, G. W., Gonnella, C., Marcynyszyn, L. A., Gentile, L., & Salpekar, N. (2005). The role of chaos in poverty and children's socioemotional adjustment. *Psychologial Science, 16*, 560–565.

Fabrega, H. (1990). Hispanic mental health research: A case for cultural psychiatry. *Hispanic Journal of Behavioral Science, 12*, 339–365.

Fairburn, C. G., Welch, S. I., Doll, H. A., Davies, B. A., & O'Connor, M. E. (1997). Risk factors for bulimia nervosa: A community-based case-control study. *Archives of General Psychiatry, 54*, 509–517.

Federal Register. (1999, March 12). Education Department [FR Doc 12405–12672] p. 12422, Vol. 64, No. 48. Retrieved from www.admin@gpo.gov

Federal Register (2006, August). Retrieved from http://idea.ed.gov/download/finalregulations.pdf

Ferrer, E., Bennett, A., Shaywitz, J. M., Holahan, J. M., Marchione, K., & Shaywitz, S. E. (2010). Uncoupling of reading and IQ over time: Empirical evidence for a definition of dyslexia. *Psychological Science, 21*(93), 93–101.

Fischer, R. L., & Fischer, S. (1996). Antidepressants for children: Is scientific support necessary? *Journal of Nervous and Mental Disease, 184*, 99–102.

Fitzgerald, H. E., Davies, W. H., Zucker, R. A., & Klinger, M. T. (1994). Developmental systems theory and substance abuse: A conceptual and methodological framework for analyzing patterns of variation in families. In L. L. Abate (Ed.), *Handbook of developmental family psychology and psychopathology* (pp. 350–372). New York, NY: Wiley.

Fitzpatrick, K. M., & Boldizar, J. P. (1993). The prevalence and consequences of exposure to violence among African American youth. *Journal of the American Academy of Adolescent Psychiatry, 32*, 424–430.

Flannery-Schroeder, E., & Kendall, P. C. (2000). Group and individual cognitive-behavioral treatments for youth with anxiety disorders: A randomized clinical trial. *Cognitive Therapy and Research, 244*, 251–278.

Fleming, J. E., & Offord, D. R. (1990). Epidemiology of childhood depressive disorders: A critical review. *Journal of the American Academy of Child and Adolescent Psychiatry, 29*, 571–580.

Foa, E. B., & Kozak, M. J. (1986). Emotional processing of fear: Exposure to corrective information. *Psychological Bulletin, 99*, 220–235.

Fonagy, P., & Target, M. (1996). A contemporary psychoanalytical perspective: Psychodynamic developmental therapy. In E. D. Hibbs & P. S. Jensen (Eds.), *Psychosocial treatments for child and adolescent disorders: Empirically based strategies for clinical practice* (pp. 619–638). Washington, DC: American Psychological Association.

Forehand, R., & Kotchick, B. (1996). Cultural diversity: A wake-up call for parent training. *Behavior Therapy, 27*, 187–206.

Forness, S. R., & Kavale, K. A. (1991). Social skill deficits as a primary learning disability: A note on problems with the ICLD diagnostic criteria. *Learning Disability Research and Practice, 6*, 44–49.

Fox, N. A., Henderson, H. A., Marshall, P. J., Nichols, K. D., & Ghera, M. (2005). Behavioral inhibition: Linking biology and behavior within a developmental framework. *Annual Review of Psychology, 56*, 235–262.

Fox, N. A., & Pine, D. S. (2012). Temperament and the emergence of anxiety disorders. *Journal of the American Academy of Child and Adolescent Psychiatry, 51*(2), 125–128.

Frances, A. (2011, July 22). DSM-5 approves new fad diagnosis for child psychiatry: Antipsychotic use likely to rise. *Psychiatric Times*. Retrieved from http://www.psychiatrictimes.com/print/article/10168/1912195

Francis, G., & Ollendick, T. H. (1988). Social withdrawal. In M. Hersen & C. G. Last (Eds.), *Child behavior therapy casebook* (pp. 31–41). New York, NY: Plenum Press.

Frick, P. J., & Kamphaus, R. W. (2001). Standardized rating scales in the assessment of children's behavioral and emotional problems. In C. E. Walker & M. C. Roberts (Eds.), *Handbook of clinical child psychology* (pp. 190–204). New York, NY: Wiley.

Frick, P. J., Kamphaus, R. W., Lahey, B. B., Loeber, R., Christ, M. A. G., Hart, E. L., & Tannenbaum, L. E. (1991). Academic underachievement and the disruptive behavior disorders. *Journal of Consulting and Clinical Psychology, 59*, 289–294.

Frick, P. J., Lahey, B. B., Loeber, R., Tannenbaum, L., Van Horn, Y., Christ, M. A., Hart, E. L., & Hanson, K. (1993). Oppositional defiant disorder and conduct disorder: A meta-analytic review of factor analyses and cross validation in a clinic sample. *Clinical Psychology Review, 13*, 319–340.

Frith, C. D., & Frith, U. (1999). Interacting minds—A biological basis. *Science, 286*, 1692–1696.

Fritz, G. K., Fritsch, S., & Hagino, O. (1997). Somatoform disorders in children and adolescents: A review of the past 10 years. *Journal of the American Academy of Child and Adolescent Psychiatry, 36*, 1329–1338.

Fryer, A. J., Mannuzza, S., Chapman, R. F., Liebowitz, M. R., & Klein, D. F. (1993). A direct interview family study of social phobia. *Archives of General Psychiatry, 50*, 286–293.

Fuchs, D., & Fuchs, L. (2005). Peer-assisted learning strategies: Promoting word recognition, fluency and reading comprehension in young children. *Journal of Special Education, 39*, 34–44.

Gabbard, G. O. (1990). *Psychodynamic psychiatry in clinical practice*. Washington, DC: American Psychiatric Press.

Garber, J., Walker, L. S., & Seman, J. (1991). Somatization symptoms in a community sample of children and adolescents: Further validation of the Children's Somatization Inventory. *Journal of Consulting and Clinical Psychology, 199*, 588–595.

Garber, J., Zeman, J., & Walker, L. S. (1990). Recurrent abdominal pain in children: Psychiatric diagnoses and parental psychopathology. *Journal of the American Academy of Child and Adolescent Psychiatry, 29*, 648–656.

Garland, A. F., & Zigler, E. (1993). Adolescent suicide prevention: Current research and social policy implications. *American Psychologist, 48*, 169–182.

Garner, D. M., Cooke, A. K., & Marano, H. E. (1997). The 1997 body image survey results. *Psychology Today*, (Jan.–Feb.), 30–44.

Garner, D. M., Garfinkel, P. E., & O'Shaughnessy, M. (1985). The validity of the distinction between bulimia with and without anorexia nervosa. *American Journal of Psychiatry, 142*, 581–587.

Garralda, E. E. (1999). Practitioner review: Assessment and management of somatisation in childhood and adolescence: A practical perspective. *Journal of Child Psychology and Psychiatry, 40*, 1159–1167.

Geary, D. C. (2000). Mathematical disorders: An overview for educators. *Perspectives, 26*, 6–9.

Geary, D. C. (2003). Learning disabilities in arithmetic. In H. L. Swanson, K. R. Harris, & S. Graham (Eds.), *Handbook of learning disabilities* (pp. 199–212). New York, NY: Guilford Press.

Geary, D. (2004). Mathematics and learning disabilities. *Journal of Learning Disabilities, 37*(1), 4–15.

Geller, B. (2001). A prepubertal and early adolescent bipolar disorder phenotype has poor one-year outcome. *The Brown University Child and Adolescent Psychopharmacology Update, 3*, 1–5.

Geller, B., & Luby, J. (1997). Child and adolescent bipolar disorder: A review of the past 10 years. *Journal of the American Academy of Child and Adolescent Psychiatry, 36*, 1168–1176.

Geller, B., Sun, K., Zimerman, B., Luby, J., Frazier, J., & Williams, M. (1995). Complex and rapid-cycling in bipolar children and adolescents: A preliminary study. *Journal of Affective Disorders, 34*, 259–268.

Geller, D. A., Biederman, J., Farapme, S., Agranat, A., Cradlock, K., Hagermoser, L., ... Coffey, B. (2001). Disentangling chronological age from age of onset in children and adolescents with obsessive-compulsive disorder. *International Journal of Neuropsychopharmacology, 4*, 169–178.

Geller, D. A., Biederman, J., Stewart, S., Mullin, E., Martin, B., Spencer, A., & Faraone, S. V. (2003). Which SSRI? A meta-analysis of pharmacotherapy trials in pediatric obsessive-compulsive disorder. *American Journal of Psychiatry, 160* (11), 1919–1928.

Gerber, P. J., & Reiff, H. B. (1994). *Learning disabilities in adulthood: Persisting problems and evolving issues*. Boston, MA: Andover Medical.

Gersten, R., Jordan, N. C., & Flojo, J. R. (2005). Early identification and interventions for students with mathematics difficulties. *Journal of Learning Disabilities, 38*, 293–304.

Giaconia, R. M., Reinherz, H. Z., Silverman, A. B., Pakiz, B., Frost, A. K., & Cohen, E. (1994). Ages of onset of psychiatric disorders in a community population of older adolescents. *Journal of the American Academy of Child and Adolescent Psychiatry, 33*, 706–717.

Gibbs, J. T., & Huang, L. (2001). A conceptual framework for the psychological assessment and treatment of minority youth. In J. T. Gibbs & L. A. Huang (Eds.), *Children of color* (pp. 1–32). San Francisco, CA: Jossey-Bass.

Gibbs, J. T., & Huang, L. N. (2003). *Children of color* (2nd ed.). San Francisco, CA: Jossey-Bass.

Gilliam, W. S., & Shabar, G. (2006). Preschool and child care expulsion and suspension. *Infants & Young Children, 19*, 228–245.

Gleason, M. M., Fox, N. A., Drury, S., Smyke, A., Egger, H., Nelson, C. Gregas, M. C., & Zeanah, C. H. (2011). Valildity of evidence-derived criteria for reactive attachment disorder: Indiscriminately social/ disinhibited and emotionally withdrawn/ inhibited types. *Journal of the American Academy of Child and Adolescent Psychiatry, 50*(3), 216–231.

Goh, H. L., Iwata, B. A., Shore, B. A., Deleon, I. G., Lerman, D. C., Ulrich, S. M., & Smith, R. G. (1995). An analysis of the reinforcing properties of hand mouthing. *Journal of Applied Behavior Analysis, 28*, 269–283.

Goldstein, A. (1994). *Addiction: From biology to drug policy*. New York, NY: W. H. Freeman.

Goldstein, S. (2005). Current literature on ADHD. *Journal of Attention Disorders, 9*(2), 452-456.

Golub, A., & Johnson, B. D. (1994). The shifting importance of alcohol and marijuana as gateway substances among serious drug abusers. *Journal of Studies on Alcohol, 55*, 607–614.

Goodwin, R. D., & Gotlib, I. H. (2004). Panic attacks and psychopathology among youth. *Acta Psychiatry Scandanavia, 109*, 216–221.

Gould, S. J. (1981). *The mismeasure of man*. New York, NY: W. W. Norton.

Graham, S., Harris, K. R., & Larsen, L. (2001). Prevention and intervention of writing difficulties for students with learning disabilities. *Learning Disabilities Research and Practice, 16*, 74–84.

Graham-Bermann, S. A., Howell, K., Habarath, J., Krishnan, S., Loree, A., & Bermann, E. A. (2008). Toward assessing traumatic events and stress symptoms in preschool children from low-income families. *American Journal of Orthopsychiatry, 78*(2), 220–228.

Grant, K. E., Compas, B. E., Thurm, A. E., & McMahon, S. D. (2004). Stressors and child and adolescent psychopathology: Measurement issues and prospective effects. *Journal of Clinical Child and Adolescent Psychology, 33*, 412–425.

Gravenstock, S. (2000). Eating disorders in adults with intellectual disabilities. *Journal of Intellectual Disability Research, 44* (6), 625–637.

Greenberg, M. T. (1999). Attachment and psychopathology in childhood. In J. Cassidy & P. R. Shaver (Eds.), *Handbook of attachment* (pp. 469–496). New York, NY: Guilford Press.

Greene, R. W., & Ablon, J. S. (2004). *The collaborative problem-solving approach: Cognitive-behavioral treatment of oppositional defiant disorder*. New York, NY: Guilford Press.

Greene, R. W., Ablon, J. S., Goring, J. C., Fazio, V., & Morse, L. R. (2003). Treatment of oppositional defiant disorder in children and adolescents. In P. M. Barrett & T. H. Ollendick (Eds.), *Handbook of interventions that work with children and adolescents* (pp. 369–393). Chichester, England: Wiley.

Greene, R. W., Biederman, J., Faraone, S. V., Sienna, M., & Garcia-Jetton, J. (1997). Adolescent outcome of boys with attention-deficit/hyperactivity disorder and social disability: Results from a 4-year longitudinal follow-up study. *Journal of Consulting and Clinical Psychology, 65*, 758–787.

Gresham, F. M., & Elliott, S. N. (1990). *Social skills rating system*. Circle Pines, MN: American Guidance Service.

Griffin, K. W., Botvin, G. J., Nichols, T. R., & Doyle, M. M. (2003). Effectiveness of a universal drug abuse prevention approach for youth at high risk for substance use initiation. *Preventive Medicine, 36*, 1–7.

Gross, J. (2002). Emotion regulation: Affective, cognitive, and social consequences. *Psychophysiology, 39*, 281–291.

Gross-Tsur, V., Shalev, R. S., Manor, O., & Amir, N. (1995). Developmental right hemisphere syndrome: Clinical spectrum of the nonverbal learning disability. *Journal of Learning Disabilities, 28*, 80–86.

Guerra, N. G., Graham, S., & Tolan, P. H. (2011). Raising healthy children: Translating child development into research and practice. *Child Development, 82*(1), 7–16.

Guralnick, M. J. (1998). Effectiveness of early intervention for vulnerable children: A developmental perspective. *American Journal of Mental Retardation, 102*, 319–345.

Guyer, B., MacDorman, M. F., Martin, J. A., Peters, K. D., & Strobino, D. M. (1998). Annual summary of vital statistics—1997. *Pediatrics, 102*, 1333–1349.

Hagopian, L. P., & Adelinis, J. D. (2001). Response blocking with and without redirection for the treatment of pica. *Journal of Applied Behavior Analysis, 34*, 527–530.

Hall, G. S. (1904). *Adolescence*. New York, NY: Appleton.

Hallowell, E. M. (1995). Coaching: An adjunct of the treatment of ADHD. *The ADHD Report*, *3*, 7–9.

Halmi, K. A. (1995). Current concepts and definitions. In G. Szmukler, C. Dare, & J. Treasure (Eds.), *Handbook of eating disorders: Theory, treatment, and research* (pp. 5–27). Chichester, UK: Wiley.

Hammen, C. (1991). The family-environmental context of depression: A perspective on children's risk. In D. Cicchetti & S. L. Toth (Eds.), *Rochester symposium on developmental psychopathology*, *4*, 251–281.

Handen, B. L. (1998). Mental retardation. In E. J. Mash & R. A. Barkley (Eds.), *Treatment of childhood disorders* (pp. 369–415). New York, NY: Guilford Press.

Hankin, B. L., & Abramson, L. Y. (2001). Development of gender differences in depression: An elaborated cognitive vulnerability–transactional stress theory. *Psychological Bulletin*, *127*, 773–796.

Harter, S., & Marold, D. (1994). Psychosocial risk factors contributing to adolescent suicidal ideation. In G. G. Noam & S. Borst (Eds.), *Children, youth, and suicide: Developmental perspectives* (pp. 71–92). San Francisco, CA: Jossey-Bass.

Haynes, S. N., & O'Brien, W. H. (1990). Functional analysis in behavior therapy. *Clinical Psychology Review*, *10*(6), 649–668.

Hayward, C., Wilson, K. A., Lagle, K., Killen, J. D., & Taylor, C. B. (2004). Parent-reported predictors of adolescent panic attacks. *Journal of the American Academy of Child and Adolescent Psychiatry*, *43*, 613–620.

Henggeler, S. W., & Borduin, C. M. (1990). *Family therapy and beyond: A multisystemic approach to treating the behavior problems of children and adolescents*. Pacific Grove, CA: Brooks/Cole.

Henggeler, S. W., Melton, G. B., & Smith, L. A. (1992). Family preservation using multisystemic therapy: An effective alternative to incarcerating serious juvenile offenders. *Journal of Consulting and Clinical Psychology*, *60*, 953–961.

Henggeler, S. W., Schoenwald, S. K., Borduin, C. M., Rowland, M. D., & Cunninghan, P. B. (1998). *Multisystemic treatment of antisocial behavior in youth*. New York, NY: Guilford Press.

Herzog, D. B., Sacks, N. R., Keller, M. B., Lavori, P. W., von Ranson, K. B., & Gray, H. N. (1993). Patterns and predictors of recovery in anorexia nervosa and bulimia nervosa. *Journal of Child Psychology and Psychiatry*, *32*, 962–966.

Herzog, W., Schellberg, D., & Deter, H. C. (1997). First recovery in anorexia nervosa patients in the long-term course: A discrete-time survival analysis. *Journal of Consulting and Clinical Psychology*, *65*, 169–177.

Hibell, B., Guttormsson, U., Ahlström, S., Balakireva, O., Bjarnason, T., Kokkevi, A., & Kraus, L. (2009). The 2007 ESPAD report: Substance use among students in 35 European countries. Stockholm, Sweden: The Swedish Council for Information on Alcohol and Other Drugs.

Hinshaw, S. P., Heller, T., & McHale, J. P. (1992). Covert antisocial behavior in boys with attention deficit hyperactivity disorder: External validation and effects of methylphenidate. *Journal of Consulting and Clinical Psychology*, *60*, 274–281.

Hinshaw-Fuselier, S., Boris, N. W., & Zeanah, C. H. (1999). Reactive attachment disorder in maltreated twins. *Infant Mental Health Journal*, *20*, 42–59.

Hirschfeld, R. M., Holzer, C., Calabrese, J. R., Weissman, M., Reed, M., Davies, M., … Hazard, E. (2003). Validity of the mood disorder questionnaire: A general population study. *American Journal of Psychiatry*, *160*(1), 178–180.

Hocutt, A. M. (1996). Effectiveness of special education: Is placement the critical factor? *The Future of Children*, *6*, 77–102.

Hoffman, E. C., & Mattis, S. G. (2000). A developmental adaptation of panic control treatment for panic disorder in adolescence. *Cognitive and Behavioral Practice, 7*, 253–261.

Hofstede, G. (1980). *Culture's consequences: International differences in work-related values.* Beverly Hills, CA: Sage.

Holmbeck, G. N., Greenley, R. N., & Franks, E. A. (2004). Developmental issues in evidence-based practice. In P. M. Barrett & E. H. Ollendick (Eds.), *Handbook of interventions that work with children and adolescents: Prevention and treatment* (pp. 27–48). Chichester, UK: Wiley.

Hooper, S. R., Swartz, C. W., Wakely, M. B., de Kruif, R. E., & Montgomery, J. W. (2002). Executive functions in elementary school children with and without problems in written expression. *Journal of Learning Disabilities, 35*(1), 57–68.

Horowitz, K., Weine, S., & Jekel, J. (1995). PTSD symptoms in urban adolescent girls: Compounded community trauma. *Journal of the American Academy of Child and Adolescent Psychiatry, 34*, 1353–1361.

Hotopf, M. (2002). Childhood experience of illness as a risk factor for medically unexplained symptoms. *Scandinavian Journal of Psychology, 43*, 139–146.

Howlin, P. (1987). Asperger's syndrome—Does it exist and what can be done about it? In *Proceedings of the First International Symposium on Specific Speech and Language Disorders in Children*. London, UK: AFASIC.

Hsieh, M., & Stright, A. D. (2012). Adolescents' emotion regulation strategies, self-concept, and internalizing problems. *Journal of Early Adolescence, 32*(6), 876–901.

Hudson, J. L., & Rapee, R. M. (2000). The origins of social phobia. *Behavior Modification, 24*, 102–129.

Hurth, J., Shaw, E., Izeman, S., Whaley, K., & Rogers, S. (1999). Areas of agreement about effective practices among programs serving young children with autism spectrum disorders. *Infants and Young Children, 12*, 17–26.

Imhof, M. (2004). Effects of color stimulation on handwriting performance of children with ADHD without and with additional learning disabilities. *European Child & Adolescent Psychiatry, 13*, 191–198.

Interagency Committee on Learning Disabilities (ICLD). (1987). *Learning disabilities: A report to the U.S. Congress*. Bethesda, MD: National Institutes of Health.

Jick, H., & Kaye, J. (2003). Epidemiology and possible causes of autism. *Pharmacotherapy, 23*, 1524–1530.

Joe, J. R., & Malach, R. S. (2004). Families with Native American roots. In E. W. Lynch & M. J. Hanson (Eds.), *Developing cross-cultural competence* (3rd ed., pp. 109–140). Baltimore, MD: Paul H. Brookes.

Johnson, E. E., Humphrey, M., Mellard, D. F., Woods, K., & Swanson, H. L. (2010). Cognitive processing deficits and students with specific learning disabilities: A selective meta-analysis of the literature. *Learning Disability Quarterly, 33*, 3–18.

Johnson, V., & Pandina, R. (2000). Alcohol problems among a community sample: Longitudinal influences of stress, coping, and gender. *Substance Use and Misuse, 35*, 669–686.

Johnston, L. D., O'Malley, P. M., Bachman, J. G., & Schulenberg, J. E. (2008). *Monitoring the Future national results on adolescent drug use: Overview of key findings, 2007* (NIH Publication No. 08-6418). Bethesda, MD: National Institute on Drug Abuse.

Johnston, L. D., O'Malley, P. M., Bachman, J. G., & Schulenberg, J. E. (2013, December 18). American teens more cautious about using synthetic drugs. Ann Arbor, MI: University of Michigan News Service. Retrieved from http://www.monitoringthefuture.org

Jones, A. P., Laurens, K. R., Herba, C. M., Barker, G., & Viding, E. (2009). Amygdala hypoactivity to fearful faces in boys with conduct problems and callous-unemotional traits. *The American Journal of Psychiatry, 166*(1), 95–102.

Jones, M. B., & Offord, D. R. (1989). Reduction of antisocial behavior in poor children in nonschool skill development. *Journal of Child Psychology and Psychiatry, 30*, 737–750.

Joseph, S. A., Brewin, C. R., Yule, W., & Williams, R. (1993). Causal attributions and post-traumatic stress in adolescents. *Journal of Child Psychology and Psychiatry, 34*, 247–253.

Kadesjo, B., & Gillberg, C. (1999). Developmental coordination disorder in Swedish 7-year-old children. *Journal of the American Academy of Child and Adolescent Psychiatry, 38*, 820–828.

Kaij, L. (1960). *Alcoholism in twins: Studies on the etiology and sequels of abuse of alcohol*. Stockholm, Sweden: Almquist & Wiksell.

Kandel, D. B. (2002). Examining the gateway hypothesis. In D. B. Kandel (Ed.), *Stages and pathways of drug involvement* (pp. 3–15). Cambridge, UK: Cambridge University Press.

Kaplan, A. (1998). Practice parameters offer guidance on substance use disorders in children, adolescents. *Psychiatric Times, XV*(4).

Kaslow, N. J., & Thompson, M. P. (1998). Applying the criteria for empirically supported treatments to studies of psychosocial interventions for child and adolescent depression. *Journal of Clinical Child Psychology, 27*, 146–155.

Kassel, J. D., & Jackson, S. I. (2001). Twelve-step-based interventions for adolescents. In E. F. Wagner & H. B. Waldron (Eds.), *Innovations in adolescent substance abuse interventions* (pp. 329–342). Oxford, UK: Elsevier Science.

Kavale, K. A. (2005). Identifying specific learning disability: Is response to intervention the answer? *Journal of Learning Disabilities, 38*, 553–562.

Kavale, K. A., & Forness, S. R. (1996). Social skill deficits and learning disabilities: A meta-analysis. *Journal of Learning Disabilities, 29*, 226–237.

Kavale, K. A., Forness, S. R., & MacMillan, D. L. (1998). The politics of learning disabilities: A rejoinder. *Learning Disability Quarterly, 21*, 306–317.

Kazdin, A. E. (1996). Problem solving and parent management in treating aggressive and antisocial behavior. In E. D. Hibbs & P. S. Jensen (Eds.), *Psychosocial treatments for child and adolescent disorders* (pp. 377–408). Washington, DC: American Psychological Association.

Kazdin, A. E., Esveldt-Dawson, K., French, N. H., & Unis, A. S. (1987). Problem-solving skills training and parent management training in the treatment of antisocial behavior in children. *Journal of Consulting and Clinical Psychology, 55*, 76–85.

Kearney, C. A., Albano, A. M., Eisen, A. R., Allan, E. D., & Barlow, D. H. (1997). The phenomenology of panic disorder in youngsters: An empirical study of a clinical sample. *Journal of Anxiety Disorders, 11*, 49–62.

Kelley, M., Power, T. G., & Wimbush, D. D. (1992). Determinants of disciplinary practices in low-income Black mothers. *Child Development, 63*, 573–582.

Kendall, P. C. (1994). Treating anxiety disorders in children: Results of a randomized clinical trial. *Journal of Consulting and Clinical Psychology, 62*, 100–110.

Kendall, P. C. (2000). *Cognitive behavioral therapy for anxious children: Treatment manual* (2nd ed.). Aramore, PA: Workbook.

Kendall, P. C., Chansky, T. E., Kane, M. T., Kim, R. S., Kortlander, E., Ronan, K. R., Sessa, F. M., & Siqueland, L. (1992). *Anxiety disorders in youth: Cognitive behavioral interventions*. Needham Heights, MA: Allyn & Bacon.

Kendall, P. C., & Ronan, K. R. (1990). Assessment of children's anxieties, fears, and phobias: Cognitive-behavioral models and methods. In C. R. Reynolds & R. W. Kamphaus (Eds.), *Handbook of psychological and educational assessment of children* (Vol. 2, pp. 223–244). New York, NY: Guilford Press.

Kendler, K. S., Gallagher, T. J., Abelson, J. M., & Kessler, R. C. (1996). Lifetime prevalence, demographic risk factors, and diagnostic validity of nonaffective psychosis as assessed in a

U.S. community sample: The National Comorbidity Survey. *Archives of General Psychiatry, 53*, 1022–1031.

Kiernan, C., & Kiernan, D. (1994). Challenging behaviour in schools for pupils with severe learning difficulties. *Mental Handicap Research, 7*, 117–201.

Kiernan, C., & Qureshi, H. (1993). Challenging behaviour. In C. Kiernan (Ed.), *Research to practice? Implications of research on the challenging behaviour of people with learning disabilities* (pp. 53–87). Kidderminster, UK: British Institute of Learning Disabilities.

Kilpatrick, D. G., Ruggiero, K. J., Acierno, R., Saunders, B. E., Resnick, H. S., & Best, C. L. (2003). Violence and risk of PTSD, major depression, substance abuse/dependence, and comorbidity: Results from the National Survey of Adolescents. *Journal of Consulting and Clinical Psychology, 71*(4), 692–700.

Kilpatrick, K. L., & Williams, L. M. (1997). Post-traumatic stress disorder in child witness to domestic violence. *Journal of Orthopsychiatry, 67*, 639–644.

Kim, A.-H., Vaughn, S., Wanzek, J., & Wei, S. (2004). Graphic organizers and their effects on the reading comprehension of students with LD: A synthesis of research. *Journal of Learning Disabilities, 37*, 105–118.

Kim, W. J. (1995). A training guideline of cultural competence for child and adolescent psychiatric residencies. *Child Psychiatry and Human Development, 26*, 125–136.

King, N. J., Ollendick, T. H., Mattis, S. G., Yang, B., & Tonge, B. (1997). Nonclinical panic attacks in adolescents: Prevalence symptomatology and associated features. *Behaviour Change, 13*, 171–183.

Kinzl, J. F., Traweger, C., & Biebi, W. (1995). Family background and sexual abuse associated with somatization. *Psychotherapy and Psychosomatic Disorders, 64*, 82–87.

Kirby, A., Sugden, D. A., Beveridge, S., & Edwards, L. (2008). Support and identification of students with developmental coordination disorder (DCD) in further and higher education. *Journal of Research in Special Educational Needs, 3*(8), 120–131.

Klinger, L. G., & Dawson, G. (1996). Autistic disorder. In E. J. Mash & R. A. Barkley (Eds.), *Child psychopathology* (pp. 311–313). New York, NY: Guilford Press.

Knopik, V. (2001). Differential genetic etiology of reading-related difficulties as a function of IQ. *Dissertation Abstracts International: Section B: The Sciences & Engineering, 61*, 6729.

Koocher, G. P., & Keith-Spiegel, P. C. (1990). *Children, ethics, and the law: Professional issues and cases*. Lincoln: University of Nebraska Press.

Kotchick, B. A., & Forehand, R. (2002). Putting parenting in perspective: A discussion of the contextual factors that shape parenting practices. *Journal of Child and Family Studies, 11*, 255–270.

Kouzis, A. C., & Labouvie, E. W. (1992). Use intensity, functional elaboration, and contextual constraint as facets of adolescent alcohol and marijuana use. *Psychology of Addictive Behaviors, 6*, 188–195.

Kovacs, M., Akiskal, H. S., Gatsonis, C., & Parrone, P. L. (1994). Childhood dysthymic disorder: Clinical features and prospective naturalistic outcome. *Archives of General Psychiatry, 51*, 365–374.

Kovacs, M., & Devlin, B. (1998). Internalizing disorders in childhood. *Journal of Child Psychology and Psychiatry and Allied Disciplines, 39*, 47–63.

Kovas, Y., Haworth, C. M., Harlaar, N., Petrill, S. A., Dale, P. S., & Plomin, R. (2007). Overlap and specificity of genetic and environmental influences on mathematics and reading disability in 10-year-old-twins. *Journal of Child Psychology and Psychiatry, 48*(9), 914–922.

Kronenberger, W. G., & Meyer, R. G. (2001). *The child clinician's handbook* (2nd ed.). Needham Heights, MA: Allyn & Bacon.

Kuhn, M., & Stahl, S. (2003). Fluency: A review of developmental and remedial practices. *Journal of Educational Psychology, 95*, 3–21.

Kunce, L., & Mesibov, G. B. (1998). Educational approaches to high-functioning autism and Asperger syndrome. In E. Schopler & G. B. Mesibov (Eds.), *Asperger syndrome or high-functioning autism? Current issues in autism* (pp. 227–261). New York, NY: Plenum Press.

LaFromboise, T. D., & Graff Low, K. (2001). American Indian children and adolescents. In J. T. Gibbs & L. N. Huang (Eds.), *Children of color* (pp. 112–142). San Francisco, CA: Jossey-Bass.

La Greca, A. M., Silverman, W. K., Vernberg, E. M., & Prinstein, M. (1996). Symptoms of posttraumatic stress in children after Hurricane Andrew: A prospective study. *Journal of Consulting and Clinical Psychology, 64*, 712–723.

Laing, S. V., Fernyhough, C., Turner, C., & Freeston, M. H. (2009). Fear, worry, and ritualistic behaviour in childhood: Developmental trends and interrelations. *Infant and Child Development, 18* (4), 351–366.

Larson, J., & Lochman, J. E. (2002). *Helping school children cope with anger: A cognitive-behavioral intervention*. New York, NY: Guilford Press.

Last, C. G., Hersen, M., Kazdin, A. E., Finkelstein, R., & Strauss, C. C. (1987). Comparison of DSM-III separation anxiety and overanxious disorder: Demographic characteristics and patterns of comorbidity. *Journal of the American Academy of Child and Adolescent Psychiatry, 26*, 527–531.

Last, C. G., Hersen, M., Kazdin, A. E., Orvaschel, H., & Perrin, S. (1991). Anxiety disorders in children and their families. *Archives of General Psychiatry, 48*(10), 928–934.

Last, C. G., Perrin, S., Hersen, M., & Kazdin, A. E. (1992). *DSM-III-R* anxiety disorders in children: Sociodemographic and clinical characteristics. *Journal of the American Academy of Child and Adolescent Psychiatry, 31*, 1070–1076.

Last, C. G., Perrin, S., Hersen, M., & Kazdin, A. E. (1996). A prospective study of child anxiety disorders. *Journal of the American Academy of Child and Adolescent Psychiatry, 35*, 1502–1510.

Lawford, B., Young, R. M, Powell, J. A., Gibson, J. N., Feeney, G. F. X., Ritchie, T. L., … Noble, E. P. (1997). Association of the D2 dopamine receptor A1 allele with alcoholism: Medical severity of alcoholism and type of controls. *Biology and Psychiatry, 41*, 386–393.

Lazear, K., Doan, J., & Roggenbaum, S. (2003). *Youth suicide prevention school-based guide—Issue brief 9: Culturally and linguistically diverse populations*. Tampa, FL: Department of Child and Family Studies, Division of State and Local Support, Louis de la Parte Florida Mental Health Institute, University of South Florida. (FMHI Series Publication #218–9).

Learning Disabilities Association of America. (2010). The Learning Disabilities Association of America's white paper on evaluation, identification and eligibility criteria for students with specific learning disabilities. Retrieved from http://ldaamerica.org/wp-content/uploads/2013/10/LDA-White-Paper-on-IDEA-Evaluation-Criteria-for-SLD.pdf

LeCroy, C. W. (1994). Social skills training. In C. W. LeCroy (Ed.), *Handbook of child and adolescent treatment manuals* (pp. 170–199). New York, NY: Lexington.

Lee, C. C. (1997). *Multicultural issues in counseling: New approaches to diversity* (2nd ed.). Alexandria, VA: American Counseling Association.

Lehmkuhl, G., Blanz, B., Lehmkuhl, U., & Braun-Scharm, H. (1989). Conversion disorder (*DSM-III* 300.11): Symptomatology and course in childhood and adolescence. *European Archives of Psychiatry and Neurological Sciences, 238*, 155–160.

Leinbenluft, E. (2011). Severe mood dysregulation, irritability, and the diagnostic boundaries of bipolar disorder in youths. *American Journal of Psychiatry, 168*, 129–142.

Leslie, A. (1988). Diagnosis and treatment of hysterical conversion reactions. *Archives of Disease in Childhood, 63*, 506–511.

Levine, M. (1999). How can we differentiate between ADHD, bipolar disorder in children? *The Brown University Child and Adolescent Psychopharmacology Update, 8*, 4–5.

Lewinsohn, P. M., Clarke, G. N., Rhode, P., Hops, H., & Seeley, J. (1996). A course in coping: A cognitive-behavioral approach to the treatment of adolescent depression. In E. D. Hibbs & P. S. Jensen (Eds.), *Psychosocial treatments for child and adolescent disorders: Empirically based strategies for clinical practice* (pp. 109–135). Washington, DC: American Psychological Association.

Lewinsohn, P. M., Clarke, G. N., Seeley, J. R., & Rohde, P. (1994). Major depression in community adolescents: Age at onset, episode duration, and time of recurrence. *Journal of the American Academy of Child and Adolescent Psychiatry, 33*, 809–818.

Liddle, H. A. (2009). Treating adolescent substance abuse using multidimensional family therapy. In J. R. Weisz & A. E. Kazdin (Eds.), *Evidence-based psychotherapies for children and adolescents* (2nd ed., pp. 416–434). New York, NY: Guilford Press.

Liddle, H. A., & Hogue, A. (2001). Multidimensional family therapy for adolescent substance abuse. In E. F. Wagner & H. B. Waldron (Eds.), *Innovations in adolescent substance abuse interventions* (pp. 229–261). Oxford, UK: Elsevier Science.

Liddle, H. A., Rowe, C. L., Dakof, G., Henderson, C. E., & Greenbaum, P. (2009). Multidimensional family therapy for young adolescent substance abuse: Twelve-month outcomes of a randomized controlled trial. *Journal of Consulting and Clinical Psychology, 77*, 12–25.

Liebman, W. M. (1978). Recurrent abdominal pain in children: A retrospective survey of 119 patients. *Clinical Pediatrics, 17*, 149–153.

Linehan, M. M., Comtois, K. A., Murray, A., Brown, N. Z., Gallop, R. J., & Heard, H. L. (2001). Two-year randomized trial + follow-up of a dialectical behavior therapy vs. therapy by experts for suicidal behaviors and borderline personality disorder. *Archives of General Psychiatry, 63*, 757–766.

Litz, B. T. (1992). Emotional numbing in combat-related post-traumatic stress disorder: A critical review and reformulation. *Clinical Psychology Review, 12*, 417–432.

Lloyd, G. K., Fletcher, A., & Minchin, M. C. W. (1992). GABA agonists as potential anxiolytics. In C. D. Burows, S. M. Roth, & R. Noyes, Jr., (Eds.), *Handbook of anxiety* (Vol. 5, pp. 35–58). Oxford, UK: Elsevier.

Lochman, J. E., Burch, P. R., Curry, J. F., & Lampron, L. B. (1984). Treatment and generalization effects of cognitive-behavioral and goal-setting interventions with aggressive boys. *Journal of Consulting and Clinical Psychology, 53*, 915–916.

Loeber, R., Green, S. M., Lahey, B. B., Christ, M. A., & Frick, P. J. (1992). Developmental sequences in the age of onset of disruptive child behaviors. *Journal of Child and Family Studies, 1*, 21–41.

Loeber, R., & Keenan, K. (1994). Interaction between conduct disorder and its comorbid conditions: Effects of age and gender. *Clinical Psychology Review, 14*, 497–523.

Loeber, R., & Stouthamer-Loeber, M. (1998). Development of juvenile aggression and violence: Some common misconceptions and controversies. *American Psychologist, 53*, 242–259.

Lonigan, C. J., Carey, M. P., & Finch, A. J. Jr. (1994). Anxiety and depression in children and adolescents: Negative affectivity and the utility of self reports. *Journal of Consulting and Clinical Psychology, 62*, 1000–1008.

Lonigan, C. J., Shannon, M. P., Saylor, C. M., Finch, A. J., & Sallee, F. R. (1994). Children exposed to disaster: II. Risk factors for the development of post-traumatic symptomatology. *Journal of the American Academy of Child and Adolescent Psychiatry, 33*, 94–105.

Lovaas, O. I. (1987). Behavioral treatment and normal educational and intellectual functioning of young autistic children. *Journal of Consulting and Clinical Psychology, 55*, 3–9.

Lovett, M., Barron, R. W., & Benson N. (2003). *Effective remediation of word identification and decoding difficulties in school-age children with reading disabilities.* New York, NY: Guilford Press.

Luby, J. L., Heffelfinger, A., Mrakotsky, C., Brown, K., Hessler, M., Wallis, J., & Spitznagel, E. (2003). The clinical picture of depression in preschool children. *Journal of the American Academy of Child and Adolescent Psychiatry, 42*, 340–348.

Luby, J. L., Sullivan, J., Belden, A., Stalets, M., Blankenship, S., & Spitznagel, E. (2006). An observational analysis of behavior in depressed preschoolers: Further validation of early onset depression. *Journal of the American Academy of Child and Adolescent Psychiatry, 45*, 203–212.

Lynch, E. W. (2004). Developing cross-cultural competence. In E. W. Lynch & M. J. Hanson (Eds.), *Developing cross-cultural competence* (3rd ed., pp. 41–78). Baltimore, MD: Paul H. Brookes.

Lyon, G. R., & Shaywitz, S. E. (2003). Part I: Defining dyslexia, comorbidity, teachers' knowledge of language and reading. *Annals of Dyslexia, 53*, 1–14.

Lyons-Ruth, K., & Jacobvitz, D. (1999). Attachment disorganization: Unresolved loss, relational violence, and lapses in behavioral and attentional strategies. In J. Cassidy & P. R. Shaver (Eds.), *Handbook of attachment: Theory, research, and clinical applications* (pp. 520–554). New York, NY: Guilford Press.

MacArthur, C. A. (2000). New tools for writing: Assistive technology for students with writing difficulties. *Topics in Language Disorders, 20*, 85–100.

Macintosh, K. E., & Dissanayake, C. (2004). Annotation: The similarities and differences between autistic disorder and Asperger's disorder. A review of the empirical evidence. *Journal of Child Psychology and Psychiatry, 45*(3), 421–434.

Macklem, G. (2008). The importance of emotional regulation in child and adolescent functioning and school success. In G. Macklem (Ed.), *Practitioner's guide to emotion regulation in school-aged children* (pp. 1–12). New York, NY: Springer.

MacMillan, D. L., & Forness, S. R. (1998). The role of IQ in special education placement decisions: Primary and determinative or peripheral and inconsequential. *Remedial and Special Education, 19*, 239–253.

Main, M., & Hesse, E. (1990). Parents' unresolved traumatic experiences are related to infant disorganized attachment status: Is frightened and/or frightening parental behavior the linking mechanism? In M. T. Greenberg, D. Cicchetti, & E. M. Cummings (Eds.), *Attachment in the preschool years: Theory, research, and intervention* (pp. 161–182). Chicago, IL: University of Chicago Press.

Main, M., & Solomon, J. (1986). Discovery of a new, insecure-disorganized/disoriented attachment pattern. In T. B. Braxelton & M. W. Yogman (Eds.), *Affective development in infancy* (pp. 95–124). Norwood, NJ: Ablex.

Main, M., & Weston, D. (1981). The quality of the toddler's relationship to mother and to father: Related to conflict behavior and the readiness to establish new relationships. *Child Development, 52*, 932–940.

Mak, W., & Rosenblatt, A. (2002). Demographic influences on psychiatric diagnoses among youth served in California systems of care. *Journal of Child and Family Studies, 11*, 165–178.

Malmquist, C. P. (1986). Children who witness parental murder: Posttraumatic aspects. *Journal of the American Academy of Child and Adolescent Psychiatry, 25*, 320–325.

Malphurs, J. E., Field, T. M., Larraine, C., Pickens, J., Yando, R., & Bendell, D. (1996). Altering withdrawn and intrusive interaction behaviors of depressed mothers. *Infant Mental Health Journal, 17*, 152–160.

March, J., Amaya-Jackson, L., & Pynoos, R. S. (1994). Pediatric posttraumatic stress disorder. In J. W. Weiner (Ed.), *Textbook of child and adolescent psychiatry* (pp. 507–527). Washington, DC: American Psychiatric Press.

March, J., Frances, A., Carpenter, D., & Kahn, D. (1997). Expert consensus guidelines: Treatment of obsessive compulsive disorder. *Journal of Clinical Psychology, 58*, 1.

Margulies, D. M., Weintraub, S., Basile, J., Grover, P. J., & Carson, G. A. (2012). Will disruptive mood dysregulation disorder reduce false diagnosis of bipolar disorder in children? *Bipolar Disorders, 14*, 488–496.

Marsh, R., Gerber, A. J., & Peterson, B. S. (2008). Neuroimaging studies of normal brain development and their relevance for understanding childhood neuropsychiatric disorders. *Journal of the American Academy of Child and Adolescent Psychiatry, 47*(11), 1233–1251.

Mash, E. J., & Terdal, L. G. (1997). Assessment of child land family disturbance: A behavioral-systems approach. In E. J. Mash & L. G. Terdal (Eds.), *Assessment of childhood disorders* (3rd ed., pp. 3–70). New York, NY: Guilford Press.

Mathyssek, C. M., Olino, T. M., Verhulst, F. C., & van Oort, F. (2012). Childhood internalizing and externalizing problems predict the onset of clinical panic attacks over adolescence: The TRAILS Study. *PLOS ONE, 7*, 1–6.

Matson, L. J., & Ollendick, H. T. (1988). *Enhancing children's social skills*. New York, NY: Pergamon Press.

Matsumoto, D. (2000). *Culture and psychology* (2nd ed.). Belmont, CA: Wadsworth.

Mattson, A. J., Sheer, D. E., & Fletcher, J. M. (1992). Electrophysiological evidence of lateralized disturbances in children with learning disabilities. *Journal of Clinical and Experimental Neuropsychology, 14*, 707–716.

Mayes, S. D., & Calhoun, S. L. (2007). Challenging the assumptions about the frequency and coexistence of learning disability types. *School Psychology International, 28*(4), 437–448.

Mayes, S. D., Calhoun, S. L., & Lane, S. E. (2005). Diagnosing children's writing disabilities: Different tests give different results. *Perceptual and Motor Skills, 101*, 72–78.

Mayes, S. D., Humphrey, F., Handford, H. A., & Mitchell, J. (1988). Rumination disorder: Differential diagnosis. *Journal of the American Academy of Child and Adolescent Psychiatry, 27*(3), 300–302.

Mazzocco, M. M., Feigenson, L., & Halberda, J. (2011). Impaired acuity of the approximate number system underlies mathematical learning disability (dyscalculia). *Child Development, 82*(4), 1224–1237.

McAdoo, H. P. (1997). *Black families* (3rd ed.). Beverly Hills, CA: Sage.

McCabe, K., Yeh, M., Hough, R. L., Landsverk, J., Hurlburt, M., Culver, S., & Reynolds, B. (1999). Racial/ethnic representation across five public sectors of care for youth. *Journal of Emotional and Behavioral Disorders, 7*, 72–82.

McClennan, J. M., & Weery, J. (2003). Evidence-based treatments in child and adolescent psychiatry: An inventory. *Journal of the American Academy of Child and Adolescent Psychiatry, 42* (12), 1388–1400.

McConaughy, S. H., & Skiba, R. (1993). Comorbidity of externalizing and internalizing problems. *School Psychology Review, 22* (3), 421–436.

McDermott, B. M., & Palmer, L. J. (2002). Postdisaster emotional distress, depression, and event-related variables: Findings across child and adolescent developmental stages. *Australian and New Zealand Journal of Psychiatry, 36*, 754–761.

McFall, R. (1982). A review and reformulation of the concept of social skills. *Behavioral Assessment, 4*, 1–33.

McFarlane, A. (1987). Post-traumatic phenomena in a longitudinal study of children following a natural disaster. *Journal of the American Academy of Child and Adolescent Psychiatry, 26*, 764–769.

McLeer, S., Deblinger, E., Henry, D., & Orvaschel, H. (1992). Sexually abused children at high risk for post-traumatic stress disorder. *Journal of the American Academy of Child and Adolescent Psychiatry, 32*, 875–879.

McLoyd, C. V. (1998). Children in poverty: Development, public policy and practice. In W. Damon (Series Ed.) & E. E. Siegel & K. A. Renniger (Vol. Eds.), *Handbook of child psychology: Vol. 4. Child psychology in practice* (5th ed., pp. 135–208). New York, NY: Wiley.

McMahon, R. J., & Kotler, J. S. (2004). Treatment of conduct problems in children and adolescents. In P. M. Barrett & T. H. Ollendick (Eds.), *Handbook of interventions that work with children and adolescents* (pp. 395–425). Chichester, UK: Wiley.

Meezan, W., & McCroskey, J. (1996). Improving family functioning through family preservation services: Results of the Los Angeles experiment. *Family Preservation Journal, 46*, 21–32.

Mellin, L. M., Irwin, C., & Scully, S. (1992). Prevalence of disordered eating in girls: A survey of middle class children. *Journal of the American Dietetic Association, 92*, 851–853.

Michaelson, R. (1993). Flood volunteers build emotional levees. *APA Monitor, 24*, 30.

Mikolajewski, A., Allan, N. P., Hart, S., Lonigan, C. J., & Taylor, J. (2013). Negative affect shares genetic and environmental influences with symptoms of childhood internalizing and externalizing disorders. *Journal of Abnormal Child Psychology, 41*, 411–423.

Miller, J. N., & Ozonoff, S. (2000). The external validity of Asperger disorder: Lack of evidence from the domain of neuropsychology. *Journal of Abnormal Psychology, 109*, 227–238.

Miller, M. N., & Pumariega, B. (1999). Culture and eating disorders. *Psychiatric Times, XVI*(2). Retrieved from www.psychiatrictimes.com/p990238.html

Minuchin, S. (1985). Families and individual development: Provocations from the field of family therapy. *Child Development, 56*, 289–302.

Minuchin, S., Rosman, B. L., & Baker, L. (1978). *Psychosomatic families: Anorexia nervosa in context*. Cambridge, MA: Harvard University Press.

Mitchell, J. E., Pyle, R. L., & Miner, R. A. (1982). Gastric dilation as a complication of bulimia. *Psychosomatics, 23*, 96–97.

Moffit, E. E. (1990). Juvenile delinquency and attention deficit disorder: Boys' developmental trajectories from age 3 to 15. *Child Development, 61*, 893–910.

Moffit, T. E., & Henry, B. (1989). Neurological assessment of executive functions in self-reported delinquents. *Development and Psychopathology, 1*, 105–118.

Molina, B. S., Hinshaw, S. P., Swanson, J. M., Arnold, L. E., Vitiello, B., Jensen, P. S., … Houck, P. R. (2009). The MTA at 8 years: Prospective follow-up of children treated for combined-type ADHD in a multisite study. *Journal of the American Academy of Child and Adolescent Psychiatry, 48*(5), 484–500.

Molina, B. S., & Pelham, W. E. (2003). Childhood predictors of adolescent substance use in a longitudinal study of children with ADHD. *Journal of Abnormal Psychology, 112*, 497–507.

Monti, P. M., Abrams, D. B., Kadden, R. M., & Cooney, N. L. (1989). *Treating alcohol dependence: A coping skills guide*. New York, NY: Guilford Press.

Morris, C. A. (2006a). The dysmorphology, genetics, and natural history of Williams-Beuren syndrome. In C. A. Morris, H. M. Lenhoff, & P. P. Wang (Eds.), *Williams-Beuren syndrome: Research, evaluation and treatment* (pp. 3–17). Baltimore, MD: Johns Hopkins University Press.

Morris, C. A. (2006b). Genotype-phenotype correlations in Williams-Beuren syndrome. In C. A. Morris, H. M. Lenhoff, & P. P. Wang (Eds.), *Williams-Beuren Syndrome: Research, evaluation and treatment* (pp. 59–82). Baltimore, MD: Johns Hopkins University Press.

Morris, R. D., Stuebing, K. K., Fletcher, J. M., Shaywitz, S. E., Lyon, G. R., Shankweiler, D. P., ... Shaywitz, B. A. (1998). Subtypes of reading disability: Variability around a phonological core. *Journal of Educational Psychology, 90*, 347–373.

MTA Cooperative Group. (1999). A 14-month randomized clinical trial of treatment strategies for attention-deficit/hyperactivity disorder. *Archives of General Psychiatry, 56*, 1073–1086.

Muris, P., Luermans, J., Merckelbach, E., & Mayer, R. (2000). Danger is lurking everywhere: the relation between anxiety and threat perception abnormalities in normal children. *Journal of Behavior Therapy and Experimental Psychiatry, 31*, 123–136.

Muris, P., Meesters, C., Merekelbach, H., Sermon, A., & Zwakhalen, S. (1998). Worry in normal children. *Journal of the American Academy of Child and Adolescent Psychiatry, 37*, 703–710.

Nachmias, M., Gunnar, M., Mangelsdorf, S., Parritz, R., & Buss, K. (1996). Behavioral inhibition and stress reactivity: The moderating role of attachment security. *Child Development, 67*, 508–522.

Nagata, D. K. (2001). The assessment and treatment of Japanese American children and adolescents. In J. T. Gibbs & L. N. Huang (Eds.), *Children of color* (pp. 68–111). San Francisco, CA: Jossey-Bass.

National Institute on Drug Abuse (NIDA). (2003a). *Preventing drug use among children and adolescents: A research-based guide for parents, educators, and community leaders* (2nd ed.). Bethesda, MD: U.S. Department of Health and Human Services, National Institutes of Health, National Institute on Drug Abuse

National Institute on Drug Abuse (NIDA). (2003b). *Monitoring the future*. Survey results for 2003. Retrieved online at www.drugabuse.gov/related-topics/trends-statistics/monitoring-future

National Institute of Mental Health (NIMH). (2000a). *Depression in children and adolescents: A fact sheet for physicians*. Retrieved online at www.nimh.nih.gov

National Institute of Mental Health (NIMH). (2000b). *Fact sheet—Child and adolescent bipolar disorder: An update from the National Institute of Mental Health*. Retrieved from www.nimh.nih.gov

National Joint Committee on Learning Disabilities (NJCLD). (1987). Learning disabilities: Issues on definition. *Journal of Learning Disabilities, 20*, 107–108.

Newacheck, P. E., & Halfon, N. (2000). Prevalence, impact and trends in childhood disability due to asthma. *Archives of Pediatric and Adolescent Medicine, 154*(3), 287–293.

Newcomb, M. D., & Felix-Ortiz, M. (1992). Multiple protective and risk factors for drug use and abuse: Cross-sectional and prospective findings. *Journal of Personality and Social Psychology, 63*, 280–296.

Nicholls, D., Chater, R., & Lask, B. (2000). Children into DSM don't go: A comparison of classification systems for eating disorders in childhood and early adolescence. *International Journal of Eating Disorders, 28*, 317–324.

Nietzel, M. T., Bernstein, D. A., & Milich, R. (1994). *Introduction to clinical psychology* (4th ed.). Englewood Cliffs, NJ: Prentice Hall.

Norgate, R. (1998). Reducing self-injurious behavior in a child with severe learning difficulties: Enhancing predictability and structure. *Educational Psychology in Practice 14*, 176–182.

Offord, D. R., Boyle, M. W., & Szatmari, P. (1987). Ontario Child Health Study, II: Six-month prevalence of disorder and rates of service utilization. *Archives of General Psychiatry, 44*, 832–836.

Offord, D. R., Boyle, M. W., & Racine, Y. (1989). Ontario Child Health Study: Correlates of disorder. *Journal of the American Academy of Child and Adolescent Psychiatry, 28*, 855–860.

Ogbu, J. U. (1981). Origins of human competence: A cultural-ecological perspective. *Child Development, 52*, 413–429.

Okamoto, Y., & Case, R. (1996). Exploring the microstructure of children's central conceptual structures in the domain of number. *Monographs of the Society for Research in Child Development, 61*, 27–59.

Olds, D., Henderson, C., Kitzman, H., Eckenrode, J., Cole, R., & Tatelbaum, R. (1998). The promise of home visitation: Results of two randomized trials. *Journal of Community Psychology, 26*, 5–21.

Ollendick, T. H. (2001). Self reported anxiety in children and adolescents: A three-year follow-up study. *Journal of Genetic Psychology, 162*, 5–19.

Ollendick, T. H., & King, N. J. (1998). Empirically supported treatment for children with phobic and anxiety disorders: Current status. *Journal of Clinical Child Psychology, 27*, 156–167.

Ollendick, T. H., & King, N. J. (2004). Empirically supported treatments for children and adolescents: Advances toward evidence-based practice. In P. M. Barrett & T. H. Ollendick (Eds.), *Handbook of interventions that work with children and adolescents* (pp. 3–26). West Sussex, UK: Wiley.

Ollendick, T. H., Mattis, S. G., & King, N. J. (1994). Panic in children and adolescents: A review. *Journal of Child Psychology and Psychiatry and Allied Disciplines, 35*, 113–134.

Ostrov, E., Offer, D., & Howard, K. I. (1989). Gender differences in adolescent symptomatology: A normative study. *Journal of the American Academy of Child and Adolescent Psychiatry, 28*, 394–398.

Overholser, J., Hemstreet, A. H., Spirito, A., & Vyse, S. (1989). Suicide awareness programs in the schools: Effects of gender and personal experience. *Journal of the American Academy of Child and Adolescent Psychiatry, 28*, 925–930.

Panerai, S., Ferrante, L., & Zingale, M. (2002). Benefits of the Treatment and Education of Autistic and Communication Handicapped Children (TEACCH) program as compared with a non-specific approach. *Journal of Intellectual Disability Research, 46*, 318–327.

Parker, D., Hoffman, S. F., Sawilowsky, S., & Rolands, L. (2011). An examination of the effects of ADHD coaching on university students' executive functioning. *Journal of Post-secondary Education and Disability, 24*(2), 115–132.

Parker, J., & Asher, S. R. (1987). Peer relations and later personal adjustment: Are low-accepted children at risk? *Psychological Bulletin, 102*, 357–389.

Parry-Jones, B., & Parry-Jones, W. L. (1992). Pica: Symptom or eating disorder? A historical assessment. *British Journal of Psychiatry, 160*, 341–354.

Pate, J. E., Pumariega, A. J., Hester, C., & Gaarner, D. M. (1992). Cross-cultural patterns in eating disorders: A review. *Journal of the American Academy of Child and Adolescent Psychiatry, 31*, 802–808.

Patterson, C., Kupersmidt, J., & Vaden, N. (1990). Income level, gender, ethnicity and household composition as predictors of children's school-based competence. *Child Development, 61*, 485–494.

Patterson, G., Reid, J., Jones, R., & Conger, R. (1975). *A social learning approach to family intervention, Vol. 1: Families with aggressive children.* Eugene, OR: Castalia.

Patterson, G. R., & Capaldi, D. M. (1990). A mediational model for boys' depressed mood. In J. Rolf, A. S. Masten, D. Cicchetti, K. H. Nuechterlein, & S. Weintraub (Eds.), *Risk and protective factors in the development of psychopathology* (pp. 141–163). Cambridge, UK: Cambridge University Press.

Patterson, G. R., Capaldi, D., & Bank, L. (1991). An early starter model for predicting delinquency. In D. Pepler & K. H. Rubin (Eds.), *The development and treatment of childhood aggression* (pp. 139–168). Hillsdale, NJ: Erlbaum.

Patterson, G. R., & Gullion, M. E. (1968). *Living with children: New methods for parents and teachers*. Champaign, IL: Research Press.

Patterson, G. R., & Yoerger, K. (2002). A developmental model for early- and late-onset delinquency. In J. B. Reid, G. R. Patterson, & J. Snyder (Eds.), *Antisocial behavior in children and adolescents: A developmental analysis and model for intervention* (pp. 147–172). Washington, DC: American Psychological Association.

Pelham, E. E., & Milich, R. (1991). Individual differences in response to Ritalin in classwork and social behavior. In L. L. Grennhill & B. B. Osmon (Eds.), *Ritalin: Theory and patient management* (pp. 203–221). New York, NY: Mary Ann Liebert.

Pelham, W. E. Jr., Wheeler, T., & Chronis, A. (1998). Empirically supported psychosocial treatments for attention-deficit/hyperactivity disorder. *Journal of Clinical Child Psychology, 27*, 190–205.

Pennington, B. (2009). *Diagnosing learning disorders: A neuropsychological framework* (2nd ed.). New York, NY: Guilford Press.

Pennington, G., & Gilger, J. (1996). *How is dyslexia transmitted?* Baltimore, MD: York.

Perez-Edgar, K., & Fox, N. A. (2005). Temperament and anxiety disorders. *Child and Adolescent Psychiatry Clinics of North America, 14*, 681–706.

Peterson, L., & Roberts, M. C. (1991). Treatment of children's problems. In C. E. Walker (Ed.), *Clinical psychology: Historical and research foundations*. New York, NY: Plenum Press.

Pfefferbaum, B. (1997). Posttraumatic stress disorder in children: A review of the past 10 years. *Journal of the American Academy of Child and Adolescent Psychiatry, 36*, 1503–1511.

Pickersgill, M. J., Valentine, J. D., Pincus, T., & Foustok, H. (1999). Girls' fearfulness as a product of mothers' fearfulness and fathers' authoritarianism. *Psychological Reports, 85*, 759–760.

Pine, D. S., Helfinstein, S. M., Bar-Haim, Y., Nelson, E., & Fox, N. A. (2009). Challenges in developing novel treatments for childhood disorders: Lessons from research on anxiety. *Neuropsychopharmacology, 34*, 213–228.

Pionek-Stone, B., Kratochwill, T. R., Sladezcek, L., & Serlin, R. C. (2002). Treatment of selective mutism: A best evidence synthesis. *School Psychology Quarterly, 17*, 168–190.

Pittman, L. D., & Chase-Lansdale, P. L. (2001). African American adolescent girls in impoverished communities: Parenting style and adolescent outcomes. *Journal of Research on Adolescence, 11*(2), 199–224.

Pope, H. G., Phillips, K. A., & Olivardia, R. (2000b). *The Adonis complex: The secret crisis of male body obsession*. New York: Free Press.

Prior, M., Eisenmajer, R., Leekam, S., Wing, L., Gould, J., Ong, B., & Dowe, D. (1998). Are there subgroups within the autistic spectrum? A cluster analysis of a group of children with autistic spectrum disorders. *Journal of Child Psychology and Psychiatry, 39*, 893–902.

Puig-Antich, J., Geotz, D., & Davies, M. (1989). A controlled family history study of prepubertal major depressive disorder. *Archives of General Psychiatry, 46*, 406–418.

Pynoos, R. S. (1990). Post-traumatic stress disorder in children and adolescents. In B. Grafinkel, G. Carlson, & E. Weller (Eds.), *Psychiatric disorders in children and adolescents* (pp. 48–63). Philadelphia, PA: W. B. Saunders.

Pynoos, R. S. (1994). Traumatic stress and developmental psychopathology in children and adolescents. In R. S. Pynoos (Ed.), *Posttraumatic stress disorder: A clinical review* (pp. 64–98). Lutherville, MD: Sidran Press.

Pynoos, R. S., & Nader, K. (1993). Issues in the treatment of posttraumatic stress in children and adolescents. In J. P. Wilson & B. Raphael (Eds.), *International handbook of traumatic stress syndromes* (pp. 535–549). New York, NY: Plenum Press.

Quay, H. C. (1986). Conduct disorders. In H. C. Quay & J. S. Werry (Eds.), *Psychopathological disorders of childhood* (3rd ed., pp. 1–34). New York, NY: Wiley.

Ramirez, O. (2001). Mexican American children and adolescents. In J. T. Gibbs & L. N. Huang (Eds.), *Children of color* (pp. 215–239). San Francisco, CA: Jossey-Bass.

Rao, S. M., Mayer, A., & Harrington, D. L. (2001). The evolution of brain activation during temporal processing. *Nature Neuroscience, 4*(3), 317–323.

Rapee, R. M. (1997). Potential role of childrearing practices in the development of anxiety and depression. *Clinical Psychology Review, 17*, 47–67.

Rechsley, D. J. (2003). IDEA Reauthorization: Outcomes criteria and the bright future of school psychology. Presentation to the Florida Association of School Psychologists, Palm Harbor, Florida.

Reebye, P., Moretti, M. M., & Gulliver, L. (1995). Conduct disorder and substance use disorder: Comorbidity in a clinical sample of preadolescents and adolescents. *Canadian Journal of Psychiatry, 40*, 313–319.

Regan, J. J., & Regan, W. (1989). Somatoform disorders. In C. G. Last & M. Hersen (Eds.), *Handbook of child psychiatric diagnoses* (pp. 343–355). New York, NY: Wiley.

Reid, R., & Ortiz-Lienemann, T. (2006). Self-regulated strategy development for written expression with students with attention deficit/hyperactivity disorder. *Exceptional Child, 73*(1), 53–68.

Reiss, S. (1991). Expectancy model of fear, anxiety, and panic. *Clinical Psychology Review, 11*, 141–153.

Renaud, J., Birmaher, B., Wassick, C. C., & Bridge, J. (1999). Use of selective serotonin reuptake inhibitors for the treatment of childhood panic disorder: A pilot study. *Journal of Child and Adolescent Psychopharmacology, 9*, 73–83.

Repetti, R. L., Taylor, S. E., & Seeman, T. E. (2002). Risky families: Family social environments and the mental and physical health of offspring. *Psychological Bulletin, 128*, 330–336.

Rey, J. M. (1993). Oppositional defiant disorder. *American Journal of Psychiatry, 150*, 1769–1777.

Richards, T., & Bates, C. (1997). Recognizing posttraumatic stress in children. *Journal of School Health, 67*, 441–443.

Ringwalt, C., Ennett, S., Vincus, A., Thorne, J., Rohrbach, L., & Ashley, S.-F. (2002). The prevalence of effective substance use prevention curricula in U.S. middle schools. *Prevention Science, 3*, 257–265.

Robin, A. L., Bedway, M., Diegel, P. T., & Gilroy, M. (1996). Therapy for adolescent anorexia nervosa: Addressing cognitions, feelings, and the family's role. In E. D. Hibbs & P. S. Jensen (Eds.), *Psychosocial treatments for child and adolescent disorders: Empirically-based strategies for clinical practice* (pp. 239–259). Washington, DC: American Psychological Association.

Robins, L. N., & McEvoy, L. (1990). Conduct problems as predictors of substance abuse. In L. E. Robins & M. Rutter (Eds.), *Straight and devious pathways from childhood to adulthood* (pp. 182–204). Cambridge, UK: Cambridge University Press.

Robinson, D. P., Greene, J. W., & Walker, L. S. (1988). Functional somatic complaints in adolescents: Relationship to negative life events, self concept, and family characteristics. *The Journal of Pediatrics, 113*, 588–593.

Rogers, H. R. (1986). *Poor women, poor families*. Armonk, NY: Sharpe.

Rogers, M. R., Ingraham, C. L., Bursztyn, A., Cajigas-Segredo, N., Esquivel, G., Hess, R. S., ... Lopez, E. C. (1999). Best practices in providing psychological services to racially, ethnically, culturally, and linguistically diverse individuals in the schools. *School Psychology International, 20*, 243–264.

Rogers, S. J. (1998). Empirically supported comprehensive treatments for young children with autism. *Journal of Clinical Child Psychology, 27*, 168–179.

Rogler, L. H. (1999). Methodological sources of cultural insensitivity in mental health research. *American Psychologist, 54*(6), 424–433.

Rosen, D. (2003). Eating disorders in children and young adolescents: Etiology, classification, clinical features, and treatment. *Adolescent Medicine—The Spectrum of Disordered Eating: Anorexia Nervosa, Bulimia Nervosa and Obesity: State of the Art Review, 14*, 49–59.

Rosen, L. W., McKeag, D. B., Hough, D. O., & Curley, V. (1986). Pathogenic weight-control behavior in female athletes. *The Physician and Sports Medicine, 14*(1), 79–86.

Rosenheim, M. K., & Testa, M. F. (1992). *Early parenthood and coming of age in the 1990's.* New Brunswick, NJ: Rutgers University Press.

Rosenthal, D. A., & Berven, N. L. (1999). Effects of client race on clinical judgment. *Rehabilitation Counseling Bulletin, 42*(3), 243–264.

Rosenthal, R., & Jacobson, L. (1968). *Pygmalion in the classroom: Teacher expectation and pupils' "intellectual development."* New York, NY: Rinehart & Winston.

Rothbart, M. K. (2003). Temperament and the pursuit of an integrated developmental psychology. *Merrill-Palmer Quarterly, 50*, 492–505.

Rothbart, M. K., & Bates, J. E. (2006). Temperament. In N. Eisenberg (Ed.), *Handbook of child psychology: Vol. 3. Social, emotional, and personality development* (6th ed., pp. 99–166). Hoboken, NJ: Wiley.

Rourke, B. P. (1989). *Nonverbal learning disabilities: The syndrome and the model*. New York, NY: Guilford Press.

Rourke, B. P. (1995). *Syndrome of nonverbal learning disabilities*. New York, NY: Guilford Press.

Rourke, B. P., Ahmad, S., Collins, D., Jayman-Abello, B., Hayman-Abello, S., & Warriner, E. M. (2002). Child clinical/pediatric neuropsychology: Some recent advances. *Annual Review of Psychology, 53*, 309–339.

Rubio-Stipec, M., Walker, A., Murphy, J., & Fitzmaurice, G. (2002). Dimensional measures of psychopathology: The probability of being classified with a psychiatric disorder using empirically derived symptom scales. *Social Psychiatry and Psychiatric Epidemiology, 37*, 553–560.

Rucklidge, J. J., & Tanock, R. (2001). Psychiatric, psychosocial and cognitive functioning of female adolescents with ADHD. *Journal of the American Academy of Child and Adolescent Psychiatry, 40*, 530–540.

Rutter, M. (1978). Diagnosis and definition. In M. Rutter & E. Schopler (Eds.), *Autism: A reappraisal of concepts and treatment*. New York, NY: Plenum Press.

Rutter, M., Beckett, C., Castle, J., Colvert, E., Kreppner, J., Mehta, M., Stevens, S., & Sonuga-Barke, E. (2007). Effects of profound early institutional deprivation: An overview of findings from a UK longitudinal study of Romanian adoptees. *European Journal of Developmental Psychology, 4*(3), 332–350.

Ryan, N. D., Puig-Antich, J., Ambrosini, P., Rabinovich, H., Nelson, B., Iyengar, S., & Twomey, J. (1987). The clinical picture of major depression in children and adolescents. *Archives of General Psychiatry, 44*, 854–861.

Saavedra, L. M., & Silverman, W. K. (2002). Classification of anxiety disorders in children: What a difference two decades make. *International Review of Psychiatry, 14*, 87–101.

Sameroff, A. (1993). Models of development and developmental risk. In C. H. Zeanah, Jr. (Ed.), *Handbook of infant mental health* (pp. 3–13). New York, NY: Guilford Press.

Sameroff, A. J., & Chandler, M. J. (1975). Reproductive risk and the continuum of caretaking casualty. In F. D. Horowitz, M. Hetherington, S. Scarr-Salapatek, & G. Siegel (Eds.), *Review of child development research* (Vol. 4, pp. 187–244). Chicago, IL: University of Chicago Press.

Sattler, J. (2002). *Assessment of children: Behavioral and clinical applications* (4th ed.). LaMesa, CA: Author.

Saxena, S., Brody, A. L., & Maidment, K. M. (1999). Localized orbitolfrontal and subcortical metabolic changes and predictors of response to paroxetine treatment in obsessive-compulsive disorder. *Neuropsychopharmacology, 21* (6), 683–693.

Scheeringa, M. S., & Zeanah, C. H. (2001). A relational perspective on PTSD in early childhood. *Journal of Traumatic Stress, 14*, 799–815.

Scheeringa, M. S., Zeanah, C. H., Myers, L., & Putnam, F. W. (2005). Predictive validity in a prospective follow-up of PTSD in preschool children. *Journal of the American Academy of Child & Adolescent Psychiatry, 44*(9), 561–570.

Schoenwald, S. K., Ward, D. M., Henggeler, S. W., & Rowland, M. D. (2000). Multisystemic therapy versus hospitalization for crisis stabilization of youth: Placement outcomes 4 months postreferral. *Mental Health Services Research, 2*, 3–12.

Schopler, R. (1985). Editorial: Convergence of learning disability, higher-level autism, and Asperger's syndrome. *Journal of Autism and Developmental Disorders, 15*, 359.

Schopler, R. (1994). A statewide program for the treatment and education of autistic and related communication handicapped children (TEACCH). *Psychology and Pervasive Developmental Disorders, 3*, 91–103.

Schor, E. (1986). Use of health care services by children and diagnoses received during presumably stressful life transitions. *Pediatrics, 77*, 834–841.

Seidman, E., Aber, J., & French, S. (2004). The organization of schooling and adolescent development. In, K. Maton, C. Schellenbach, B. Leadbeater, & A. Solarz (Eds.), *Investing in children and youth, families and communities: Strengths-based research and policy*, pp. 233–250. Washington, DC: American Psychological Association.

Seligman, M. E. P. (1975). *Helplessness*. San Francisco, CA: W. H. Freeman.

Seligman, M., & Peterson, C. (1986). A learned helpless perspective on childhood depression: Theory and research. In M. Rutter, C. E. Izard, & P. B. Read (Eds.), *Depression in young people* (pp. 223–249). New York, NY: Guilford Press.

Seltzer, W. (1985). Conversion disorder in childhood and adolescence: A familial/cultural approach, Part I. *Family Systems Medicine, 3*, 261–280.

Semrud-Clikeman, M. (2005). Neuropsychological aspects for evaluating learning disabilities. *Journal of Learning Disabilities, 38*, 563–568.

Semrud-Clikeman, M., Biederman, J., Sprich-Buckminster, S., Lehman, B. K., Faraone, S. V., & Norman, D. (1992). Comorbidity between ADDH and learning disability: A review and report in a clinically referred sample. *Journal of the American Academy of Child and Adolescent Psychiatry, 31*, 439–448.

Shaffer, D., & Craft, L. (1999). Methods of adolescent suicide prevention. *Journal of Clinical Psychiatry, 60*, 70–74.

Shaffer, D., Gould, M. S., Fisher, P., Trautment, P., Moreau, D., Kleinman, M., & Flory, M. (1996). Psychiatric diagnoses in child and adolescent suicide. *Archives of General Psychiatry, 53*, 339–348.

Sharrer, V. W., & Ryan-Wenger, M. (1995). A longitudinal study of age and gender differences of stressors and coping strategies in school-aged children. *Journal of Pediatric Health Care, 9*, 123–130.

Shaywitz, S. (2003). *Overcoming dyslexia: A new and complete science-based program for reading problems at any level*. New York, NY: Alfred A. Knopf.

Shaywitz, S. E., Morris, R., & Shaywitz, B. A. (2008). The education of dyslexic children from childhood to young adulthood. *Annual Review of Psychology, 59*, 451–475.

Shaywitz, S. E., & Shaywitz, B. A. (2008). Paying attention to reading: The neurobiology of reading and dyslexia. *Development and Psychopathology, 20*, 1329–1349.

Shedler, J., & Block, J. (1990). Adolescent drug use and psychological health. *American Psychologist, 45*, 612–630.

Sheeber, L., Hops, H., & Davis, B. (2001). Family processes in adolescent depression. *Clinical Child and Family Psychology Review, 4*, 19–35.

Sherman, D. K., Iacono, W. G., & McGue, M. K. (1997). Attention deficit hyperactivity disorder dimensions: A twin study of inattention and impulsivity-hyperactivity. *Journal of the American Academy of Child and Adolescent Psychiatry, 36*, 745–733.

Siegel, M., & Barthel, R. P. (1986). Conversion disorders on a child psychiatry consultation service. *Psychosomatics, 27*, 201–204.

Silverman, W. K., & Ginsburg, G. S. (1995). Specific phobias and generalized anxiety disorder. In J. S. March (Ed.), *Anxiety disorders in children and adolescents* (pp. 151–180). New York, NY: Guilford Press.

Silverman, W. K., & Nelles, W. B. (2001). The influence of gender on children's ratings of fear in self and same-aged peers. *Journal of Genetic Psychology, 148*, 17–21.

Silverman, W. K., & Saavedra, L. M. (2004). Assessment and diagnosis in evidence-based practice. In P. M. Barrett & T. H. Ollendick (Eds.), *Handbook of interventions that work with children and adolescents* (pp. 49–70). West Sussex, UK: Wiley.

Silverman, W. K., Saavedra, L. M., & Pina, A. A. (2001). Test-retest reliability of anxiety symptoms and diagnoses using the Anxiety Disorders Interview Schedule for *DSM-IV*: Child and Parent Versions (ADIS for *DSM-IV*:C/P). *Journal of the American Academy of Child and Adolescent Psychiatry, 40*, 937–944.

Slaff, B. (1989). History of child and adolescent psychiatry ideas and organizations in the United States: A twentieth-century review. In S. C. Feinstein (Eds.), *Adolescent psychiatry: Developmental and clinical studies* (Vol. 16, pp. 31–52). Chicago, IL: University of Chicago Press.

Smucker, M. R., Craighead, W. E., Craighead, L. W., & Green, B. J. (1986). Normative and reliability data for the Children's Depression Inventory. *Journal of Abnormal Child Psychology, 14*, 25–39.

Sonuga-Barke, E. J., Daley, D., Thompson, M., Laver-Bredbury, C., & Weeks, A. (2001). Parent-based therapies for preschool attention-deficit/hyperactivity disorder: A randomized, controlled trial with a community sample. *Journal of the American Academy of Child and Adolescent Psychiatry, 40*, 402–408.

Spaccarelli, S., Cotler, S., & Penman, D. (1992). Problem-solving skills training as a supplement to behavioral parent training. *Cognitive Therapy and Research, 27*, 171–186.

Spangler, G., & Grossman, K. (1999). Individual and psychological correlates of attachment disorganization in infancy. In J. Solomon & C. George (Eds.), *Attachment disorganization* (pp. 95–126). New York, NY: Guilford Press.

Spence, S. (1997). Structure of anxiety symptoms in children: A confirmatory factor analytic study. *Journal of Abnormal Psychology, 106*, 280–297.

Spitz, A. (1946). Anaclitic depression. *Psychoanalytic Study of the Child, 2*, 313–342.

Sroufe, L. A. (2007). The concept of development in developmental psychopathology. *Child Perspectives, 3*, 178–193.

Sroufe, L. A., & Rutter, M. (1984). The domain of developmental psychopathology. *Child Development, 55*, 17–29.

Stanger, C., & Lewis, M. (1993). Agreement among parents, teachers, and children on internalizing and externalizing behavior problems. *Journal of Clinical Child Psychology, 22*, 107–115.

Stanovich, K. E. (1986). Matthew effects in reading: Some consequences of individual differences in the acquisition of literacy. *Reading Research Quarterly, 21*, 360–407.

Stanton, M. D., & Shadish, W. R. (1997). Outcome, attrition, and family/couples treatment for drug abuse: A review of the controlled, comparative studies. *Psychological Bulletin, 122*, 170–191.

Stark, K. D., Swearer, S., Jurkowski, C., Sommer, D., & Bowen, B. (1996). Targeting the child and the family: A holistic approach to treating child and adolescent depressive disorders. In E. D. Hibbs & P. S. Jensen (Eds.), *Psychosocial treatments for child and adolescent disorders: Empirically based strategies for clinical practice* (pp. 207–238). Washington, DC: American Psychological Association.

Stein, M. B., Jang, K. L., & Livesley, W. J. (1999). Heritability of anxiety sensitivity: A twin study. *American Journal of Psychiatry, 156*, 246–251.

Steiner, H. (2000). Evaluation and management of violent behavior in bipolar adolescents. In *Program and Abstracts from the American Psychiatric Association, 153rd Annual Meeting, Abstract 19D.* Retrieved from www.medscape.com/viewarticle/420304

Steinhausen, H., & Juzi, C. (1996). Elective mutism: An analysis of 100 cases. *Journal of the American Academy of Child and Adolescent Psychiatry, 35*, 606–614.

Stevenson, H. W., Chen, C., & Uttal, D. H. (1990). Beliefs and achievement: A study of Black, White, and Hispanic children. *Child Development, 16*, 508–523.

Stingaris, A. (2011). Irritability in children and adolescents: A challenge for DSM-5. *European Child and Adolescent Psychiatry, 20*, 61–66.

Stone, W. L., & La Greca, A. M. (1990). The social status of children with learning disabilities: A reexamination. *Journal of Learning Disabilities, 23*, 32–37.

Strauss, C. C., Lease, C. A., Last, C. G., & Francis, G. (1988). Overanxious disorder: An examination of developmental differences. *Journal of Abnormal Child Psychology, 16*, 433–443.

Strober, M., Morrell, W., Lanpert, C., & Burroughs, J. (1990). Relapse following discontinuation of lithium maintenance therapy in adolescents with bipolar illness: A naturalistic study. *American Journal of Psychiatry, 147*, 457–461.

Strober, M., Freeman, R., Lampert, C., Diamond, J., & Kaye, W. (2000). Controlled family study of anorexia nervosa and bulimia nervosa: Evidence of shared liability and transmission of partial syndromes. *American Journal of Psychiatry, 157*(3), 393–401.

Stuart, R. (2004). Twelve practical suggestions for achieving multicultural competence. *Professional Psychology: Research and Practice, 35*, 3–9.

Sugden, D., Kirby, A., & Dunford, C. (2008). Issues surrounding children with developmental coordination disorder. *International Journal of Disability, 2*(55), 173–187.

Swanson, H. L. (2009). Neuroscience and RTI: A complementary role. In E. Fletcher-Janzen & C. R. Reynolds (Eds.), *Neuropsychological perspectives on learning disabilities in the era of RTI: Recommendations for diagnosis and intervention* (pp. 28–53). Hoboken, NJ: Wiley.

Swanson, H. L., & Jerman, O. (2006). Math disabilities: A selective meta-analysis of the literature. *Review of Educational Research, 76*, 249–274.

Swanson, J., Arnold, L. E., Kraemer, H., Hechman, L., Molina, B., Hinshaw, S., … Wigal, T. (2008). Evidence, interpretation, and qualification from multiple reports of long-term outcomes in the Multimodal Treatment Study of Children with ADHD (MTA), Part II: Supporting details. *Journal of Attention Disorders, 12*(1), 15–43.

Swarr, A. E., & Richards, M. H. (1996). Longitudinal effects of adolescent girls' pubertal development, perceptions of pubertal timing, and parental relations on eating problems. *Developmental Psychology, 32*, 636–646.

Swift, I., Paquette, D., Davison, K., & Saeed, H. (1999). Pica and trace metal deficiencies in adults with developmental disabilities. *British Journal of Developmental Disabilities, 45*, 111–117.

Szatmari, P., Boyle, M., & Offord, D. R. (1989). ADDH and conduct disorder: Degree of diagnostic overlap and differences among correlates. *Journal of the American Academy of Child and Adolescent Psychiatry, 28*, 865–872.

Taylor, A. (1986). *Loneliness, goal orientation, and sociometric status: Mildly retarded children's adaptation to the mainstream classroom*. Paper presented at the annual meeting of the American Educational Research Association, San Francisco, CA.

Taylor, D. C., Szatmari, P., Boyle, M. H., & Offord, D. (1996). Somatization and the vocabulary of everyday bodily experiences and concerns: A community study of adolescents. *Journal of the American Academy of Child and Adolescent Psychiatry, 35*, 491–499.

Telch, C. F., Agras, W. S., & Linehan, M. M. (2001). Dialectical behavior therapy for binge eating disorder. *Journal of Consulting and Clinical Psychology, 69*(6), 1061–1065.

Teplin, L. A., Abram, K. M., McClelland, G. M., Dulcan, M. K., & Mericle, A. A. (2002). Psychiatric disorders in youth in juvenile detention. *Archives of General Psychiatry, 59*, 1133–1143.

Terr, L. C. (1991). Childhood traumas: An outline and overview. *American Journal of Psychiatry, 148*, 10–20.

Thapar, A., Harold, G., & McGuffin, P. (1998). Life events and depressive symptoms in childhood: Shared genes or shared adversity? A research note. *Journal of Child Psychology and Psychiatry, 39*, 1153–1158.

Thomas, A., & Chess, S. (1977). *Temperament and development*. New York, NY: Brunner/Mazel.

Tremblay, R. E., Japel, C., Perusse, D., McDuff, P., Boivin, M., Zoccolillo, M., & Montplaisir, J. (1999). The search for the age of "onset" of physical aggression: Rousseau and Bandura revisited. *Criminal Behaviour and Mental Health, 9*, 8–23.

Tucker, D. M., Leckman, J. F., Scahill, L., & Guita, E. (1996). A putative postreptococcal case of OCD with chronic tic disorder, not otherwise specified. *Journal of the American Academy of Child and Adolescent Psychiatry, 35* (12), 1684–1691.

Tueth, M. J., Murphy, T. K., & Evans, D. L. (1998). Special considerations: Use of lithium in children, adolescents, and elderly populations. *Journal of Clinical Psychiatry, 59*, 66–73.

U.S. Census Bureau. (1996). *Statistical abstract of the United States, 1996* (116th ed.). Washington, DC: U.S. Department of Commerce.

U.S. Census Bureau. (2009, May). Census Bureau estimates nearly half of children under age 5 are minorities. Retrieved from www.census.gov/newsroom/releases/archives/population/cb09-75.html

U.S. Department of Health and Human Services (USDHHS). (1999). *Mental health: A report of the surgeon general*. Rockville, MD: U.S. Department of Health and Human Services, Public Health Service, Office of the Surgeon General.

U.S. Department of Health and Human Services (USDHHS). (2001). *Mental health: Culture, race, and ethnicity. A supplement to Mental Health: A Report of the Surgeon General*. Rockville, MD: U.S. Department of Health and Human Services, Public Health Service, Office of the Surgeon General.

U.S. Environmental Protection Agency (EPA). (2014). Learn about lead. Retrieved on January 26, 2014, from http://www2.epa.gov/lead/learn-about-lead

Vaivre-Douret, L., Lalanne, C., Ingster-Moati, I., Boddaert, N., Cabrot, D., Dufier, J., … Falissard, B. (2011). Subtypes of developmental coordination disorder: Research on their nature and etiology. *Developmental Neurospychology, 36*(5), 614–643.

Vaughn, S., Hogan, A., Kouzekanam, K., & Shapiro, S. (1990). Peer acceptance, self-perceptions, and social skills of learning disabled students prior to identification. *Journal of Educational Psychology, 82*, 101–106.

Vaughn S., Linar-Thompson, S., & Hickman P. 2003. Response to treatment as a way of identifying students with learning disabilities. *Exceptional Children, 69*, 391–409.

Velkamp, L. J., & Miller, T. W. (1994). *Clinical handbook of child abuse and neglect*. Madison, CT: International University Press.

Vellutino, F. R., Scanlon, D. M., Small, S., & Fanuele, D. P. (2006). Response to intervention as a vehicle for distinguishing between children with and without reading disabilities: Evidence for the role of kindergarten and first-grade interventions. *Journal of Learning Disabilities, 39*, 157–169.

Versi, M. (1995). Differential effects of cognitive behavior modification on seriously emotionally disturbed adolescents exhibiting internalizing and externalizing problems. *Journal of Child and Family Studies, 4*, 279–292.

Viding, E., Jones, A. P., Frick, P. J., Moffitt, T. E., & Plomin, R. (2008). Heritability of antisocial behaviour at 9: Do callous–unemotional traits matter? *Developmental Science, 11*, 17–22.

Vik, P. W., Brown, S. A., & Myers, M. G. (1997). Adolescent substance abuse problems. In E. J. Mash & L. G. Terdal (Eds.), *Assessment of childhood disorders* (pp. 717–748). New York, NY: Guilford Press.

Waldron, H. B. (1998). Substance abuse disorders. In T. Ollendick (Ed.), *Comprehensive clinical psychology* (Vol. 5, pp. 539–563). Oxford, UK: Elsevier Science.

Waldron, H. B., & Kern-Jones, S. (2004). Treatment of substance abuse disorders in children and adolescents. In P. M. Barrett & T. H. Ollendick (Eds.), *Handbook of interventions that work with children and adolescents: Prevention and treatment* (pp. 329–342). Chichester, UK: Wiley.

Walker, L. S., Garber, J., & Greene, J. W. (1991). Psychosocial correlates of recurrent childhood pain: A comparison of pediatric patients with recurrent abdominal pain, organic illness, and psychiatric disorders. *Journal of Abnormal Child Psychology, 102*, 248–258.

Walker, S. (2002). Culturally competent protection of children's mental health. *Child Abuse Review, 2*, 380–393.

Walters, E. E., & Kendler, K. S. (1995). Anorexia nervosa and anorexia-like syndromes in a population-based female twin sample. *American Journal of Psychiatry, 152*, 64–71.

Wang, P. P. (2006). The behavioral neuroscience of Williams-Beuren syndrome: An overview. In C. A. Morris, H. M. Lenhoff, & P. P. Wang (Eds.), *Williams-Beuren syndrome: Research, evaluation and treatment* (pp. 147–158). Baltimore, MD: Johns Hopkins University Press.

Warren, S. L., Huston, L., Egeland, B., & Sroufe, L. A. (1997). Child and adolescent anxiety disorders and early attachment. *Journal of the American Academy of Child and Adolescent Psychiatry, 36*, 637–644.

Webster-Stratton, C. (1984). Randomized trial of two parent-training programs for families with conduct-disordered children. *Journal of Consulting and Clinical Psychology, 52*, 666–678.

Weddle, K. D., & McKenry, P. C. (1995). Self-destructive behaviors among Black youth: Suicide and homicide. In R. L. Taylor (Ed.), *African American youth: Their social and economic status in the United States* (pp. 203–224). New York, NY: Praeger.

Weems, C. F., Saltzman, K. M., Reiss, A. L., & Carrion, V. G. (2003). A prospective test of the association between hyperarousal and emotional numbing in youth with a history of traumatic stress. *Journal of Clinical Child and Adolescent Psychology, 32*, 166–171.

Weiss, M. D., Worling, D. E., & Wasdell, M. B. (2003). A chart review study of the inattentive and combined types of ADHD. *Journal of Attention Disorders, 7*(1), 1–9.

Wenar, C., & Kerig, P. (2000). *Developmental psychopathology* (4th ed.). Boston, MA: McGraw-Hill.

Wender, P. H., & Klein, D. F. (1981). *Mind, mood and medicine*. New York, NY: Meridian.

West, S. I., & O'Neal, K. K. (2004). Project D.A.R.E.: Outcome effectiveness revisited. *American Journal of Public Health, 94*, 1027–1029.

Wielkiewicz, R. M. (1995). *Behavior management in the schools* (2nd ed.). Boston, MA: Allyn & Bacon.

Willis, W. (2004). Families with African American roots. In E. W. Lynch & M. J. Hanson (Eds.), *Developing cross-cultural competence* (3rd ed., pp. 141–178). Baltimore, MD: Paul H. Brookes.

Wilmshurst, L. (2002). Treatment programs for youth with emotional and behavioral disorders: An outcomes study of two alternate approaches. *Mental Health Services Research, 4*, 85–96.

Wilson, W. J., & Aponte, R. (1985). Urban poverty. *Annual Review of Sociology, 11*, 231–258.

Windle, M., & Tubman, J. G. (1999). Children of alcoholics. In W. K. Silverman & T. H. Ollendick (Eds.), *Developmental issues in the clinical treatment of children* (pp. 393–414). Boston, MA: Allyn & Bacon.

Wing, L. (1981). Asperger's syndrome: A clinical account. *Psychological Medicine, 11*, 115–129.

Winters, K. C., Latimer, W. W., & Stinchfield, R. (2001). Assessing adolescent substance use. In E. F. Wagner & H. B. Waldron (Eds.), *Innovations in adolescent substance abuse interventions* (pp. 1–29). Oxford, UK: Elsevier Science.

Witelson, S. (1977). Developmental dyslexia: Two right hemispheres and none left. *Science, 195*, 309–311.

Wolpe, J. (1958). *Psychotherapy by reciprocal inhibition.* Stanford, CA: Stanford University Press.

Wolraich, M. L. (2001). Current assessment and treatment practices in ADHD. In P. S. Jensen & J. R. Cooper (eds.), *Attention deficit hyperactivity disorder: State of the science-best practices.* pp. 1–23. Kingston, NJ: Civic Research Institute.

Wong, B. (1978). The effects of directive cues on the organization of memory and recall in good and poor readers. *Journal of Educational Research, 72*, 32–38.

Wong, M. G. (1995). Chinese Americans. In P. G. Min (Ed.), *Asian Americans: Contemporary trends and issues* (pp. 58–94). Beverly Hills: Sage.

Wooley, S. C., & Wooley, O. W. (1985). Intense outpatient and residential treatment for bulimia. In D. M. Garner & P. E. Garfinkel (Eds.), *Handbook of psychotherapy for anorexia nervosa and bulimia* (pp. 391–430). New York, NY: Guilford Press.

World Health Organization (WHO). (1993). *The ICD-10 classification of mental and behavioral disorders: Clinical descriptions and diagnostic guidelines.* Geneva, Switzerland: Author.

Yeh, C. J., & Huang, K. (2000). Interdependence in ethnic identity and self: Implications for theory and practice. *Journal of Counseling and Development, 78*, 420–429.

Yehuda, R., & McFarlane, A. C. (1995). Conflict between current knowledge about posttraumatic stress disorder and the original conceptual basis. *American Journal of Psychiatry, 152*, 1705–1713.

Ysseldyke, J. E., Thurlow, M. L., Christenson, S. L., & Muyskens, P. (1991). Classroom and home learning differences between students labeled as educable mentally retarded and their peers. *Education and Training in Mental Retardation, 26*, 3–17.

Zeanah, C. H., Boris, N. W., & Larrieu, J. A. (1997). Infant development and developmental risk: A review of the past 10 years. *Journal of the American Academy of Child and Adolescent Psychiatry, 36*, 165–178.

Zeanah, C. H., Smyke, A. T., & Dumitrescu, A. (2002). Attachment disturbances in young children. II: Indiscriminate behavior and institutional care. *Journal of the American Academy of Child and Adolescent Psychiatry, 41*, 983–989.

Zeman, J., Cassano, M., Perry-Parrish, C., & Stegall, S. (2006). Emotion regulation in children and adolescents. *Journal of Developmental and Behavioral Pediatrics, 27*, 155–168.

Zoccolillo, M., & Cloniger, C. R. (1985). Parental breakdown associated with somatization disorder (hysteria). *British Journal of Psychiatry, 147*, 443–446.

Zolog, T. C., Jane-Ballabriga, M. C., Bonillo-Martin, A., Canals-Sans, J., Hernandez-Martinez, C., Romero-Acosta, K., & Domenech-Llaberia, E. (2011). Somatic complaints and symptoms of anxiety and depression in a school-based sample of preadolescents and early adolescents: Functional impairment and implications for treatment. *Journal of Cognitive and Behavioral Psychotherapies, 11*, 191–208.

Index

MPM 250321
Printed in Singapore